fashionable clothing from the sears catalogs
MID 1980s

Tammy Ward

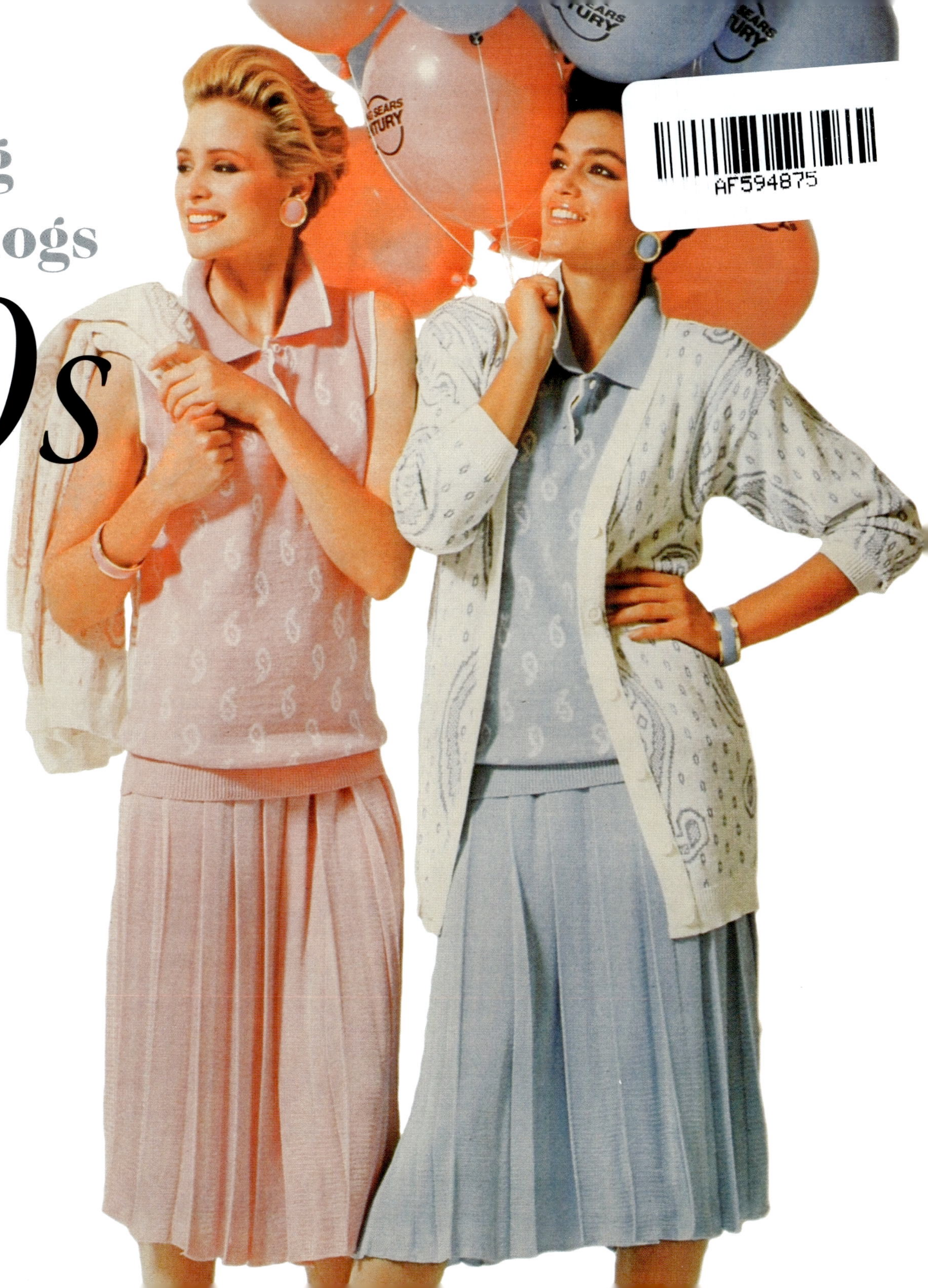

Schiffer Publishing Ltd®
4880 Lower Valley Road, Atlgen, Pennsylvania 19310

Images used in this book are from the Sears Catalogs ©Sears, Roebuck and Co., and are used with permission.

Spring/Summer 1984
28, 33, 36, 37, 39, 41, 47, 49, 53, 59, 61, 65, 75, 83, 88, 93, 96, 97, 103, 106, 118, 125, 141, 145, 146, 155, 163, 173, 185, 186, 191, 195, 230, 275, 275B, 276, 277, 285, 288, 299, 304, 310, 317, 324, 330, 333, 335, 339, 343, 352, 353, 362, 363, 379, 382, 383, 384, 385, 389, 403, 411, 421, 423, 427, 433, 434, 447, 453, 457, 459, 462, 463

Fall/Winter 1984
33, 51, 52, 53, 55, 61, 62, 66, 67, 71, 87, 93, 97, 119, 143, 144, 157, 159, 161, 162, 164, 165, 167, 170, 174, 177, 179, 187, 191, 197, 200, 203, 209, 234, 237, 245, 253, 287, 289, 293, 295, 300, 303, 305, 307, 309, 335, 342, 343, 344, 358, 371, 373, 375, 381, 383, 393, 398, 403, 404, 409, 412, 413, 415, 416, 419, 420, 428, 432, 441, 444, 447, 453, 462, 465, 466, 467, 482, 488, 491, 494, 495, 507, 511, 514, 515, 523, 533, 543, 547, 549, 571, 581, 593, 605, 608, 611, 613

Spring/Summer 1985
27, 29, 31, 36, 41, 43, 52, 66, 70, 76, 81, 83, 103, 109, 123, 136, 157, 161, 168, 170, 171, 177, 179, 298, 299, 305, 326, 337, 353, 359, 407, 432, 433, 434, 435, 436, 438, 440, 441, 442, 443, 472, 480, 501, 506

Fall/Winter 1985
26, 28, 33, 34, 40, 41, 42, 43, 47, 51, 53, 54, 75, 77, 89, 92, 104, 110, 144, 160, 169, 173, 180, 196, 199, 209, 233, 295, 309, 311, 313, 314, 321, 324, 330, 334, 402, 403, 458, 467, 475, 490, 497, 511, 512, 514, 526, 528, 534, 537, 541, 556, 558, 562, 566, 571, 580, 581, 583, 586, 594, 596, 613, 620, 621, 622, 629

Library of Congress Control Number: 2008929332

Designed by John P. Cheek
Cover design by Bruce Waters

Type set in Eras Bk BT/Aldine 721 BT

ISBN: 978-0-7643-2960-9
Printed in China

Spring/Summer 1986
7, 11, 15, 20, 21, 22, 28, 32, 36, 43, 47, 59, 75, 83, 105, 115, 127, 151, 158, 167, 193, 217, 281, 285, 286, 295, 297, 298, 300, 301, 309, 315, 316, 320, 321, 323, 329, 329B, 350, 353, 355, 361, 365, 391, 392, 402, 406, 408, 409, 412, 425E, 429, 432, 435, 456, 458, 464, 467

Fall/Winter 1986
13, 19, 27, 29, 38, 39, 41, 43, 45, 49, 52, 53, 57, 69, 71, 91, 97, 117, 119, 127, 131, 133, 134, 135, 136, 137, 139, 140, 145, 147, 157, 159, 173, 177, 185, 223, 264, 272, 274, 278, 284, 293, 294, 295, 303, 309, 311, 315, 328, 337, 353, 355, 382, 384, 385, 402, 453, 455, 497, 512, 524

Schiffer Books are available at special discounts for bulk purchases for sales promotions or premiums. Special editions, including personalized covers, corporate imprints, and excerpts can be created in large quantities for special needs. For more information contact the publisher:

Published by Schiffer Publishing Ltd.
4880 Lower Valley Road
Atglen, PA 19310
Phone: (610) 593-1777; Fax: (610) 593-2002
E-mail: Info@schifferbooks.com

For the largest selection of fine reference books on this and related subjects, please visit our web site at **www.schifferbooks.com**
We are always looking for people to write books on new and related subjects. If you have an idea for a book please contact us at the above address.

This book may be purchased from the publisher.
Include $5.00 for shipping.
Please try your bookstore first.
You may write for a free catalog.

In Europe, Schiffer books are distributed by
Bushwood Books
6 Marksbury Ave.
Kew Gardens
Surrey TW9 4JF England
Phone: 44 (0) 20 8392-8585; Fax: 44 (0) 20 8392-9876
E-mail: info@bushwoodbooks.co.uk
Website: www.bushwoodbooks.co.uk
Free postage in the U.K., Europe; air mail at cost.

Contents

Introduction

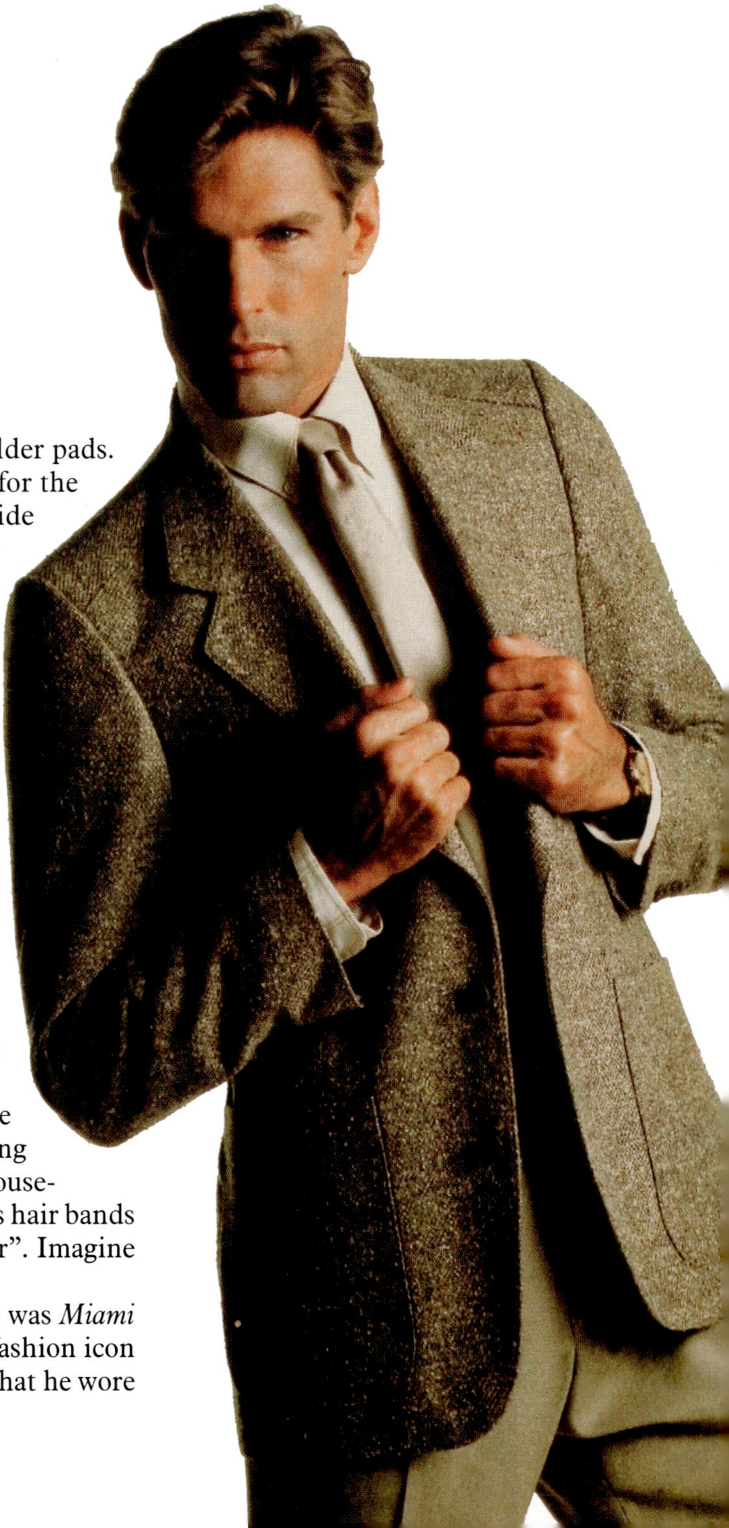

One of the most widely appearing styles of the 1980s was achieved with shoulder pads. The evening soap opera *Dynasty* held a global audience, and the film set designer for the show promoted the wide shoulder look because of star Linda Evans' naturally wide shoulders. Members of the cast were promptly attired in shoulder pads. Another very popular evening soap, *Dallas,* was also broadcast worldwide and this style of clothing was seen on that show as well. Soon, everyone was wearing shoulder pads. Women loved this style of clothing because shoulder pads smoothed out any body postural imperfections. It seemed almost impossible to find clothing that didn't contain them! Designers eventually tried to drop this style but the public demanded it. They started making garments with detachable shoulder pads and a woman could then decide whether she wanted to keep them or not.

This style carried over into the women's work force with mannish looking suits, and was termed "power dressing". The idea was that big shoulders got noticed and women would be taken seriously in the business world. Women started to model their business attire after such successful women as Margaret Thatcher, and yuppies followed what Princess Diana of Wales was wearing. An accessory that went along with business attire for women were large, square scarves in wool or acrylic. They were adorned in paisley and exotic patterns, and were draped just so about a woman's shoulders. If you had any trouble with understanding the draping of these scarves, leaflets were created to help a girl out!

To go along with the wide shoulder look, "big hair" was another essential for the '80s. This was influenced also by *Dallas* and *Dynasty*, whose hair stylists were creating bigger and bigger hair styles. Also, MTV was becoming more widely available to households in the 1980s and we got to watch music videos featuring extremely popular '80s hair bands like Bon Jovi, Cinderella, Def Leppard and Poison who truly epitomized "Big Hair". Imagine the amount of gel, mousse, and hair spray needed to hold those hair styles!

Another widely popular television show that influenced fashion styles for men was *Miami Vice.* For the man of the '80s, who didn't want the "Don Johnson" look? He was a fashion icon and thus he started a fashion revolution as many men copied his look. The clothes that he wore on this show had a huge impact on clothing being designed for men at this time. Men began sporting three-day stubble, espadrilles and loafers without socks, no belt, unconstructed Italian blazers over tee shirts, linen pants, and wearing them in pastel colors became the "macho" way to dress.

As for teen girls, styles were highly influenced by a superstar named Madonna, the ultimate material girl. Her impact on fashion was indisputable as she burst into the music scene wearing lace tops with short skirts over Capri pants. She made wearing lingerie on the outside popular. Her wildly teased and colored hair, and her fashion statements were copied by adoring fans all over the world. She was definitely another fashion icon of this time.

You will find many memorable and very distinctive fashions as you flip through these pages. Take a look down memory lane and remember the fun of exercise clothing (*Flash Dance*), leg warmers, banana clips, punk fashions (including hairstyles and music), designer jeans, parachute pants (break dancing), jelly bracelets, rat tails, mullets, and Michael Jackson's still strong music video *Thriller.* All of these and more influenced and became the styles of the mid-1980s.

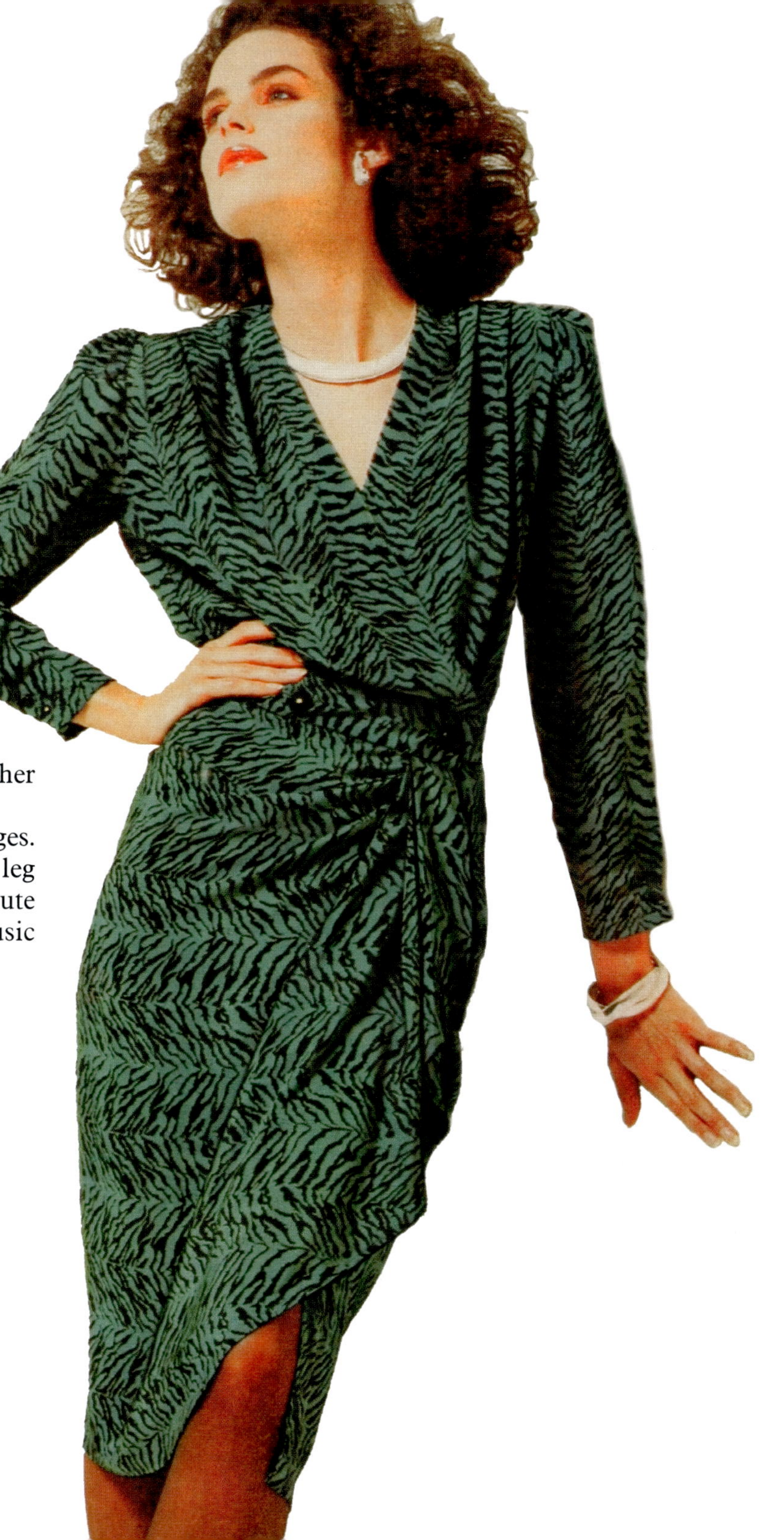

Women's Fashions

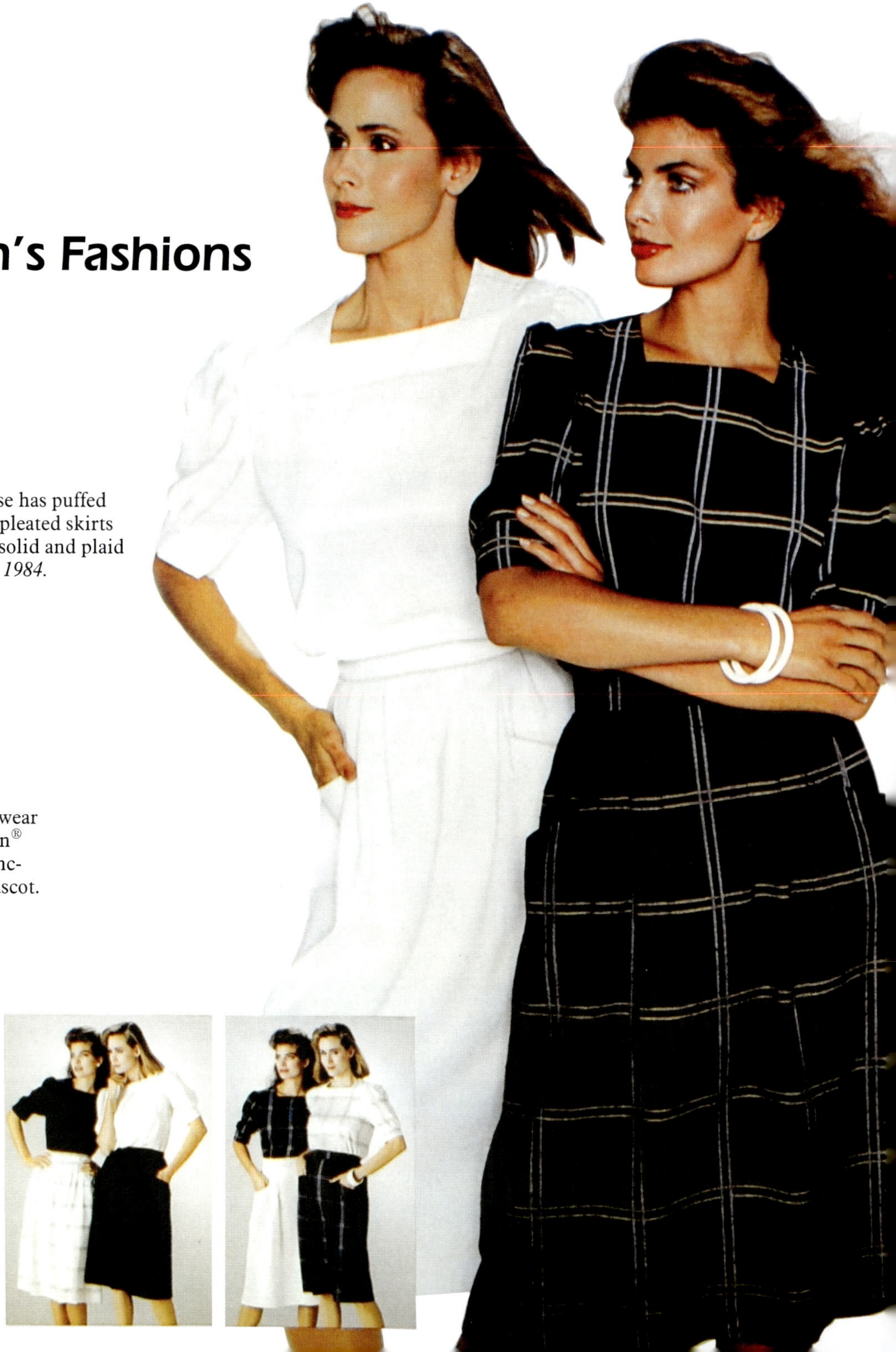

Square neckline blouse has puffed sleeves, coordinating pleated skirts have drop pockets in solid and plaid styles. *Spring/Summer 1984.*

Career/Work Wear

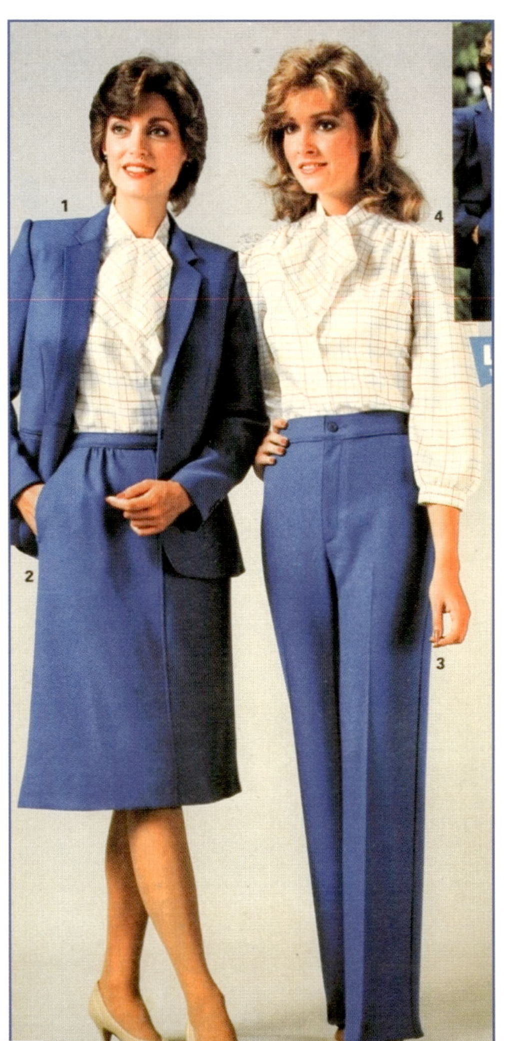

Levi's Bend Over womenswear woven of texturized Dacron® polyester. Blouse by Provinc-etown with handkerchief ascot. *Spring/Summer 1984.*

Double knit gabardine blazer and matching skirt requires no ironing. *Spring/Summer 1984.*

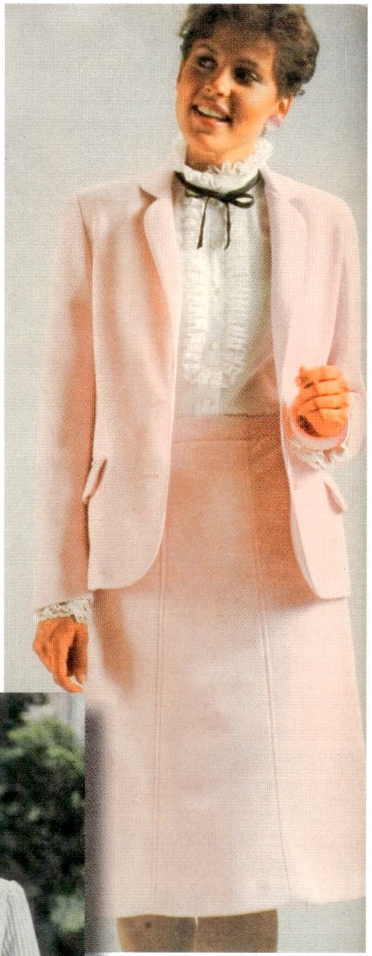

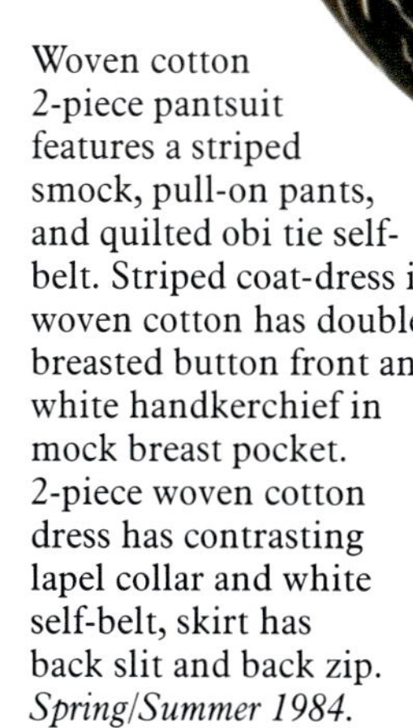

Woven cotton 2-piece pantsuit features a striped smock, pull-on pants, and quilted obi tie self-belt. Striped coat-dress in woven cotton has double-breasted button front and white handkerchief in mock breast pocket. 2-piece woven cotton dress has contrasting lapel collar and white self-belt, skirt has back slit and back zip. *Spring/Summer 1984.*

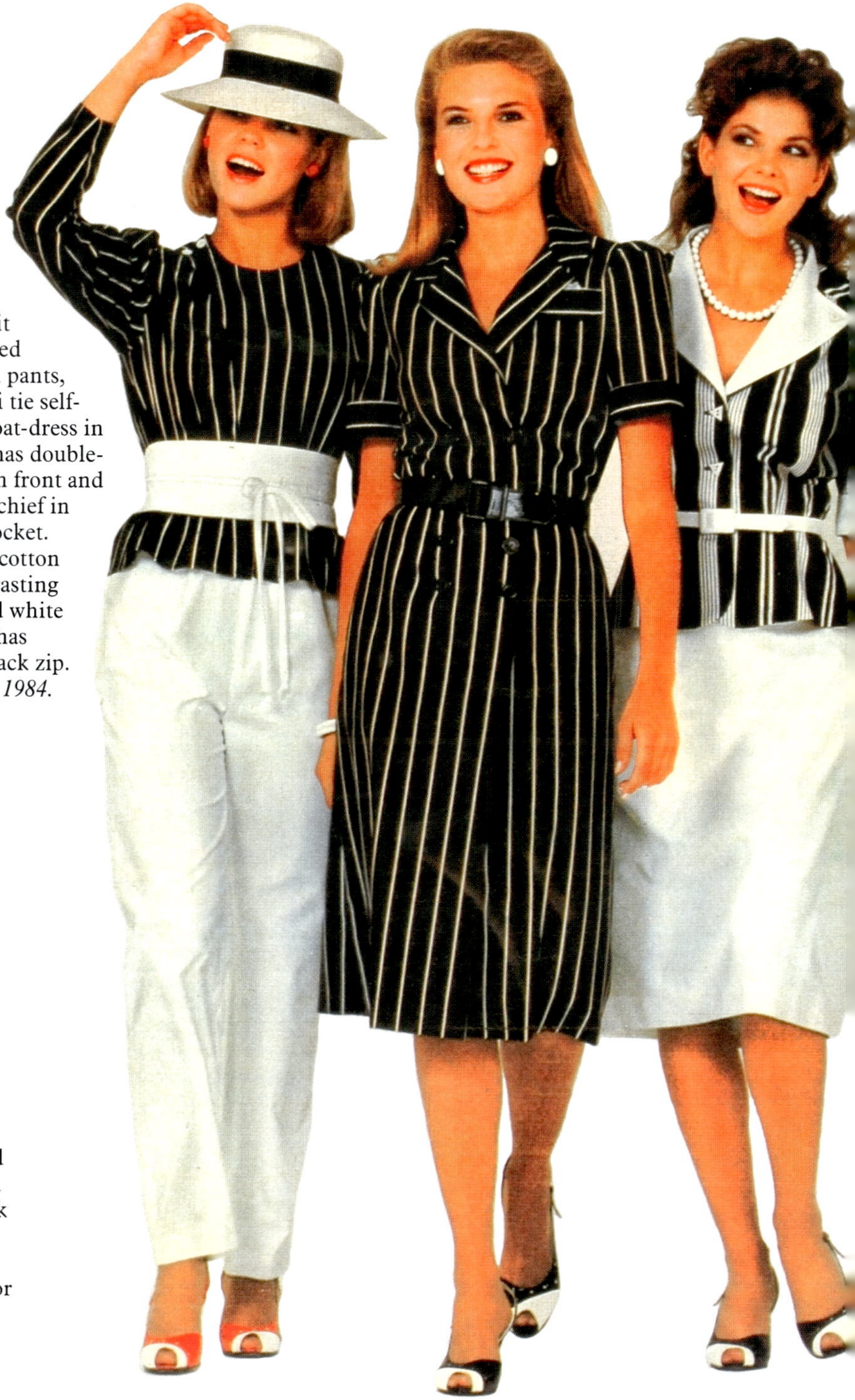

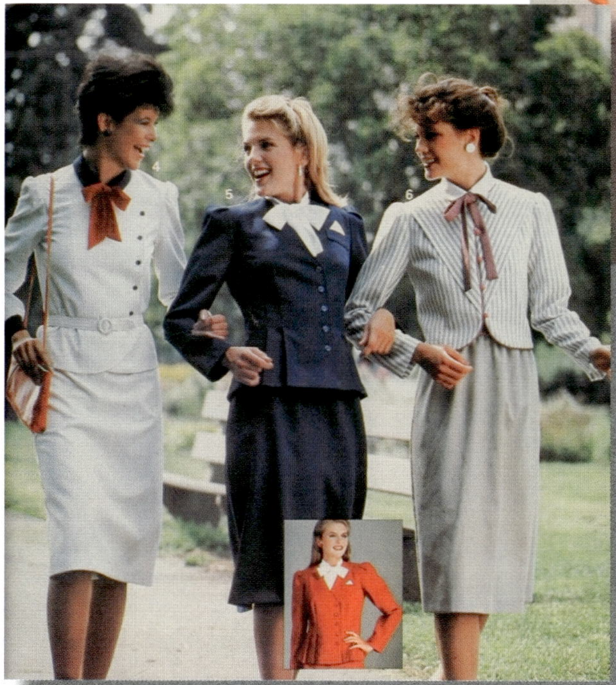

2-piece dress has asymmetrical button closure, navy pinstripes, and detachable red bow tie. Tailored 2-piece dress with peplum top has pleats and front darts, skirt has back slit and button closure. 2-piece dress has striped jacket with contrast piping and a smooth polyester and rayon skirt. Perfect for the office. *Spring/Summer 1984.*

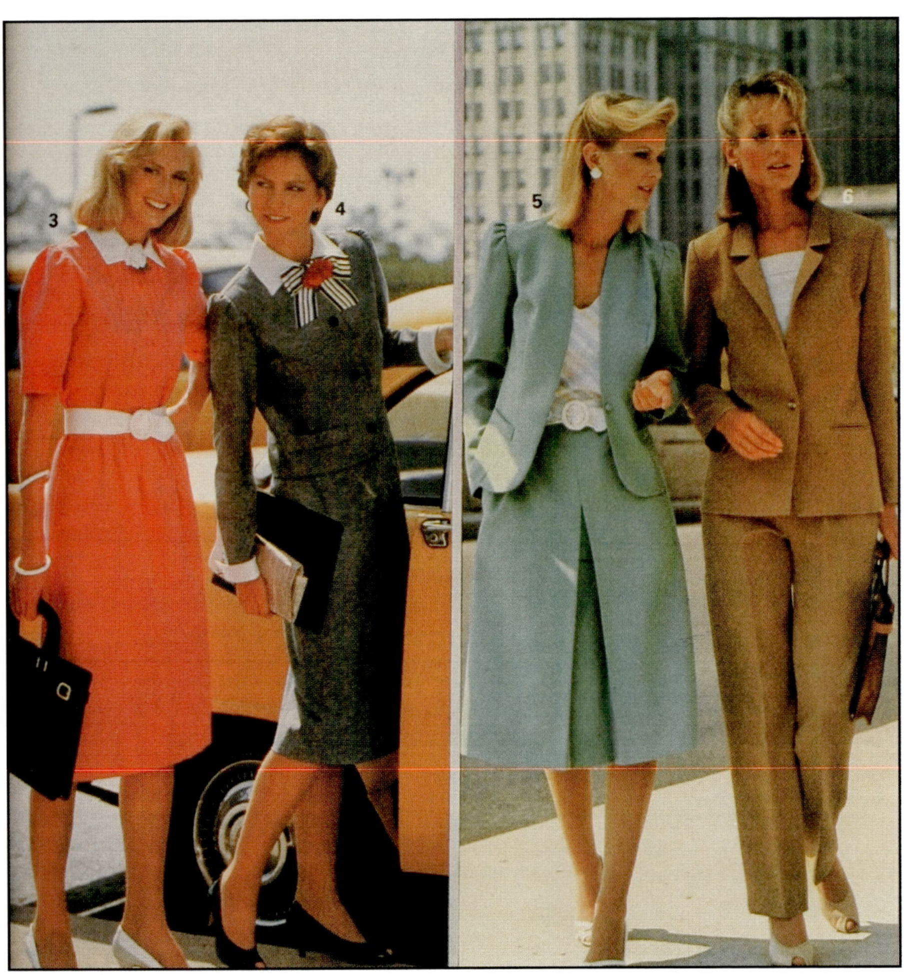

Woven Fortrel® polyester dress has stitched button-front and flower pin. Charcoal gray 2-piece suit with contrasting white trim in polyester and cotton with a woven tweed texture. 2-piece suit has jacket with mock pockets and A-line skirt in woven Dacron® polyester. Khaki pant-suit in woven polyester. *Spring/Summer 1984.*

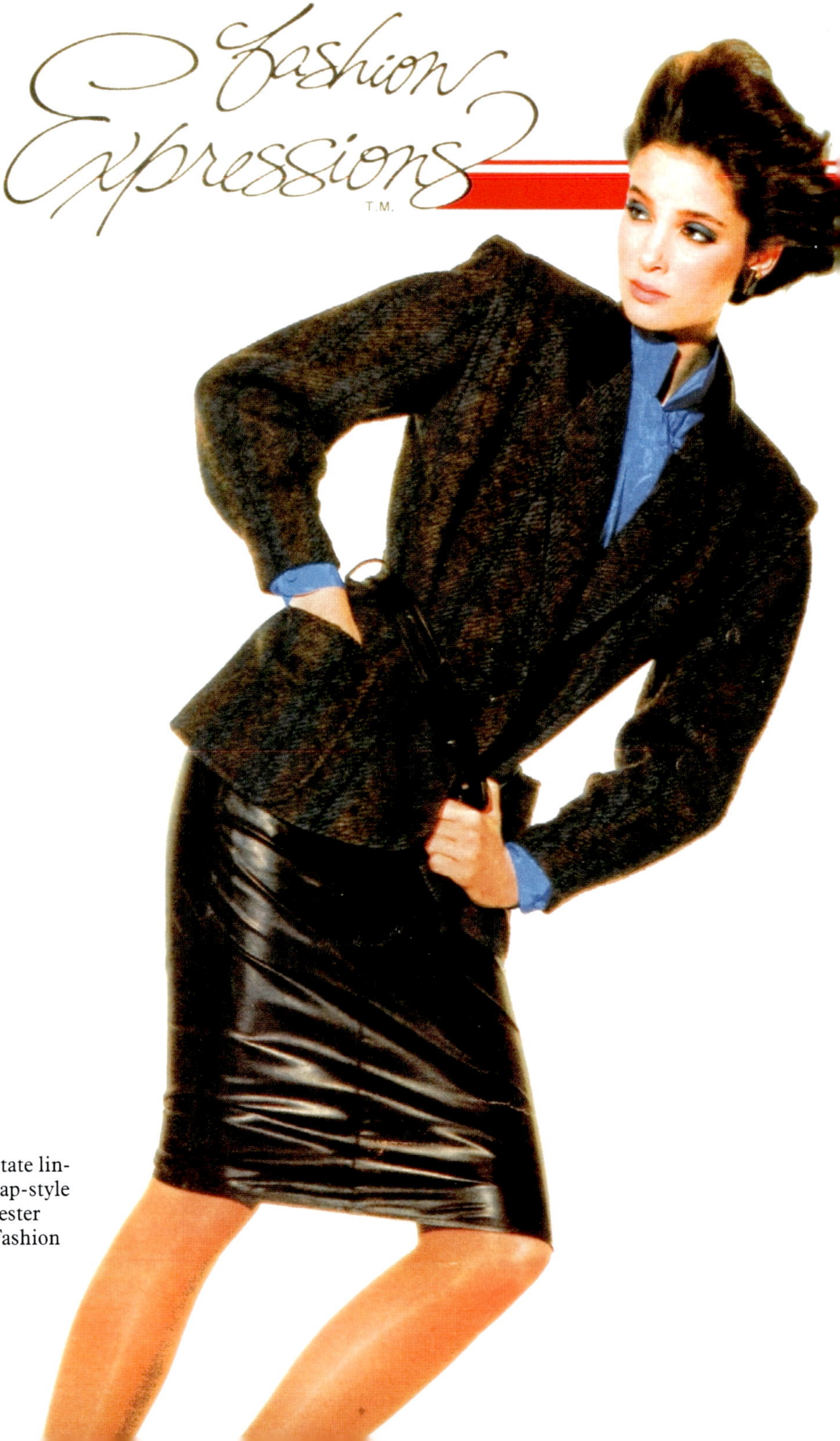

Fashion Expressions T.M.

Soft and supple 100% leather skirt with acetate lining is very sleek. It is paired here with a wrap-style jacket in a weave of wool, mohair, and polyester with a n acetate lining. Both are from the Fashion Expressions collection. *Fall/Winter 1984.*

Leather skirt and pants paired with polyester notch collar blouse and pleated polyester blouse with Victorian cuffs. *Fall/Winter 1984.*

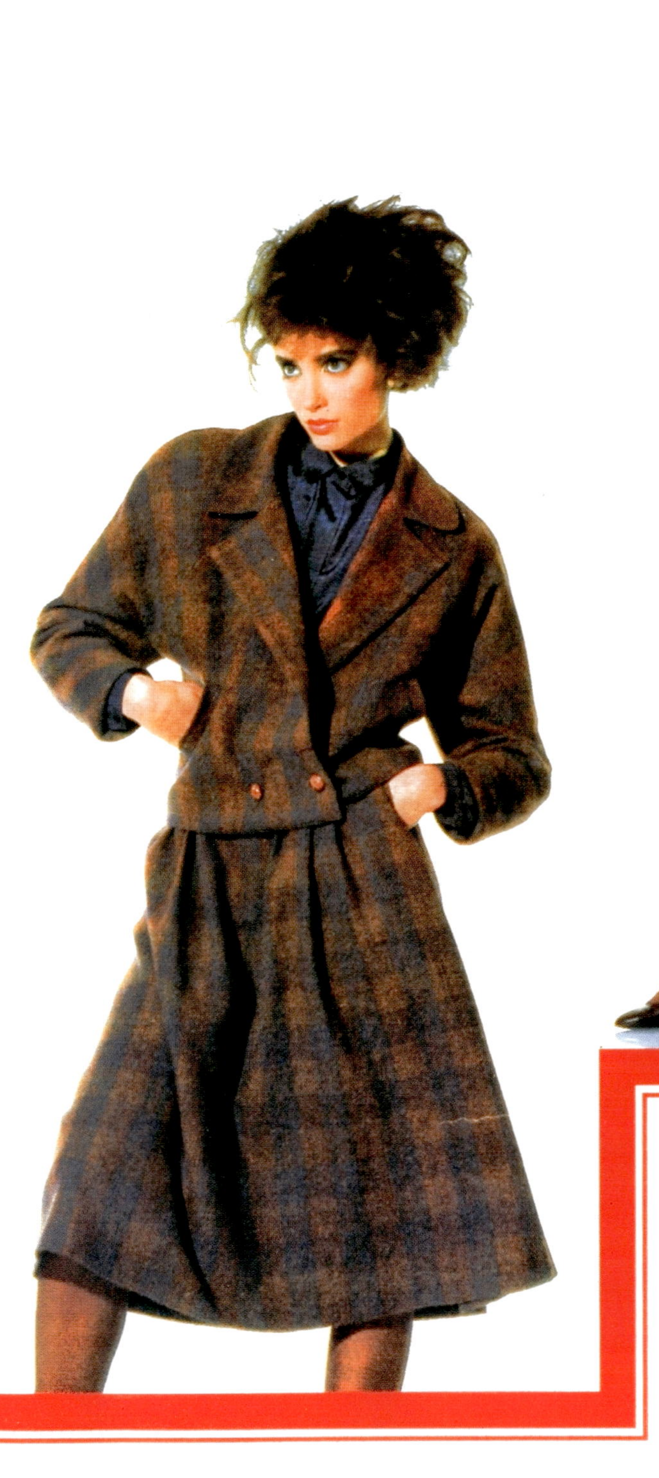

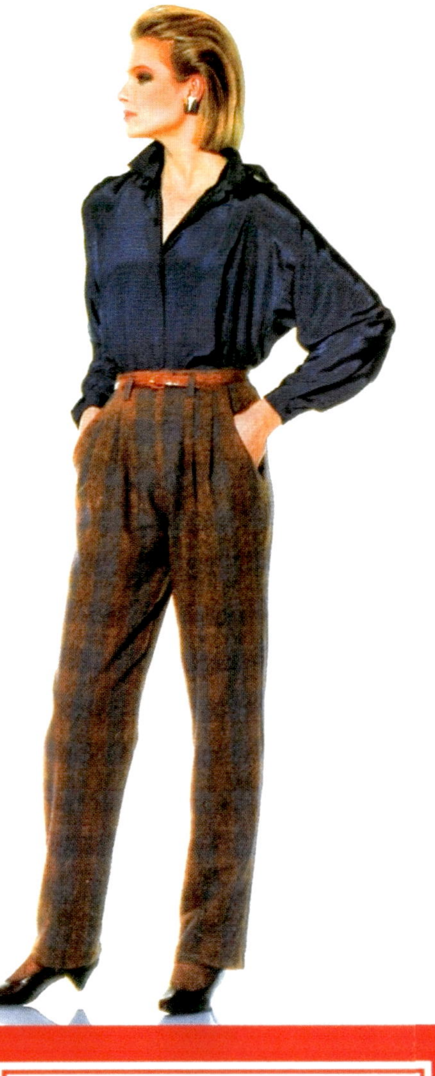

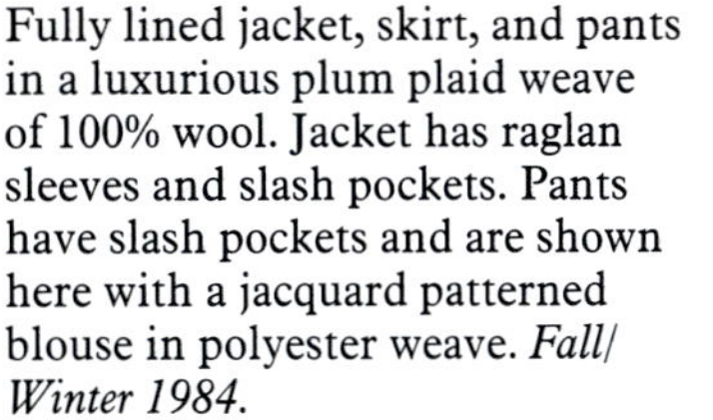

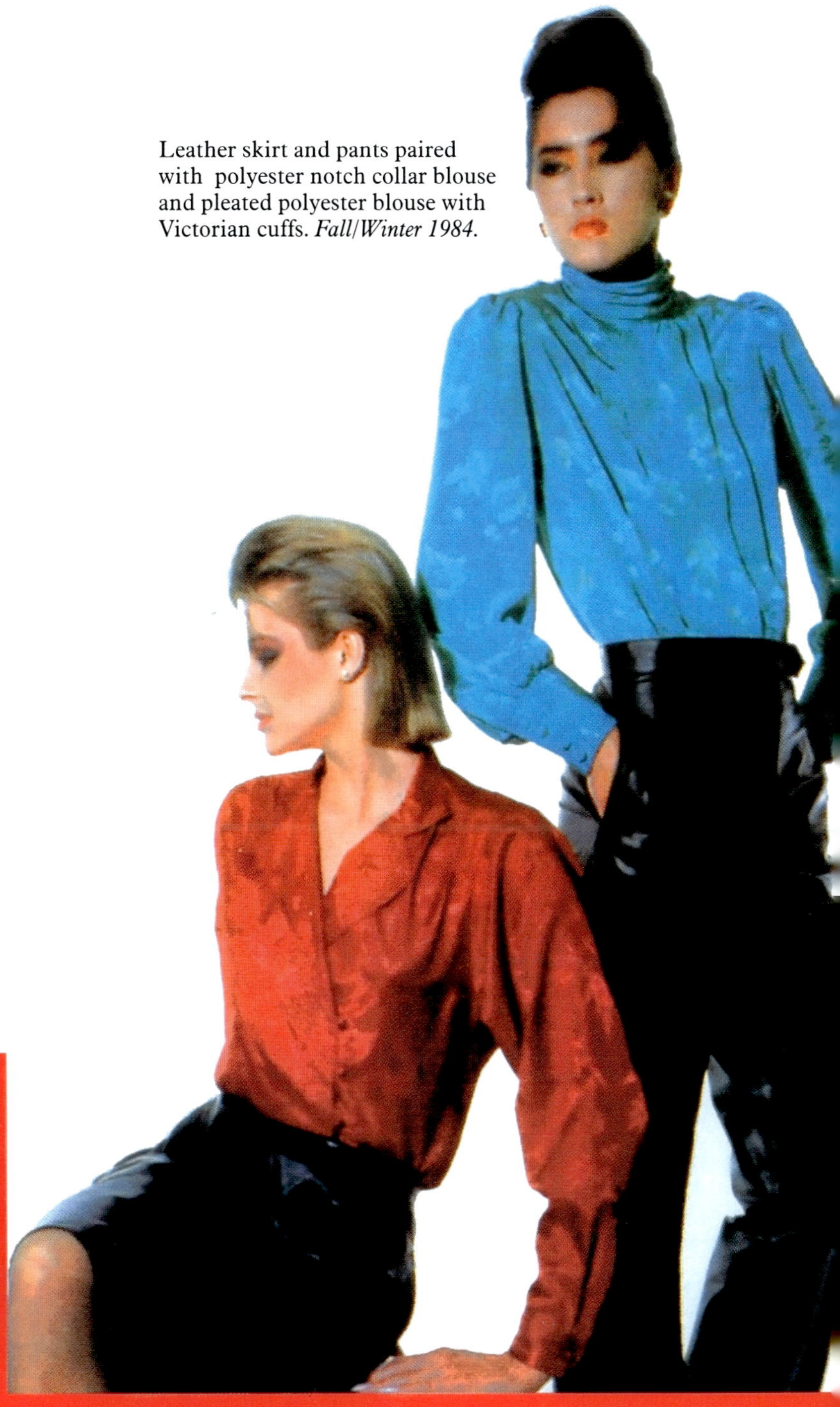

Fully lined jacket, skirt, and pants in a luxurious plum plaid weave of 100% wool. Jacket has raglan sleeves and slash pockets. Pants have slash pockets and are shown here with a jacquard patterned blouse in polyester weave. *Fall/Winter 1984.*

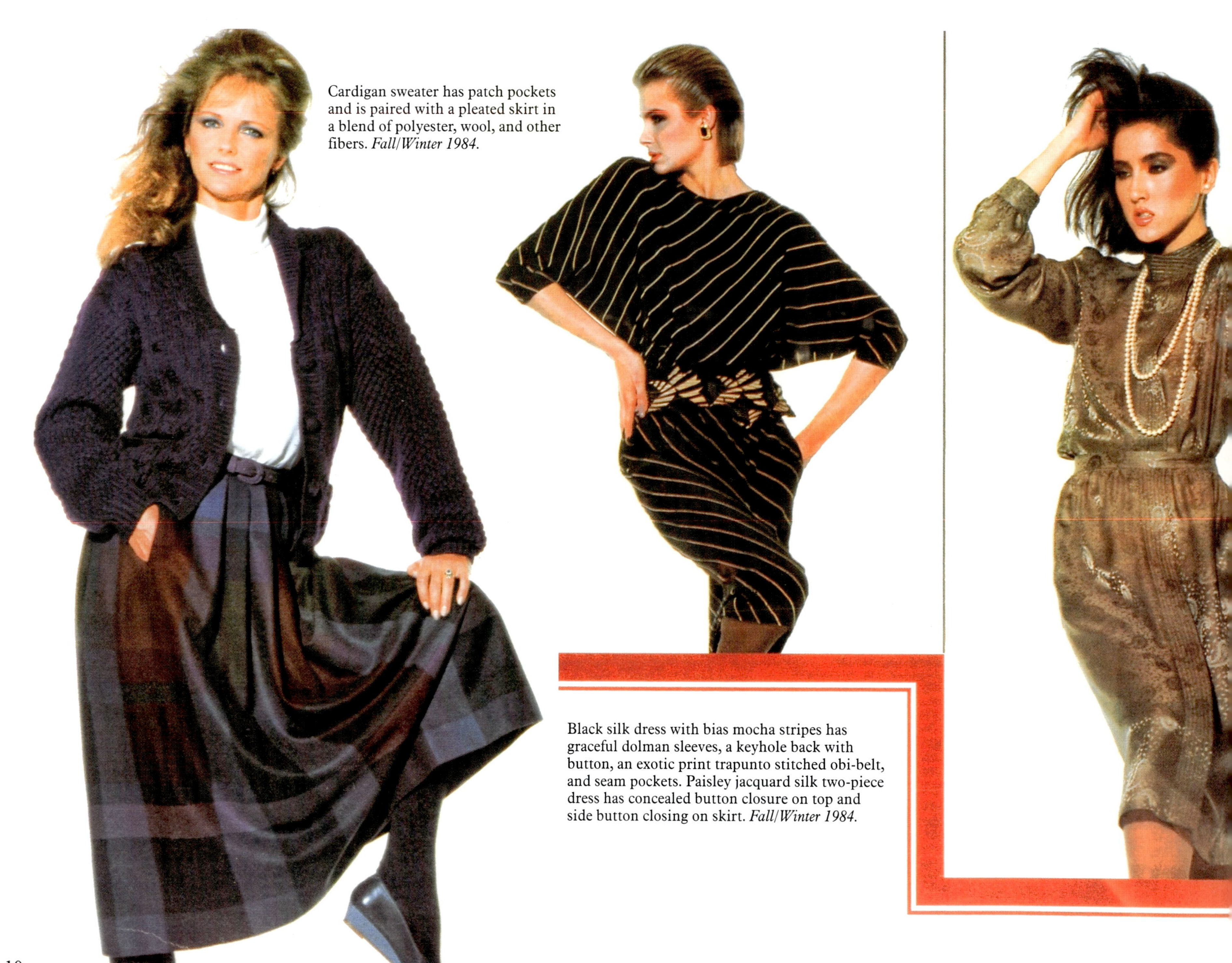

Cardigan sweater has patch pockets and is paired with a pleated skirt in a blend of polyester, wool, and other fibers. *Fall/Winter 1984.*

Black silk dress with bias mocha stripes has graceful dolman sleeves, a keyhole back with button, an exotic print trapunto stitched obi-belt, and seam pockets. Paisley jacquard silk two-piece dress has concealed button closure on top and side button closing on skirt. *Fall/Winter 1984.*

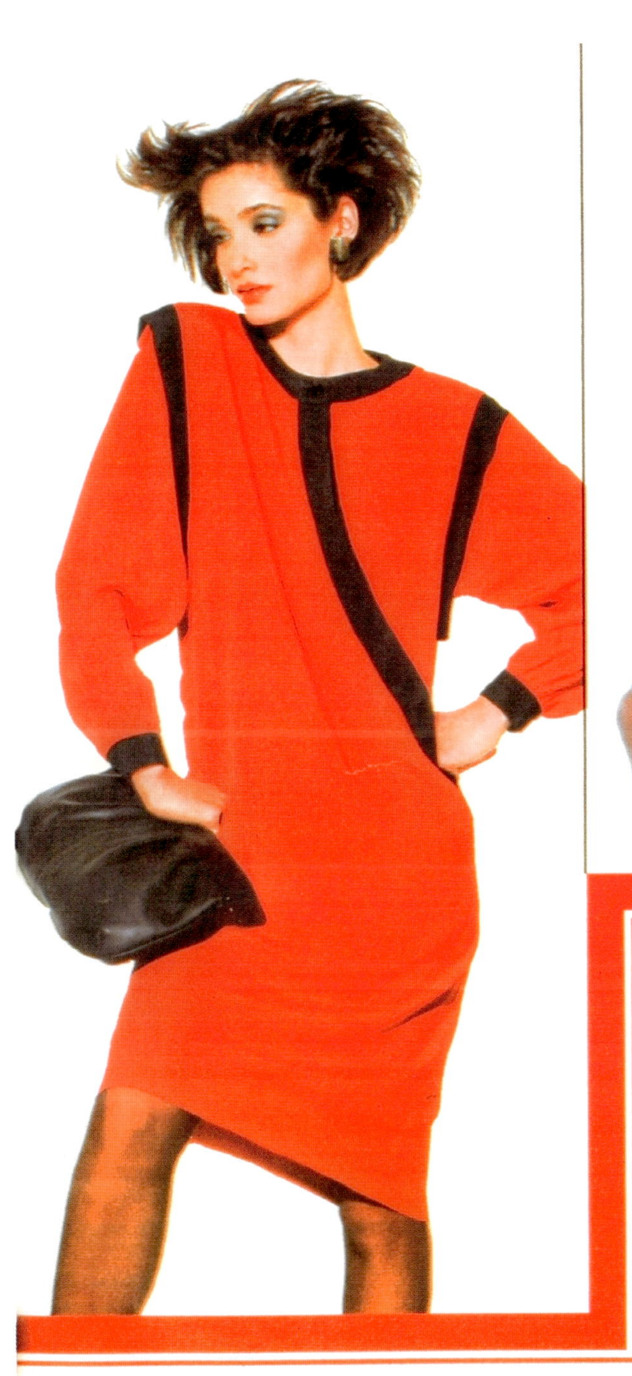

Streamlined Cherry red chemise has contrasting black neckline, shoulders, and cuffs made of woven acetate and rayon tissue faille. Shimmering jacquard patterned polyester chemise is styled with a mandarin neck, keyhole-button closure, and long sleeves have double-button cuffs. *Fall/Winter 1984.*

Blouse has soft draping cowl and an adjustable side tie, blouse with soft shirring is paired with a flattering neckline and bow, blouse with soft shirring has a back keyhole opening. All are made in polyester georgette. *Fall/Winter 1984.*

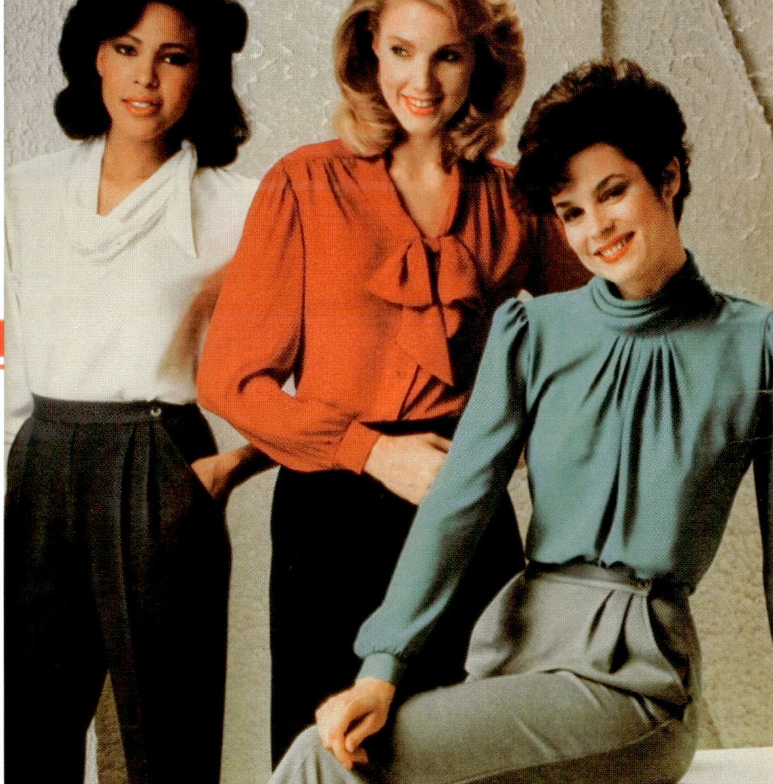

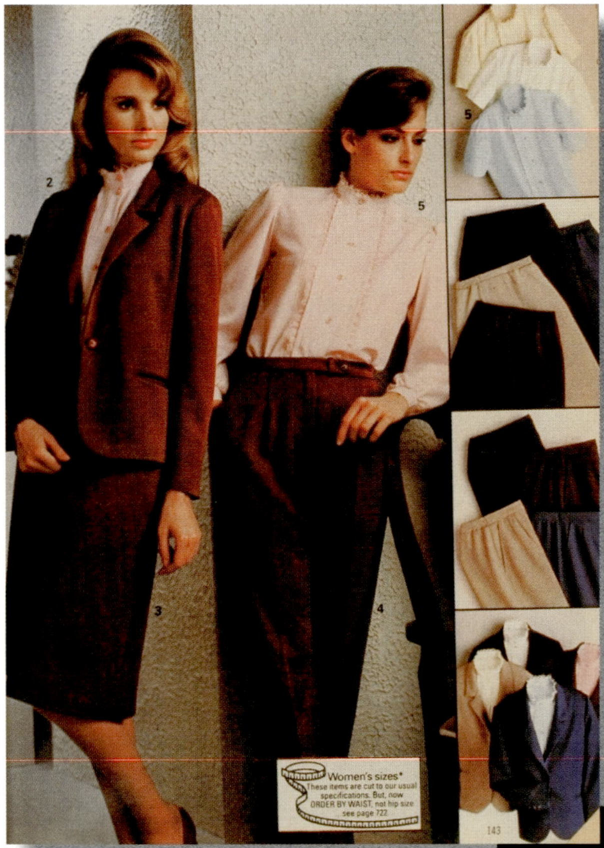

Blazer, skirt, and pants are knit of Celanese Fortrell polyester, shirt in long and short sleeves is woven of Dacron polyester. *Fall/Winter 1984.*

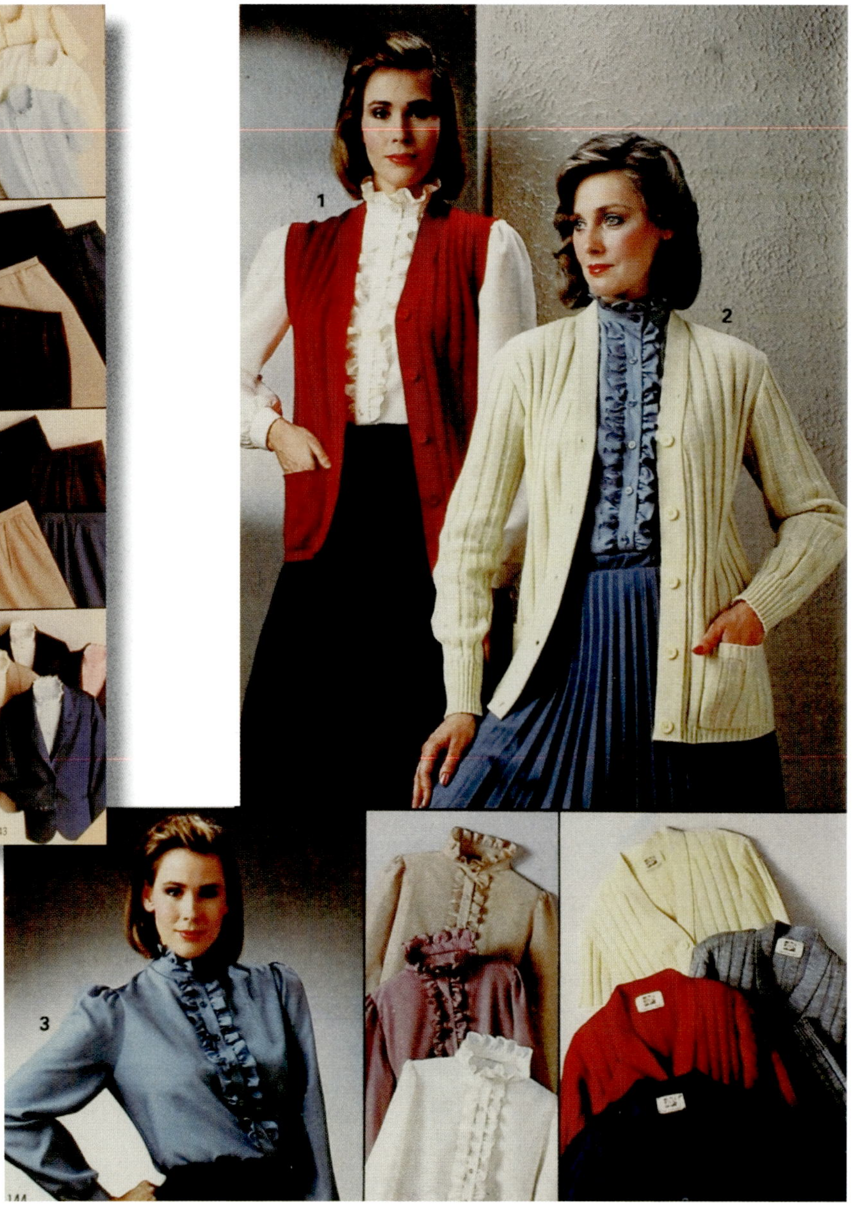

Vest and cardigan button-front sweaters are knit of soft acrylic and are paired with ruffled polyester blouses with bib fronts. *Fall/Winter 1984.*

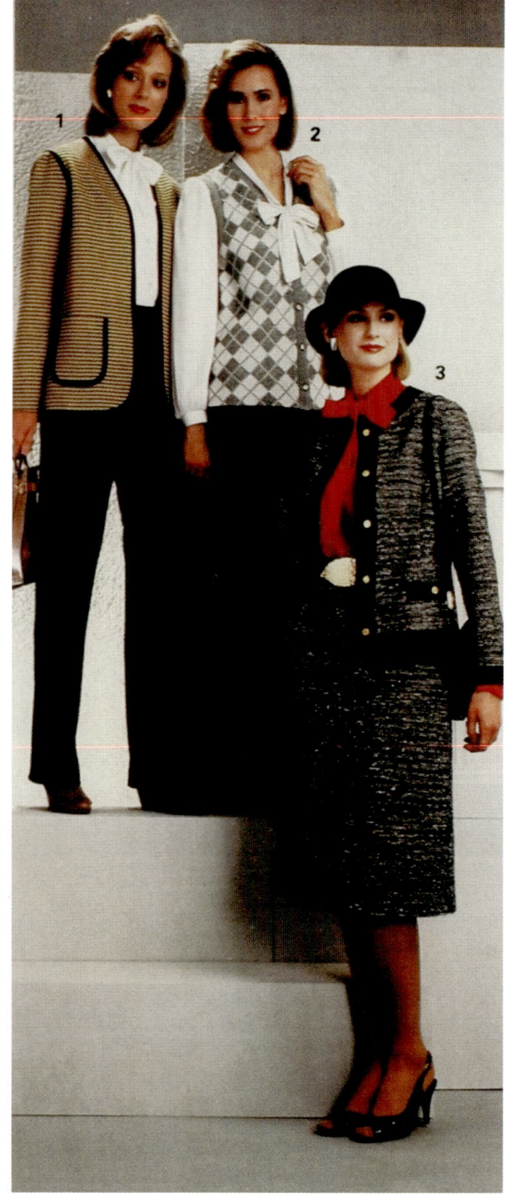

Polyester pants suit has a long-sleeved camel jacket with trim and patch pockets and button-front blouse with soft tie neck. Gray polyester pantsuit has a button-front cardigan and low bow collar blouse. Black and gray tweed suit has contrasting black trim on jacket and an elasticized waistband on skirt. *Fall/Winter 1984.*

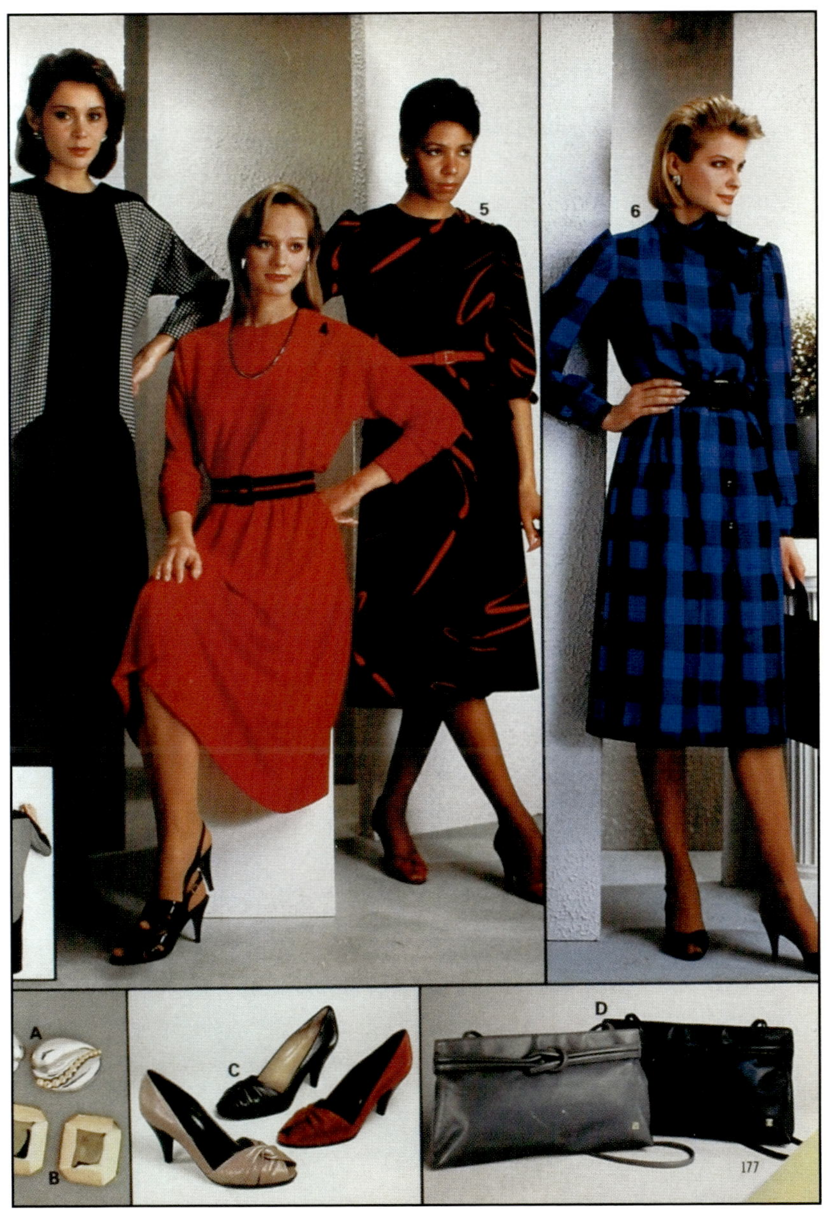

Black chemise with black and white block checked body has padded shoulders and 5-button back closure; red knit dress has dolman sleeves, buttoned keyhole back, and elastic waist; black and red print peplum has button trimmed shoulder and elastic cuffed push-up sleeves; royal and black checked dress with stand-up collar and contrasting tie and belt. *Fall/Winter 1984.*

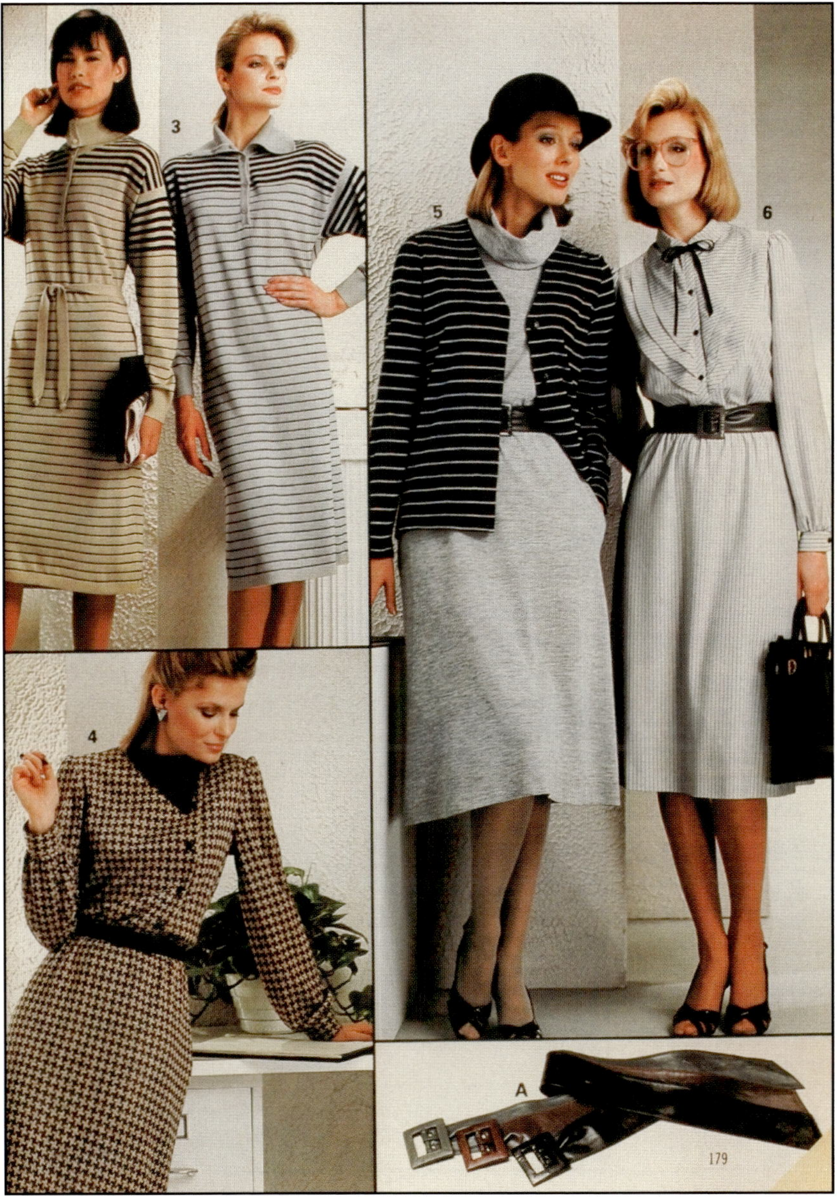

100% Merino wool striped dress with ribbed collar and cuffs and button placket closure, camel and navy checked dress with asymmetrical button front and collar and navy slide belt, waistless gray dress with cowl neck paired with a gray and black striped jacket, gray and black crepe dress has peter pan collar and ribbon tie. *Fall/Winter 1984.*

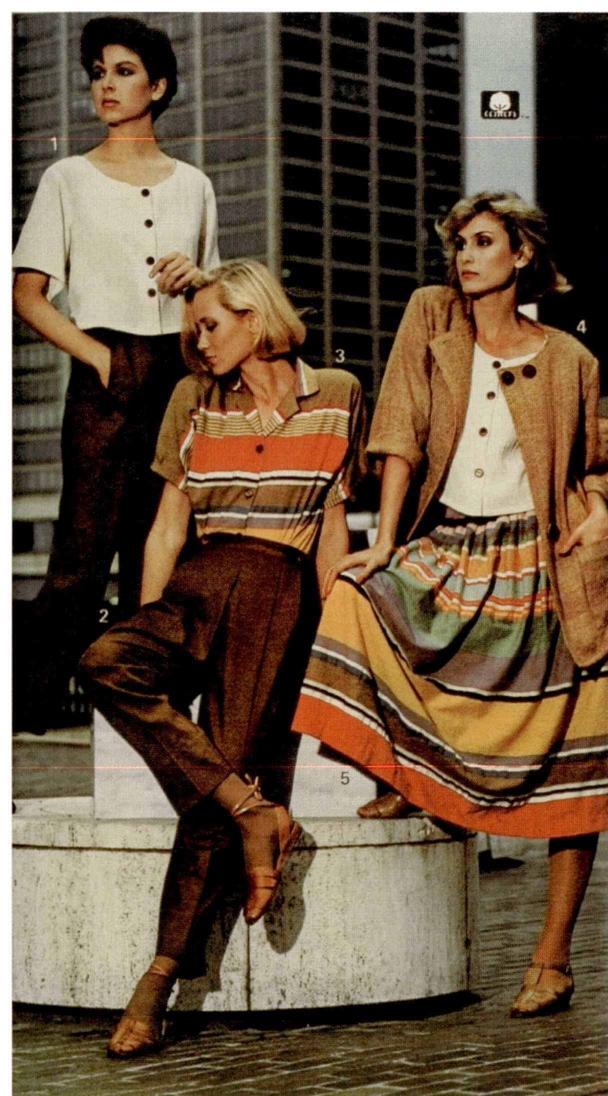

Tops, pants, skirt, and jacket from the Sierra Madre collection in all cotton fabric. *Spring/Summer 1985*

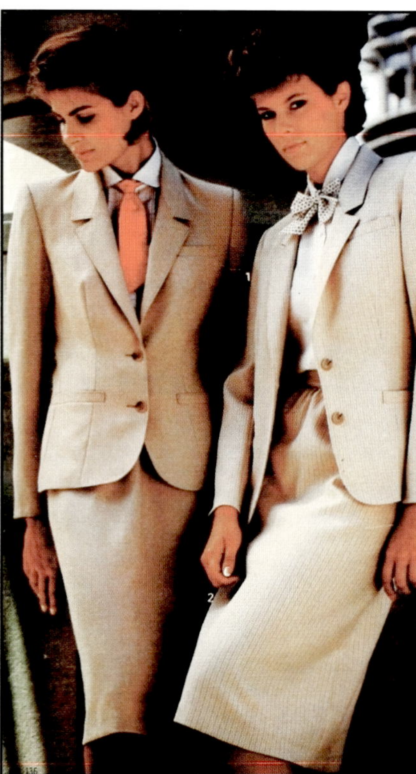

Polyester stretch blazers and skirts for a polished look. *Spring/Summer 1985*

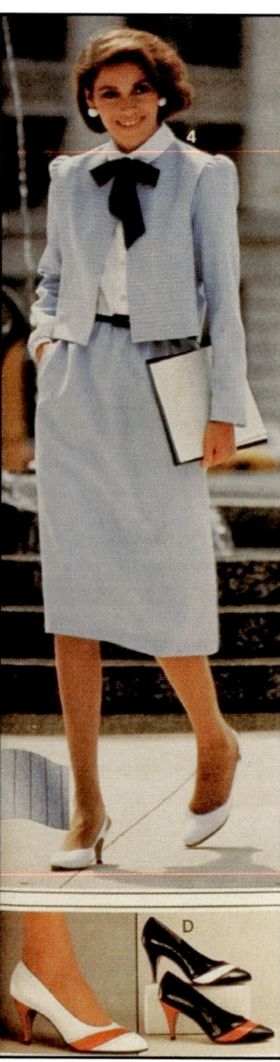

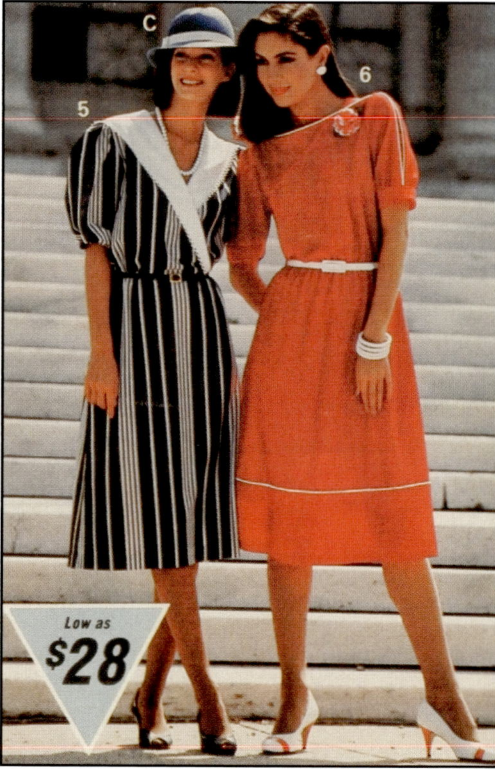

Blue with navy stripes jacket dress, navy and white surplice-front style dress has white sailor style collar, red duco-dot dress has fresh white piping. *Spring/Summer 1985*

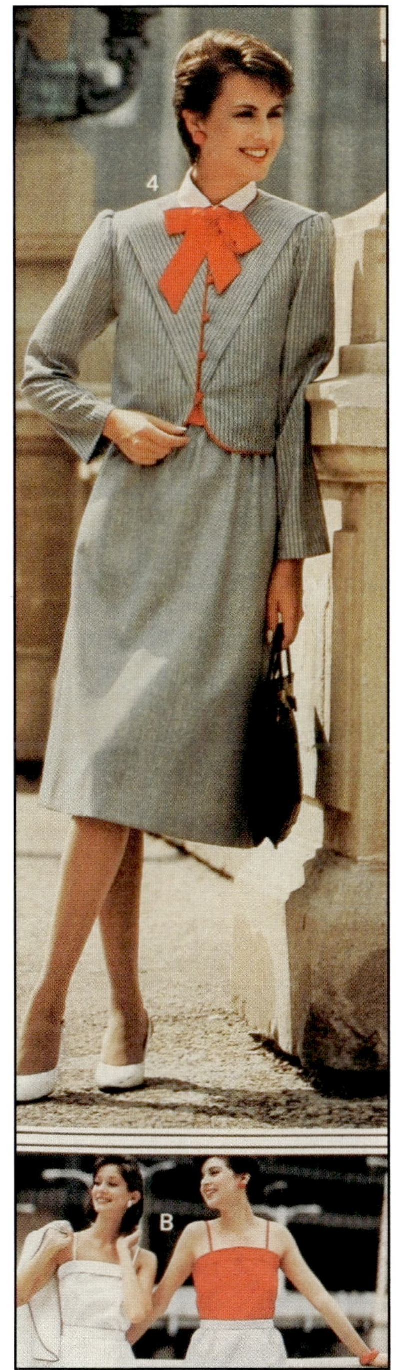

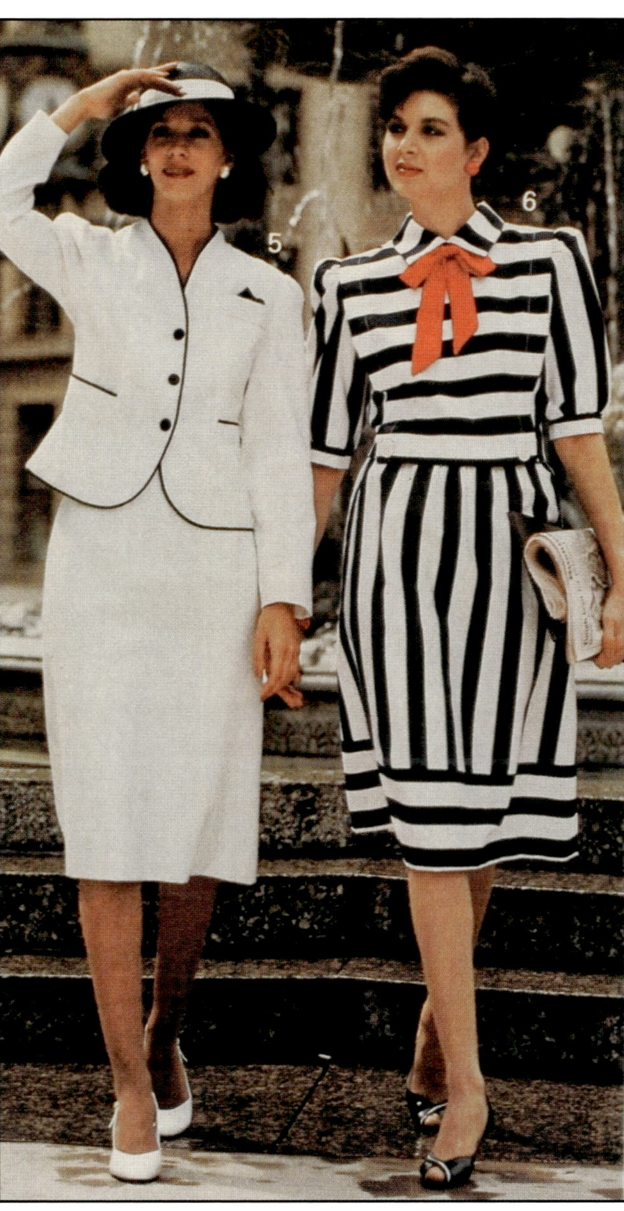

Gray jacket dress accented with red buttons, piping, and detachable bow. Classic white suit with navy piping and buttons. Navy and white striped dress. *Spring/Summer 1985*

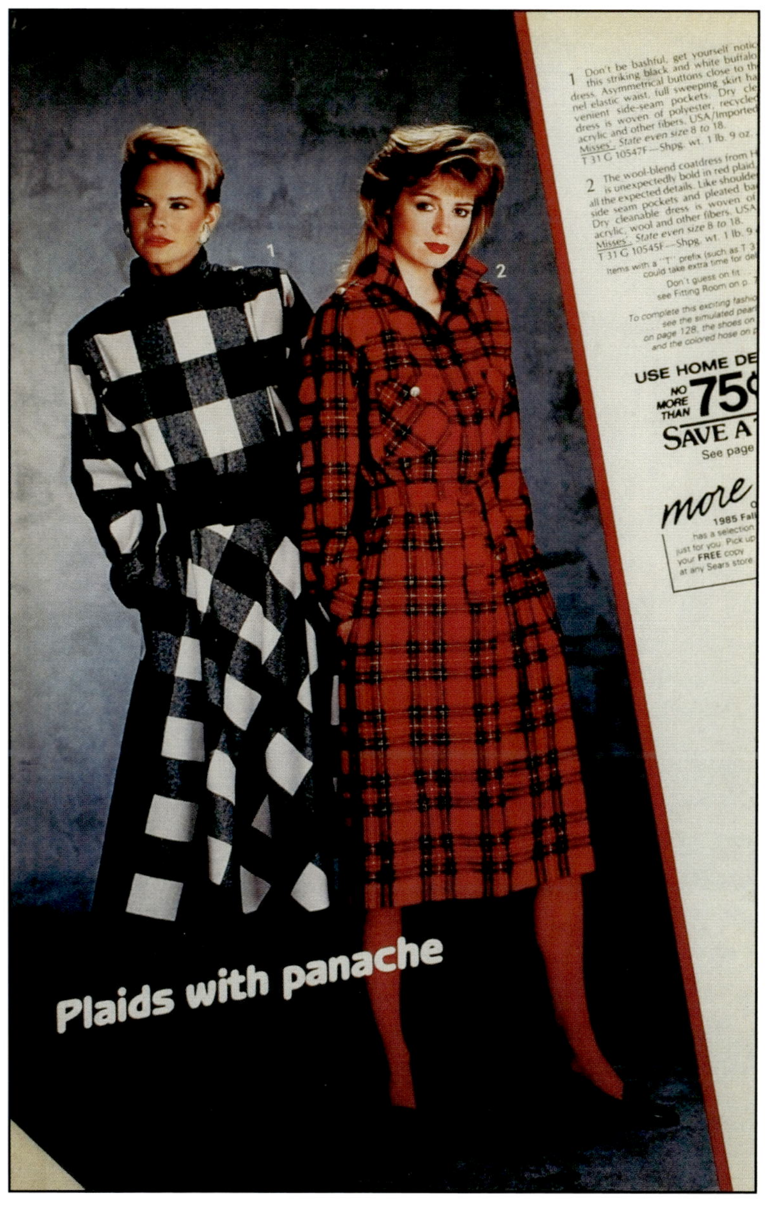

Black and white buffalo plaid dress with asymmetrical buttons. Coatdress in red plaid with side seam pockets and pleated back bodice. *Fall/Winter 1985*

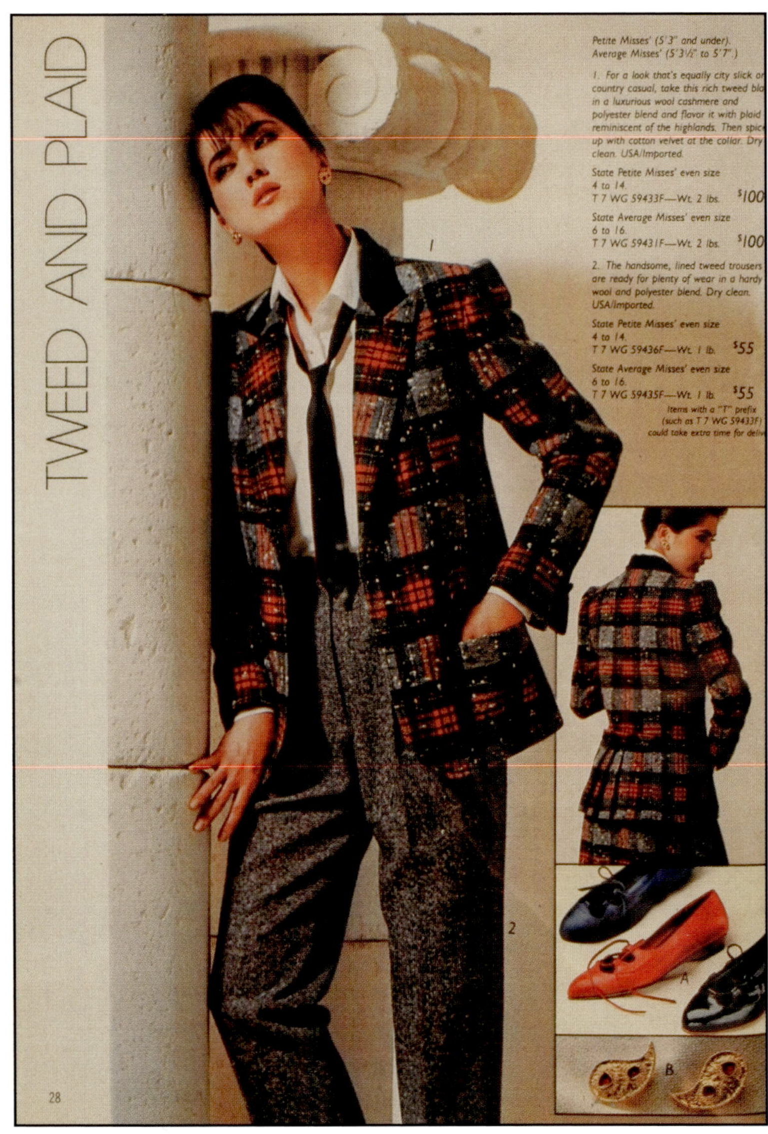

Wool cashmere and polyester blazer with cotton velvet at the collar, lined tweed trousers. *Fall/Winter 1985*

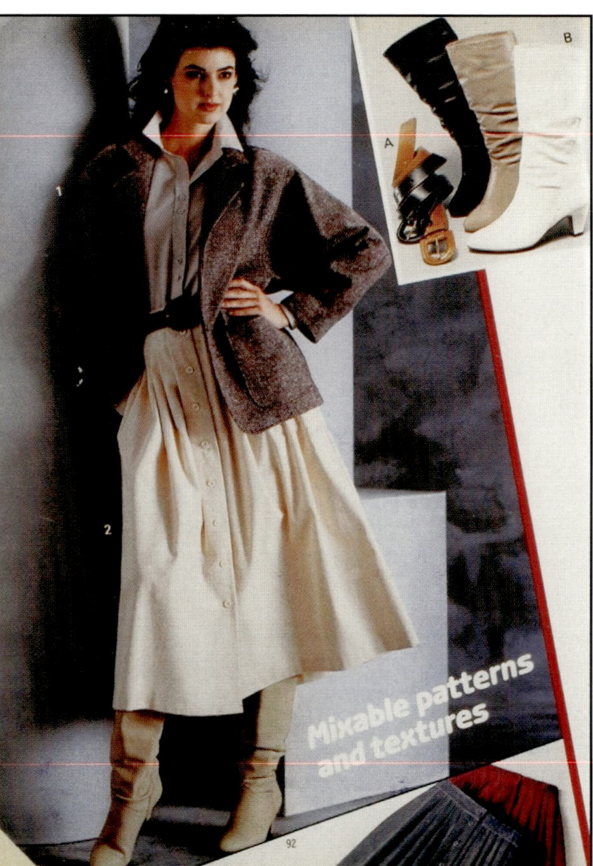

Long tweed blazer is worn with a swingy wide-wale corduroy skirt. *Fall/Winter 1985*

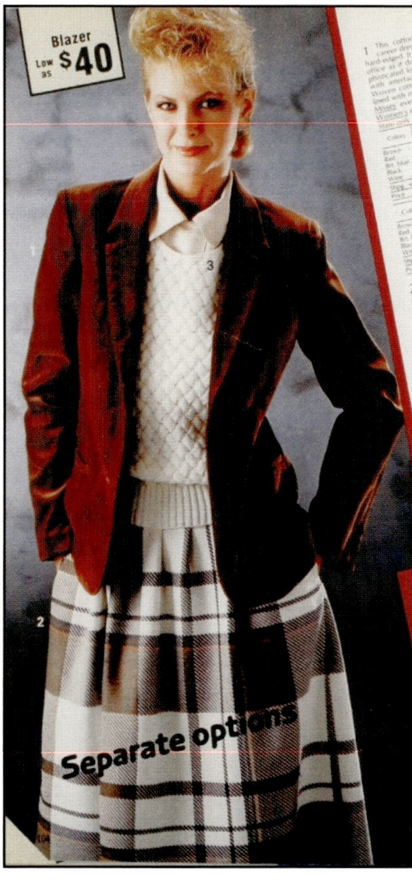

Cotton velvet blazer is worn over an acrylic pullover vest and a softly pleated wool and polyester plaid skirt. *Fall/Winter 1985*

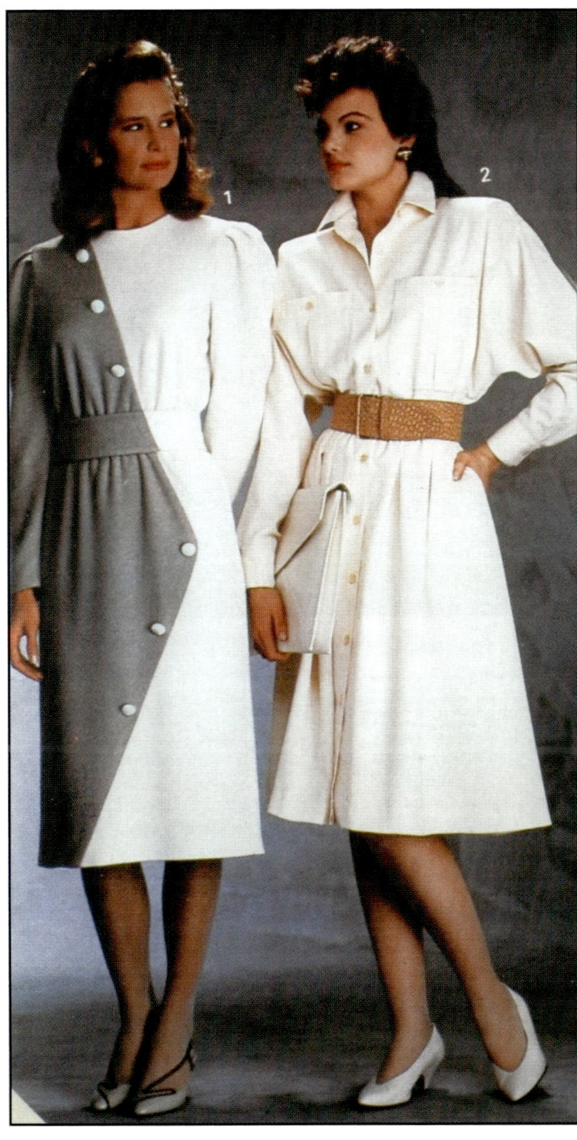

Carriage Court dress in white and gray is knit of acrylic, polyester and rabbit hair. Shirtdress with padded drop shoulders in polyester gabardine. *Fall/Winter 1985*

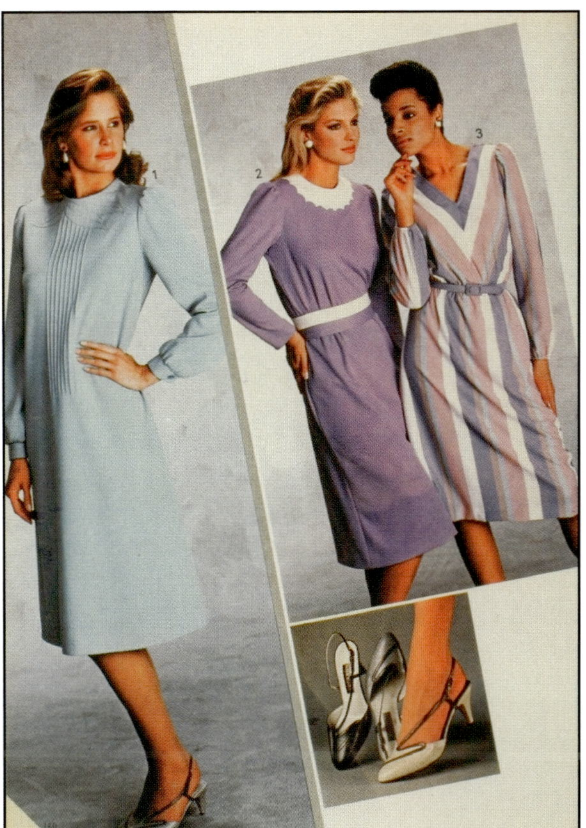

Dusty blue chemise from Sunshine Alley® in polyester and wool knit. Lilac spun polyester dress with cream neck insert. Purple, mauve, and cream stripes on a shoulder-buttoned pullover dress. *Fall/Winter 1985*

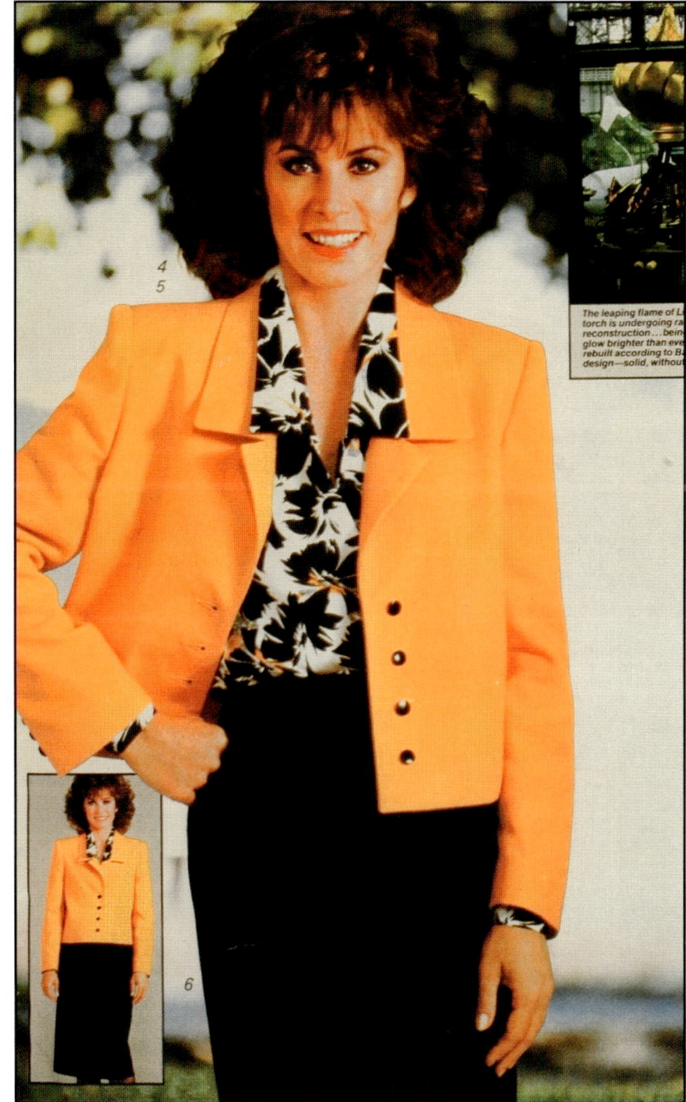

Polyester and rayon weave marigold jacket, button front blouse with shoulder pads, and black linen-look skirt. *Spring/Summer 1986*

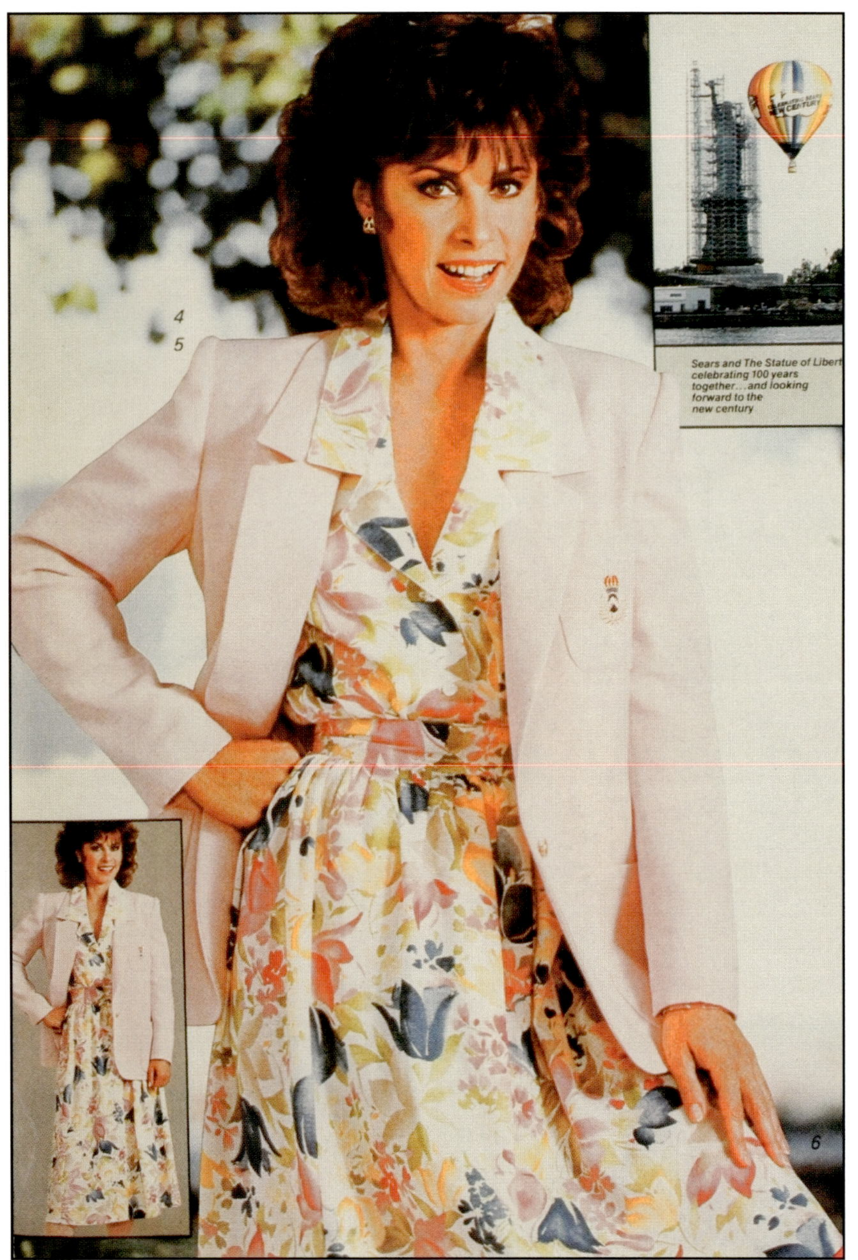

Soft pink blazer has shoulder pads in polyester and rayon weave. Polyester and cotton shirt and skirt are done in a leno weave that feels like linen. *Spring/Summer 1986*

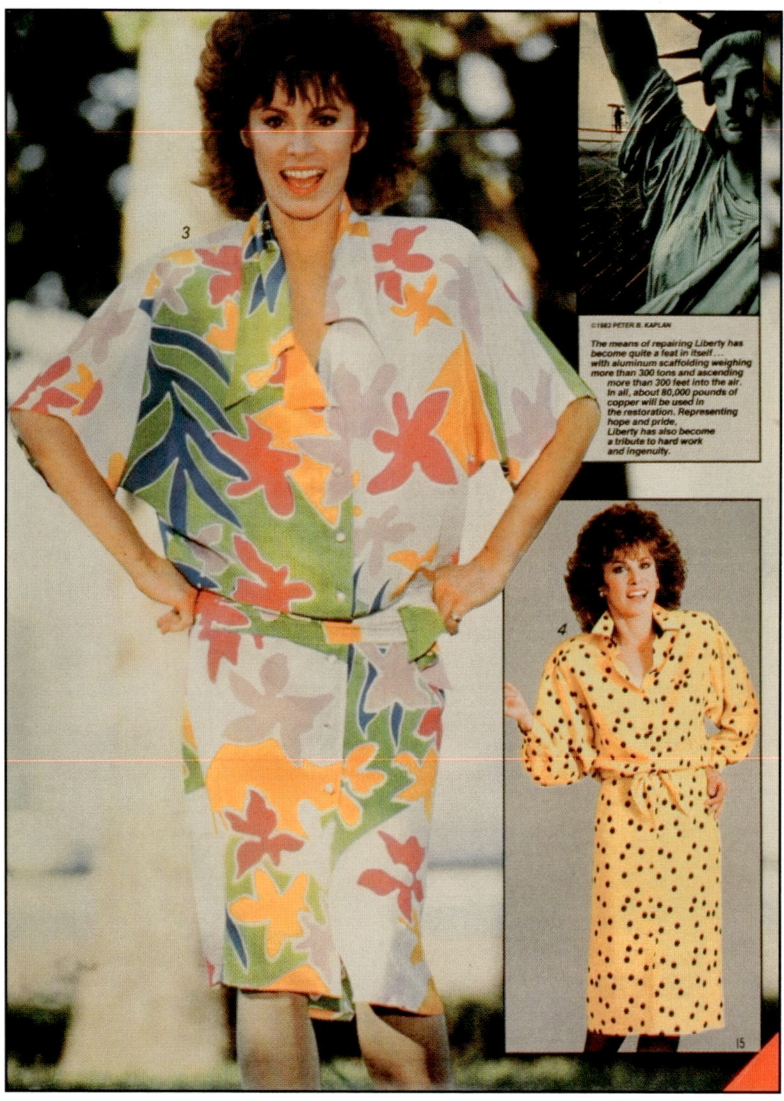

Floral print dress has an oversized collar, shoulder pads, and dolman sleeves. Coin dot coat style dress in woven polyester crepe. *Spring/Summer 1986*

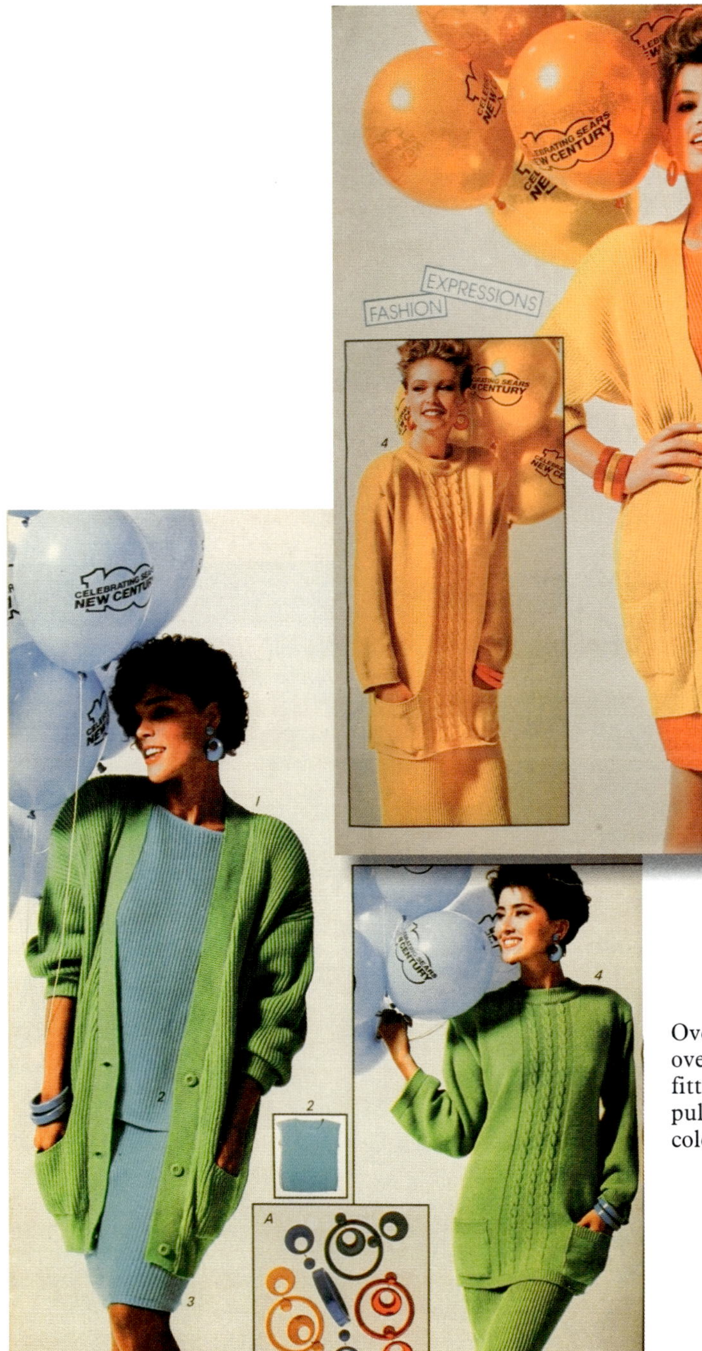

Oversized cardigan, slightly oversized sleeveless top, snug fitting skirt, and cable knit pullover sweater in exciting colors. *Spring/Summer 1986*

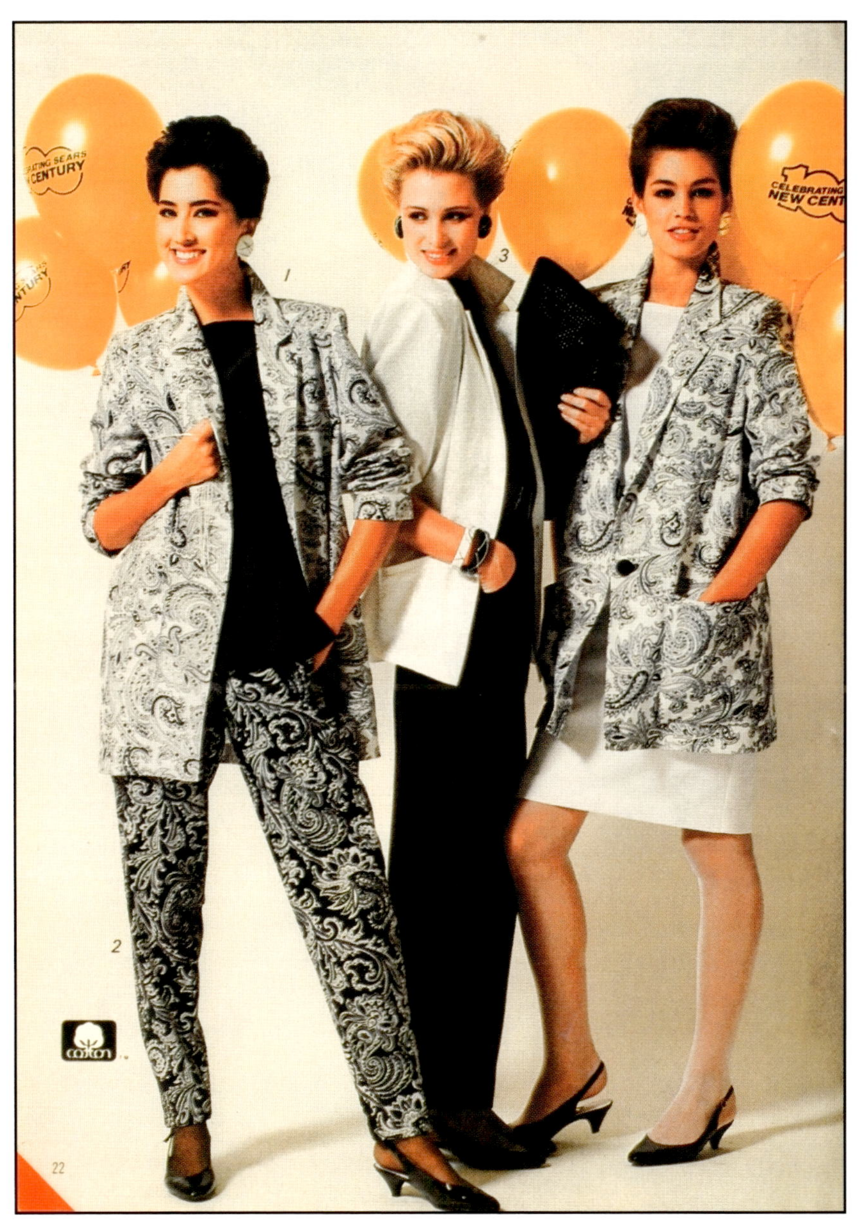

Paisley printed blazer and pants, or black and white solids, mix and match for a variety of styles. *Spring/Summer 1986*

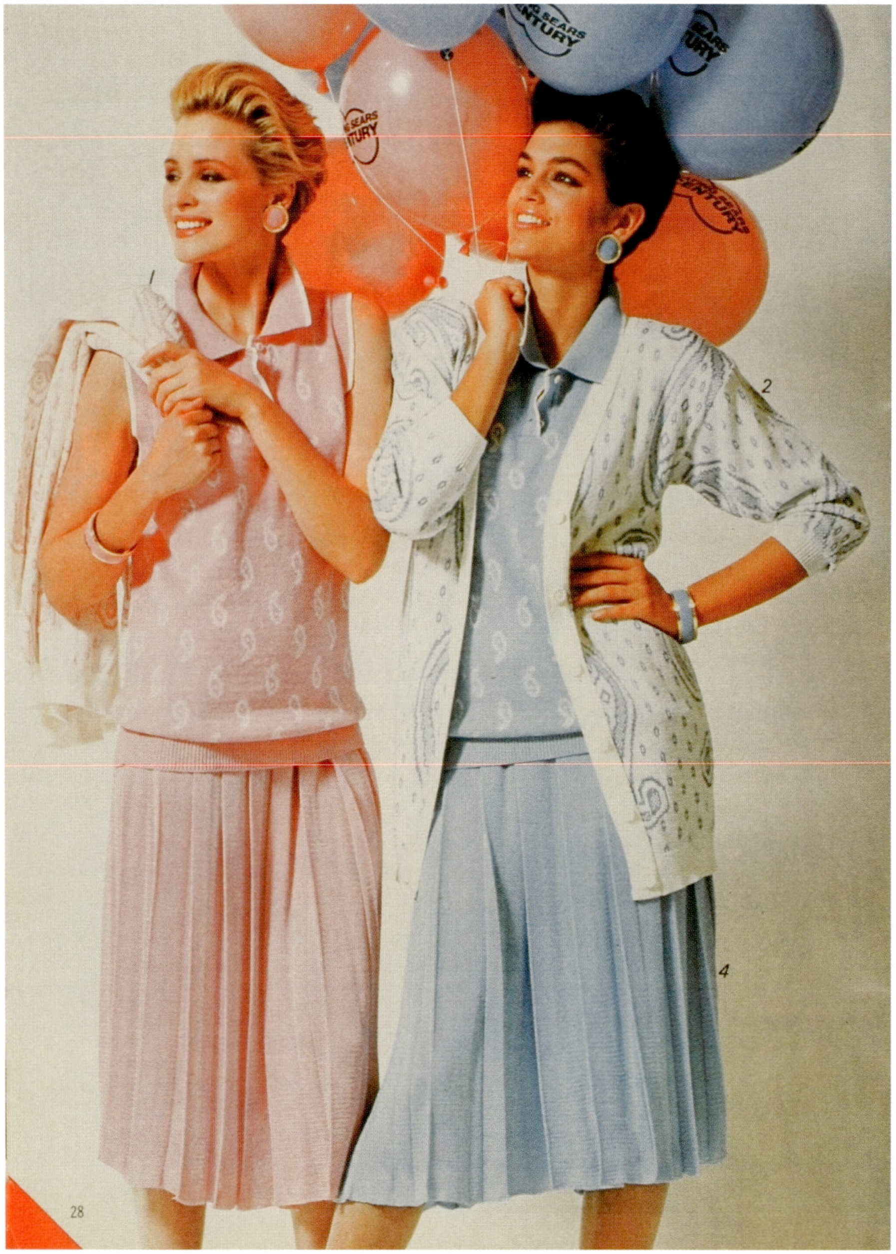

Slightly oversized sleeveless pullover with subtle paisley print, coordinating cardigan, and box-pleated skirt in blue or pink. *Spring/Summer 1986*

Lamb's wool and nylon knit sweater dress has cable stitched accents on the raglan sleeves, ribbed finish at the neck, sleeves, and hem. *Fall/Winter 1986*

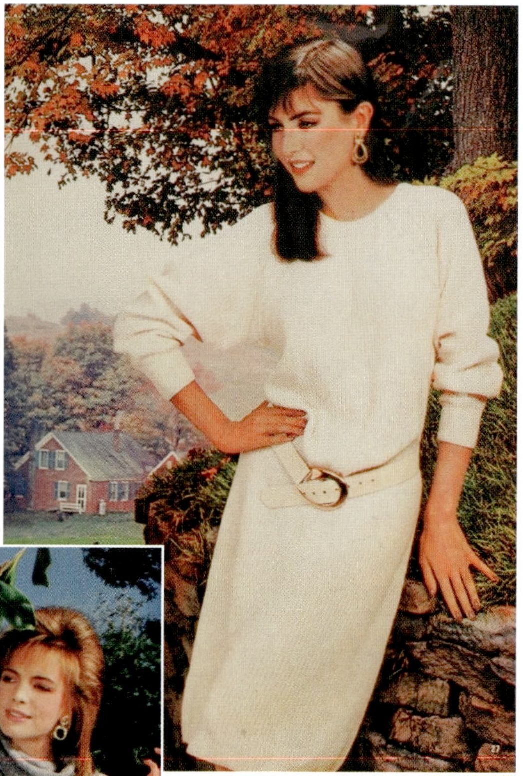

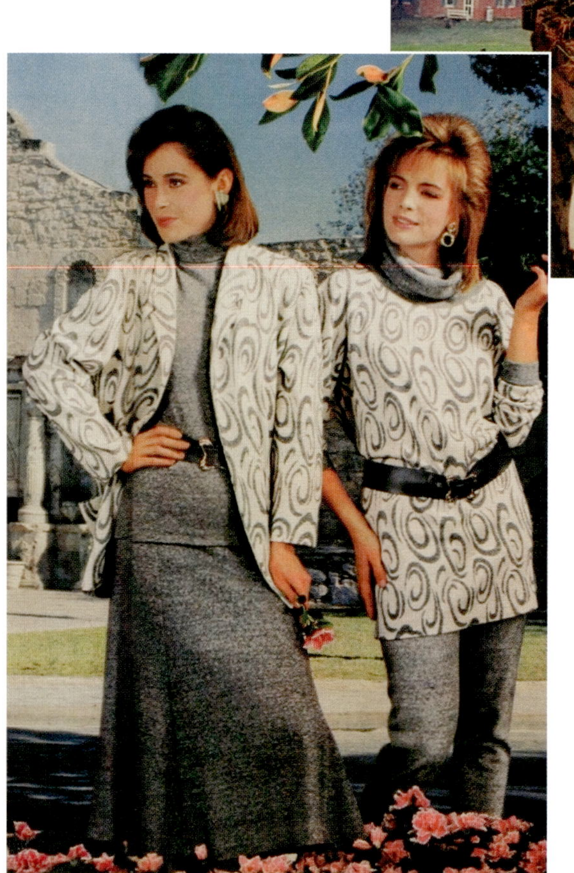

Five interchangeable pieces of jersey knits in a gray and white pattern or all gray. *Fall/Winter 1986*

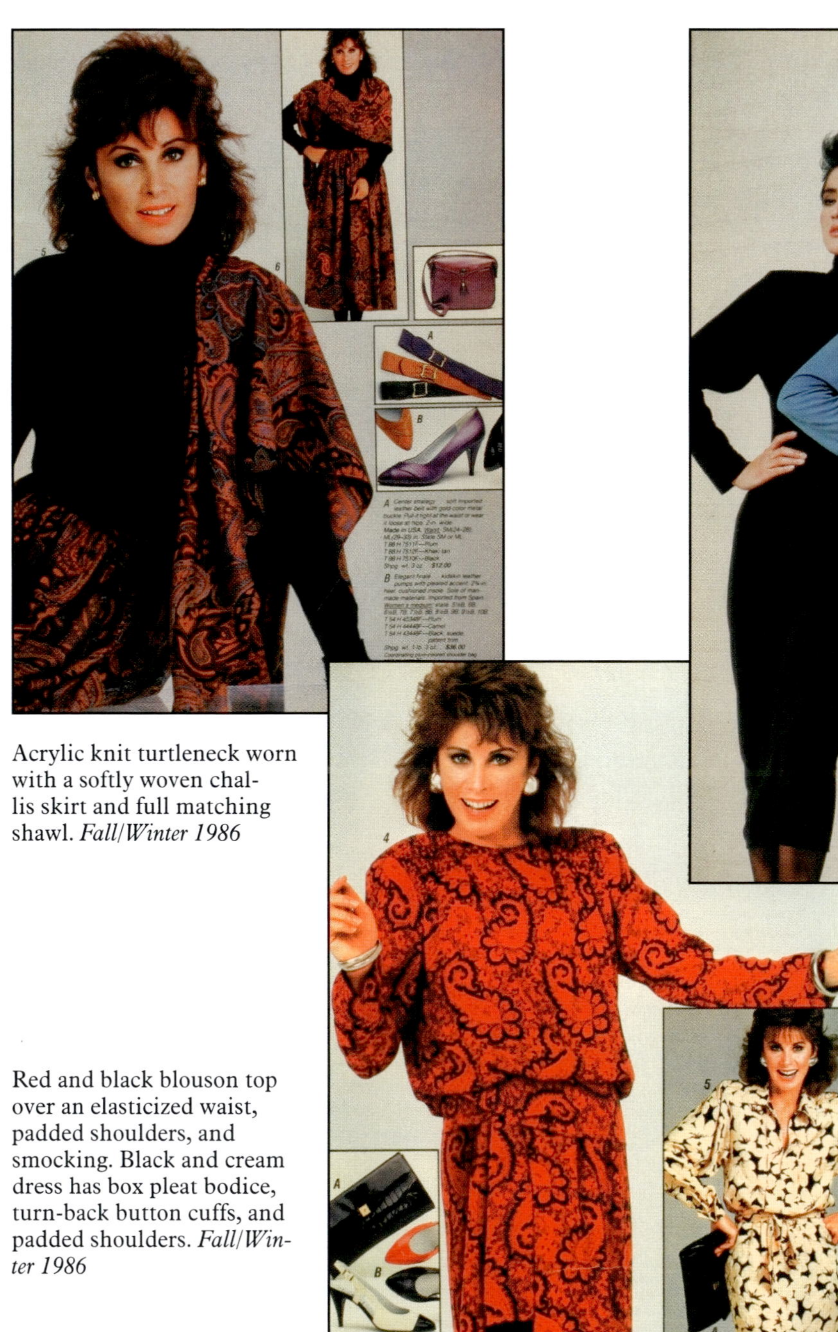

Acrylic knit turtleneck worn with a softly woven challis skirt and full matching shawl. *Fall/Winter 1986*

Red and black blouson top over an elasticized waist, padded shoulders, and smocking. Black and cream dress has box pleat bodice, turn-back button cuffs, and padded shoulders. *Fall/Winter 1986*

Bodysuit with shoulder pads and snap closure crotch, sarong skirt has a button closure. *Fall/Winter 1986*

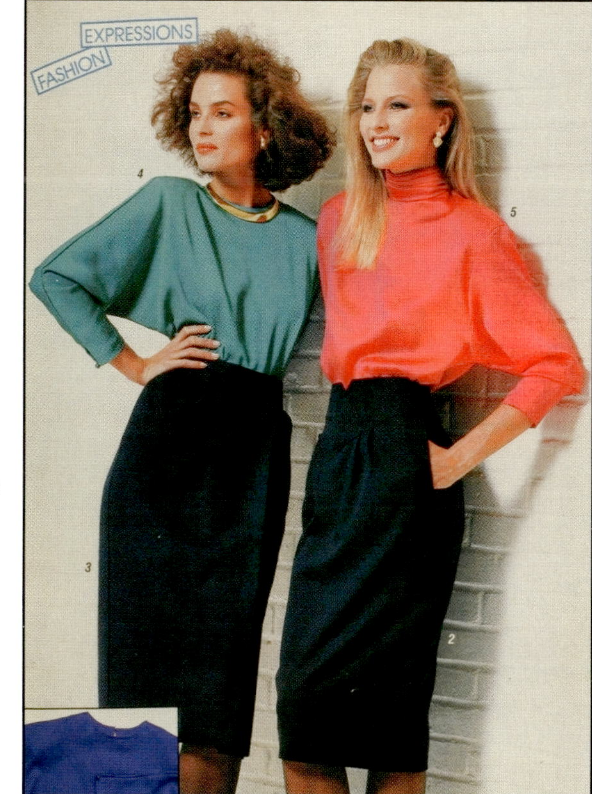

Satiny woven polyester blouses in a jewel-neck and crushed collar style, worn with polyester and wool gabardine skirts. *Fall/Winter 1986*

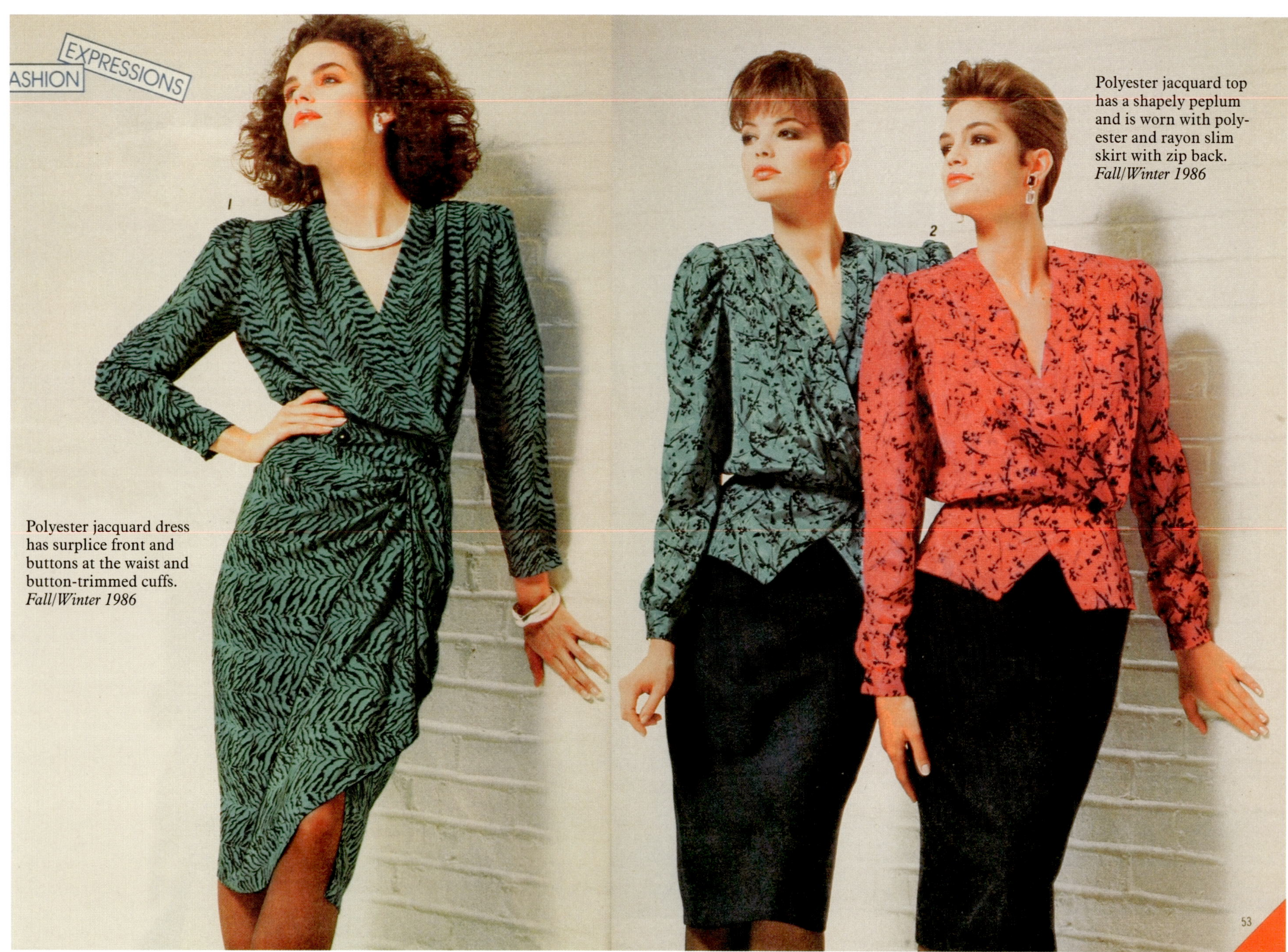

Polyester jacquard dress has surplice front and buttons at the waist and button-trimmed cuffs. *Fall/Winter 1986*

Polyester jacquard top has a shapely peplum and is worn with polyester and rayon slim skirt with zip back. *Fall/Winter 1986*

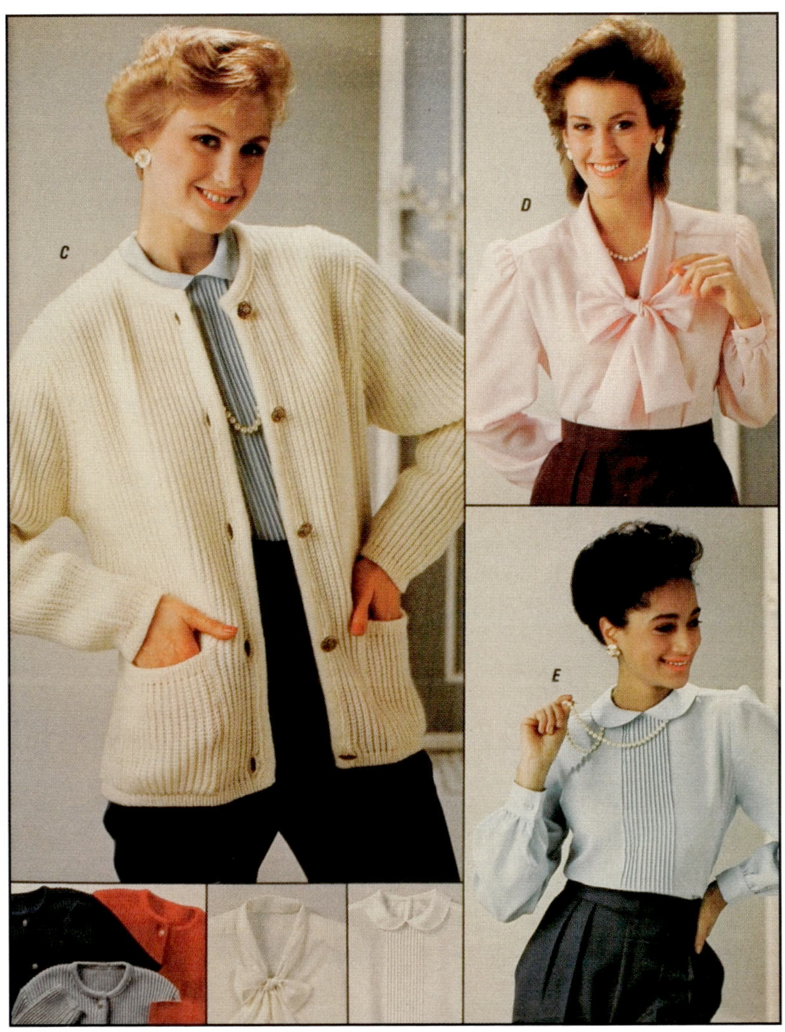

Shaker stitch cardigan sweater knit of acrylic, self-fabric bow blouse has self covered buttons on cuffs and is woven of Dacron polyester, pleated shirt has keyhole back closure and button cuffs woven of Dacron polyester. *Fall/Winter 1986*

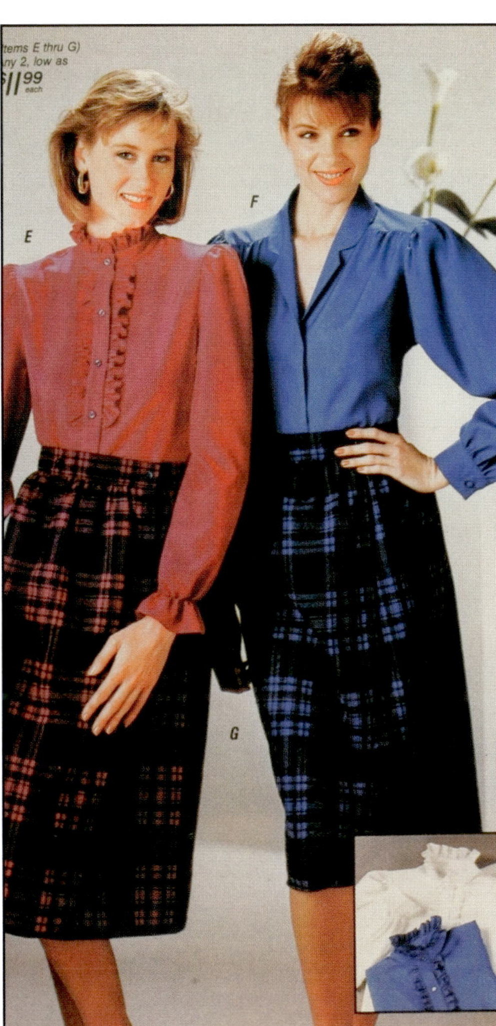

Ruffled blouse and notch-collar blouse are woven of Dacron polyester and worn with a front wrap skirt. *Fall/Winter 1986*

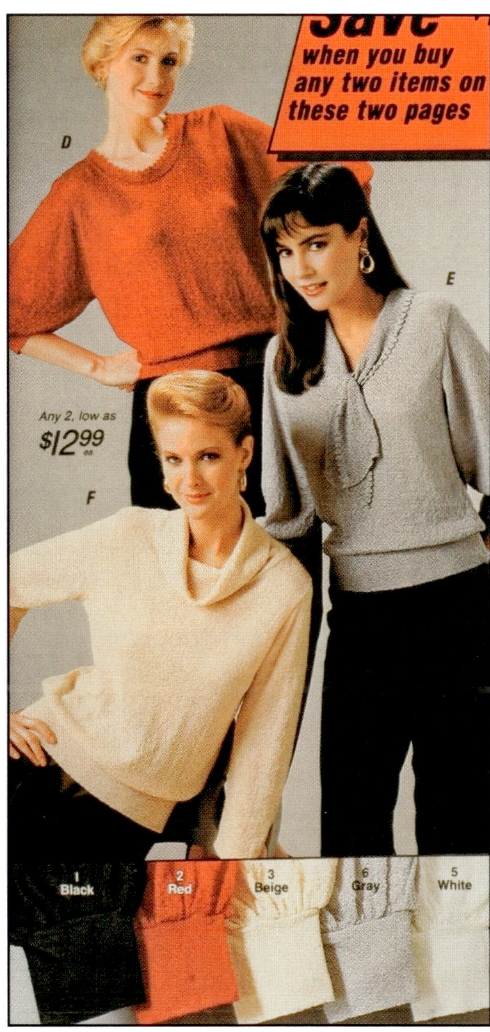

Knit tops and woven pull-on pants. *Fall/Winter 1986*

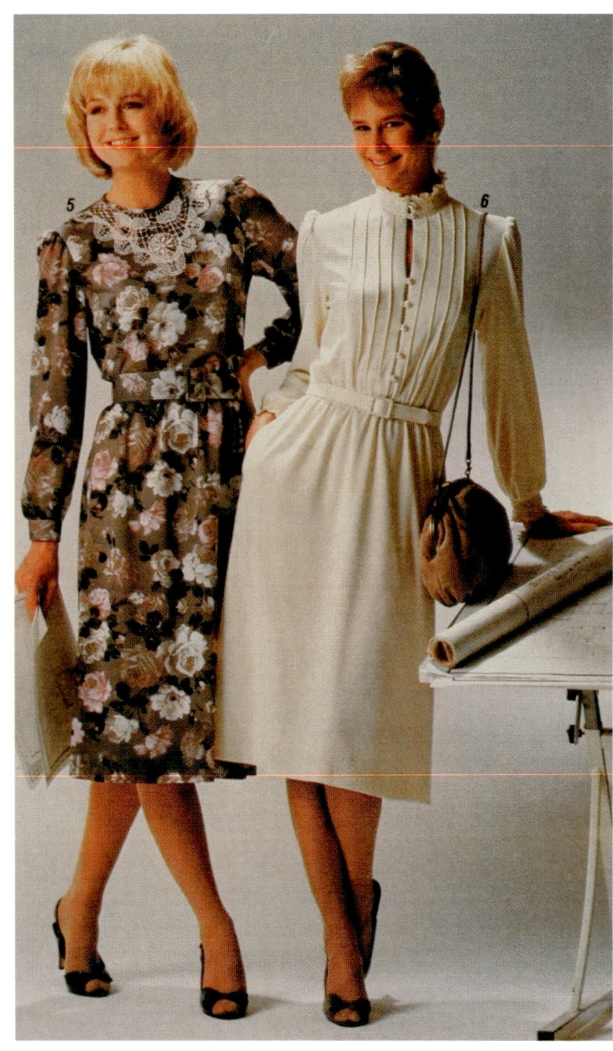

Rose printed crepe dress has an elegant lace collar. Button-front dress has feminine tucks and smocking. *Fall/Winter 1986*

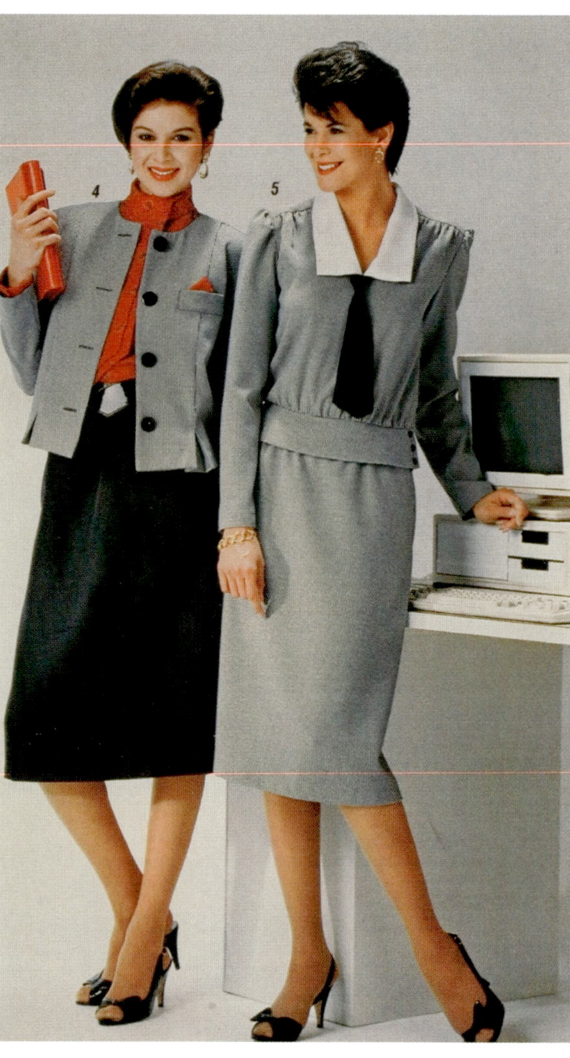

3-piece suit with hounds tooth patterned jacket, red paisley print shirt, and slim skirt. Hounds tooth checked peplum suit has a crisp white collar and removable tie. *Fall/Winter 1986*

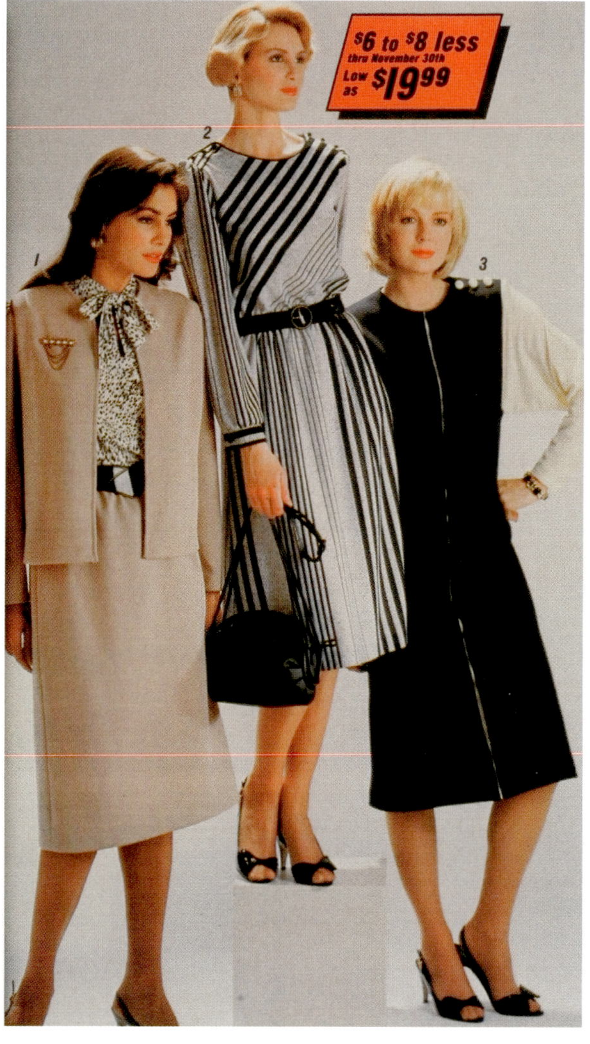

Beige jacket dress has cardigan style jacket, and a printed top with tie neck closure. Scoop neck pullover dress has contrast piping and buttons trimming the shoulders. Black chemise has a contrast inverted front pleat, dolman sleeves, and a back button closure. *Fall/Winter 1986*

Dressy

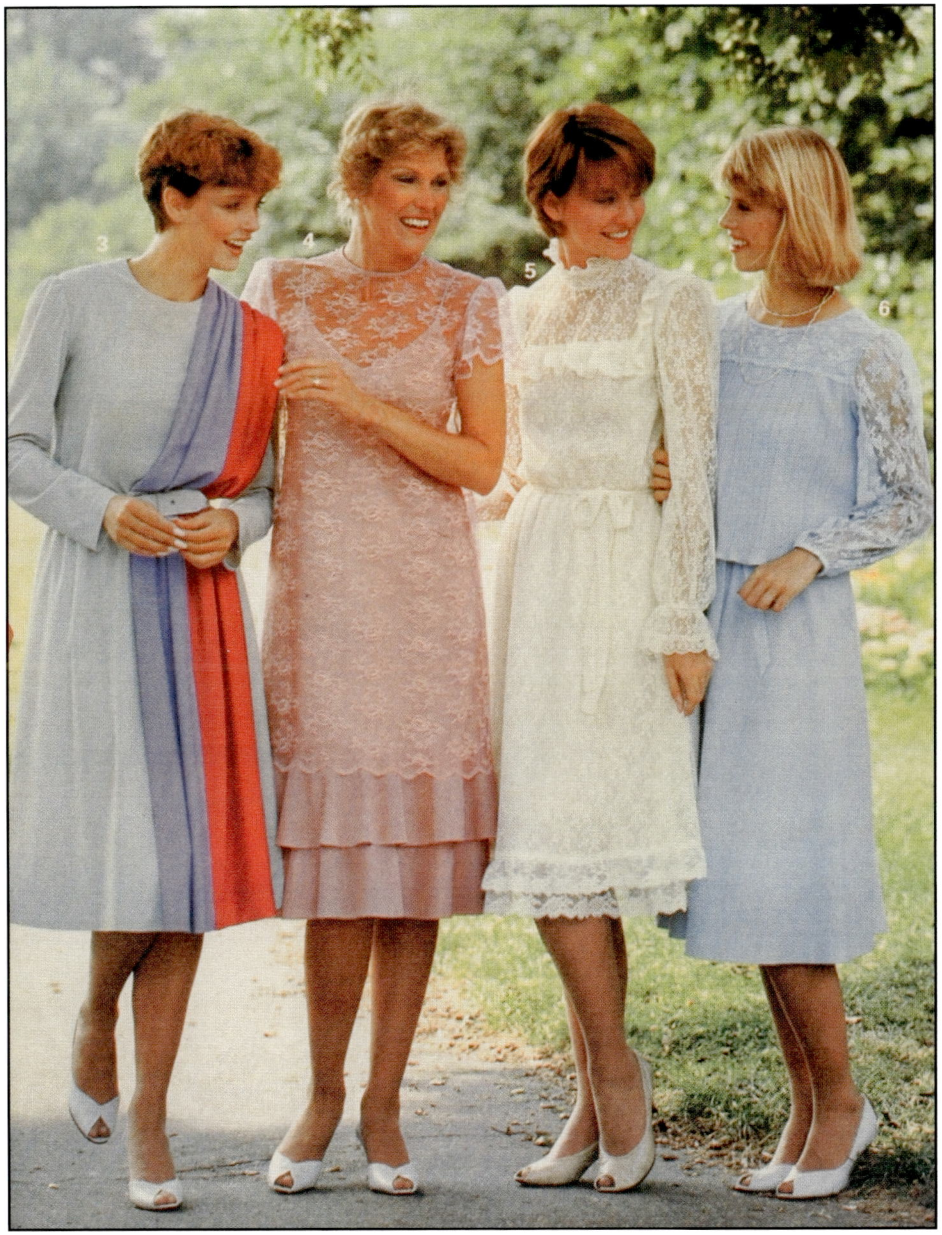

Grecian surplice of lilac and fuchsia drapes over a gray dress. Mauve chemise dress with enchanting lace tunic. Demure romantic lace dress with ruffled trim. Pale blue polyester dress with crystal pleats and lace. *Spring/Summer 1984.*

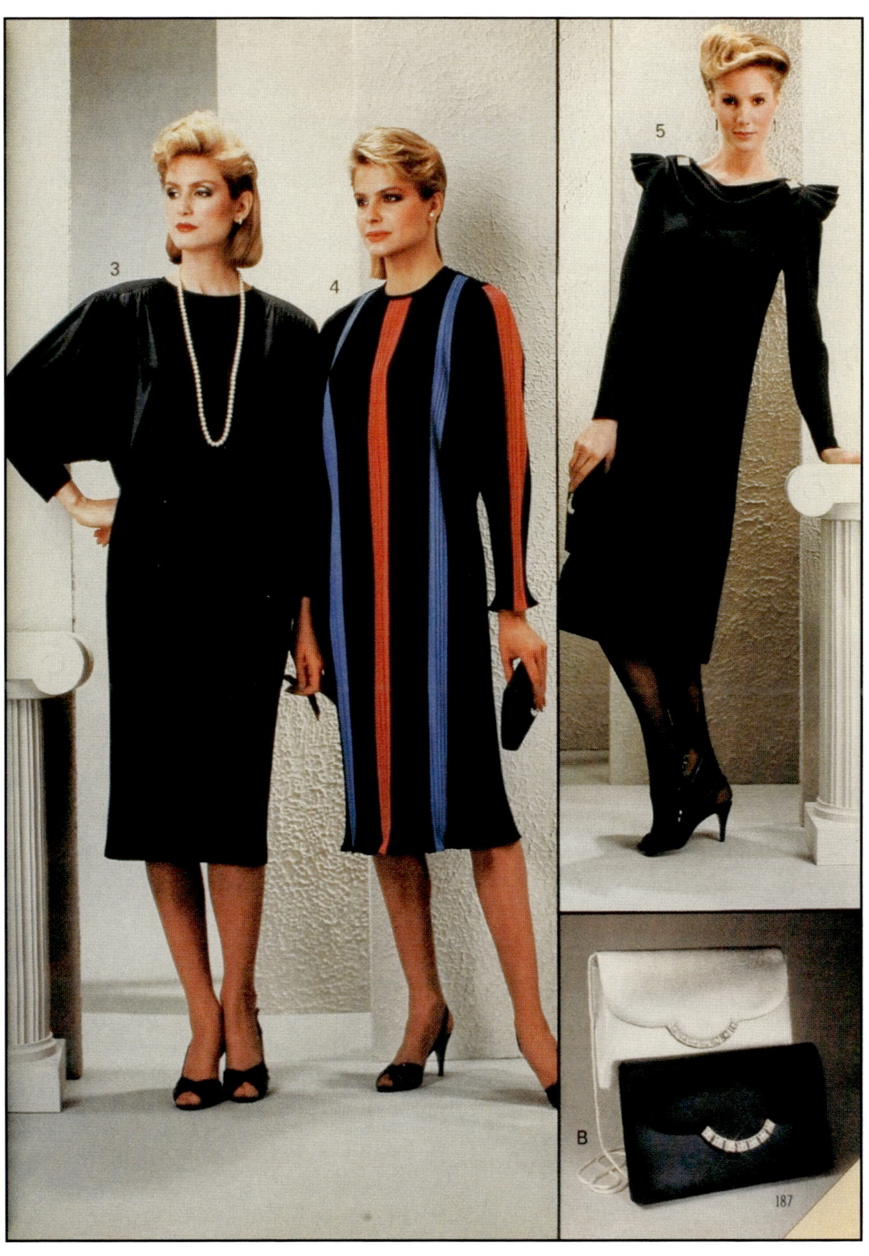

Dramatic black chemise has shirred padded shoulders and deep dolman sleeves, gorgeous periwinkle and raspberry striped dress is crystal pleated, elegant black crepe chemise with detachable rhinestone pins and cowl draped neck. *Fall/Winter 1984.*

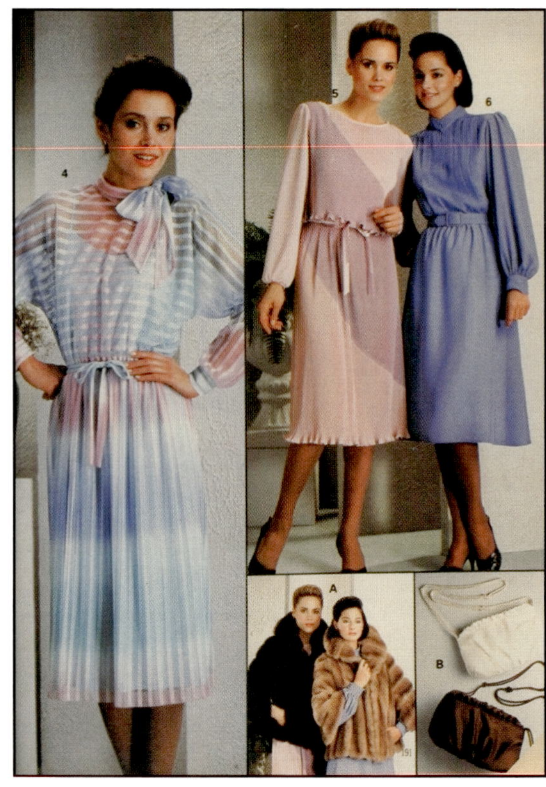

Water-colored striped ribbonette dress has dolman sleeves and side-tie keyhole neck that snaps at the shoulder, crystal pleated color-spliced dress in misty pink and mauve crepe has 2-tone ribbon belt, periwinkle georgette has 2-button stand-up collar and 2-button cuffs. *Fall/Winter 1984.*

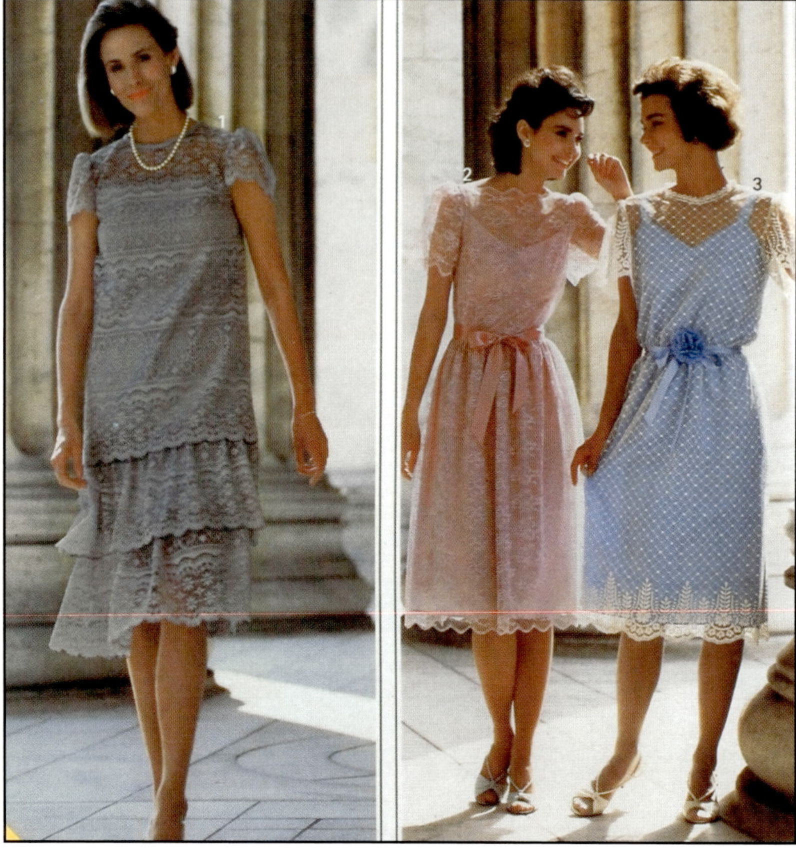

Pearl gray lace tunic with scalloped edges atop a lace-tiered, slip-top chemise. Mauve lace dress with satin ribbon sash. Ivory lace with patterned sleeves over a blue taffeta v-neck lining, satin ribbon sash has a blue flower. *Spring/Summer 1985*

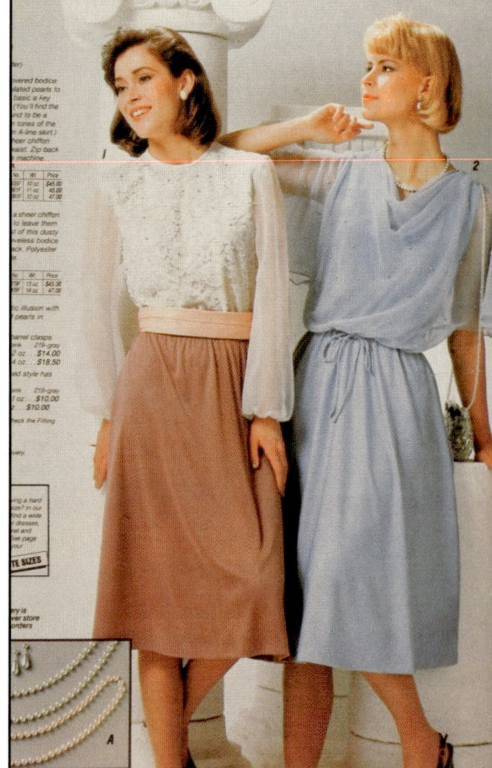

Dress with lace-covered bodice is trimmed in simulated pearls, has sheer chiffon sleeves, an A-line skirt, and cummerbund. Sheer chiffon overlay has simulated pearls, sleeveless bodice, and pleated skirt. *Fall/Winter 1986*

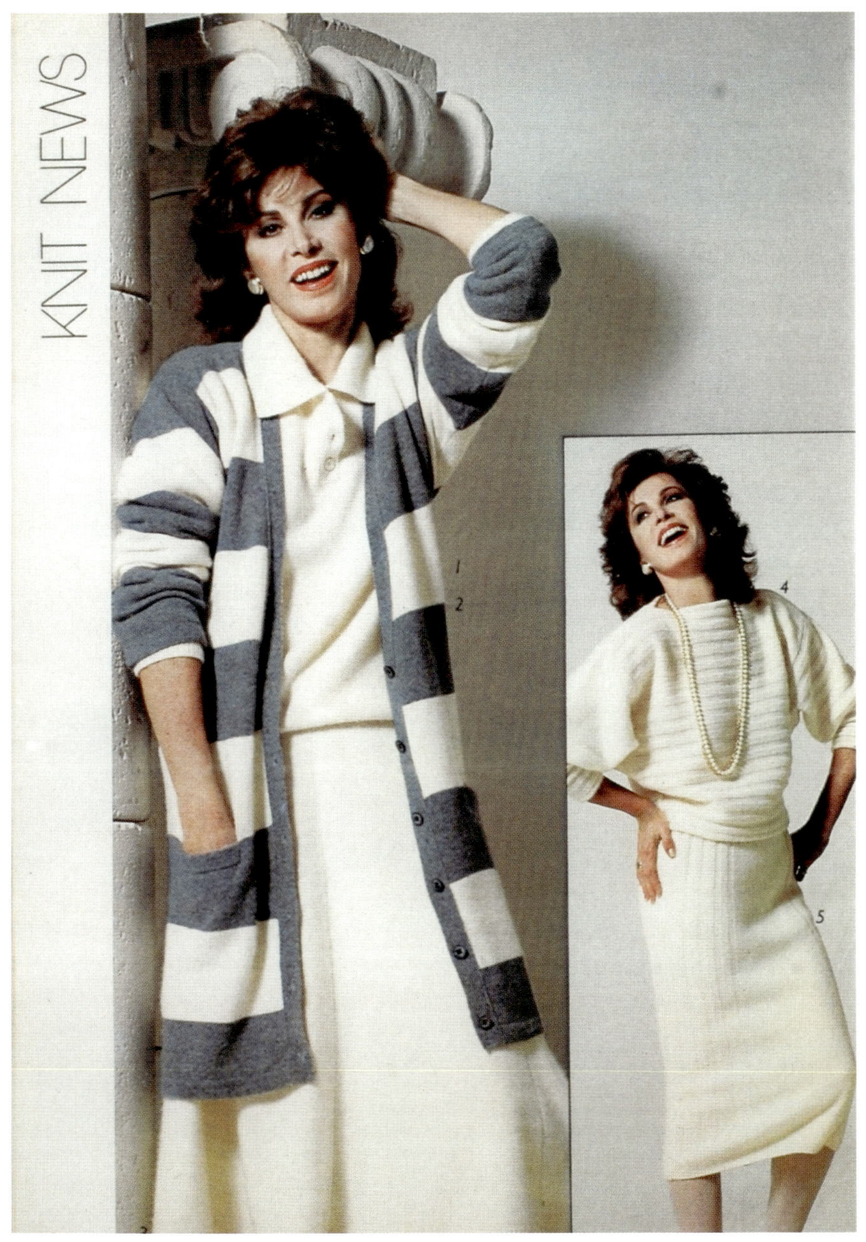

Oversized cardigan sweater with heather gray stripe, long sleeve polo, and 6-gore flared skirt. Boat neck sweater has horizontal ribbing worn with vertical textured slim skirt. *Fall/Winter 1985*

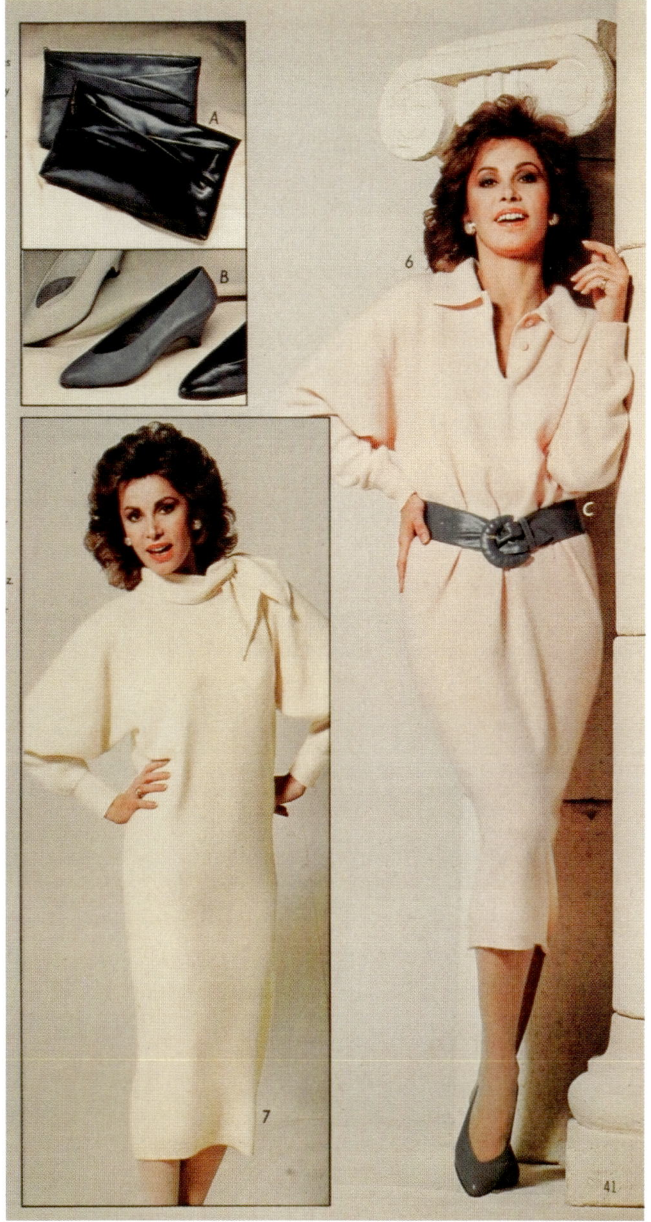

Polo style sweater dress knit of wool, nylon, and angora rabbit hair. Elegant winter white dress in wool, nylon, and angora rabbit hair. *Fall/Winter 1985*

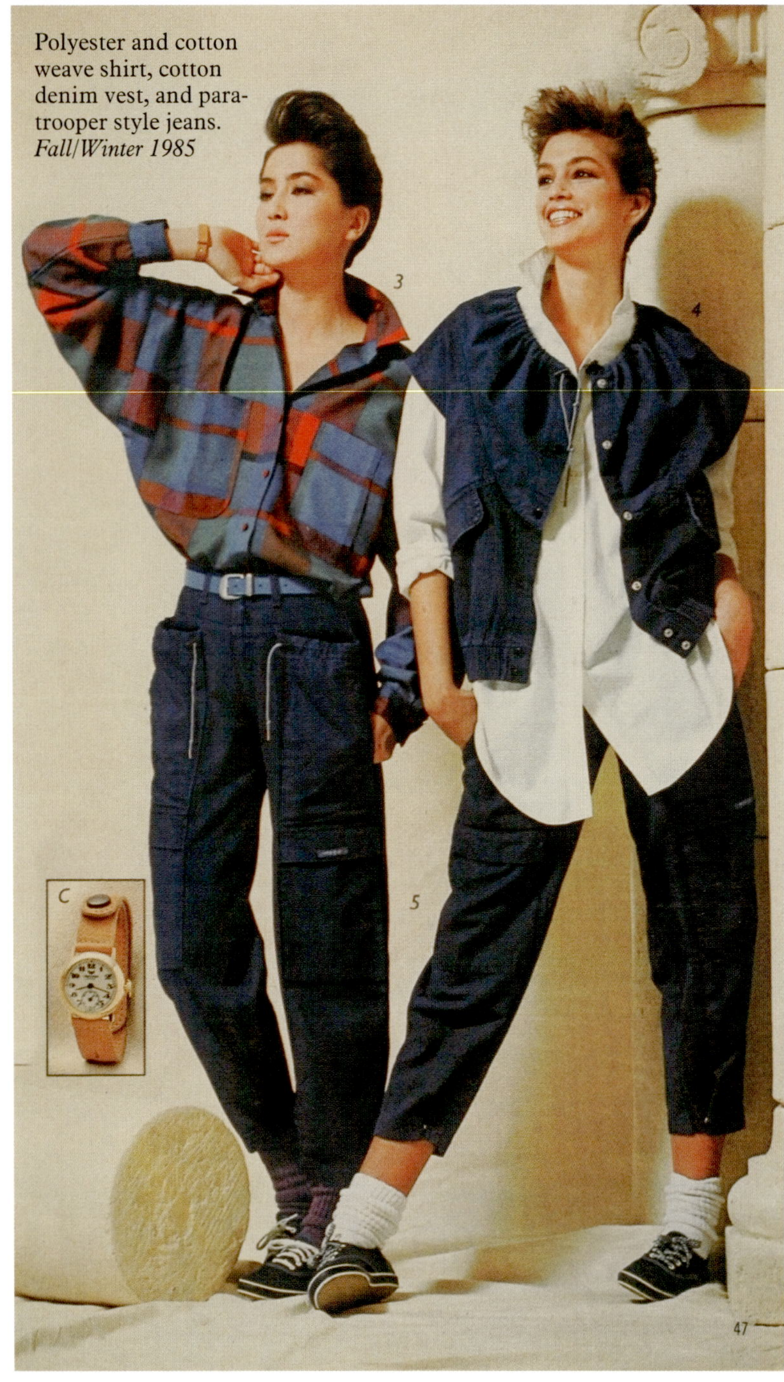

Polyester and cotton weave shirt, cotton denim vest, and paratrooper style jeans. *Fall/Winter 1985*

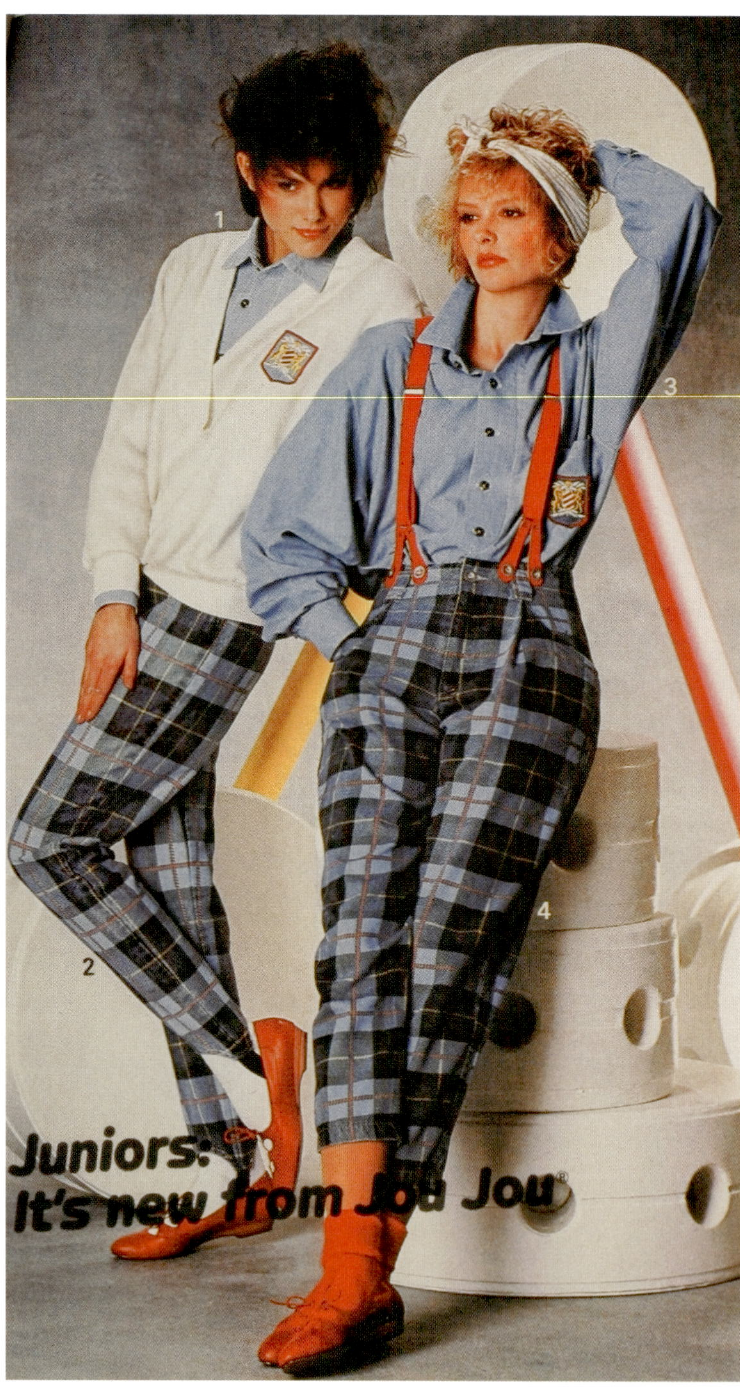

Varsity prep-style shirt and sweater, plaid stirrup pants, and printed cotton denim plaid pants. *Fall/Winter 1985*

Double V pullover shirt with shoulder pads and button trim on the collar worn with a wool skirt. Cotton shirt with removable tie is worn with plaid skirt with side seam pockets. *Fall/Winter 1985*

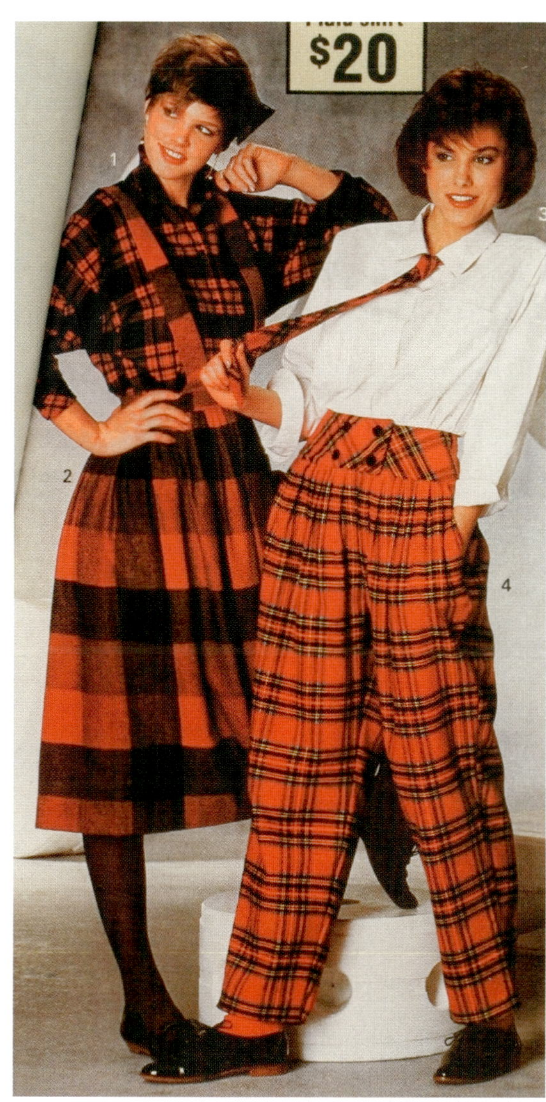

Brush plaid shirt worn with plaid suspender skirt. Oversized white shirt with tartan tie worn with flannel pants. *Fall/Winter 1985*

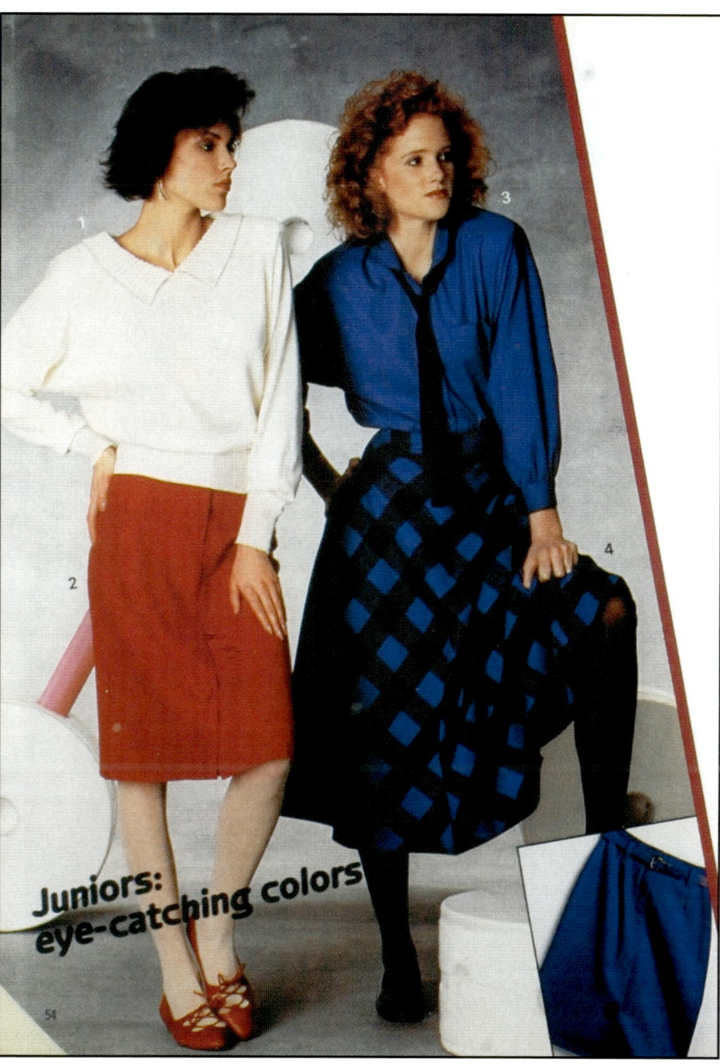

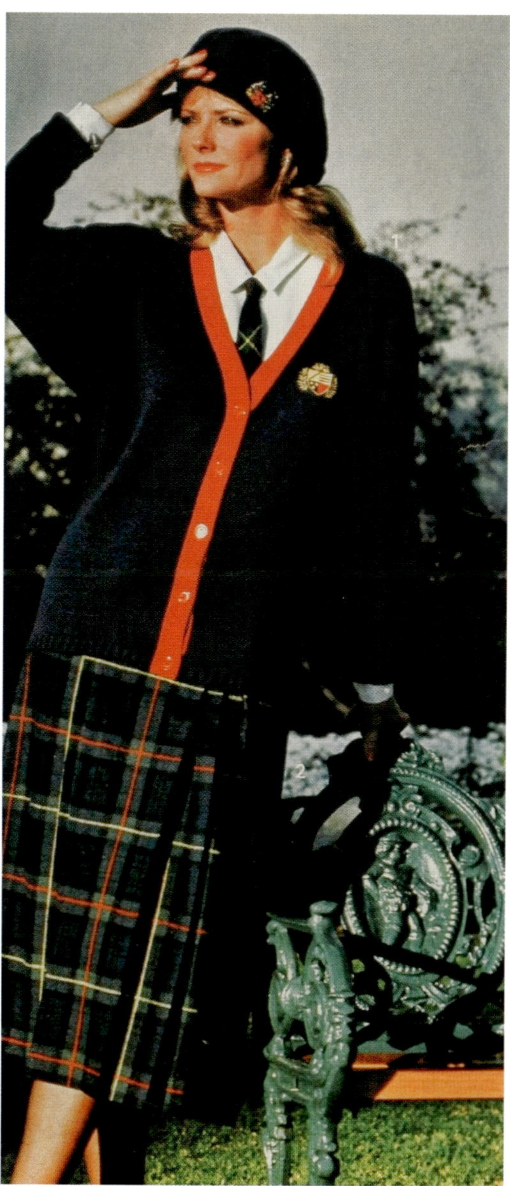

Cardigan sweater is soft and unconstructed, tartan plaid kilt has side button closure. *Fall/Winter 1985*

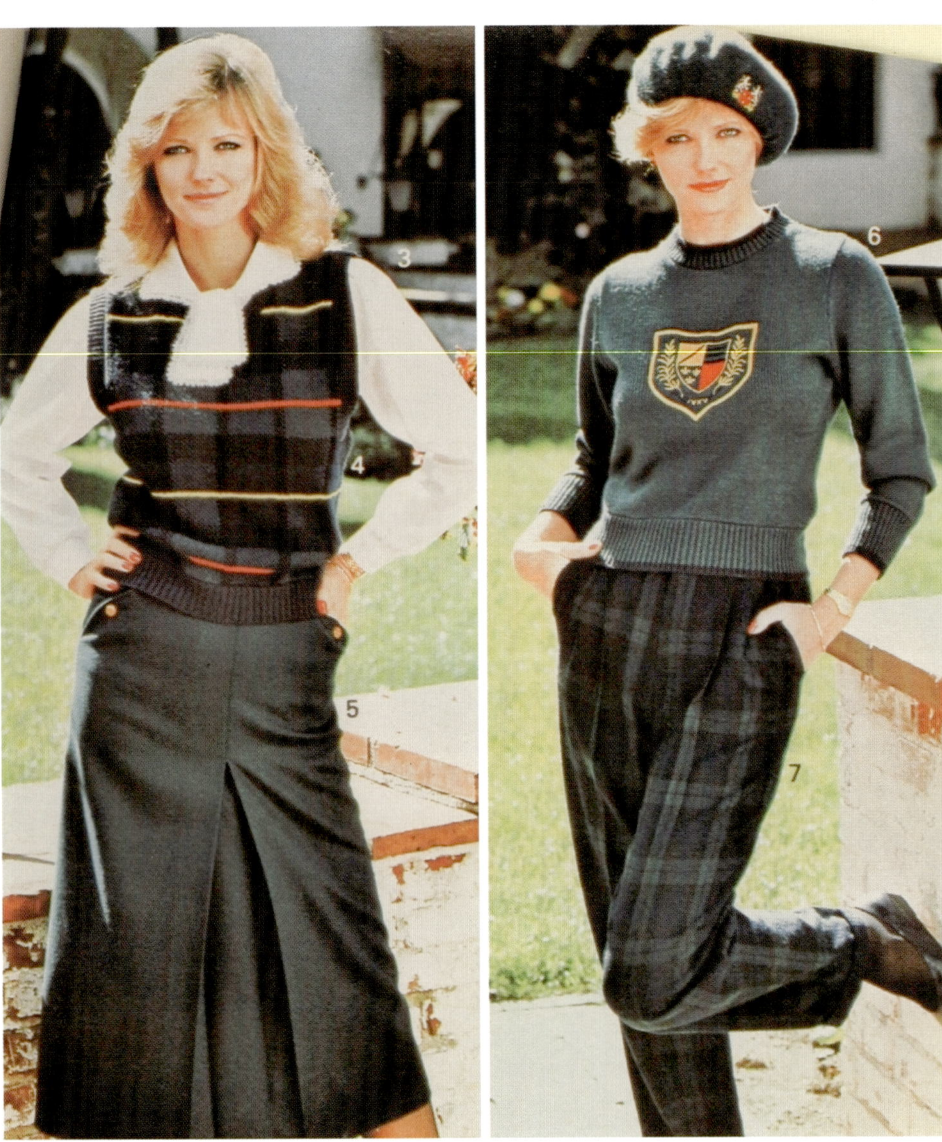

Jabot blouse worn under a tartan vest with an inverted front pleated skirt. Pullover sweater has embroidered crest worn with cuffed tartan man-tailored trousers. *Fall/Winter 1985*

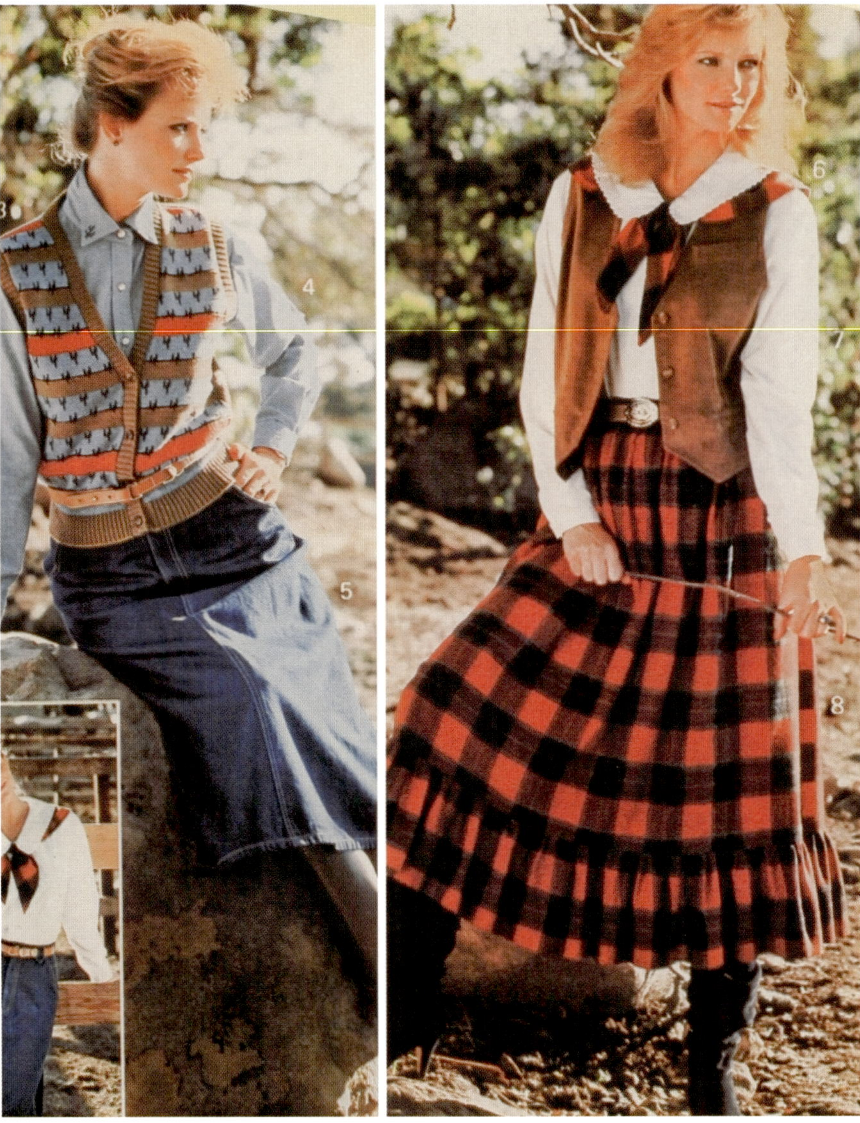

Cactus pattern acrylic sweater vest, chambray cotton and polyester shirt, and denim skirt. Corduroy vest has 3 pockets and adjustable back belt, blouse with plaid kerchief, and a bright country plaid skirt with true prairie charm. *Fall/Winter 1985*

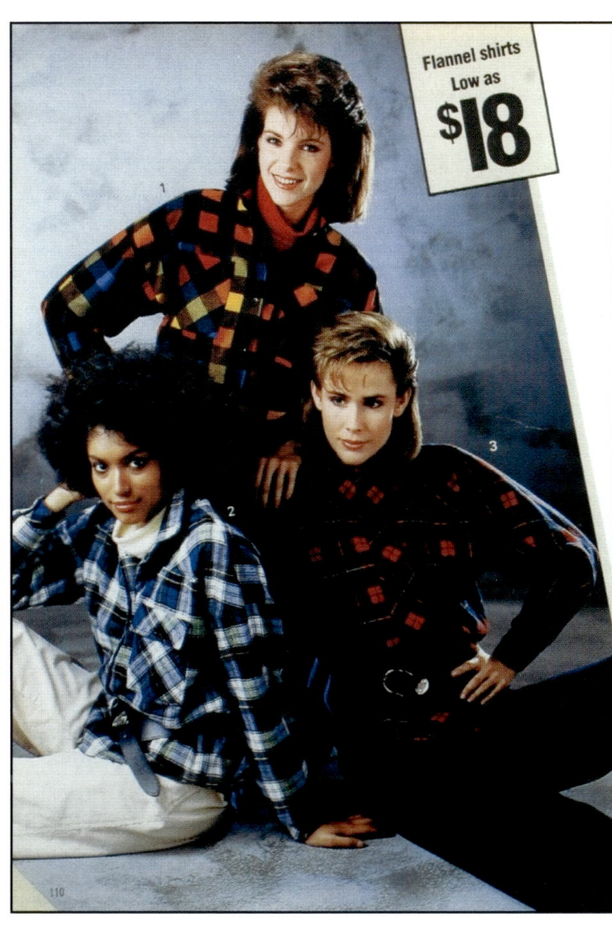

Woven cotton flannel shirts in warm fall colors.
Fall/Winter 1985

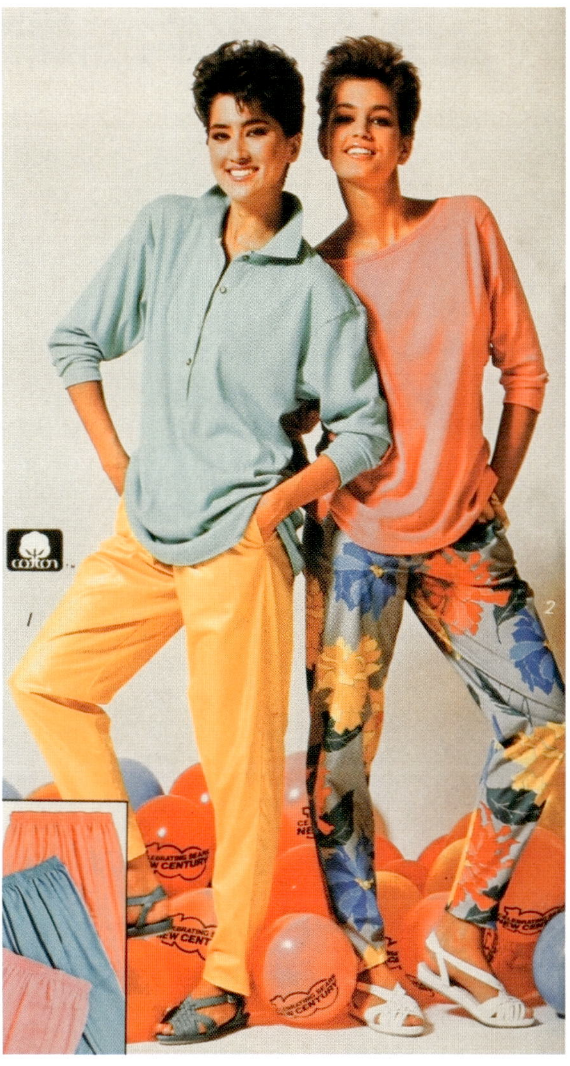

Boat neck or oversized polo shirts worn with solid or floral chintz pants. *Spring/Summer 1986*

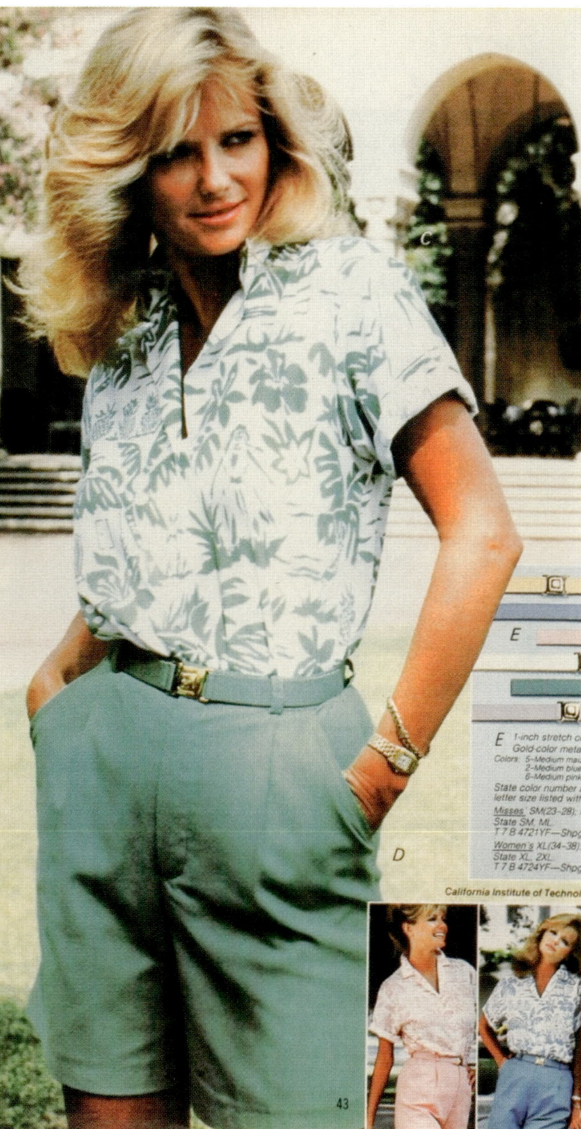

Hawaiian print camp shirt woven of polyester and cotton paired with Bermuda shorts woven of Celanese Fortrel® polyester and cotton.
Spring/Summer 1986

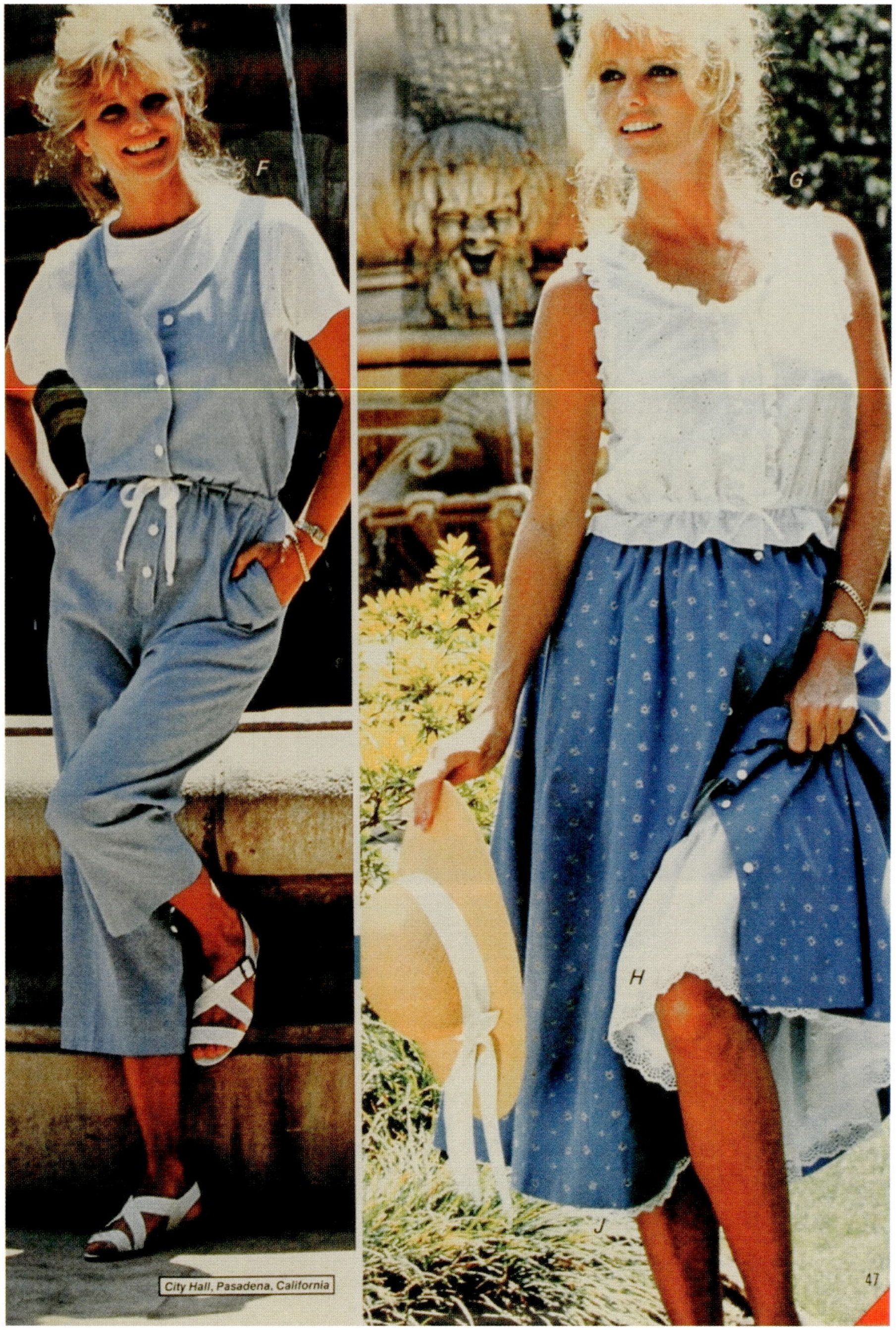

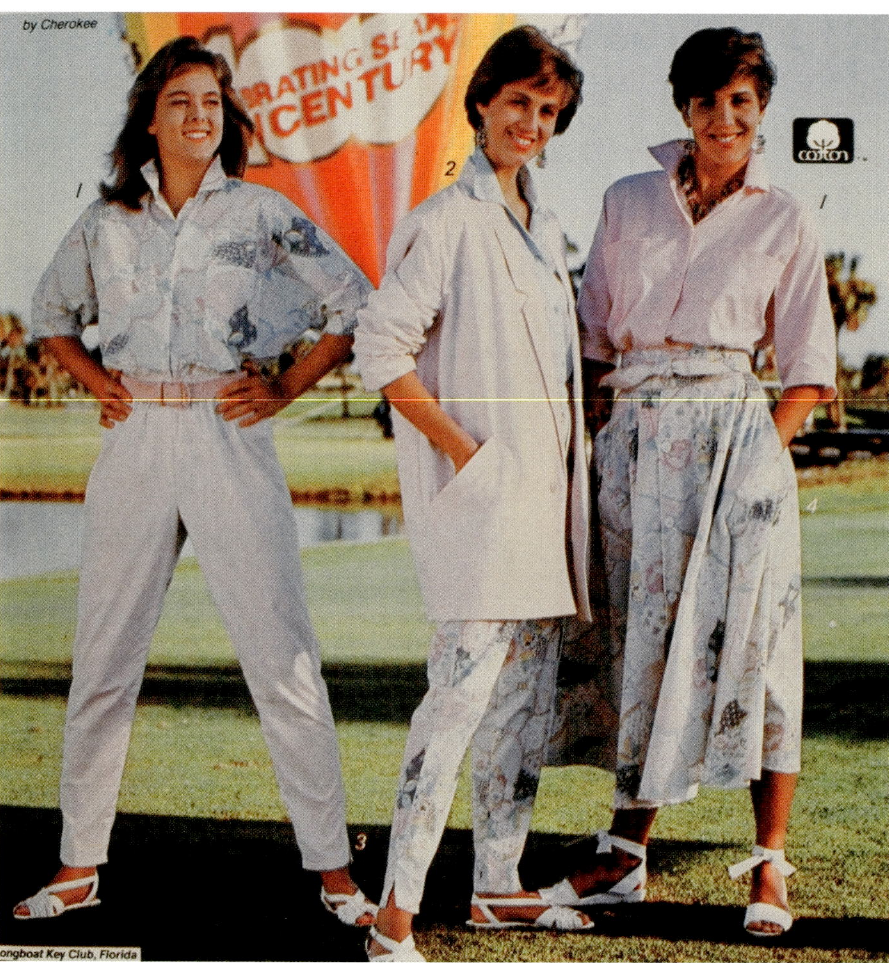

Oversized camp shirt worn with slim pants, oversized boxy blazer worn with printed slim pants, oversized camp shirt worn with a full swingy skirt. All are woven cotton. *Spring/ Summer 1986*

Chambray sleeveless jumpsuit in polyester and cotton fabric. Camisole, flounced petti-skirt, and rosette print skirt. *Spring/ Summer 1986*

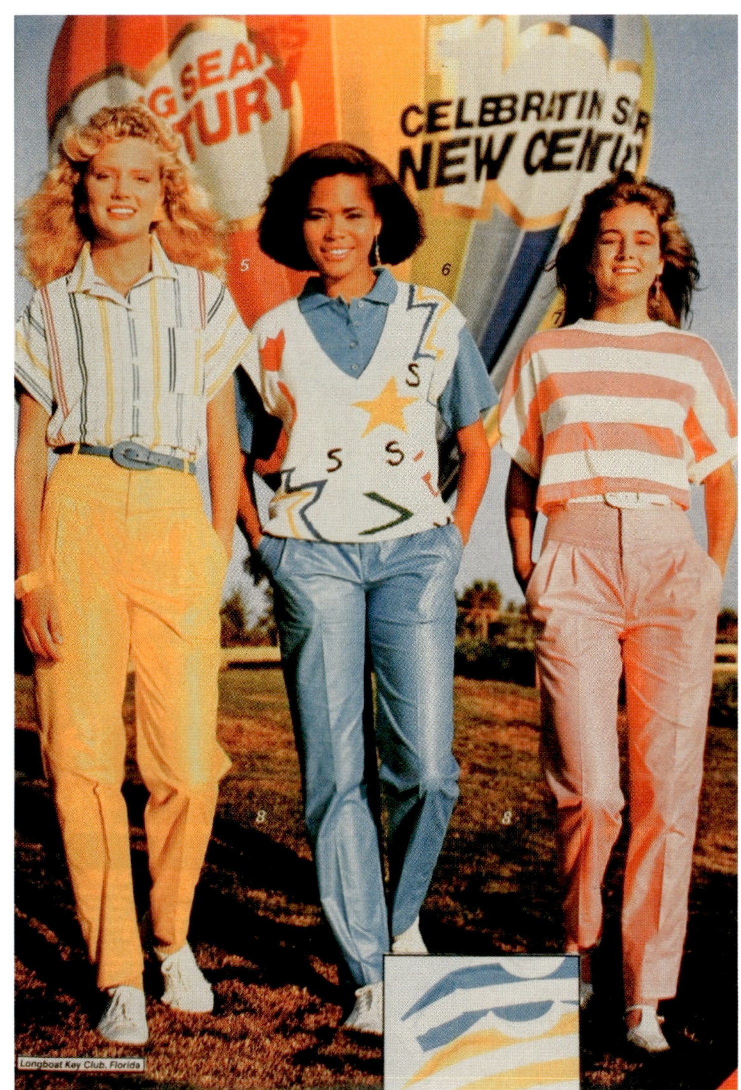

Cotton and polyester striped shirt, sweater vest is knit intarsia of ramie and cotton, oversized cropped top in polyester and cotton, all paired with baggy style shiny pants in woven polyester and cotton. *Spring/Summer 1986*

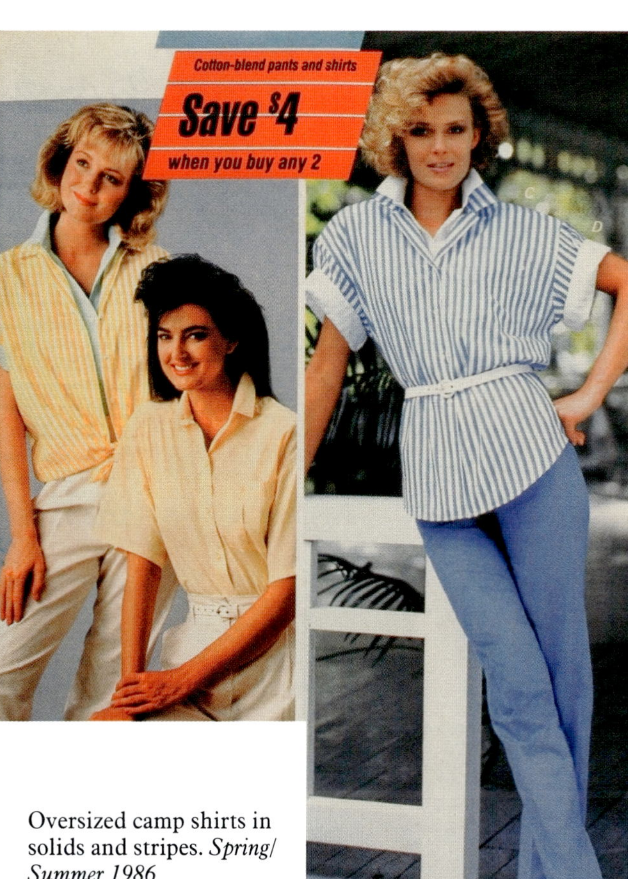

Oversized camp shirts in solids and stripes. *Spring/Summer 1986*

Polyester and cotton polo shirts in solids or stripes paired with pleated Lee® and western style Levi's® jeans. *Spring/Summer 1986*

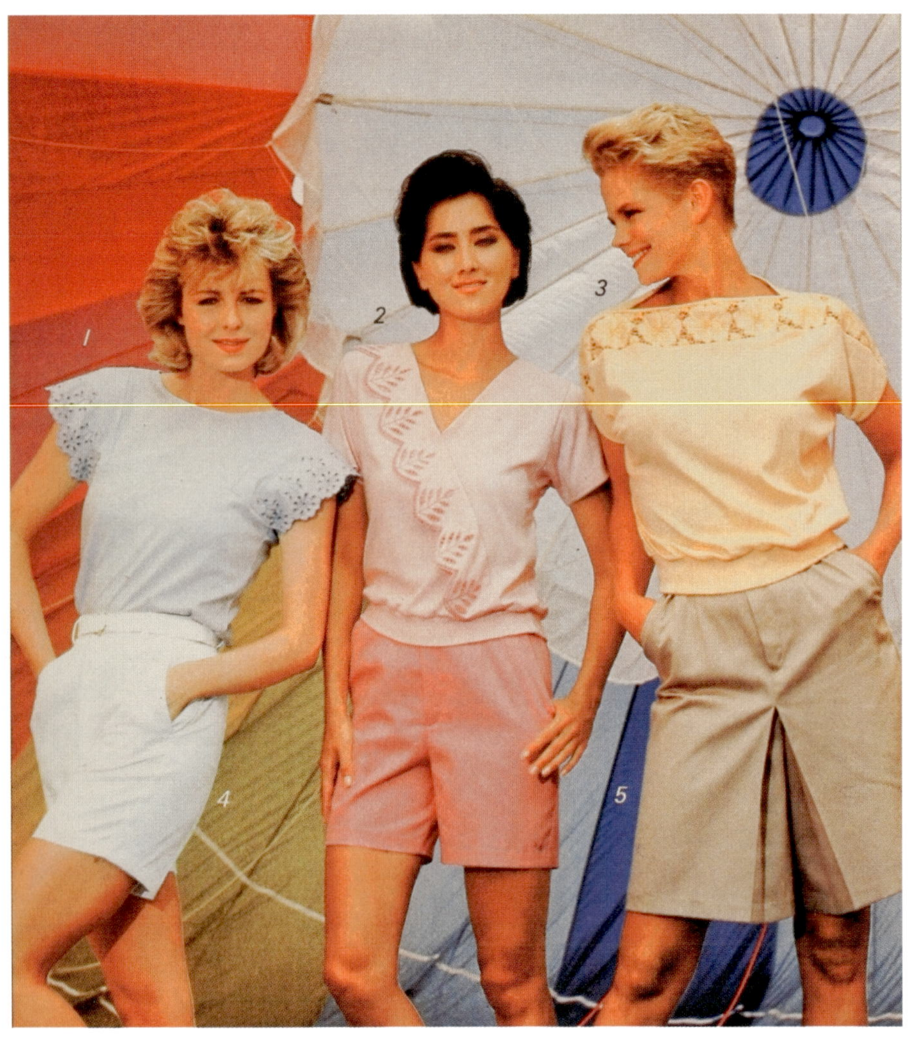

Polyester and cotton tops are accented with embroidery and worn here with cotton and polyester shorts and culottes. *Spring/Summer 1986*

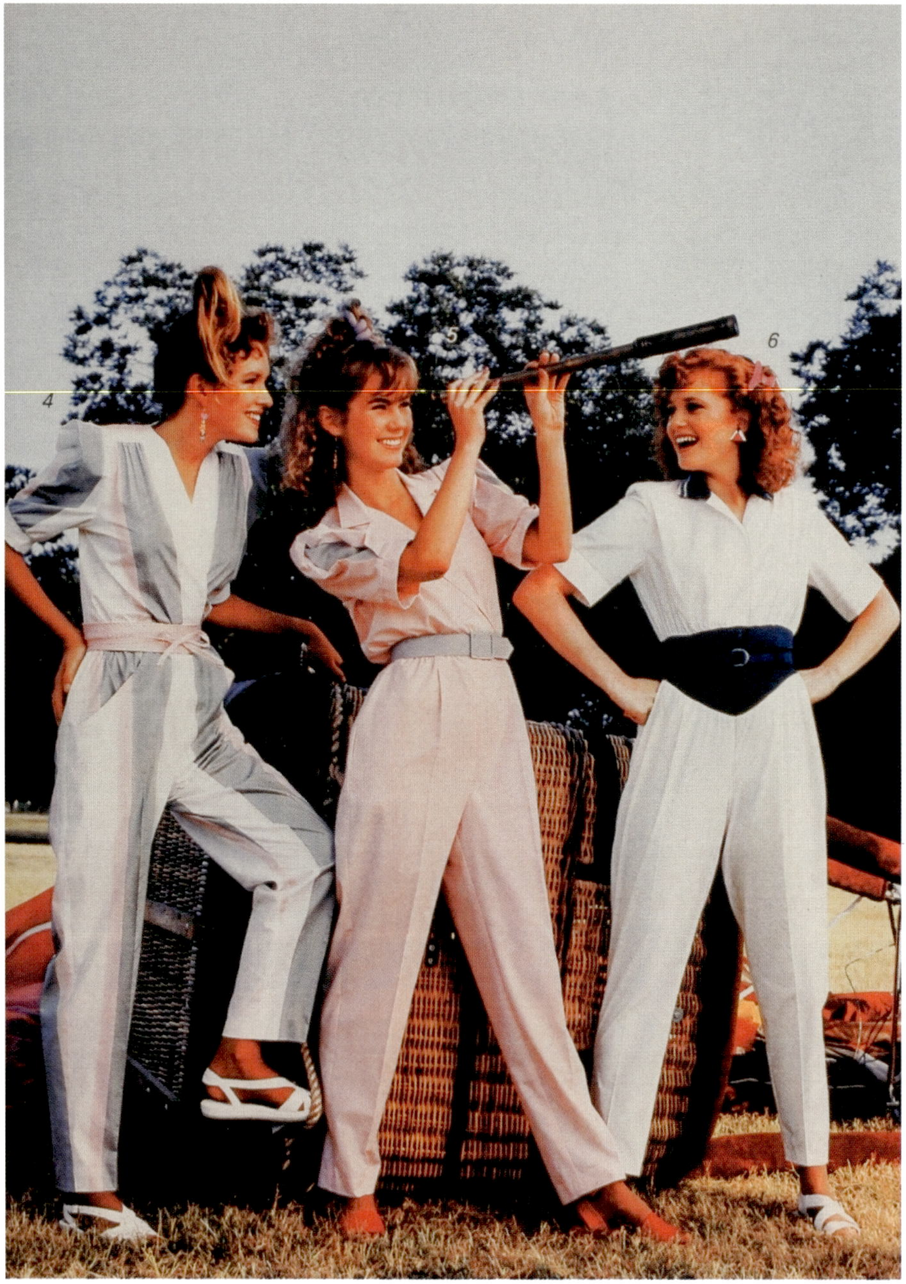

Jumpsuits in pink, gray, and white stripes, pink with contrasting insert on the sleeves, or white has a navy rib knit collar and waist. *Spring/Summer 1986*

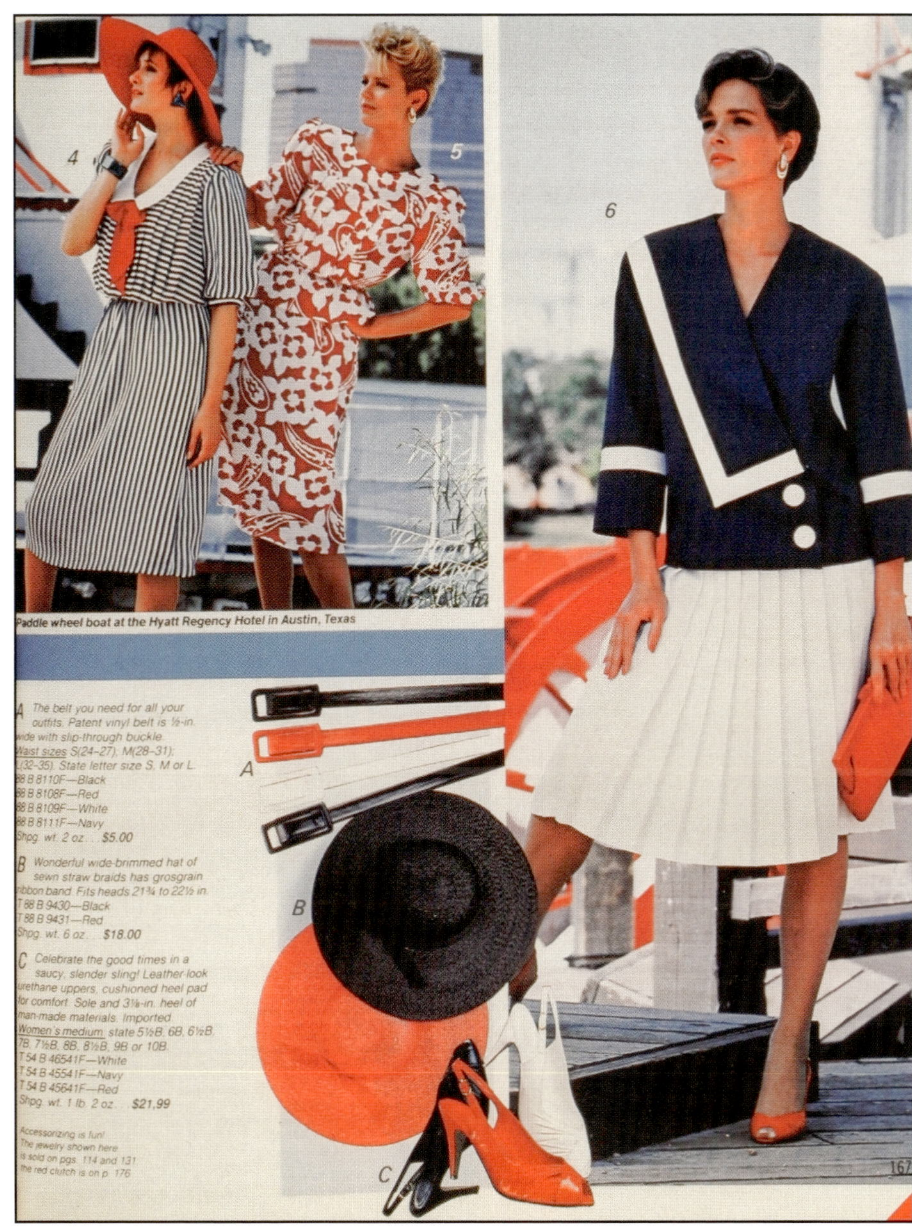

Navy and white georgette dress has shoulder pads, pleats, and an elasticized waist. 2-piece dress has a peplum top, shoulder pads, self covered belt, and skirt has elasticized waist and back slit. 2-piece dress of navy and white has pleated skirt and jacket with shoulder pads. *Spring/Summer 1986*

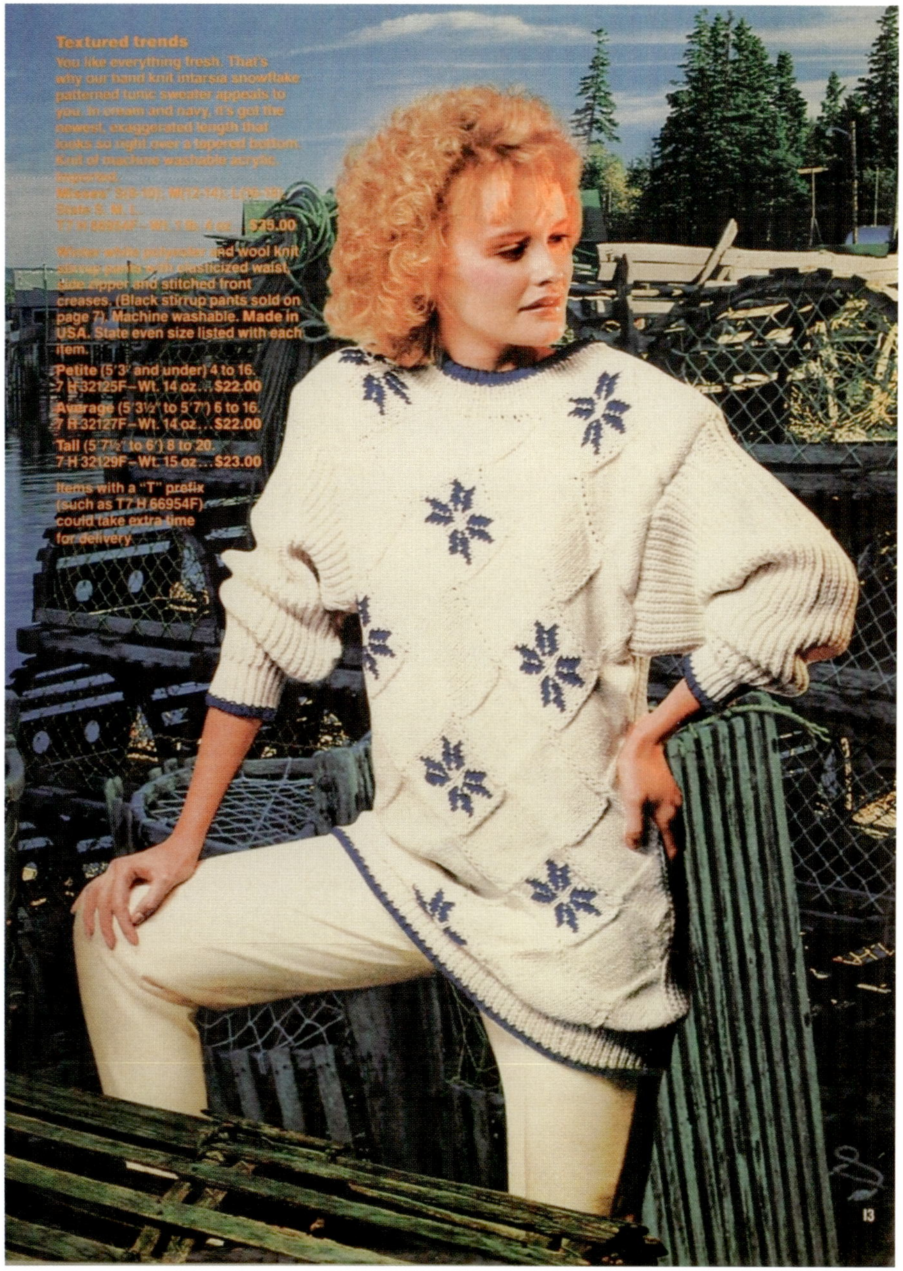

Hand-knit, intarsia snowflake-patterned tunic sweater worn with winter white polyester and wool stirrup pants. *Fall/Winter 1986*

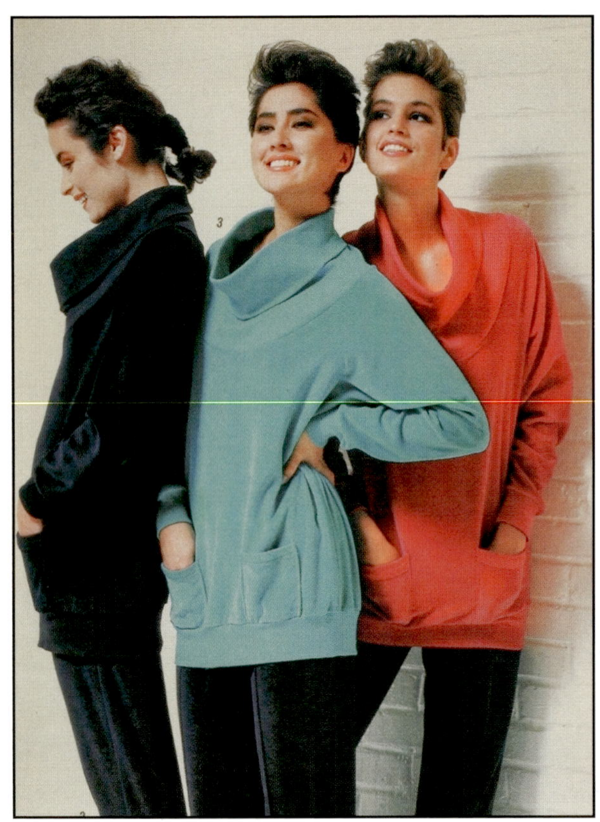

Plush woven cotton and polyester velour oversized tops with cowl neckline, worn with same fabric stirrup pants. *Fall/Winter 1986*

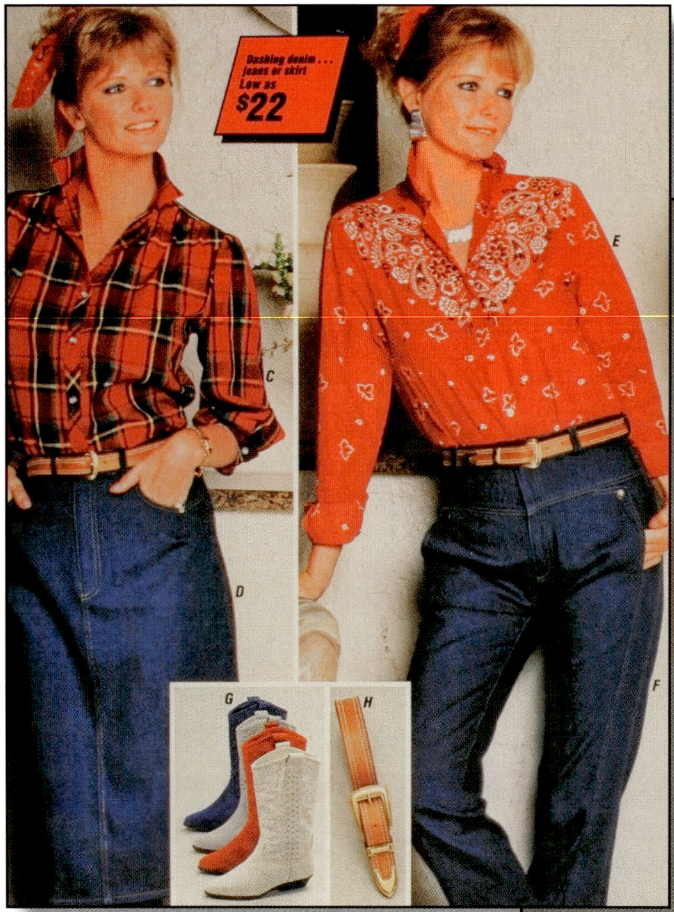

Plaid blouse in woven Kodel® polyester and cotton worn with a cotton denim skirt with back slit. Bandana print polyester and rayon shirt worn with cotton denim jeans. *Fall/Winter 1986*

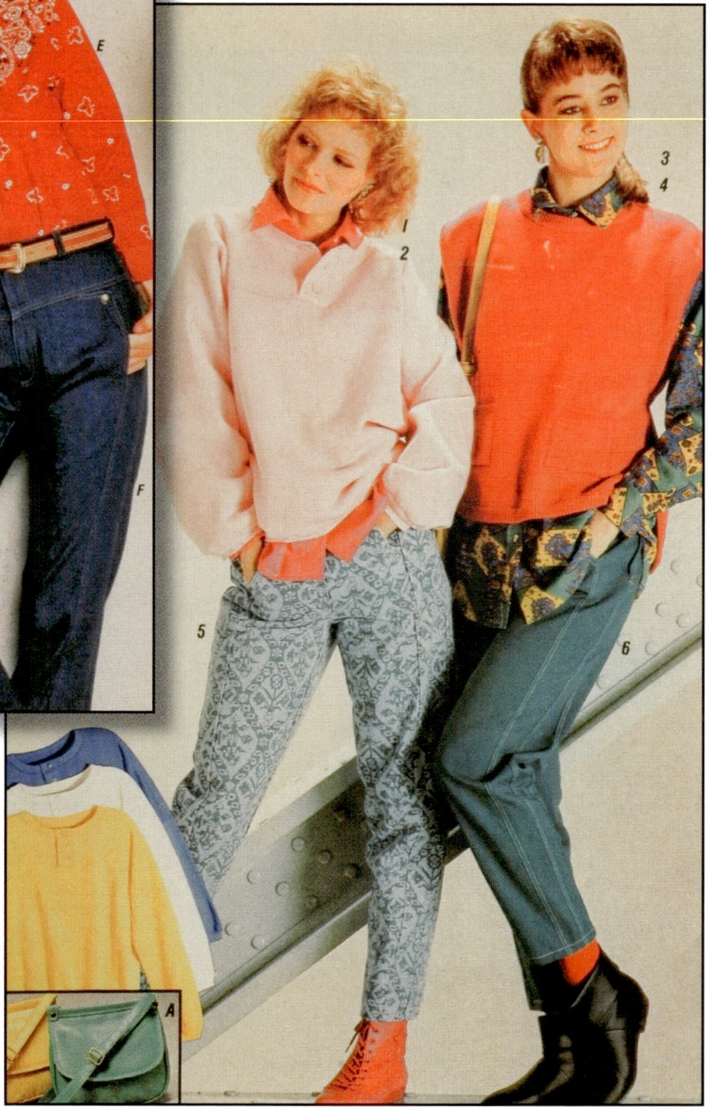

Shirts and pants from the Bold Spirit collection are worn here in the popular layer look. *Fall/Winter 1986*

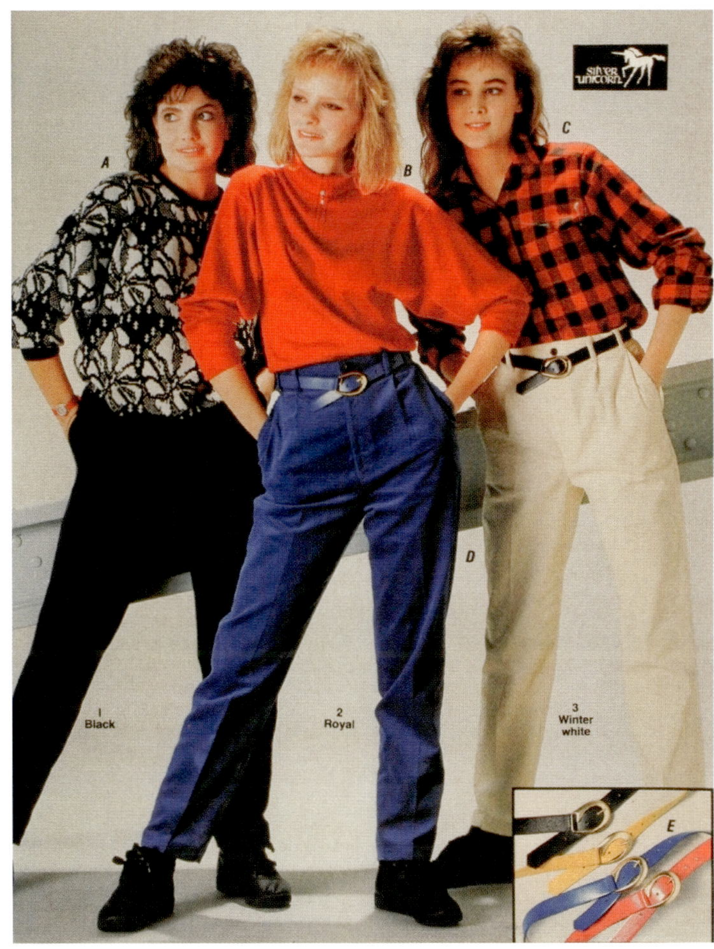

Acrylic and wool jacquard knit sweater, zip front turtleneck, polyester and cotton flannel shirt, all worn with corduroy pants. *Fall/Winter 1986*

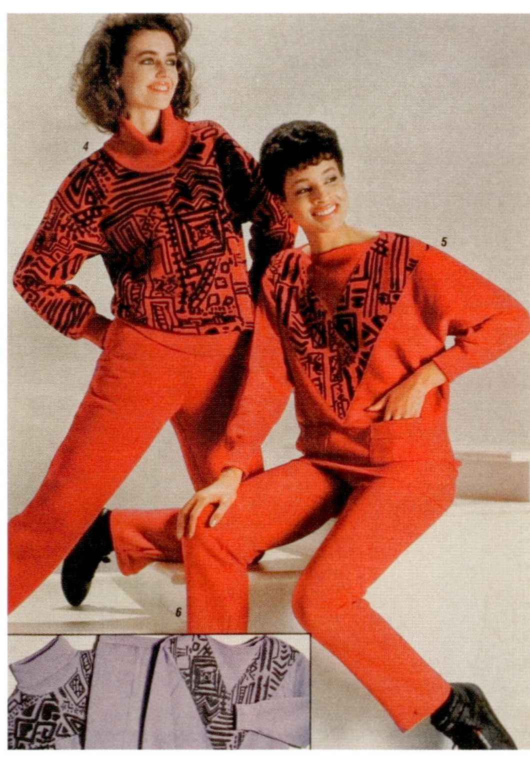

Aztec printed fleece wear tops in polyester and cotton fabric are worn with slim pants of same material. *Fall/Winter 1986*

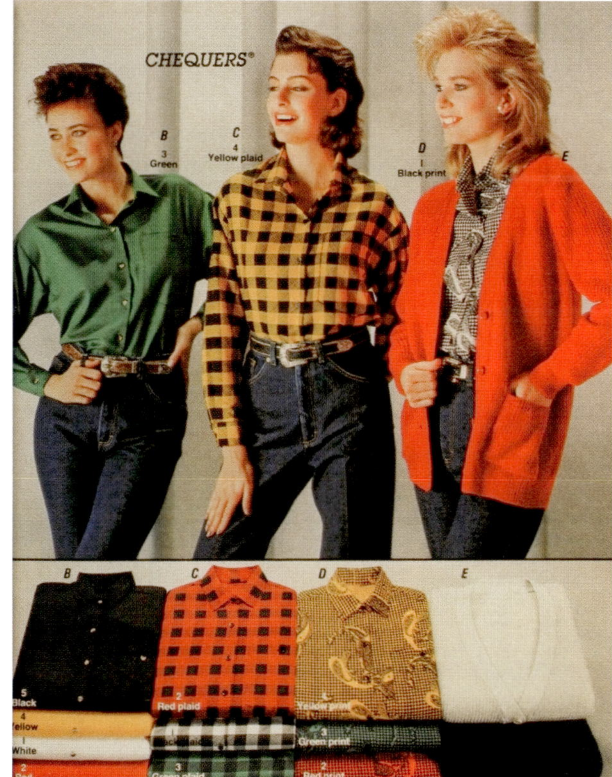

Chequers® twill shirts and Shaker stitched sweaters. *Fall/Winter 1986*

Sporty & Exercise Wear

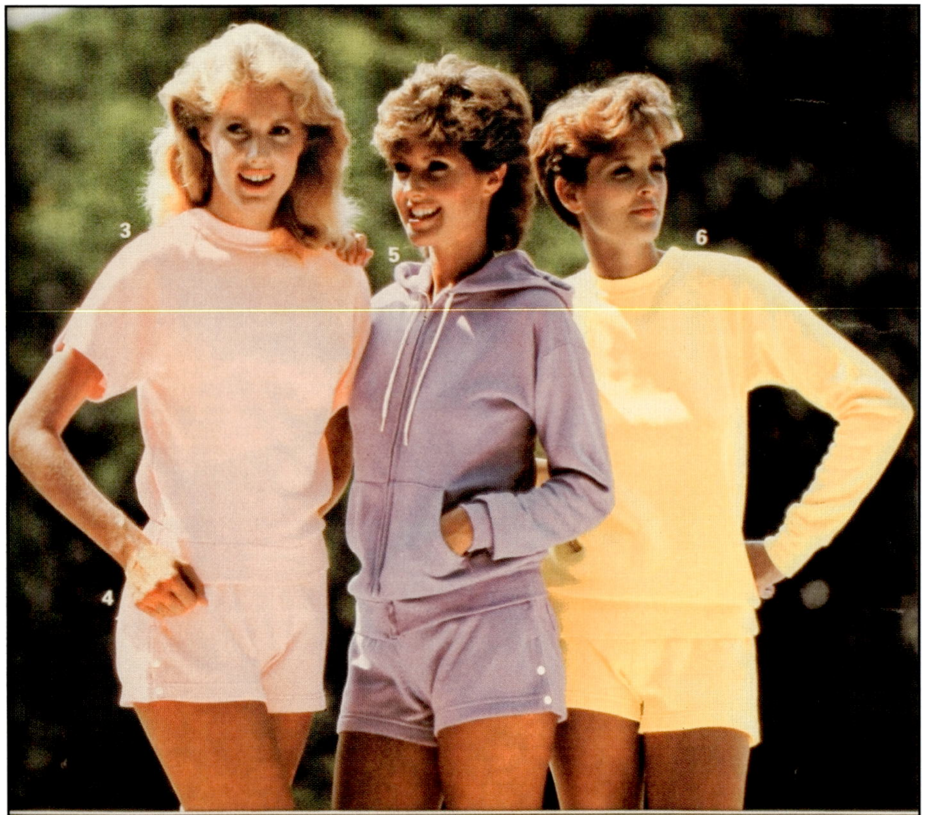

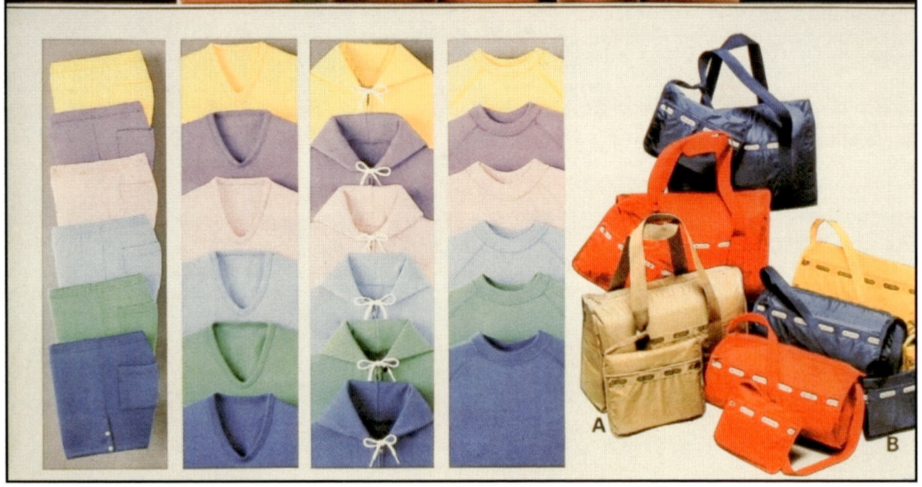

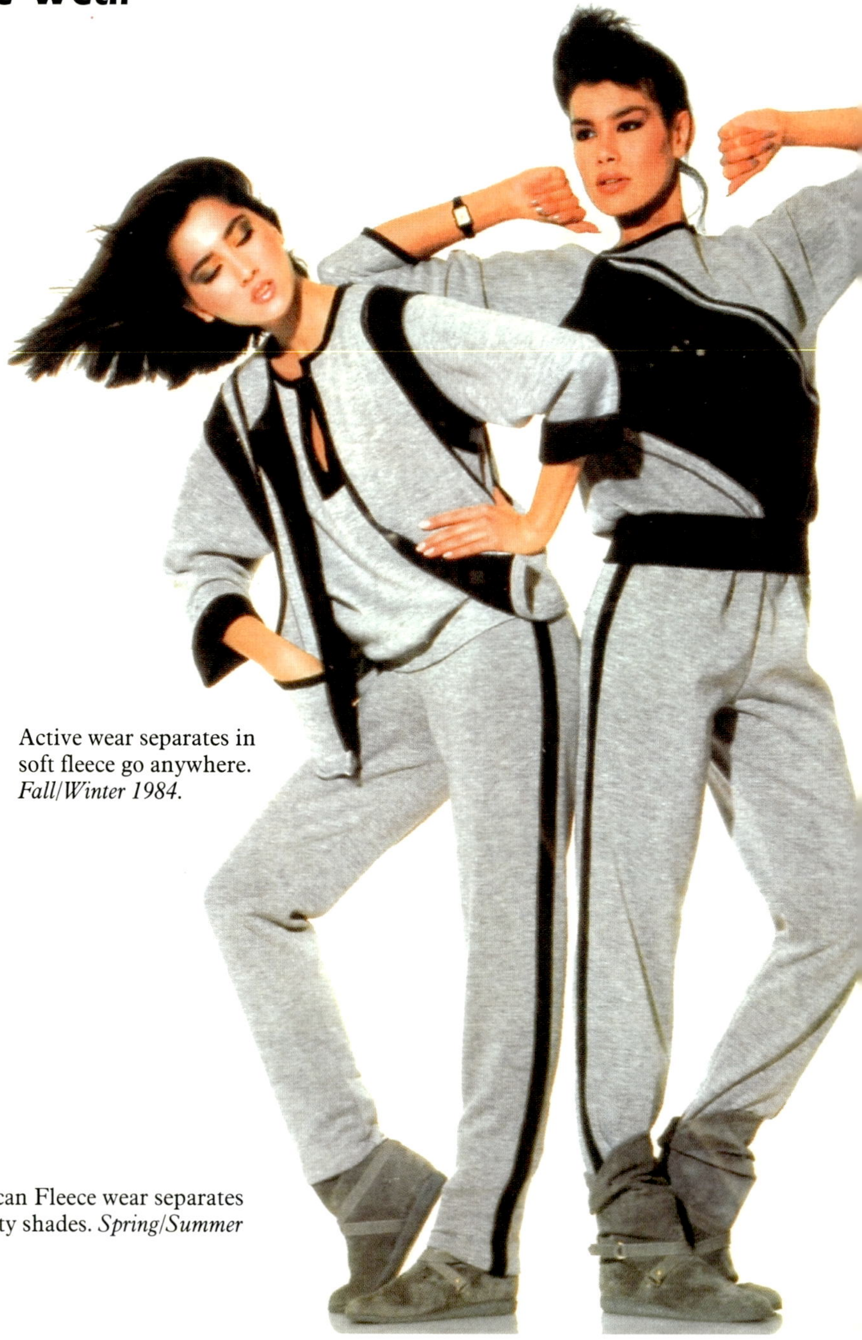

Active wear separates in soft fleece go anywhere. *Fall/Winter 1984.*

American Fleece wear separates in pretty shades. *Spring/Summer 1984.*

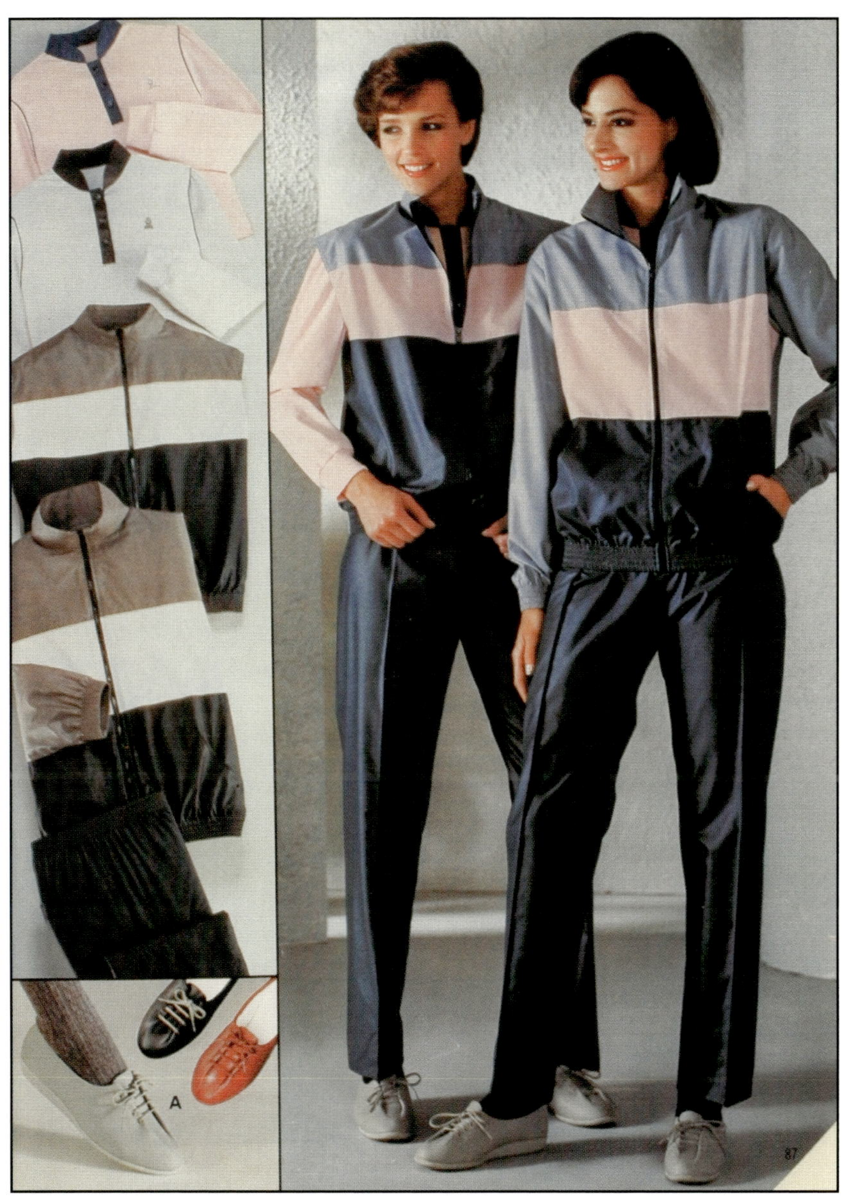

Goolagong active wear paired with casual oxfords. *Fall/Winter 1984.*

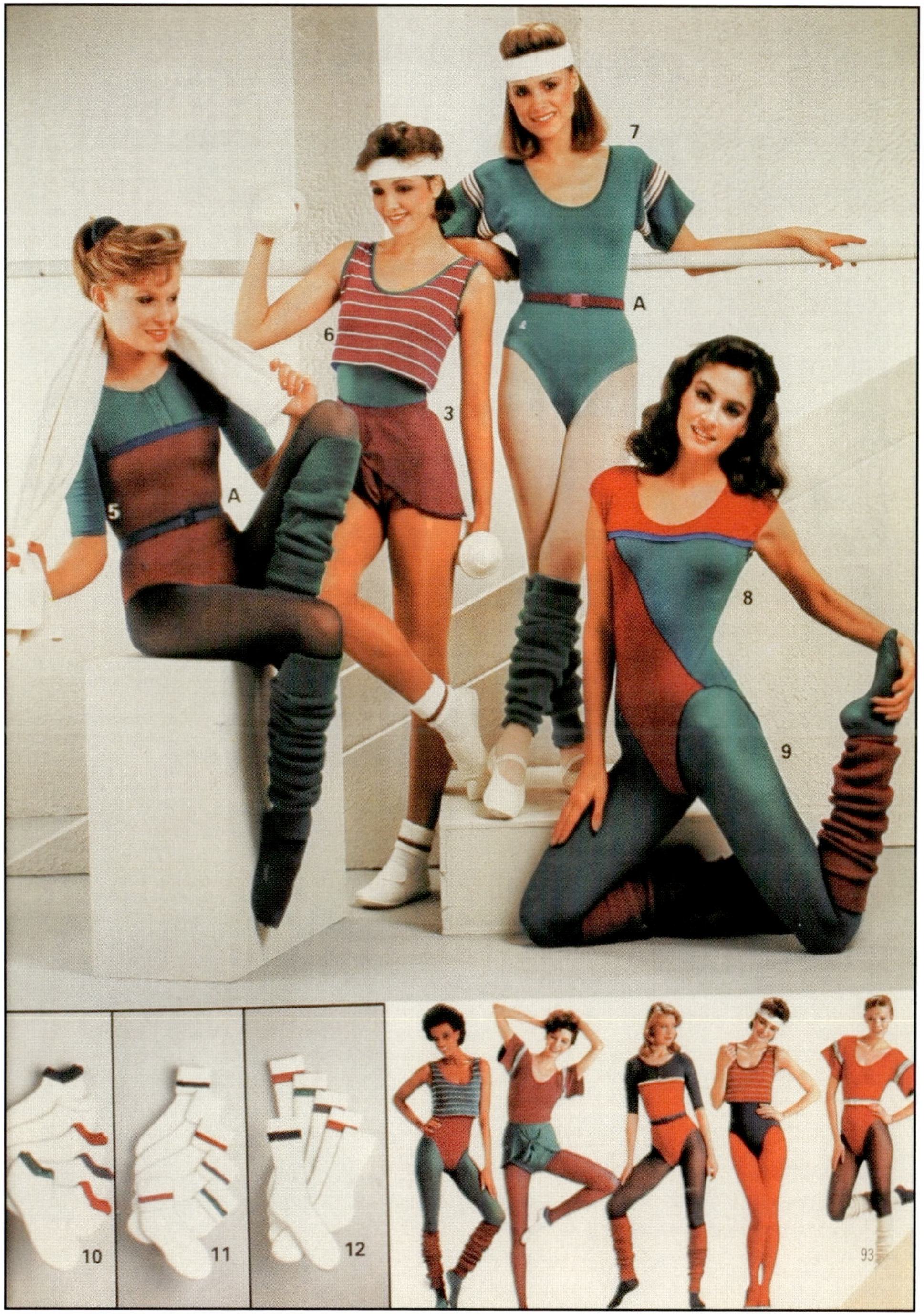

Evonne Goolagong's cotton blend fabrics offers unique coordinates in spliced, striped, blocked, meshed, and layered looks. *Fall/Winter 1984.*

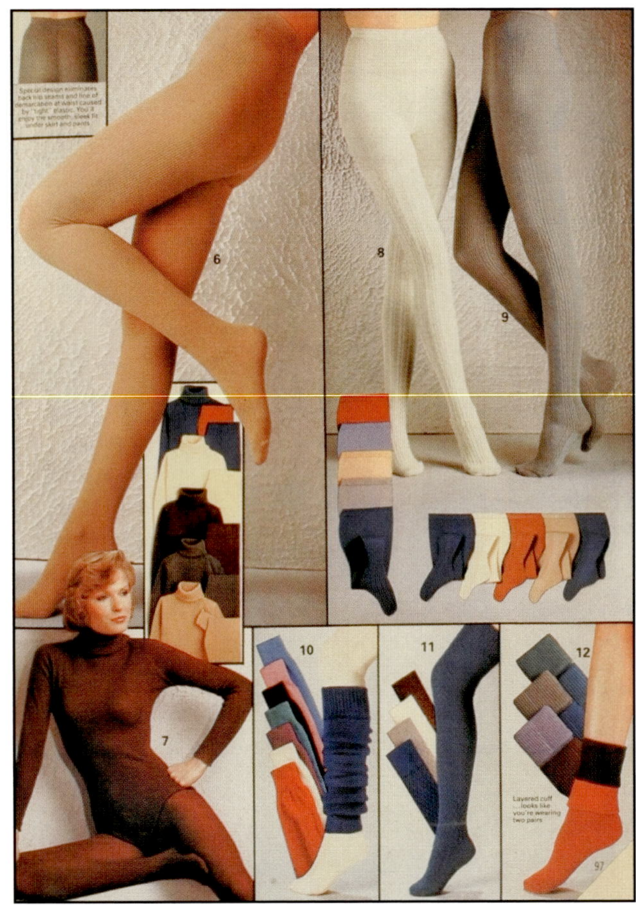

Rib-knit and cable-knit tights, bodysuits, leg warmers, over-the-knee socks, and sports socks help to achieve the popular layered look. *Fall/Winter 1984.*

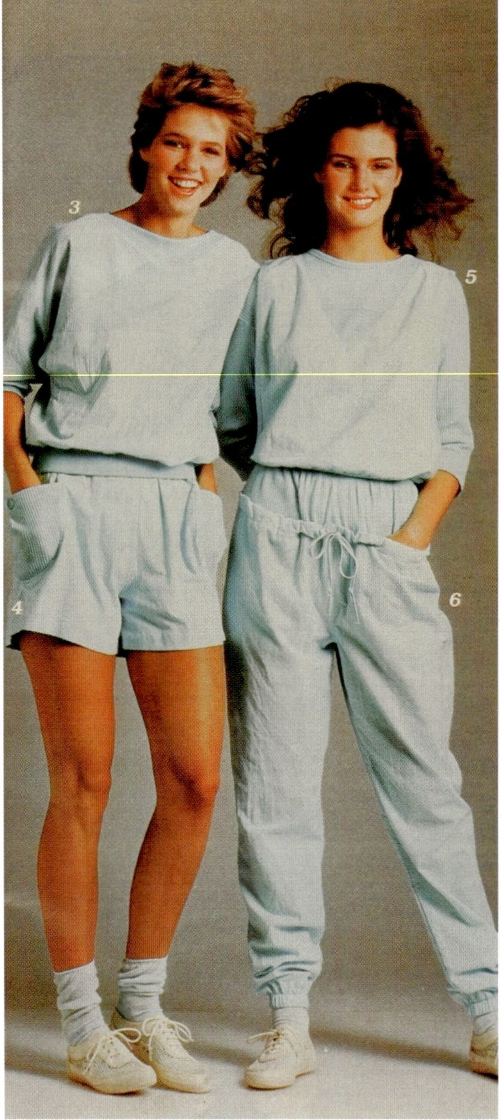

Laundered-look cotton active wear in polyester and cotton. *Spring/Summer 1985*

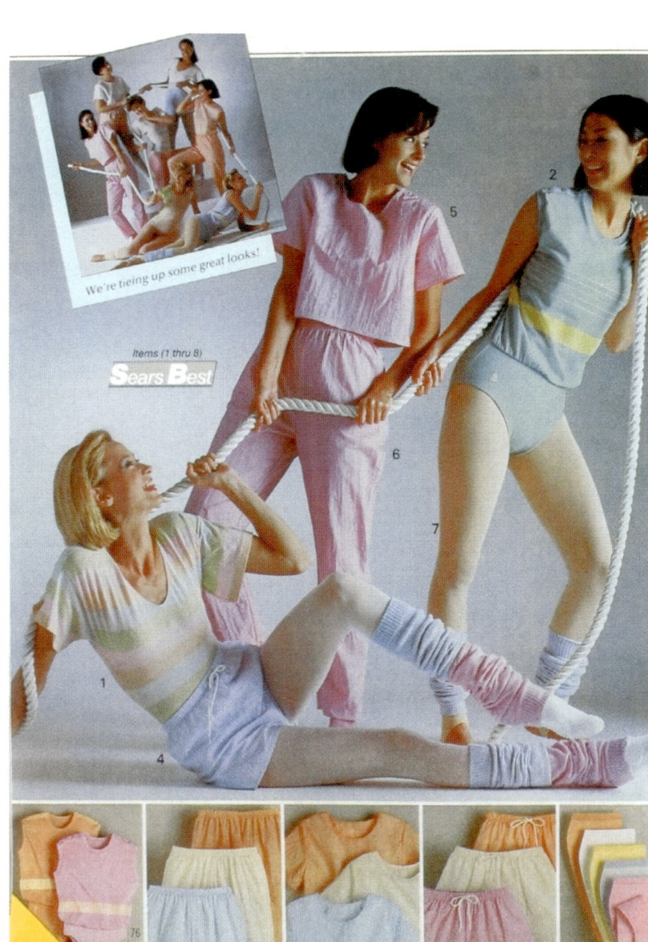

Goolagong exercise wear for fun and fitness. *Spring/Summer 1985*

Champagne long gown of sensuous Captiva® nylon, blue floral print long gown with elasticized empire waist, Zefran® nylon tricot gown, and Captiva® nylon tricot gown. *Spring/Summer 1984.*

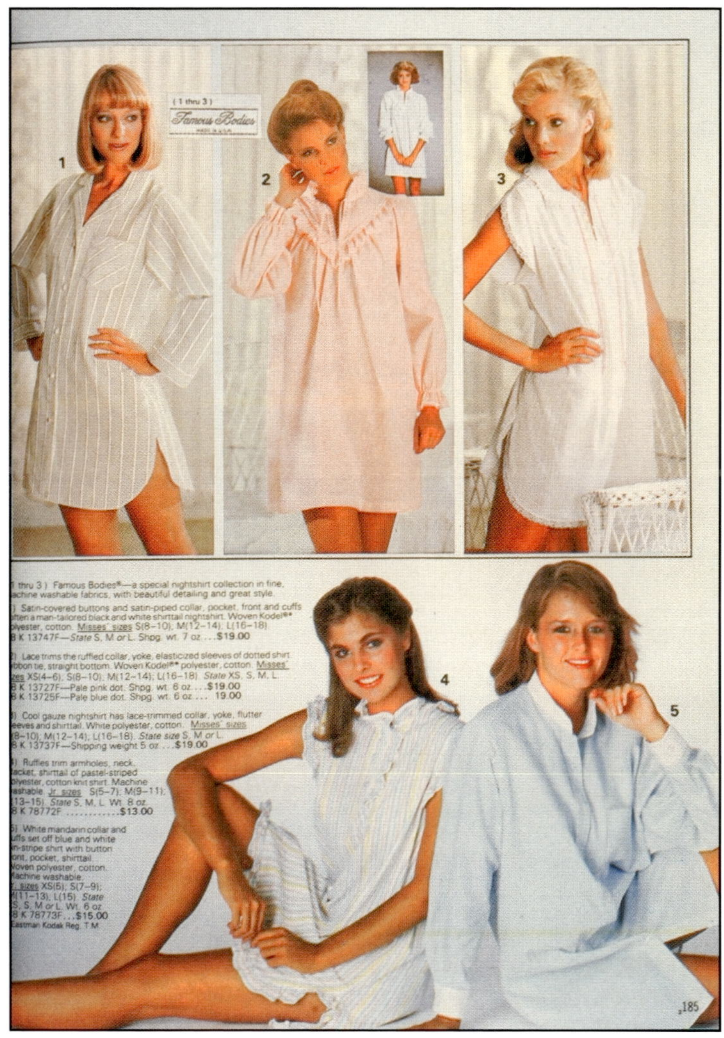

Famous Bodies® nightshirt collection. *Spring/Summer 1984.*

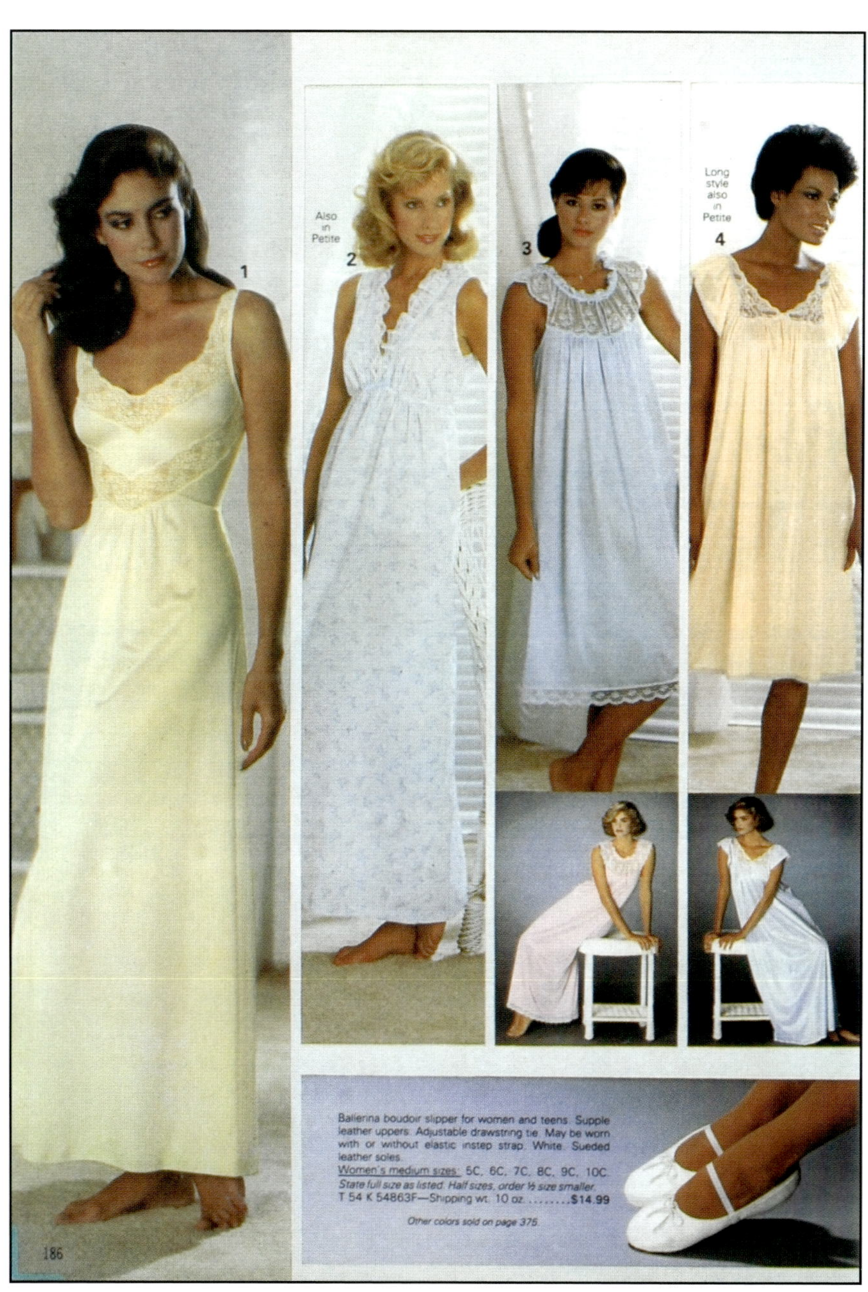

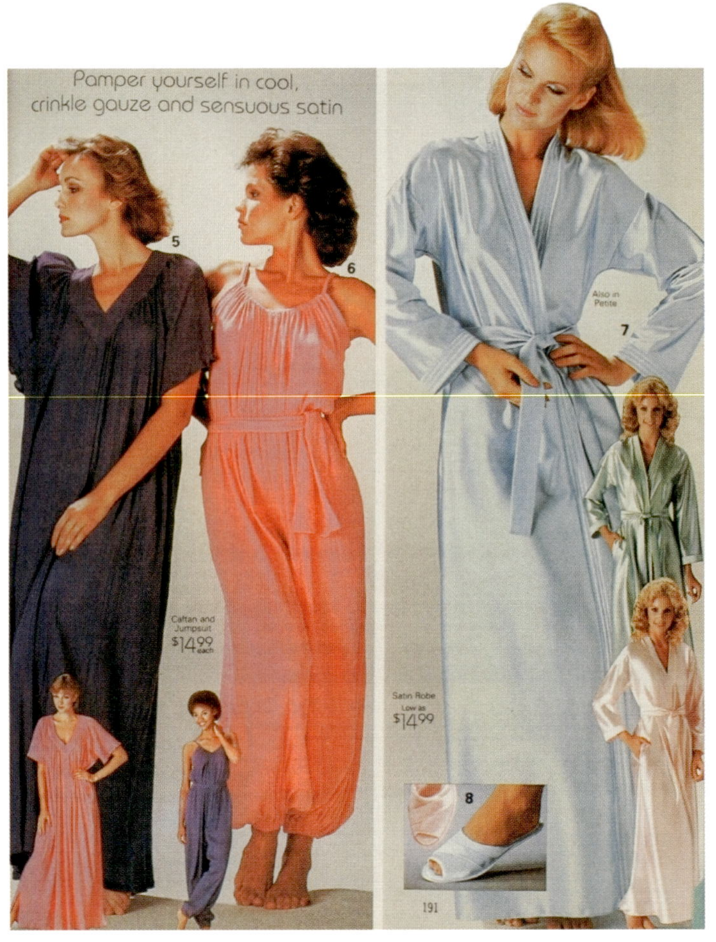

Crinkle-gauze Caftan in 100% cotton, jumpsuit in cool cotton gauze, and Amel® triacetate satin wrap robe. *Spring/Summer 1984.*

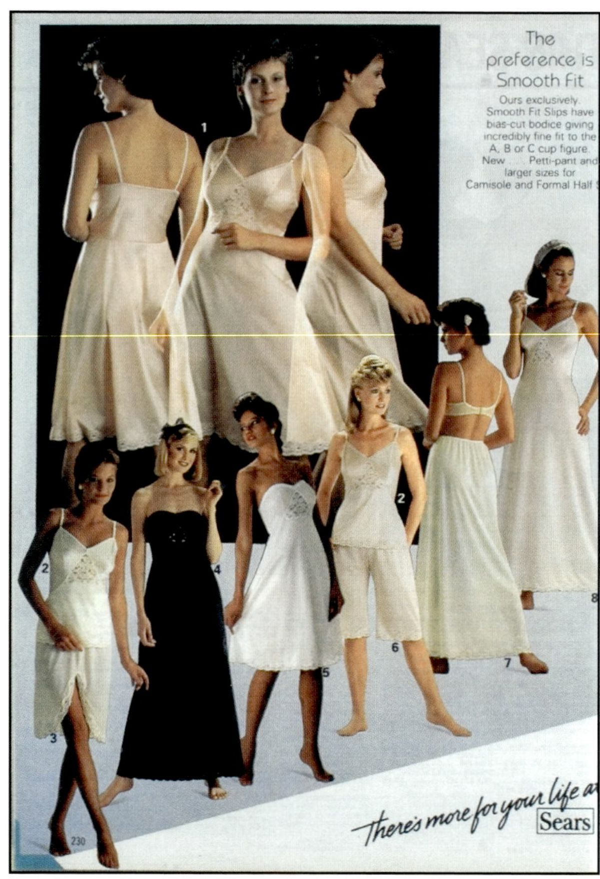

Slips from the Smooth Fit collection. Made of satiny Antron® III nylon tricot. *Spring/Summer 1984.*

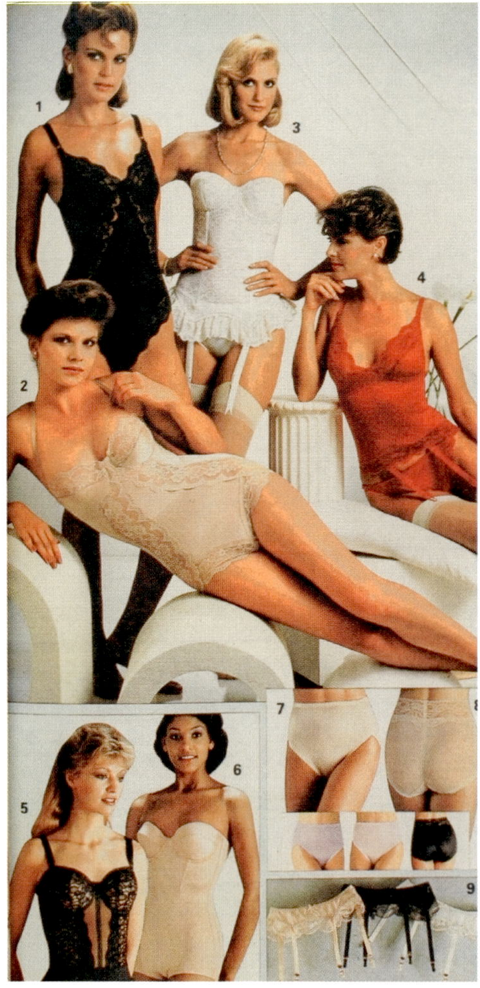

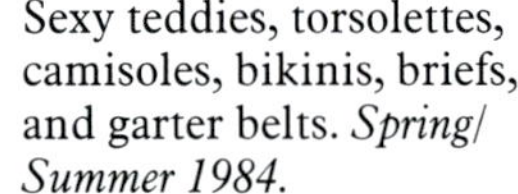

Sexy teddies, torsolettes, camisoles, bikinis, briefs, and garter belts. *Spring/Summer 1984.*

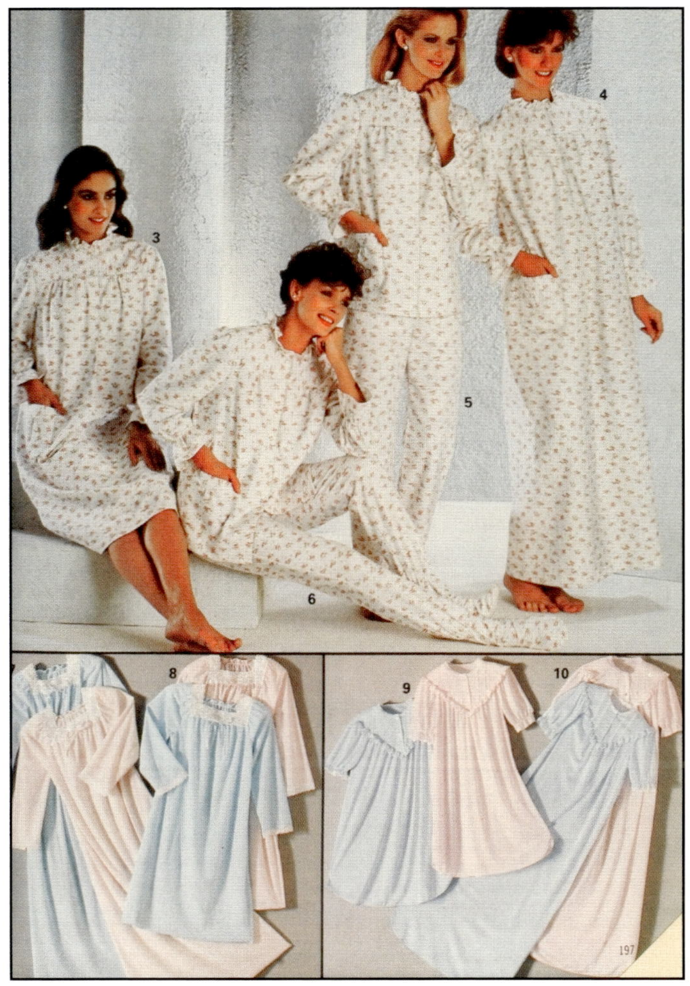

Nightwear in assorted styles. *Fall/Winter 1984.*

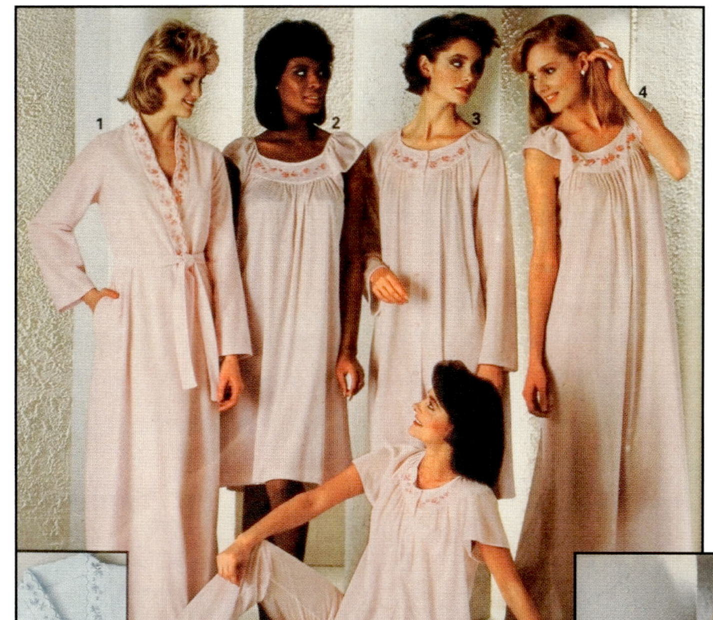

Fleece robe, long and short gowns, and pajamas in 100% nylon. *Fall/Winter 1984.*

Chenille robes in solids or stripes, in button front or wrap styles. *Fall/Winter 1984.*

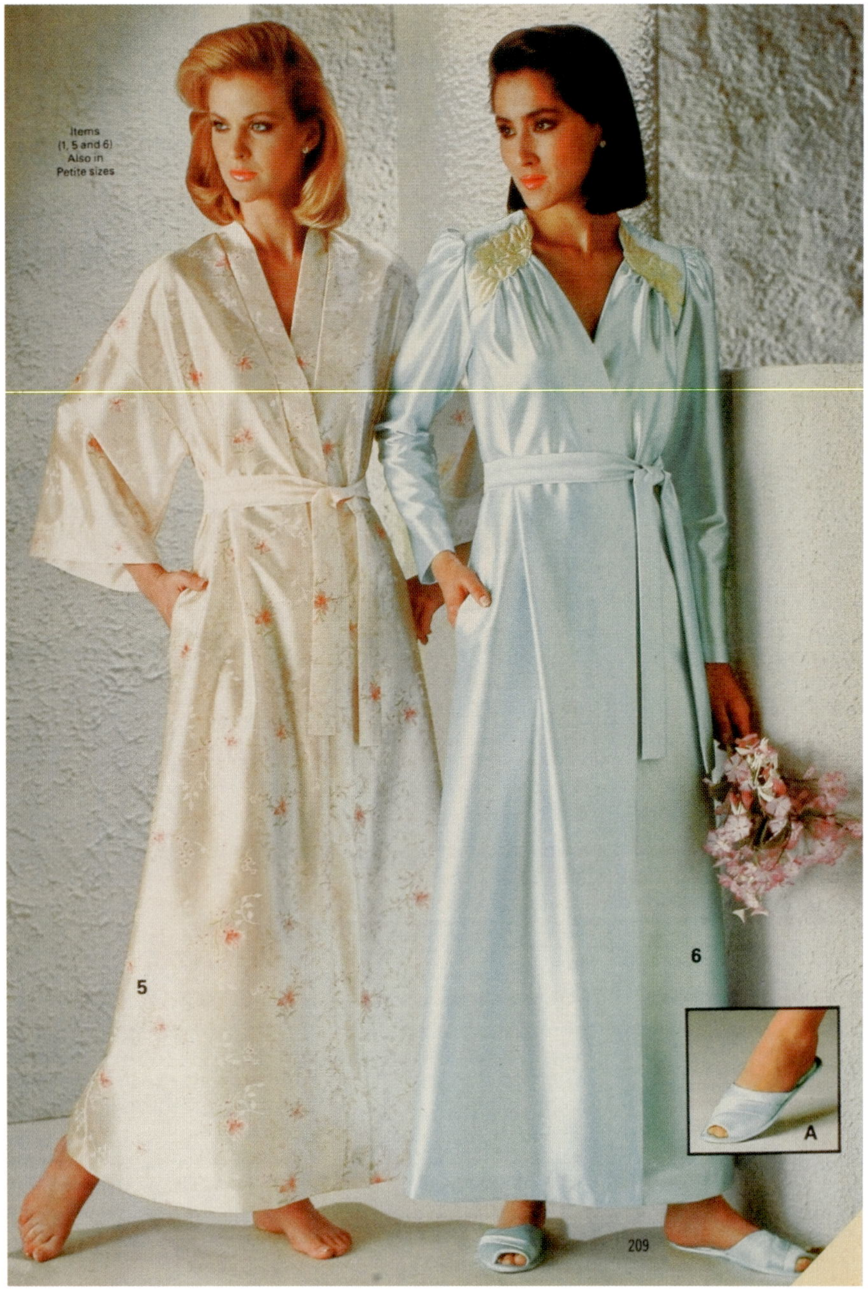

Satin print wrap robe and aqua blue boudoir coat with coordinating satin scuffs. *Fall/ Winter 1984.*

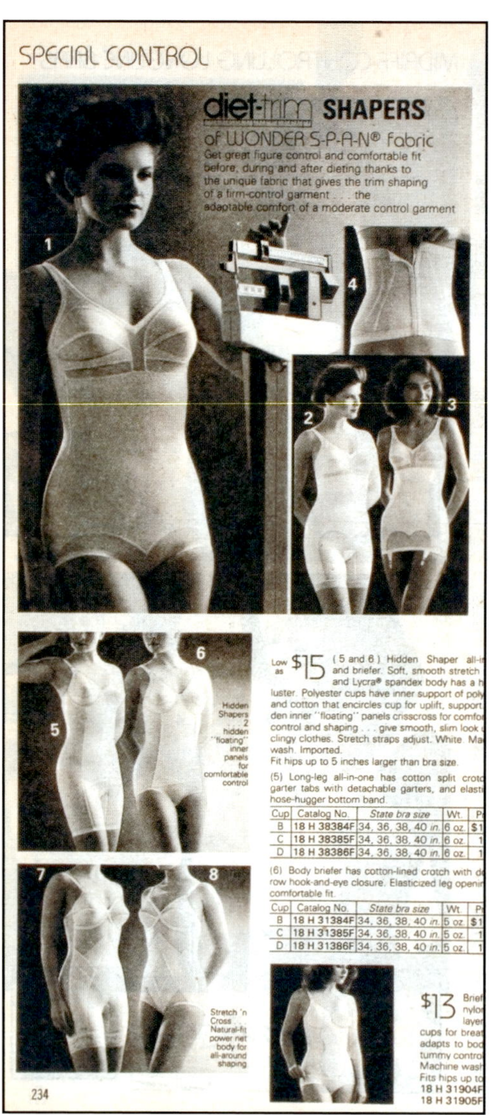

SPECIAL CONTROL

diet-trim SHAPERS

of WONDER S-P-A-N® fabric

Get great figure control and comfortable fit before, during and after dieting thanks to the unique fabric that gives the trim shaping of a firm-control garment . . . the adaptable comfort of a moderate control garment

Hidden Shapers 2 hidden "floating" inner panels for comfortable control

Low as $15 (5 and 6) Hidden Shaper all-i and briefer. Soft, smooth stretch and Lycra® spandex body has a h luster. Polyester cups have inner support of poly and cotton that encircles cup for uplift, support den inner "floating" panels crisscross for comfo control and shaping . . . give smooth, slim look clingy clothes. Stretch straps adjust. White. Ma wash. Imported.

Fit hips up to 5 inches larger than bra size.

(5) Long-leg all-in-one has cotton split crotc garter tabs with detachable garters, and elasti hose-hugger bottom band.

Cup	Catalog No.	*State bra size*	Wt.	P
B	18 H 38384F	34, 36, 38, 40 *in.*	6 oz.	$1
C	18 H 38385F	34, 36, 38, 40 *in.*	6 oz.	1
D	18 H 38386F	34, 36, 38, 40 *in.*	6 oz.	1

(6) Body briefer has cotton-lined crotch with d row hook-and-eye closure. Elasticized leg openi comfortable fit.

Cup	Catalog No.	*State bra size*	Wt.	P
B	18 H 31384F	34, 36, 38, 40 *in.*	5 oz.	$1
C	18 H 31385F	34, 36, 38, 40 *in.*	5 oz.	1
D	18 H 31386F	34, 36, 38, 40 *in.*	5 oz.	1

Stretch 'n Cross . . . Natural-fit power net body for all-around shaping

$13 Brief nylo layer cups for brea adapts to bod tummy contro Machine wash Fits hips up to 18 H 31904F 18 H 31905F

234

WONDER S-P-A-N® and Natural Fit Stretch 'n Cross body briefers offers firm control. *Fall/ Winter 1984.*

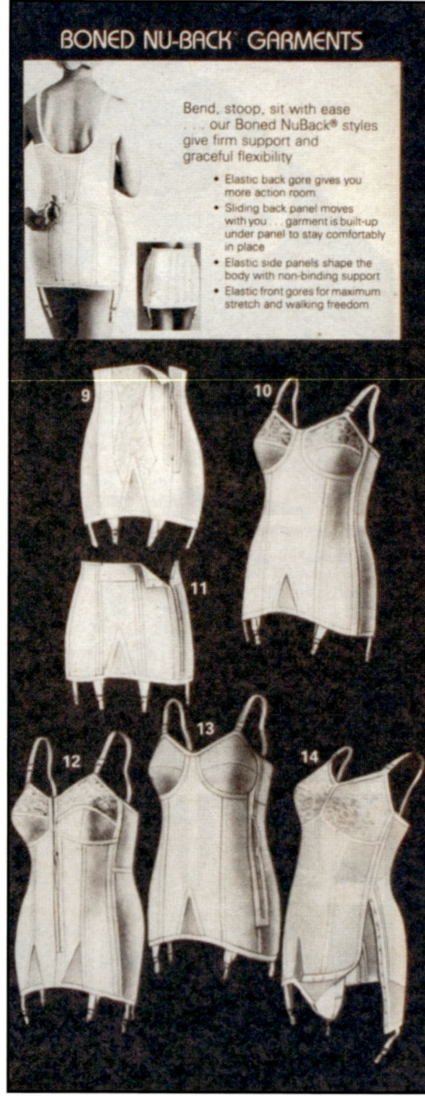

BONED NU-BACK GARMENTS

Bend, stoop, sit with ease . . . our Boned NuBack® styles give firm support and graceful flexibility

- Elastic back gore gives you more action room
- Sliding back panel moves with you . . . garment is built-up under panel to stay comfortably in place
- Elastic side panels shape the body with non-binding support
- Elastic front gores for maximum stretch and walking freedom

Bonded Nu-Back garments let you bend, stoop, and sit with ease. *Fall/Winter 1984.*

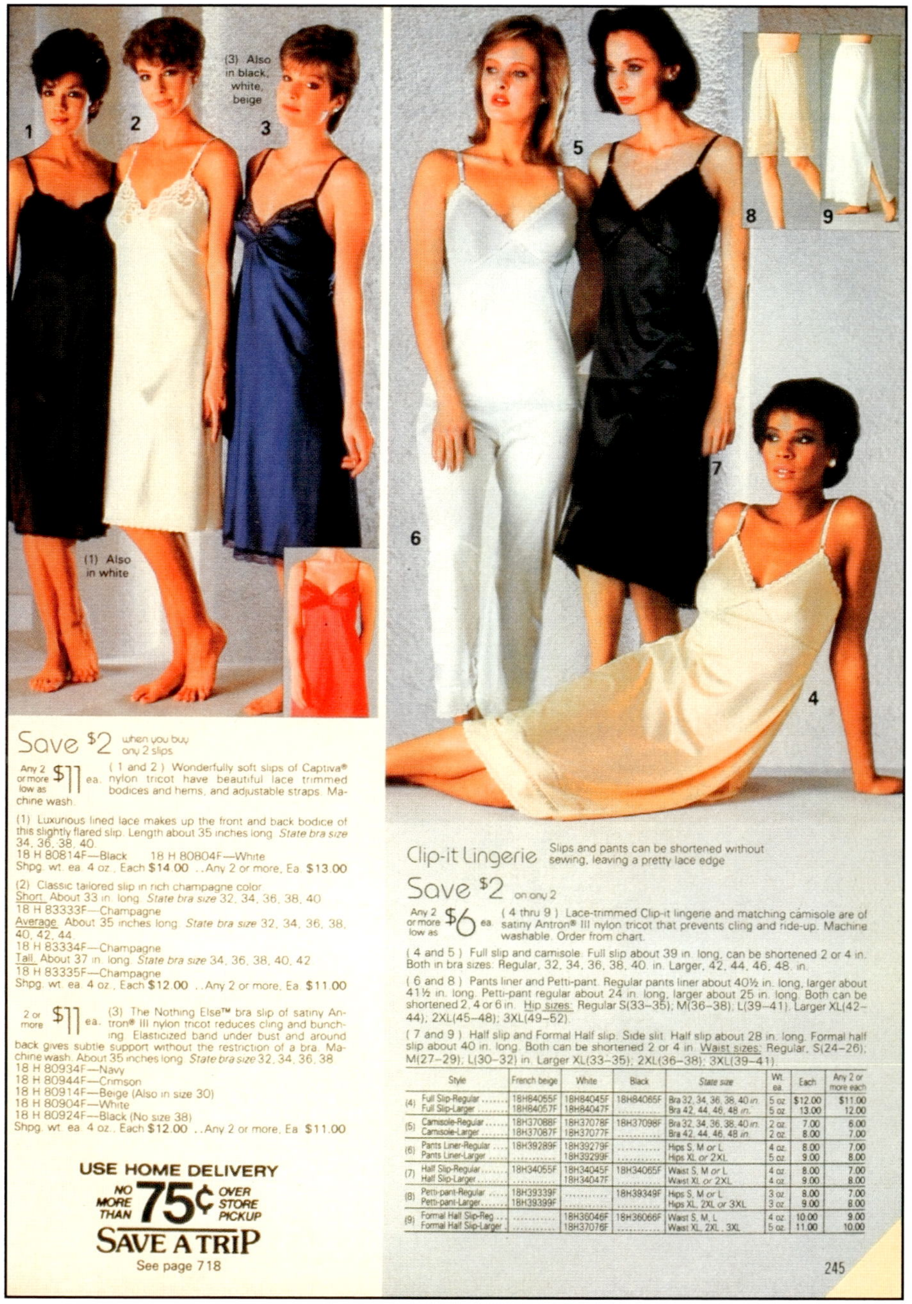

(3) Also in black, white, beige

(1) Also in white

Save $2 when you buy any 2 slips

Any 2 or more low as $11 ea. (1 and 2) Wonderfully soft slips of Captiva® nylon tricot have beautiful lace trimmed bodices and hems, and adjustable straps. Machine wash.

(1) Luxurious lined lace makes up the front and back bodice of this slightly flared slip. Length about 35 inches long. *State bra size* 34, 36, 38, 40.
18 H 80814F—Black 18 H 80804F—White
Shpg. wt. ea. 4 oz., Each **$14.00** ..Any 2 or more, Ea. **$13.00**

(2) Classic tailored slip in rich champagne color.
Short. About 33 in. long. *State bra size* 32, 34, 36, 38, 40
18 H 83333F—Champagne
Average. About 35 inches long. *State bra size* 32, 34, 36, 38, 40, 42, 44.
18 H 83334F—Champagne
Tall. About 37 in. long. *State bra size* 34, 36, 38, 40, 42
18 H 83335F—Champagne
Shpg. wt. ea. 4 oz., Each **$12.00** ..Any 2 or more, Ea. **$11.00**

2 or more $11 ea. (3) The Nothing Else™ bra slip of satiny Antron® III nylon tricot reduces cling and bunching. Elasticized band under bust and around back gives subtle support without the restriction of a bra. Machine wash. About 35 inches long. *State bra size* 32, 34, 36, 38
18 H 80934F—Navy
18 H 80944F—Crimson
18 H 80914F—Beige (Also in size 30)
18 H 80904F—White
18 H 80924F—Black (No size 38)
Shpg. wt. ea. 4 oz., Each **$12.00** ..Any 2 or more, Ea. **$11.00**

USE HOME DELIVERY
NO MORE THAN 75¢ OVER STORE PICKUP
SAVE A TRIP
See page 718

Clip-it Lingerie Slips and pants can be shortened without sewing, leaving a pretty lace edge

Save $2 on any 2

Any 2 or more low as $6 ea. (4 thru 9) Lace-trimmed Clip-it lingerie and matching camisole are of satiny Antron® III nylon tricot that prevents cling and ride-up. Machine washable. Order from chart.

(4 and 5) Full slip and camisole. Full slip about 39 in. long, can be shortened 2 or 4 in. Both in bra sizes: Regular, 32, 34, 36, 38, 40. in. Larger, 42, 44, 46, 48. in.

(6 and 8) Pants liner and Petti-pant. Regular pants liner about 40½ in. long, larger about 41½ in. long. Petti-pant regular about 24 in. long, larger about 25 in. long. Both can be shortened 2, 4 or 6 in. Hip sizes: Regular S(33–35); M(36–38); L(39–41). Larger XL(42–44); 2XL(45–48); 3XL(49–52).

(7 and 9) Half slip and Formal Half slip. Side slit. Half slip about 28 in. long. Formal half slip about 40 in. long. Both can be shortened 2 or 4 in. Waist sizes: Regular, S(24–26); M(27–29); L(30–32) in. Larger XL(33–35); 2XL(36–38); 3XL(39–41).

	Style	French beige	White	Black	State size	Wt. ea.	Each	Any 2 or more each
(4)	Full Slip-Regular	18H84055F	18H84045F	18H84065F	Bra 32, 34, 36, 38, 40 *in.*	5 oz	$12.00	$11.00
	Full Slip-Larger	18H84057F	18H84047F	....	Bra 42, 44, 46, 48 *in.*	5 oz	13.00	12.00
(5)	Camisole-Regular	18H37088F	18H37078F	18H37098F	Bra 32, 34, 36, 38, 40 *in.*	2 oz	7.00	6.00
	Camisole-Larger	18H37087F	18H37077F	....	Bra 42, 44, 46, 48 *in.*	2 oz	8.00	7.00
(6)	Pants Liner-Regular	18H39289F	18H39279F	....	Hips S, M *or* L	4 oz	8.00	7.00
	Pants Liner-Larger	....	18H39299F	....	Hips XL *or* 2XL	5 oz	9.00	8.00
(7)	Half Slip-Regular	18H34055F	18H34045F	18H34065F	Waist S, M *or* L	4 oz	8.00	7.00
	Half Slip-Larger	....	18H34047F	....	Waist XL *or* 2XL	4 oz	9.00	8.00
(8)	Petti-pant-Regular	18H39339F	....	18H39349F	Hips S, M *or* L	3 oz	8.00	7.00
	Petti-pant-Larger	18H39399F	....	....	Hips XL, 2XL *or* 3XL	3 oz	9.00	8.00
(9)	Formal Half Slip-Reg	....	18H36046F	18H36066F	Waist S, M, L	4 oz	10.00	9.00
	Formal Half Slip-Larger .	....	18H37076F	....	Waist XL, 2XL, 3XL	5 oz	11.00	10.00

245

Slips, camisoles, pants liners, petti-pants, and formal half slips for any lingerie needs. *Fall/Winter 1984.*

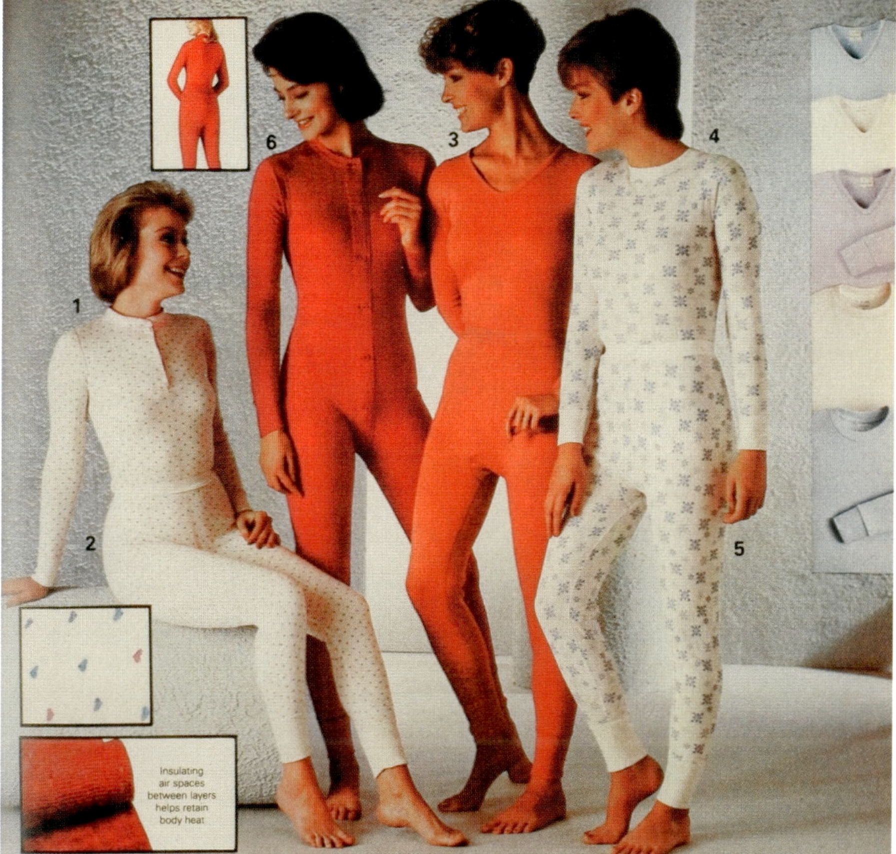

Winterskins® thermals providing the warmth your body needs in cold weather. *Fall/Winter 1984.*

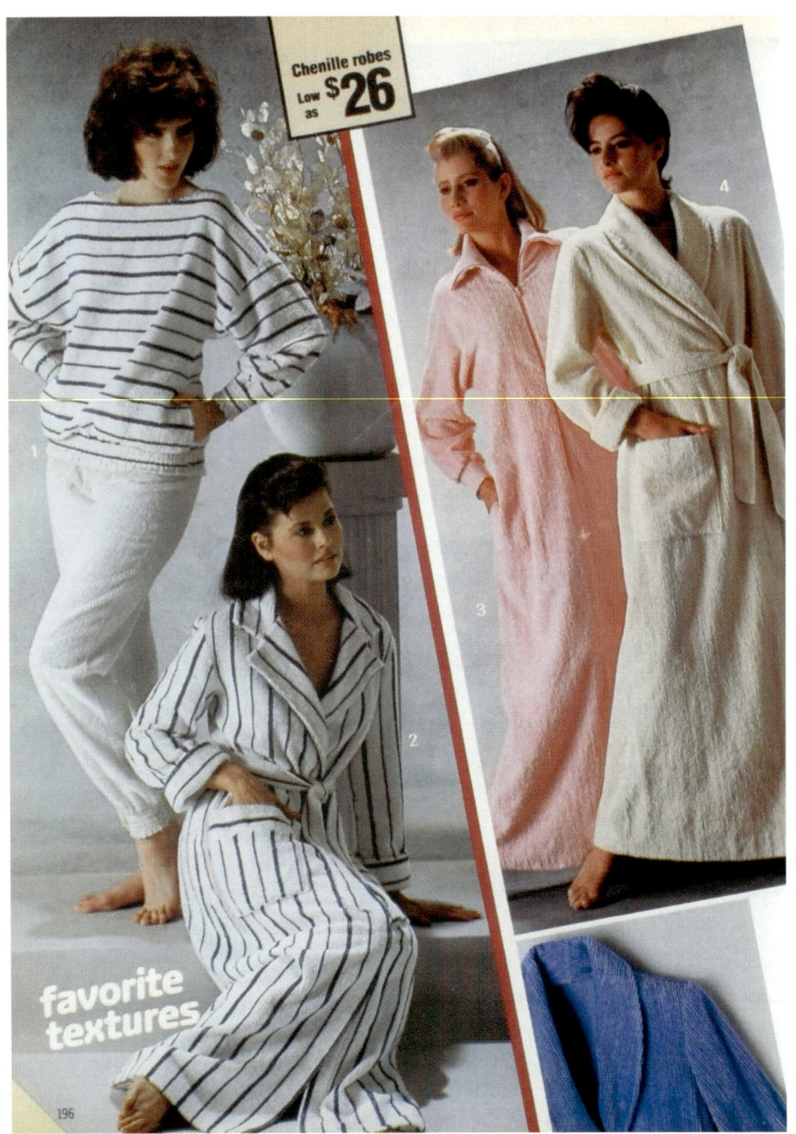

Chenille robes and two-piece lounger provides warm and comfort. *Fall/Winter 1985*

Shapely teddy, lacy torsolette, and camisole and bikini set. *Fall/Winter 1985*

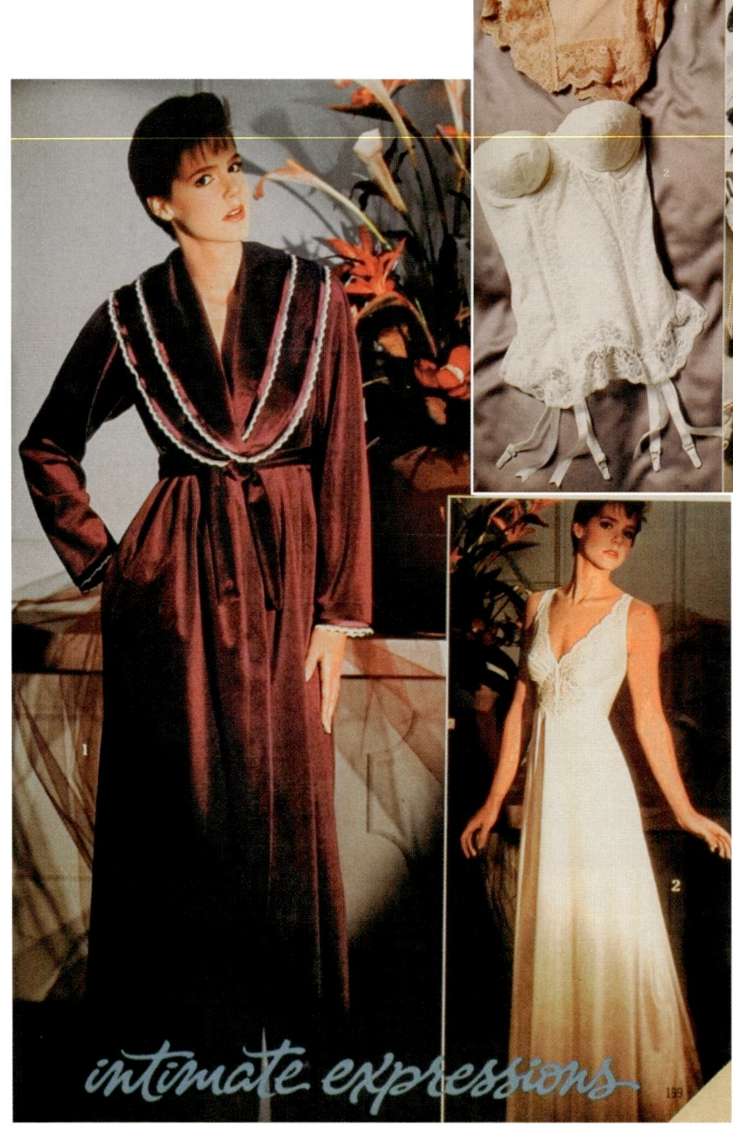

Nylon tricot gown has a touch of spandex in the bodice for support. Fleece robe in a velvety rich texture has a double collar. *Fall/Winter 1985*

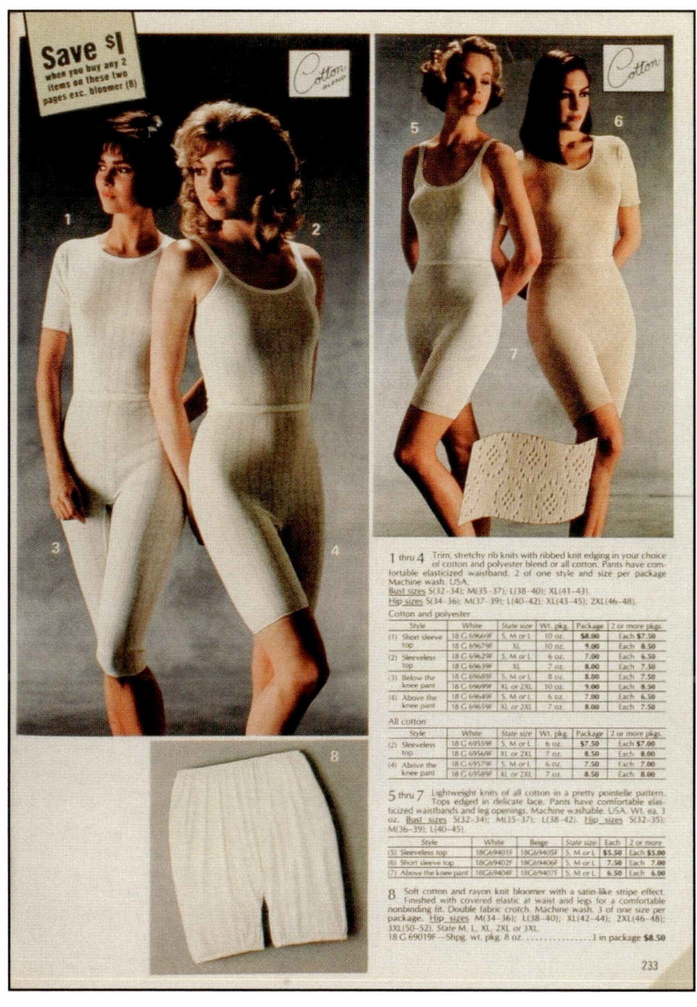

1 thru 4 Trim, stretchy rib knits with ribbed knit edging in your choice of cotton and polyester blend or all cotton. Pants have comfortable elasticized waistband. 2 of one style and size per package Machine wash. USA.
Bust sizes S(32–34); M(35–37); L(38–40); XL(41–43).
Hip sizes S(34–36); M(37–39); L(40–42); XL(43–45); 2XL(46–48).

Cotton and polyester

Style	White	State size	Wt. pkg.	Package	2 or more pkgs.
(1) Short sleeve top	18 G 69669F	S, M or L	10 oz.	$8.00	Each $7.50
	18 G 69679F	XL	10 oz.	9.00	Each 8.50
(2) Sleeveless top	18 G 69629F	S, M or L	6 oz.	7.00	Each 6.50
	18 G 69639F	XL	7 oz.	8.00	Each 7.50
(3) Below the knee pant	18 G 69689F	S, M or L	8 oz.	8.00	Each 7.50
	18 G 69699F	XL or 2XL	10 oz.	9.00	Each 8.50
(4) Above the knee pant	18 G 69649F	S, M or L	6 oz.	7.00	Each 6.50
	18 G 69659F	XL or 2XL	7 oz.	8.00	Each 7.50

All cotton

Style	White	State size	Wt. pkg.	Package	2 or more pkgs.
(2) Sleeveless top	18 G 69559F	S, M or L	6 oz.	$7.50	Each $7.00
	18 G 69569F	XL or 2XL	7 oz.	8.50	Each 8.00
(4) Above the knee pant	18 G 69579F	S, M or L	6 oz.	7.50	Each 7.00
	18 G 69589F	XL or 2XL	7 oz.	8.50	Each 8.00

5 thru 7 Lightweight knits of all cotton in a pretty pointelle pattern. Tops edged in delicate lace. Pants have comfortable elasticized waistbands and leg openings. Machine washable. USA. Wt. ea. 3 oz. Bust sizes S(32–34); M(35–37); L(38–42). Hip sizes S(32–35); M(36–39); L(40–45).

Style	White	Beige	State size	Each	2 or more
(5) Sleeveless top	18G69401F	18G69405F	S, M or L	$5.50	Each $5.00
(6) Short sleeve top	18G69402F	18G69406F	S, M or L	7.50	Each 7.00
(7) Above the knee pant	18G69404F	18G69407F	S, M or L	6.50	Each 6.00

8 Soft cotton and rayon knit bloomer with a satin-like stripe effect. Finished with covered elastic at waist and legs for a comfortable nonbinding fit. Double fabric crotch. Machine wash. 3 of one size per package. Hip sizes M(34–36); L(38–40); XL(42–44); 2XL(46–48); 3XL(50–52). State M, L, XL, 2XL or 3XL.
18 G 69019F—Shpg. wt. pkg. 8 oz. ....3 in package $8.50

233

Ribbed knits in cotton and polyester blends or pure cotton, soft cotton and rayon knit bloomers. *Fall/Winter 1985*

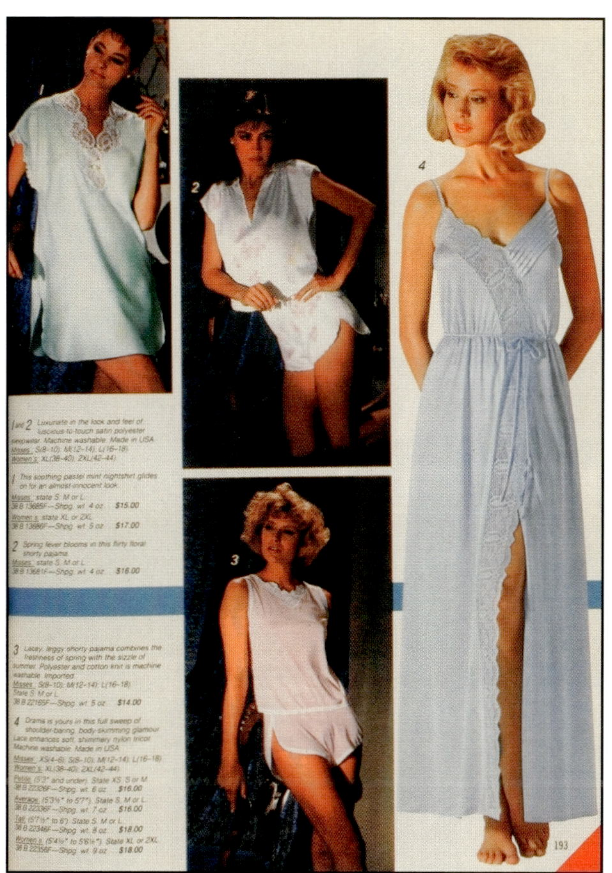

1 and 2 Luxuriate in the look and feel of luscious-to-touch satin polyester sleepwear. Machine washable. Made in USA.
Misses' S(8–10); M(12–14); L(16–18).
Women's XL(38–40); 2XL(42–44).

1 This soothing pastel mint nightshirt glides on for an almost-innocent look.
Misses' state S, M or L.
38 B 13685F—Shpg. wt. 4 oz. $15.00
Women's state XL or 2XL.
38 B 13686F—Shpg. wt. 5 oz. $17.00

2 Spring fever blooms in this flirty floral shorty pajama.
Misses' state S, M or L.
38 B 13681F—Shpg. wt. 4 oz. $16.00

3 Lacey, leggy shorty pajama combines the freshness of spring with the sizzle of summer. Polyester and cotton knit is machine washable. Imported.
Misses' S(8–10); M(12–14); L(16–18).
State S, M or L.
38 B 22165F—Shpg. wt. 5 oz. $14.00

4 Drama is yours in this full sweep of shoulder-baring, body-skimming glamour. Lace enhances soft, shimmery nylon tricot. Machine washable. Made in USA.
Misses' XS(4–6); S(8–10); M(12–14); L(16–18).
Women's XL(38–40); 2XL(42–44).
Petite (5'3" and under). State XS, S or M.
38 B 22326F—Shpg. wt. 6 oz. $16.00
Average (5'3½" to 5'7"). State S, M or L.
38 B 22336F—Shpg. wt. 7 oz. $16.00
Tall (5'7½" to 6'). State S, M or L.
38 B 22346F—Shpg. wt. 8 oz. $18.00
Women's (5'4½" to 5'6½"). State XL or 2XL.
38 B 22356F—Shpg. wt. 9 oz. $18.00

193

Nightshirt, shorty pajamas, and shoulder-baring tricot, all made in satin polyester. *Spring/Summer 1986*

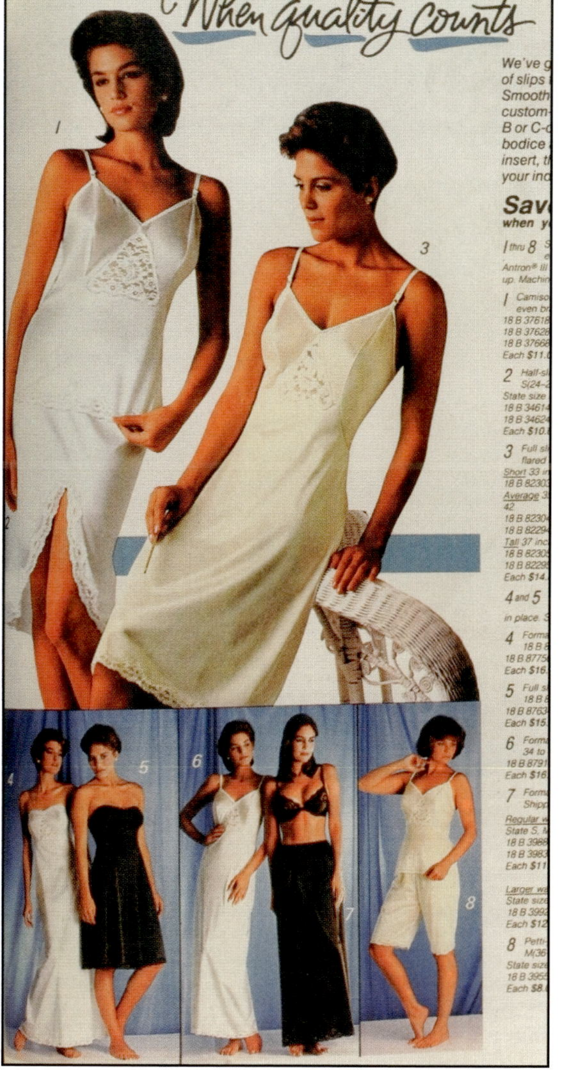

A variety of slips from the Smooth-Fit collection in Antron® III nylon tricot fabrics. *Spring/Summer 1986*

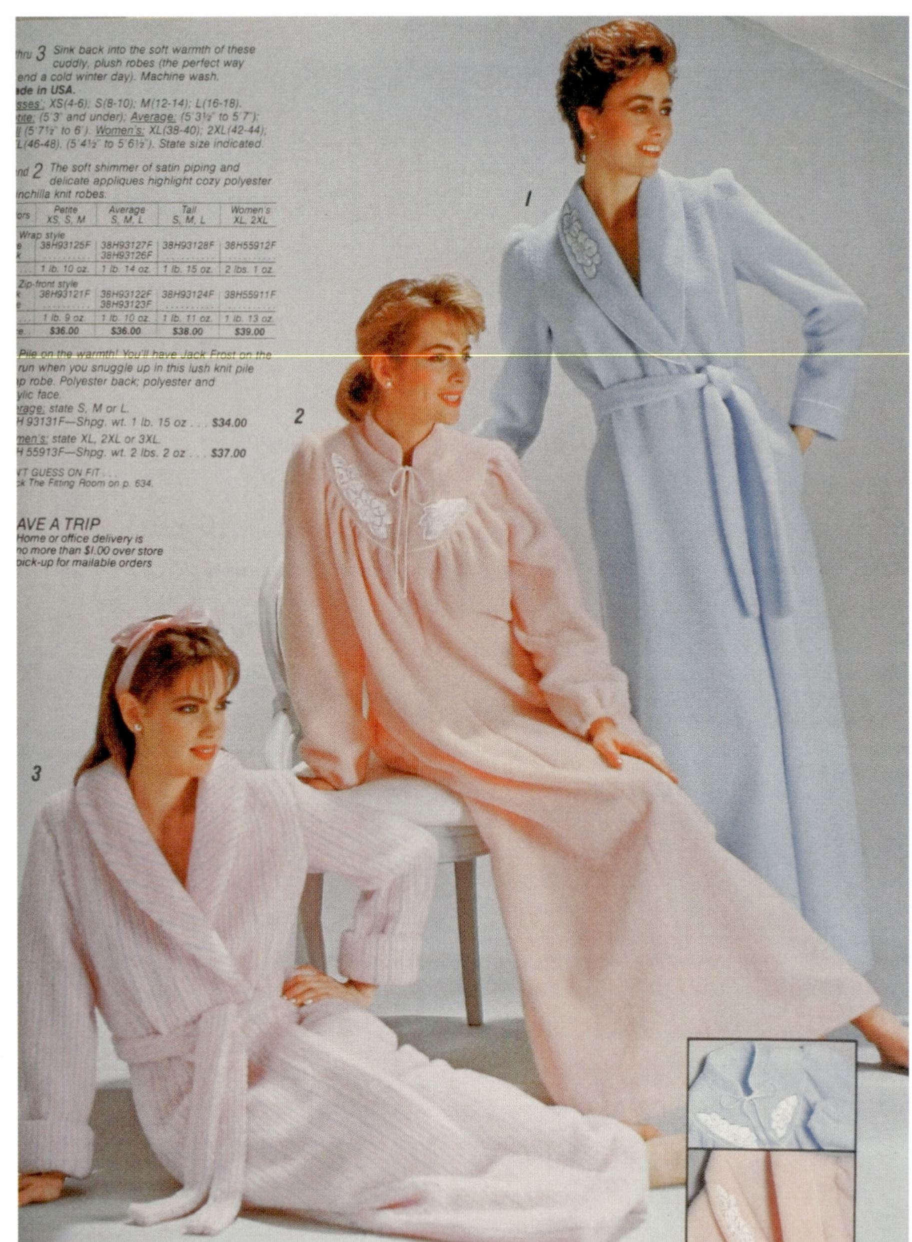

Soft, plush robes to warm up to. *Fall/Winter 1986*

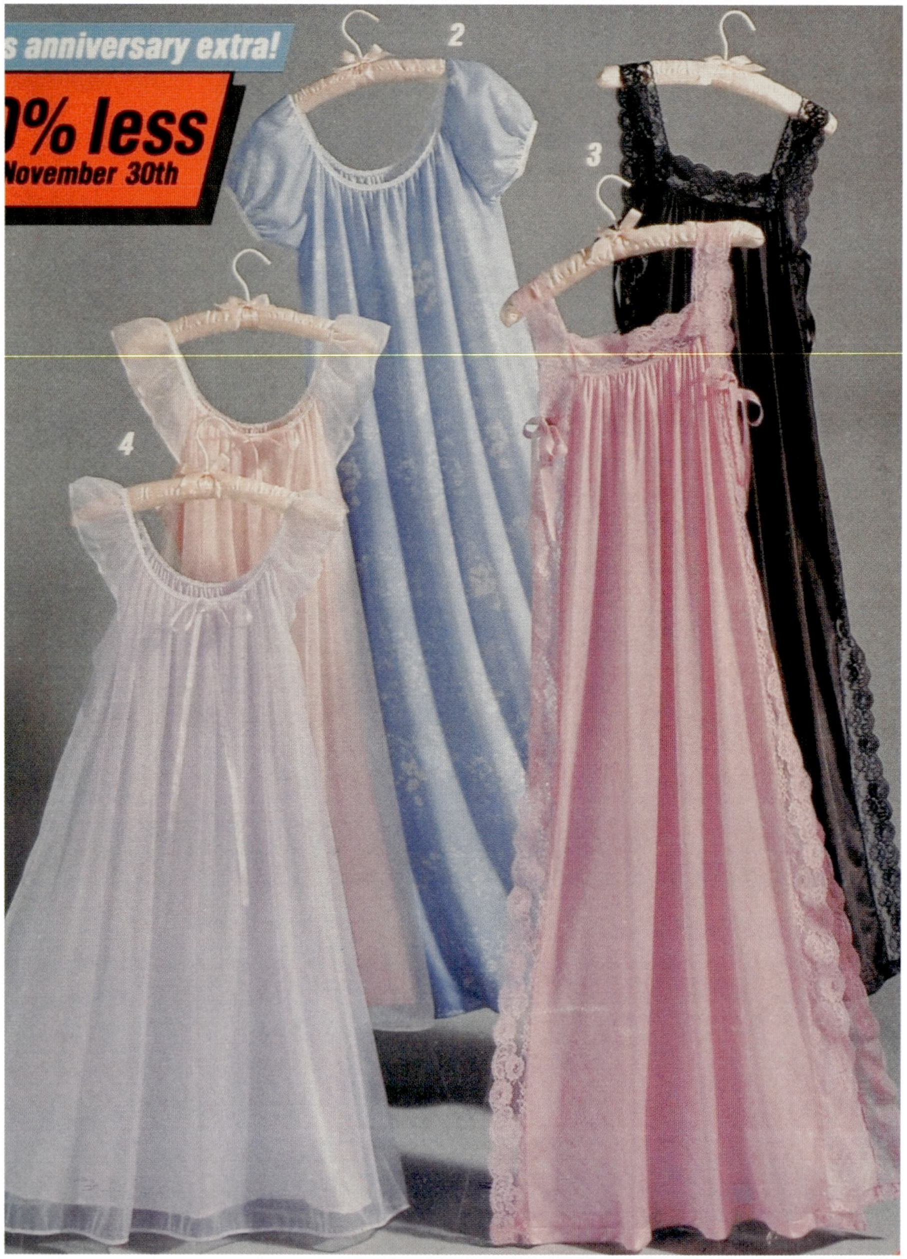

Nightgowns in dreamy colors and fabrics. *Fall/Winter 1986*

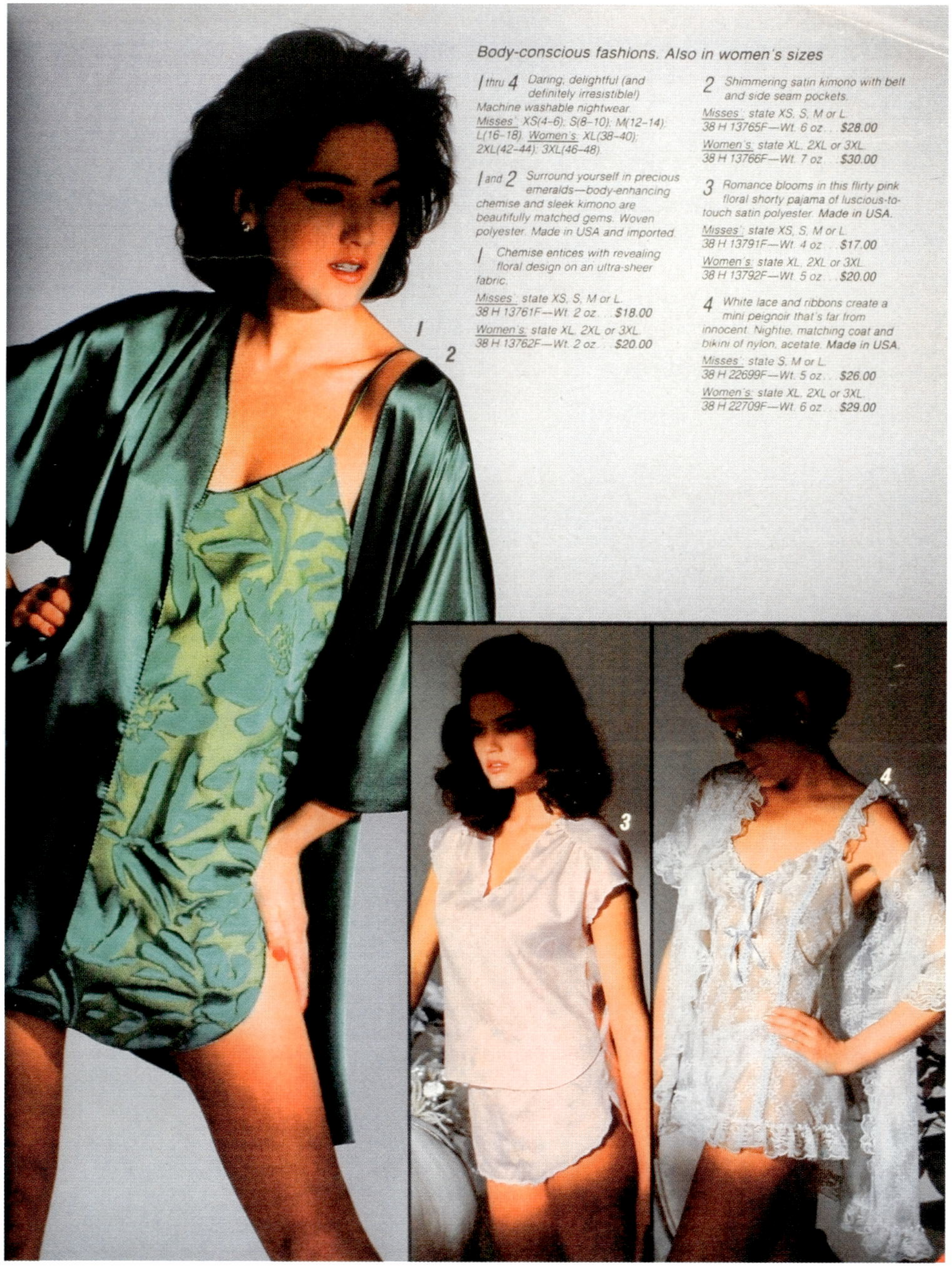

Body-conscious fashions. Also in women's sizes

1 thru 4 Daring, delightful (and definitely irresistible!) Machine washable nightwear. Misses': XS(4-6), S(8-10), M(12-14), L(16-18). Women's: XL(38-40); 2XL(42-44); 3XL(46-48).

1 and 2 Surround yourself in precious emeralds—body-enhancing chemise and sleek kimono are beautifully matched gems. Woven polyester. Made in USA and imported.

1 Chemise entices with revealing floral design on an ultra-sheer fabric.
Misses': state XS, S, M or L.
38 H 13761F—Wt. 2 oz. . . $18.00
Women's: state XL, 2XL or 3XL.
38 H 13762F—Wt. 2 oz. . . $20.00

2 Shimmering satin kimono with belt and side seam pockets.
Misses': state XS, S, M or L.
38 H 13765F—Wt. 6 oz. . . $28.00
Women's: state XL, 2XL or 3XL.
38 H 13766F—Wt. 7 oz. . . $30.00

3 Romance blooms in this flirty pink floral shorty pajama of luscious-to-touch satin polyester. **Made in USA.**
Misses': state XS, S, M or L.
38 H 13791F—Wt. 4 oz. . . $17.00
Women's: state XL, 2XL or 3XL.
38 H 13792F—Wt. 5 oz. . . $20.00

4 White lace and ribbons create a mini peignoir that's far from innocent. Nightie, matching coat and bikini of nylon, acetate. **Made in USA.**
Misses': state S, M or L.
38 H 22699F—Wt. 5 oz. . . $26.00
Women's: state XL, 2XL or 3XL.
38 H 22709F—Wt. 6 oz. . . $29.00

Body-enhancing chemise and kimono in emerald green. Flirty shorty pajamas in pink floral. Mini peignoir in white lace and ribbons with matching coat and bikini. *Fall/Winter 1986*

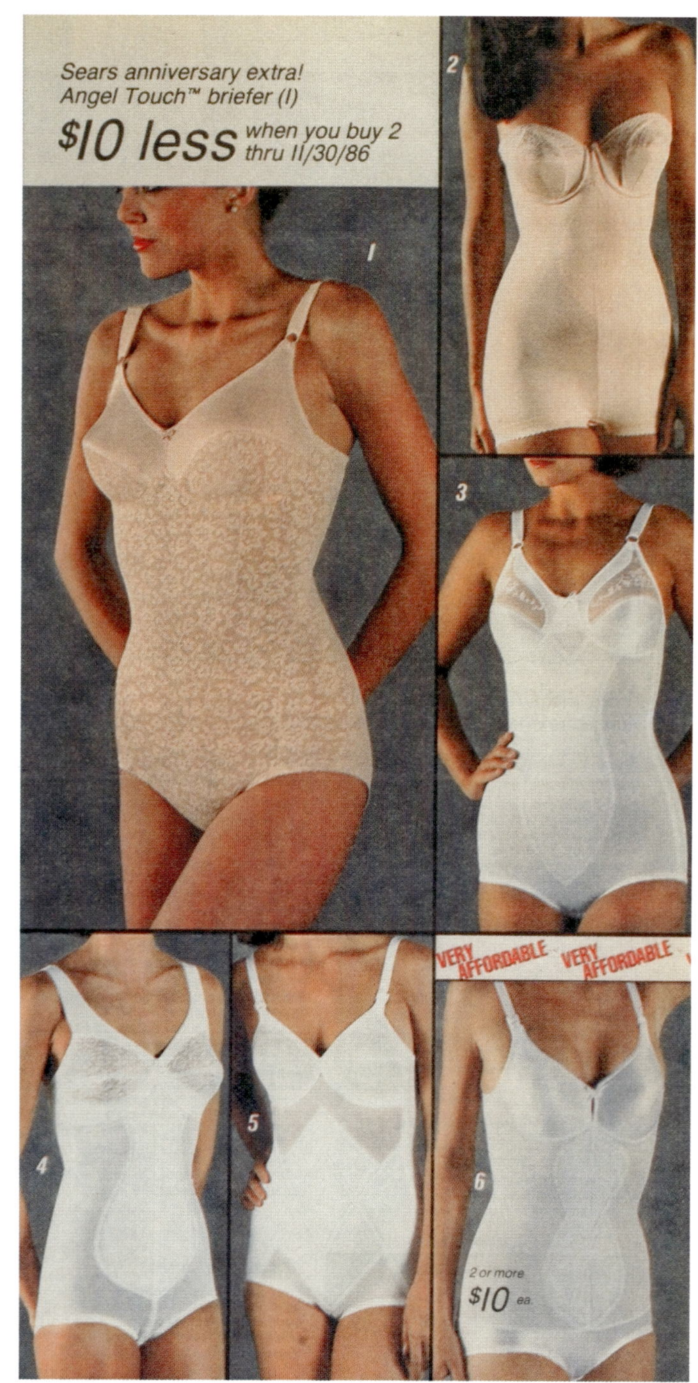

Briefers with hook-and-eye closures in fabrics such as spandex, polyester, and nylon. *Fall/Winter 1986*

Swimwear

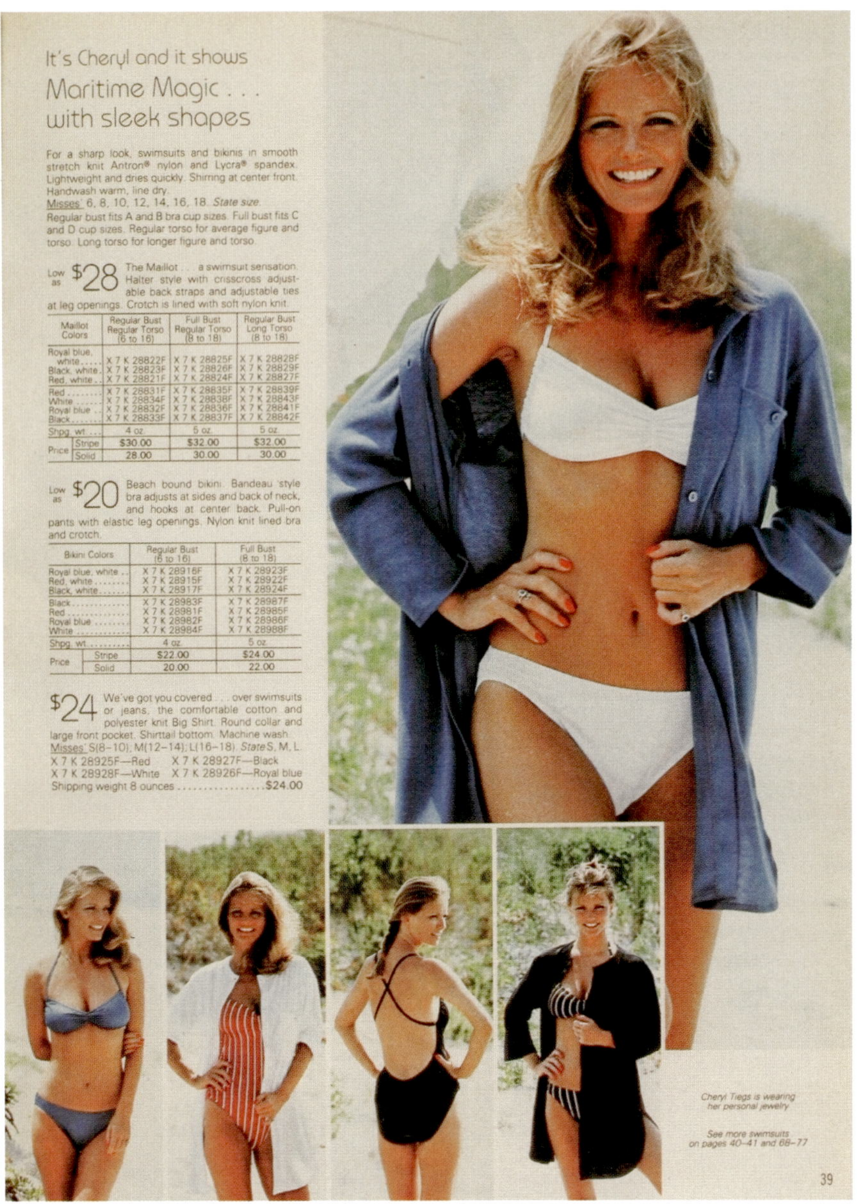

It's Cheryl and it shows
Maritime Magic . . .
with sleek shapes

For a sharp look, swimsuits and bikinis in smooth stretch knit Antron® nylon and Lycra® spandex. Lightweight and dries quickly. Shirring at center front. Handwash warm, line dry.
Misses' 6, 8, 10, 12, 14, 16, 18. *State size.*
Regular bust fits A and B bra cup sizes. Full bust fits C and D cup sizes. Regular torso for average figure and torso. Long torso for longer figure and torso.

Low as $28 The Maillot . . . a swimsuit sensation. Halter style with crisscross adjustable back straps and adjustable ties at leg openings. Crotch is lined with soft nylon knit.

Maillot Colors		Regular Bust Regular Torso (6 to 16)	Full Bust Regular Torso (8 to 18)	Regular Bust Long Torso (8 to 18)
Royal blue, white		X 7 K 28822F	X 7 K 28825F	X 7 K 28828F
Black, white		X 7 K 28823F	X 7 K 28826F	X 7 K 28829F
Red, white		X 7 K 28821F	X 7 K 28824F	X 7 K 28827F
Red		X 7 K 28831F	X 7 K 28835F	X 7 K 28839F
White		X 7 K 28834F	X 7 K 28838F	X 7 K 28843F
Royal blue		X 7 K 28832F	X 7 K 28836F	X 7 K 28841F
Black		X 7 K 28833F	X 7 K 28837F	X 7 K 28842F
Shpg. wt.		4 oz.	5 oz.	5 oz.
Price	Stripe	$30.00	$32.00	$32.00
	Solid	28.00	30.00	30.00

Low as $20 Beach bound bikini. Bandeau style bra adjusts at sides and back of neck, and hooks at center back. Pull-on pants with elastic leg openings. Nylon knit lined bra and crotch.

Bikini Colors		Regular Bust (6 to 16)	Full Bust (8 to 18)
Royal blue, white		X 7 K 28916F	X 7 K 28923F
Red, white		X 7 K 28915F	X 7 K 28922F
Black, white		X 7 K 28917F	X 7 K 28924F
Black		X 7 K 28983F	X 7 K 28987F
Red		X 7 K 28981F	X 7 K 28985F
Royal blue		X 7 K 28982F	X 7 K 28986F
White		X 7 K 28984F	X 7 K 28988F
Shpg. wt.		4 oz.	5 oz.
Price	Stripe	$22.00	$24.00
	Solid	20.00	22.00

$24 We've got you covered . . . over swimsuits or jeans, the comfortable cotton and polyester knit Big Shirt. Round collar and large front pocket. Shirttail bottom. Machine wash.
Misses' S(8–10), M(12–14); L(16–18). *State* S, M, L.
X 7 K 28925F—Red X 7 K 28927F—Black
X 7 K 28928F—White X 7 K 28926F—Royal blue
Shipping weight 8 ounces $24.00

Cheryl Tiegs is wearing her personal jewelry

See more swimsuits on pages 40–41 and 68–77

39

Swimsuits and bikinis in stretch knit Antron® nylon and Lycra® spandex are lightweight and dry quickly. *Spring/Summer 1984.*

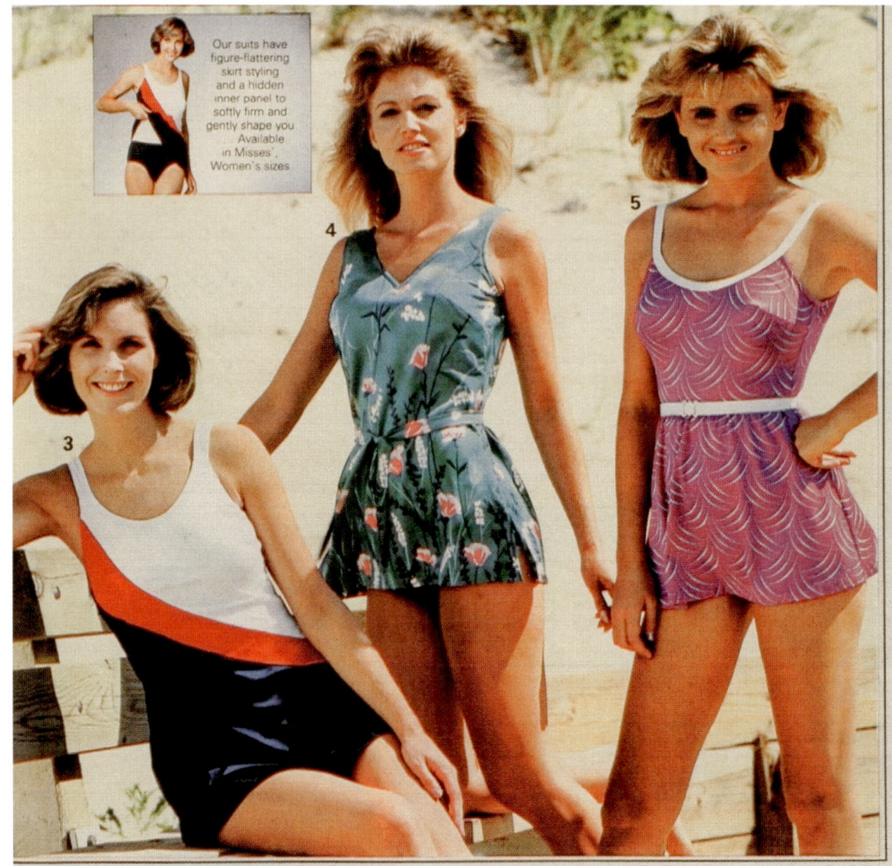

(3 thru 5) Stylish swimdresses give you the subtle support you're looking for when you put on a swim suit. Suits (4 and 5) have a lightweight power net panel of Antron® nylon and Lycra® spandex attached from under the bust to the top of the panty; panel in suit (3) is nylon and spandex. Quick drying swimdresses (4 and 5) are knit of Antron® nylon and Lycra® spandex, (3) is nylon and spandex. Hand wash.

(3) A fitting salute . . . colors of summer! Soft stretch knit bra with elastic under bust; nylon knit lined crotch. Imported.
Misses' 10, 12, 14, 16, 18
X 7 K 8391F—Wt. 8 oz. $30.00
Women's 38, 40, 42, 44, 46
X 7 K 8392F—Wt. 10 oz. $33.00

(4) The flowers that bloom in the Spring will last on through the Summer on this brightly colored V-neck swimdress. Inner bra has soft, pre-formed cups for firm support. Nylon knit lined crotch for comfort. Elasticized leg openings. Self-fabric belt.
Misses' 10, 12, 14, 16, 18
X7K8393F–Turquoise ground
X7K8394F–Navy blue ground
Wt. ea. 8 oz. . . . . . Ea. **$32.00**
Women's 38, 40, 42, 44, 46
X7K8395F–Turquoise ground
X7K8396F–Navy blue ground
Wt. ea. 10 oz. . . . Ea. **$35.00**

(5) Sprightly patterned swimdress will suit you to a "T". Contrasting belt and straps will brighten the scene. Soft stretch knit inner bra for gentle support. Nylon knit lined crotch. Straps crisscross in back. Elasticized leg openings.
Misses' 10, 12, 14, 16, 18
X7K8397F—Purple ground
X7K8398F—Black ground
Wt. ea. 7 oz. . . . Ea. **$32.00**
Women's 38, 40, 42, 44, 46
X7K8399F—Purple ground
X7K24074F–Black ground
Wt. ea. 9 oz. . . . Ea. **$35.00**

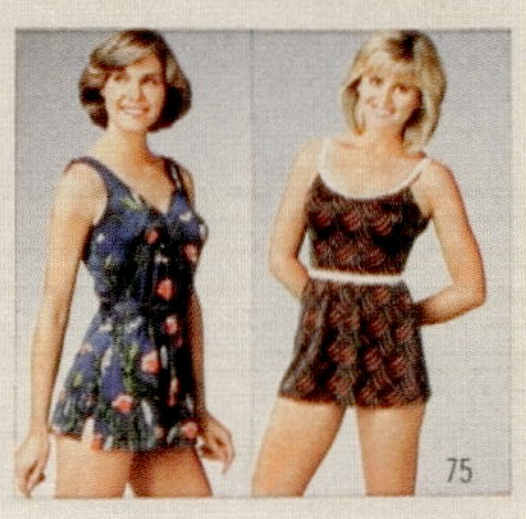

Antron® nylon and Lycra® spandex swimdresses offers stylish support. *Spring/Summer 1984.*

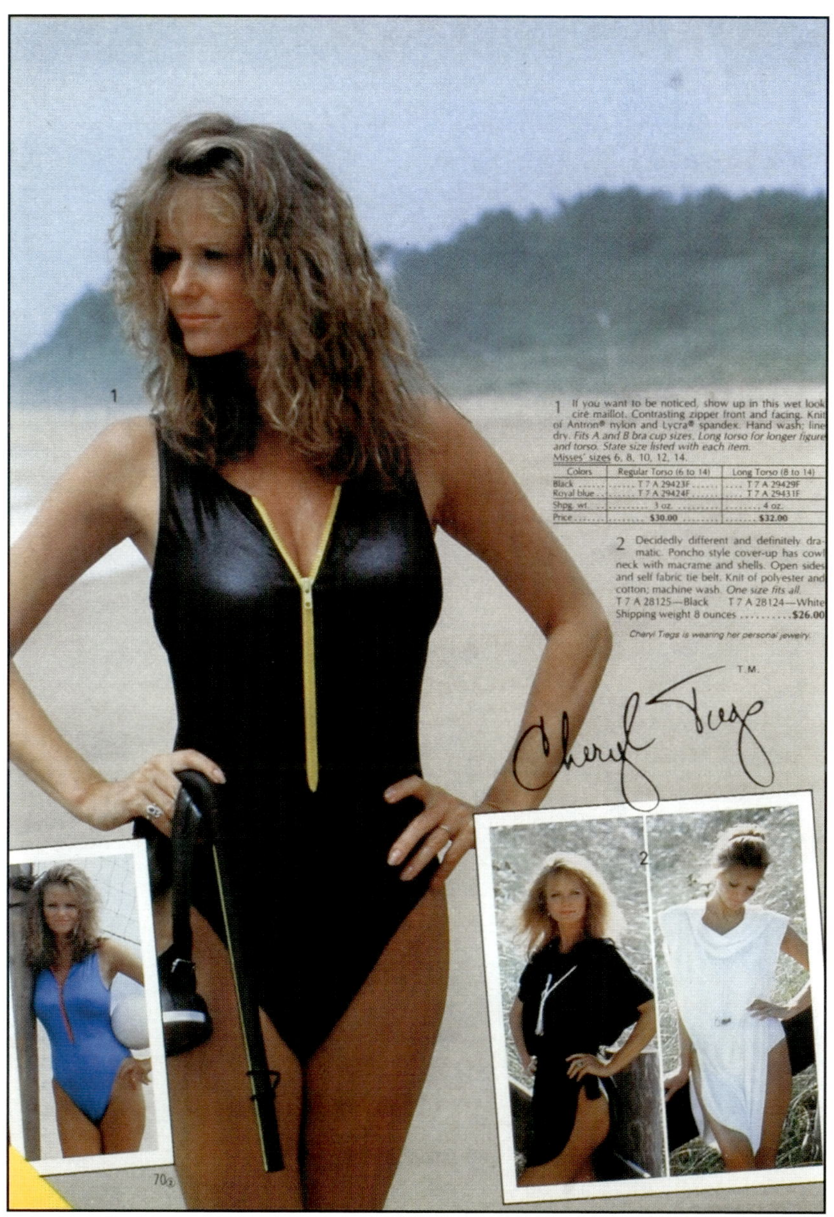

1 If you want to be noticed, show up in this wet look ciré maillot. Contrasting zipper front and facing. Knit of Antron® nylon and Lycra® spandex. Hand wash; line dry. *Fits A and B bra cup sizes. Long torso for longer figure and torso. State size listed with each item.*
Misses' sizes 6, 8, 10, 12, 14.

Colors	Regular Torso (6 to 14)	Long Torso (8 to 14)
Black	T 7 A 29423F	T 7 A 29429F
Royal blue	T 7 A 29424F	T 7 A 29431F
Shpg. wt.	3 oz.	4 oz.
Price	**$30.00**	**$32.00**

2 Decidedly different and definitely dramatic. Poncho style cover-up has cowl neck with macrame and shells. Open sides and self fabric tie belt. Knit of polyester and cotton; machine wash. *One size fits all.*
T 7 A 28125—Black T 7 A 28124—White
Shipping weight 8 ounces **$26.00**

Cheryl Tiegs is wearing her personal jewelry.

Wet look ciré maillot has contrasting zipper in nylon and spandex fabric. *Spring/Summer 1985*

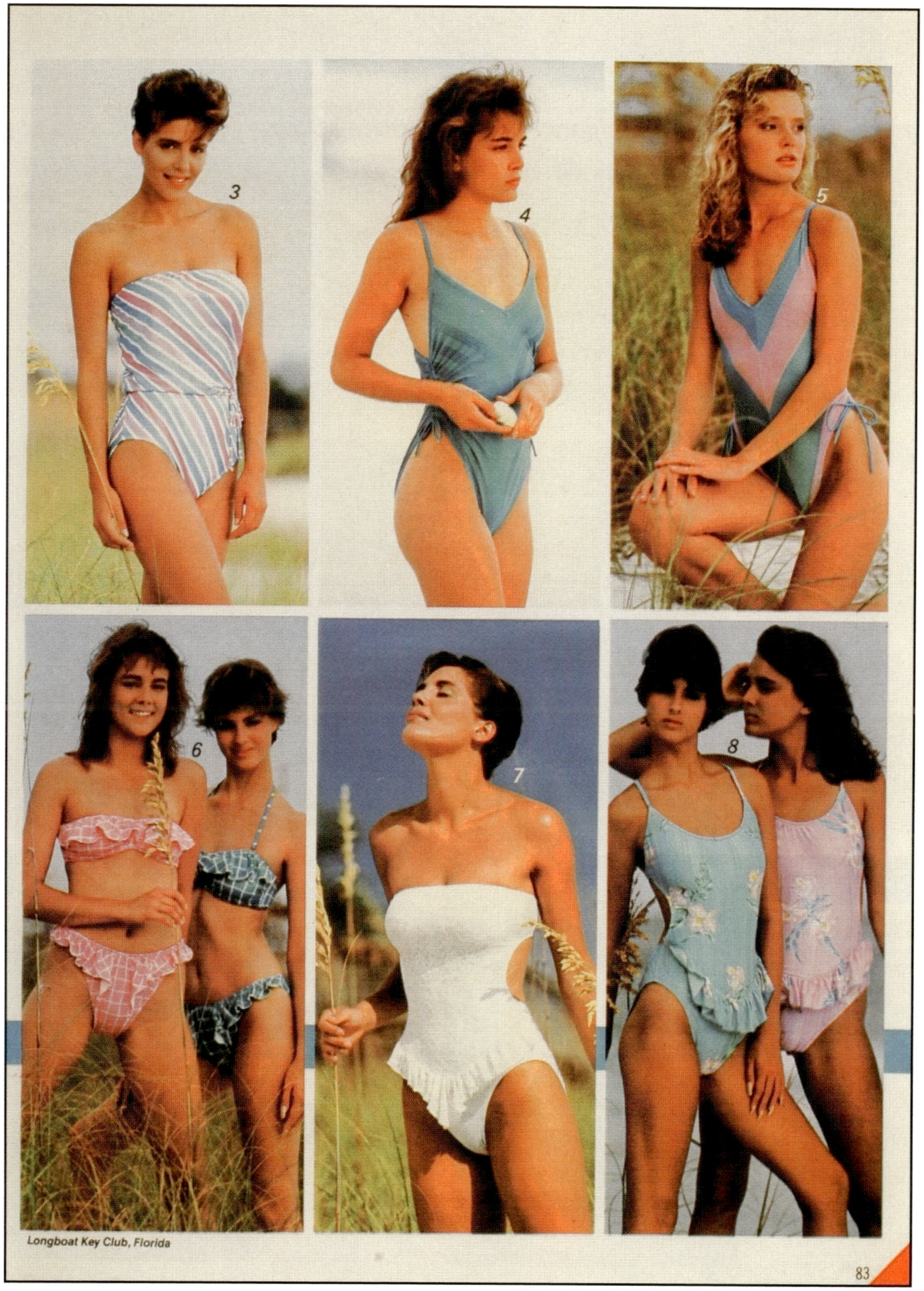

3 4 5 6 7 8

Longboat Key Club, Florida

83

Swimsuits in a variety of colors and styles. *Spring/Summer 1986*

Footwear

Athletic Shoes

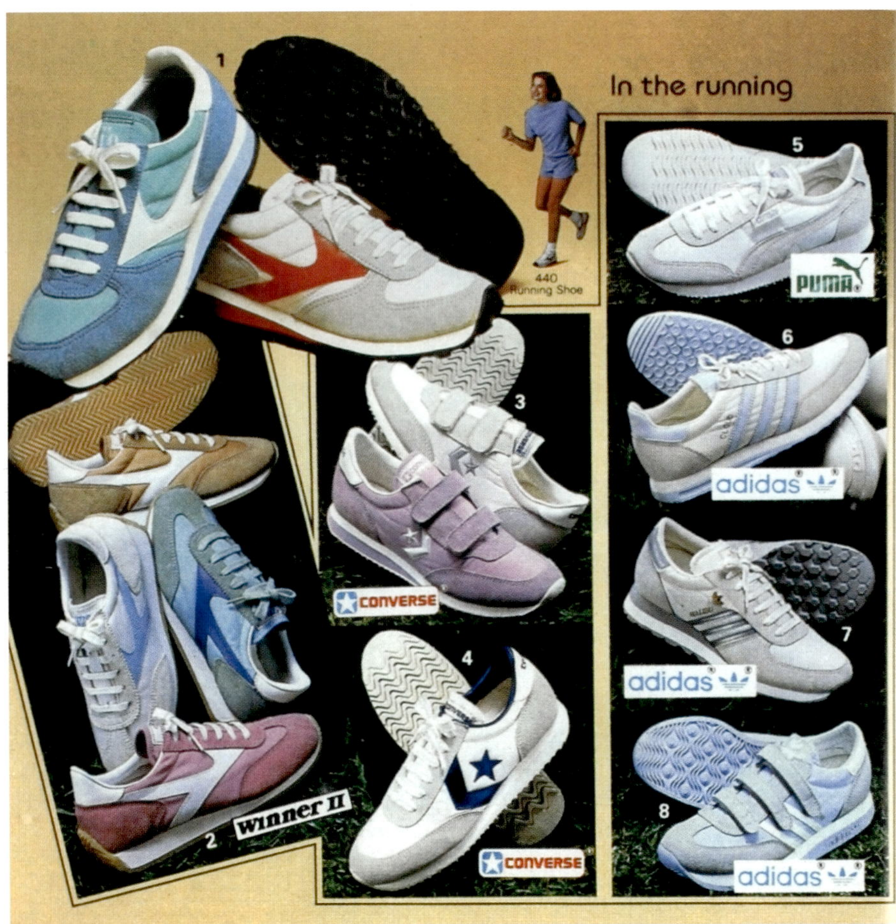

Adidas®, Converse®, Puma®, and Winner II® women's athletic running shoes. *Spring/Summer 1984.*

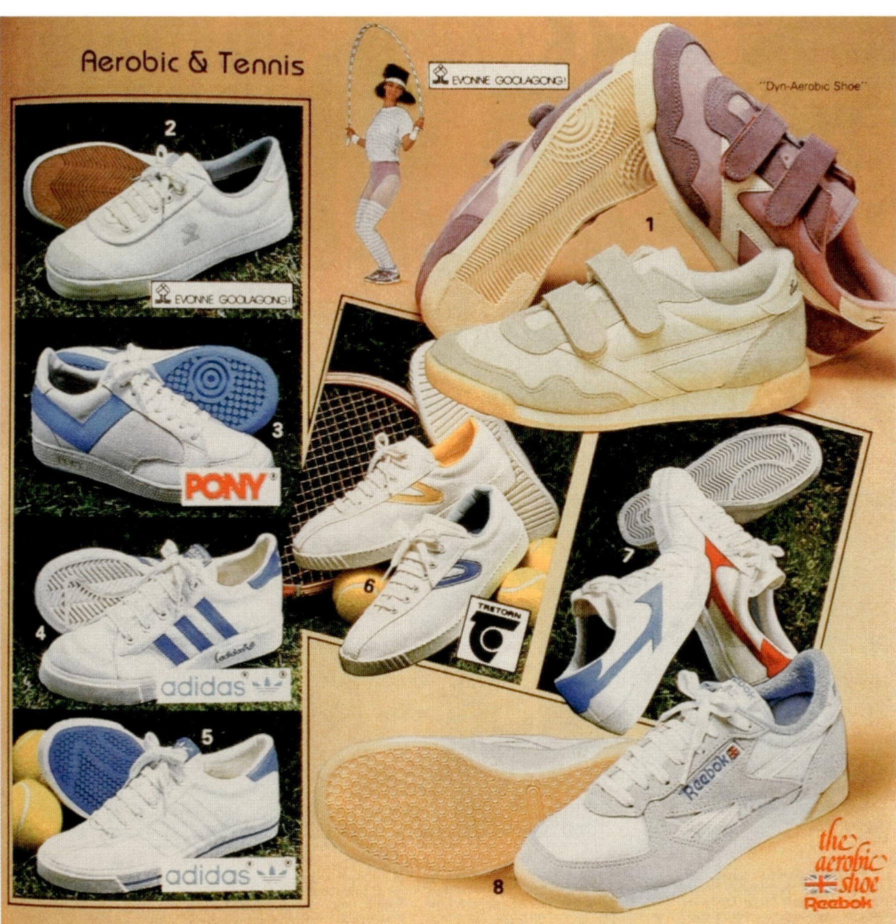

Aerobic & tennis shoes representing Adidas®, Evonne Goolagong®, Pony®, Tretorn®, and Reebok®. *Spring/Summer 1984.*

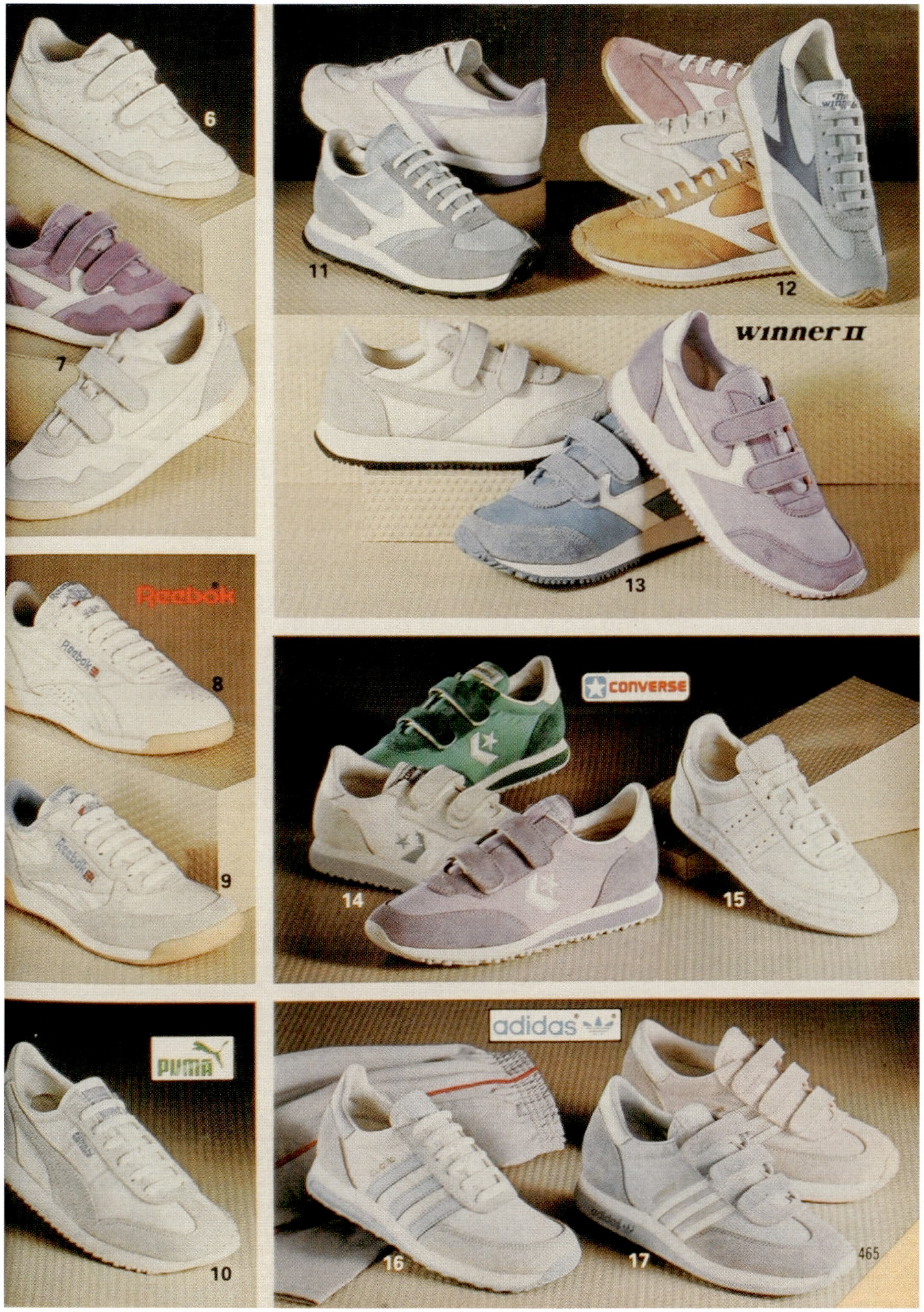

Brand name athletic shoes for the sports-minded lady. *Fall/Winter 1984.*

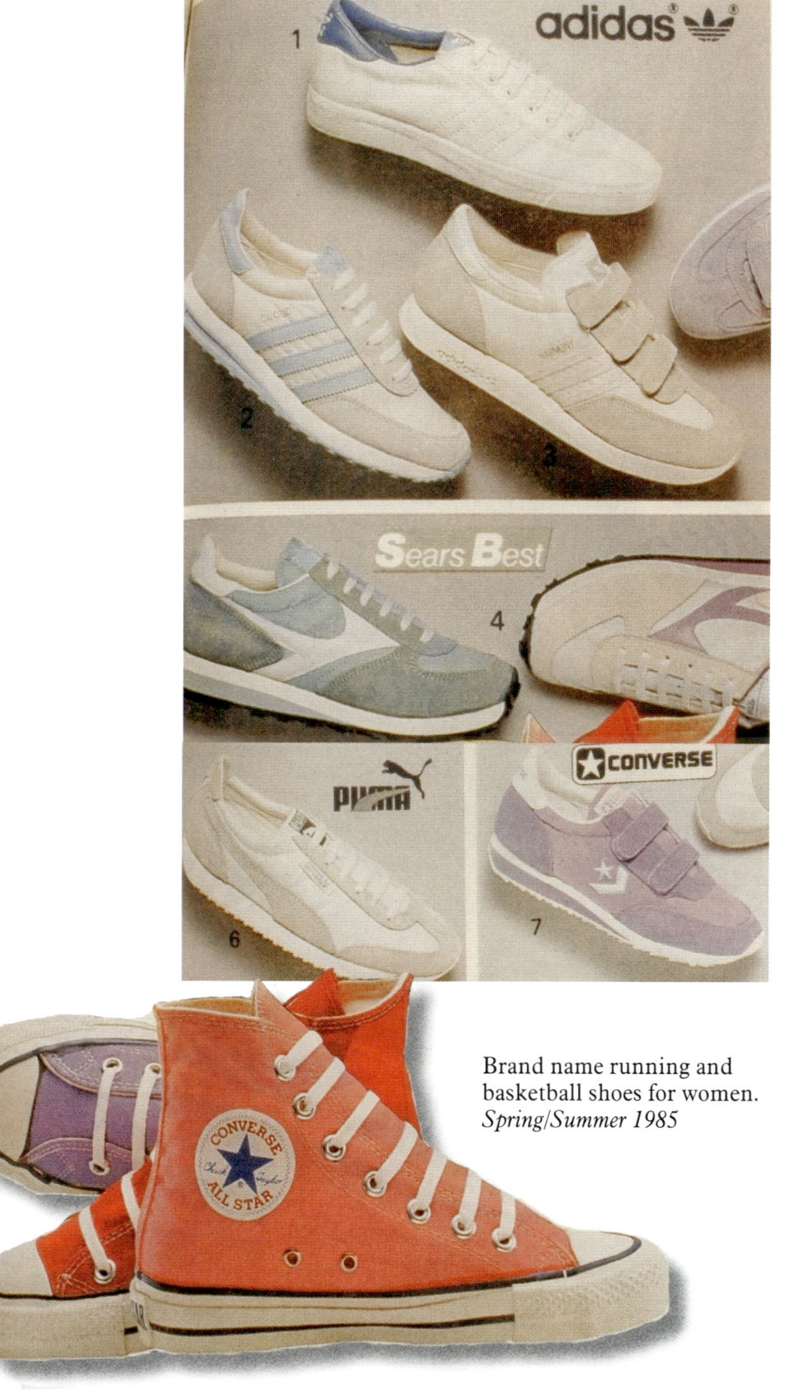

Brand name running and basketball shoes for women. *Spring/Summer 1985*

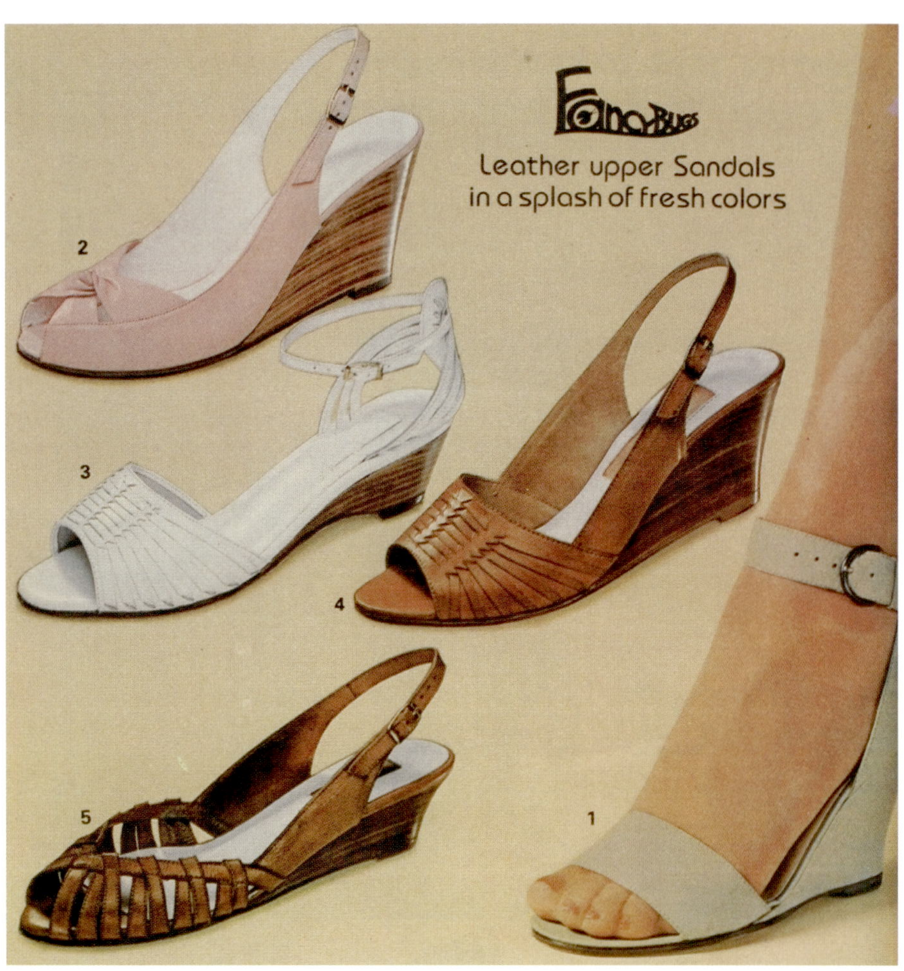

Fancy Bugs leather upper sandals with wedge heels. *Spring/Summer 1984.*

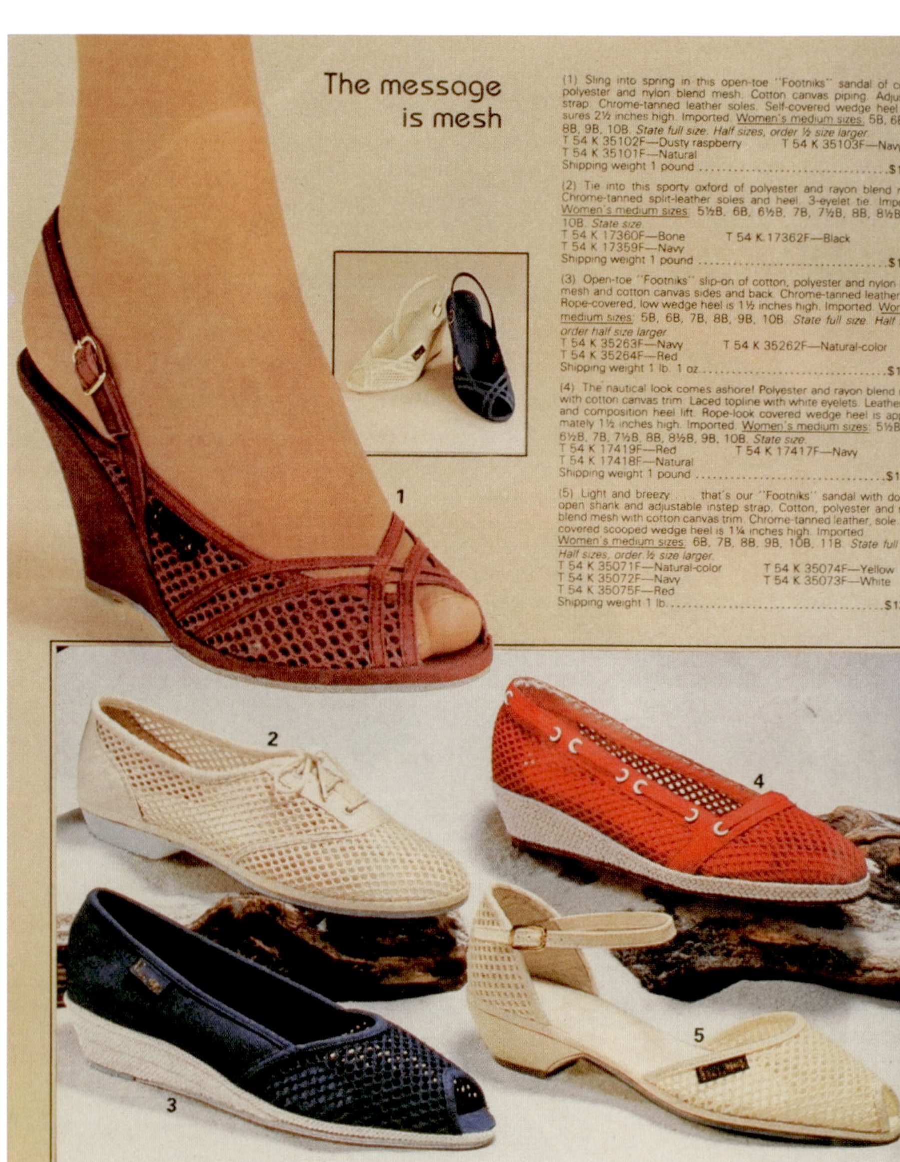

A variety of mesh sandals. *Spring/Summer 1984.*

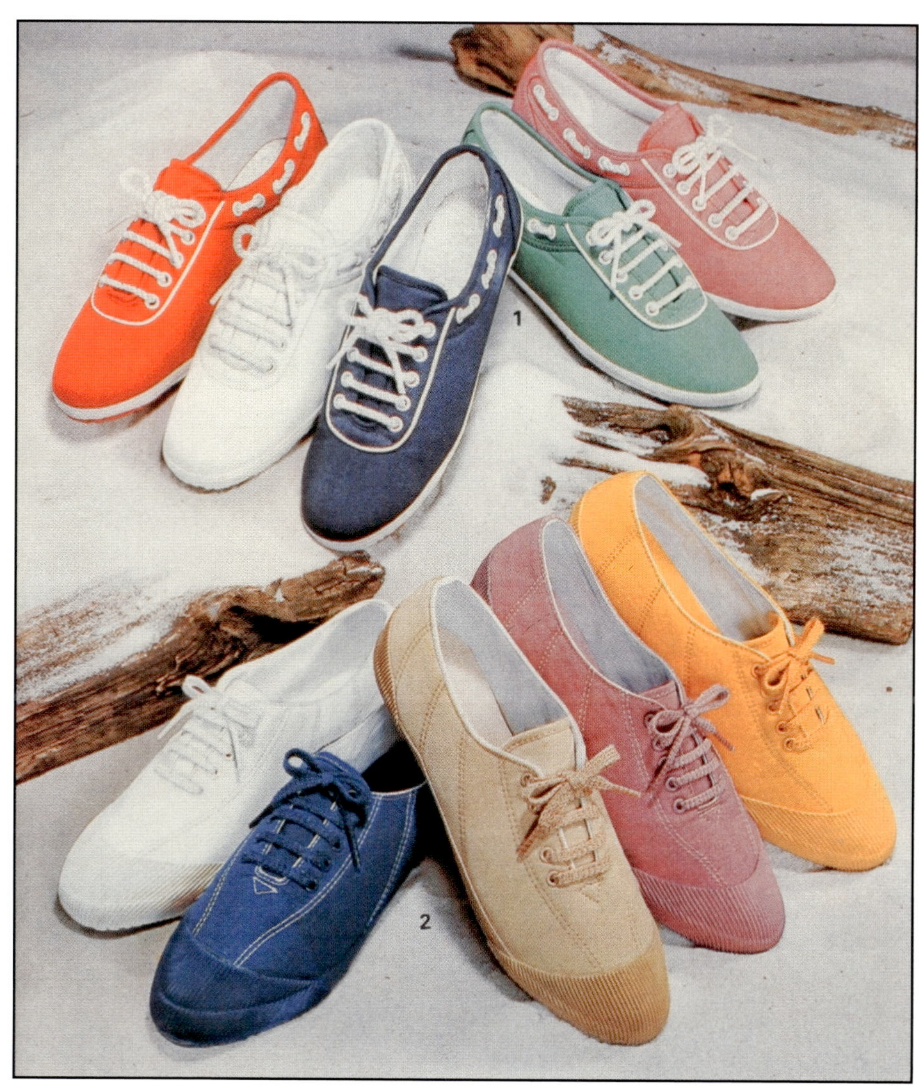

These sporty or boat-style canvas shoes go great with shorts, skirts, or slacks. *Spring/Summer 1984.*

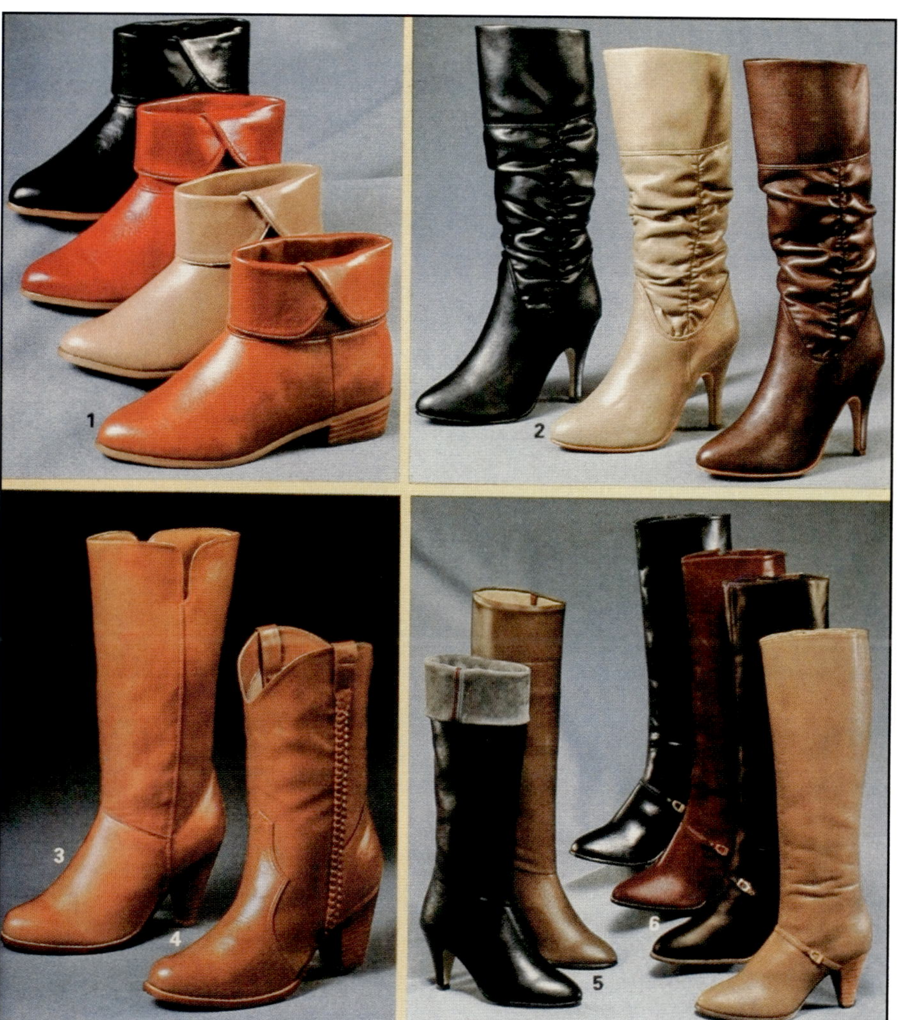

Assorted styles of boots with urethane uppers look like real leather. *Spring/Summer 1984.*

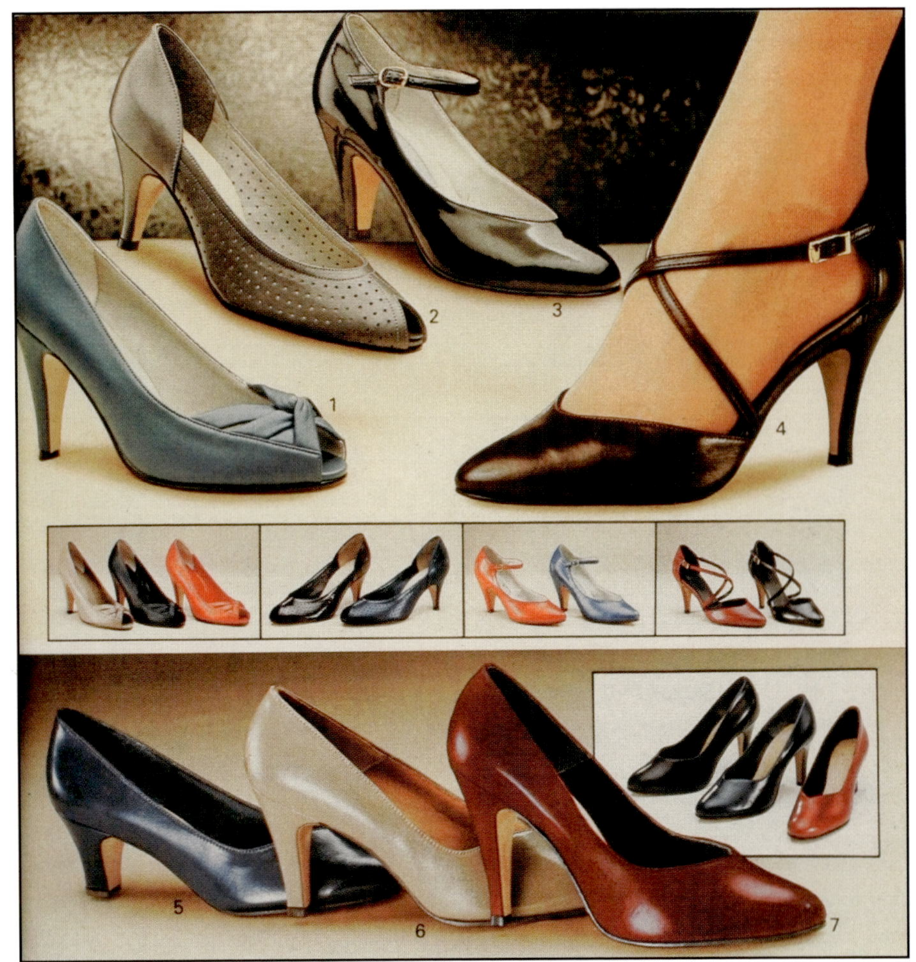

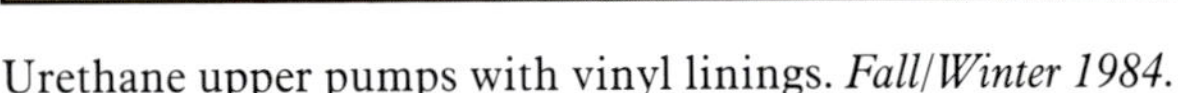
Urethane upper pumps with vinyl linings. *Fall/Winter 1984.*

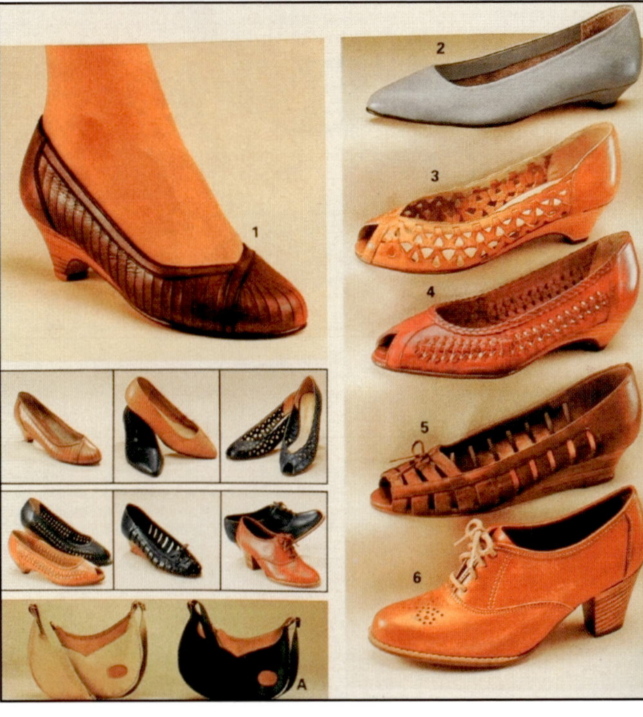

Leather upper casual shoes in a variety of styles. Hobo style shoulder bags. *Fall/Winter 1984.*

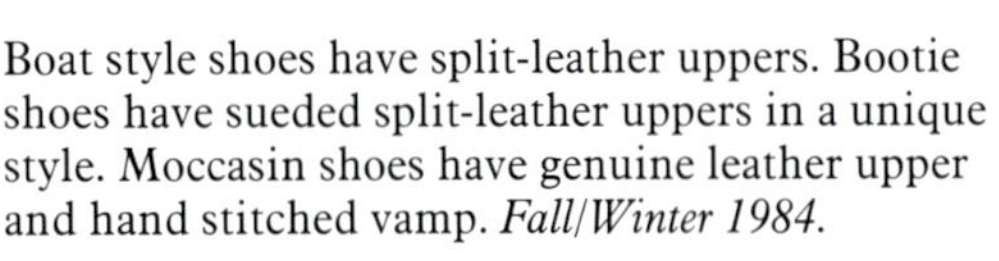
Boat style shoes have split-leather uppers. Bootie shoes have sueded split-leather uppers in a unique style. Moccasin shoes have genuine leather upper and hand stitched vamp. *Fall/Winter 1984.*

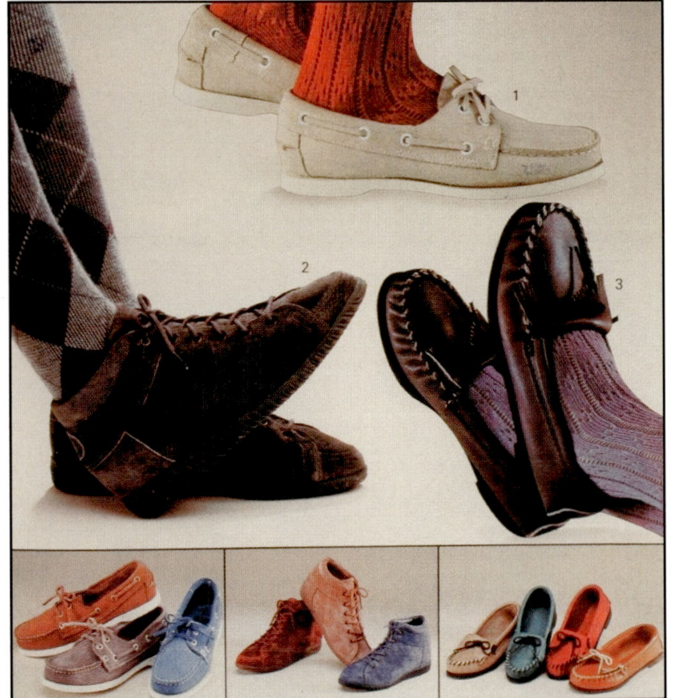

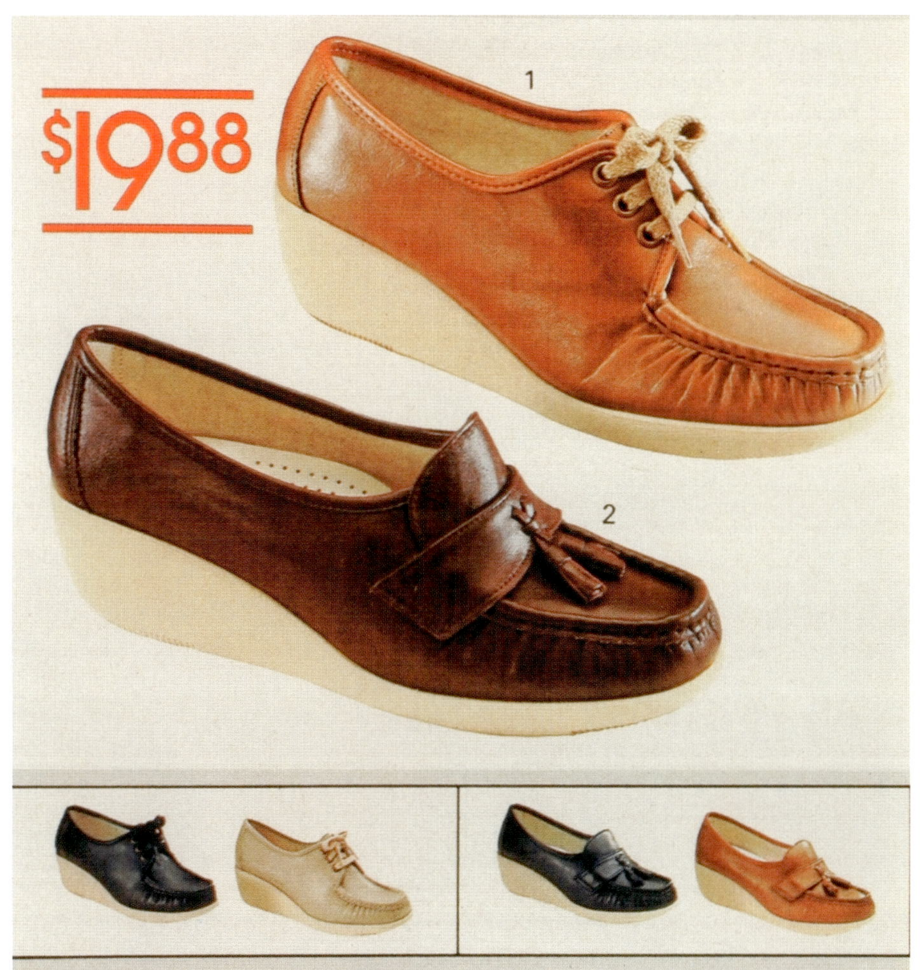

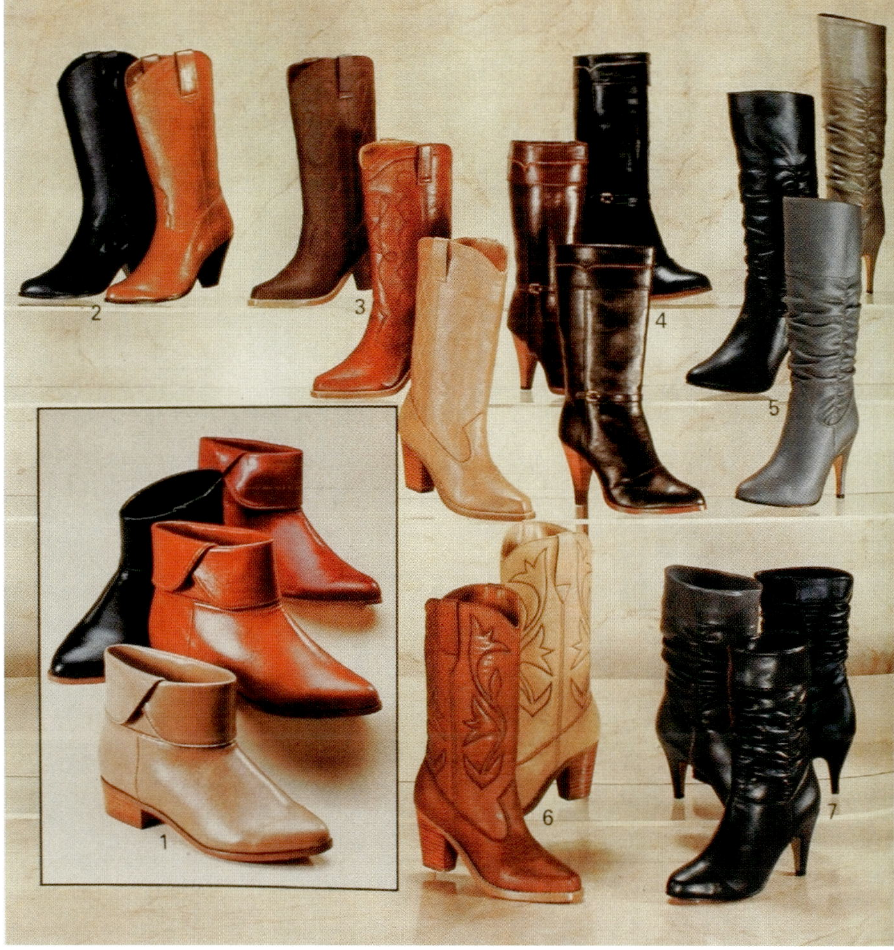

Leather-look urethane boots. *Fall/Winter 1984.*

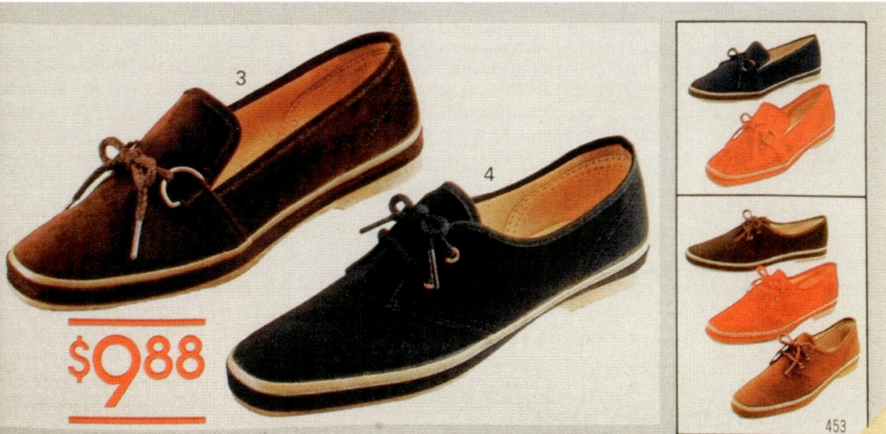

Soft Moc casuals have genuine leather uppers featuring hand-sewn moccasin construction. Sporty casual shoes in soft brushed nylon velour upper. *Fall/Winter 1984.*

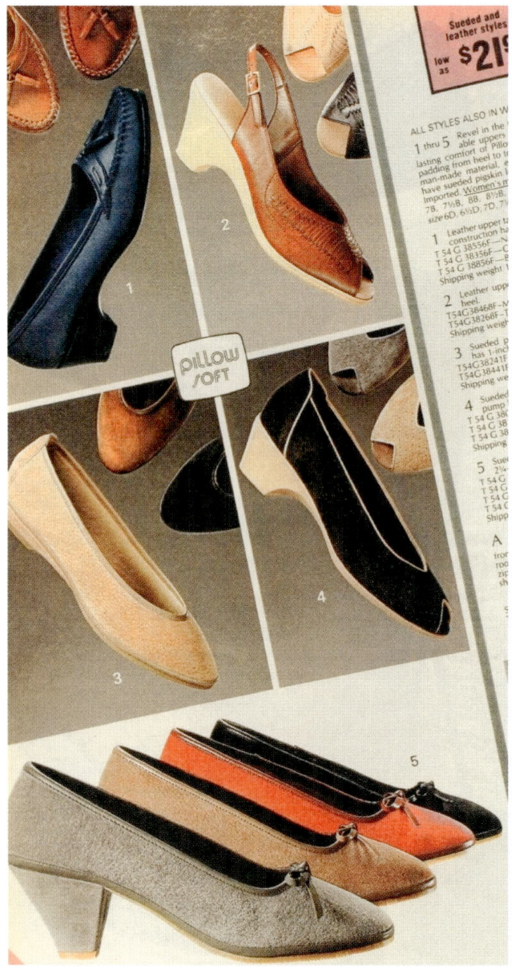

Rich and fashionable uppers have Pillow Soft® insoles from heel to toe. *Fall/Winter 1985*

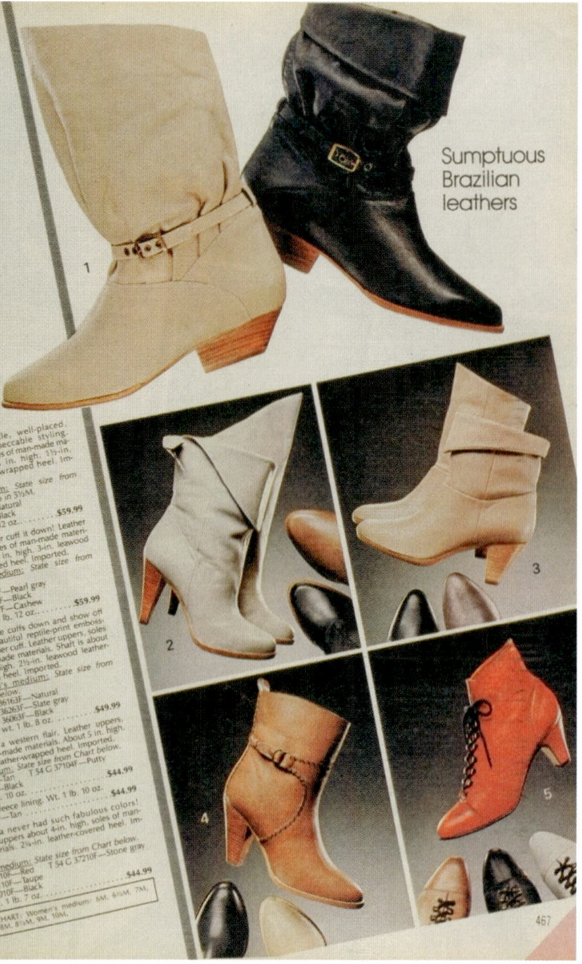

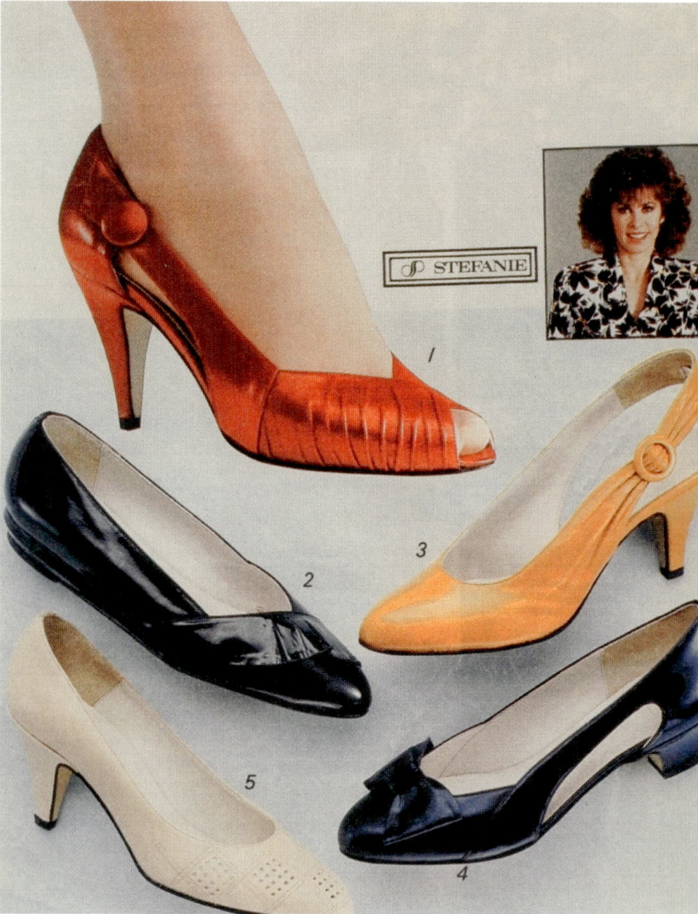

Elegant Italian calfskin leather shoes from the Stefanie collection. *Spring/Summer 1986*

Brazilian leather boots in a variety of styles features buckles, folded cuffs, western styl- ing, and tie up laces. *Fall/Winter 1985*

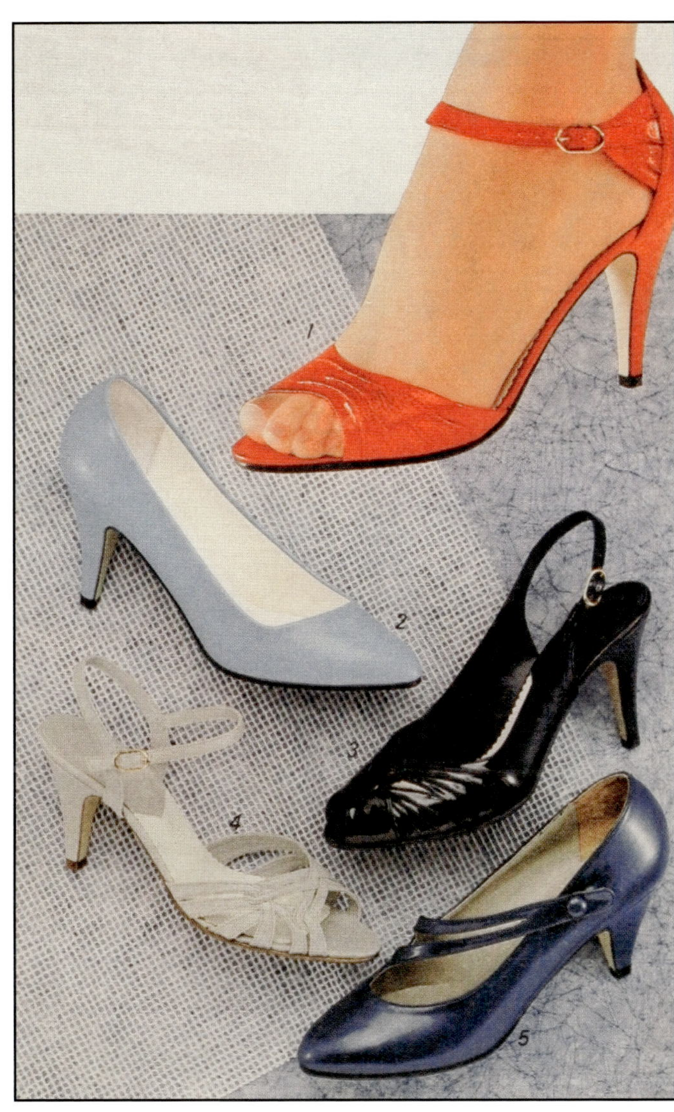

Soft leather-look urethane dress shoes all have cushioned insoles. *Spring/Summer 1986*

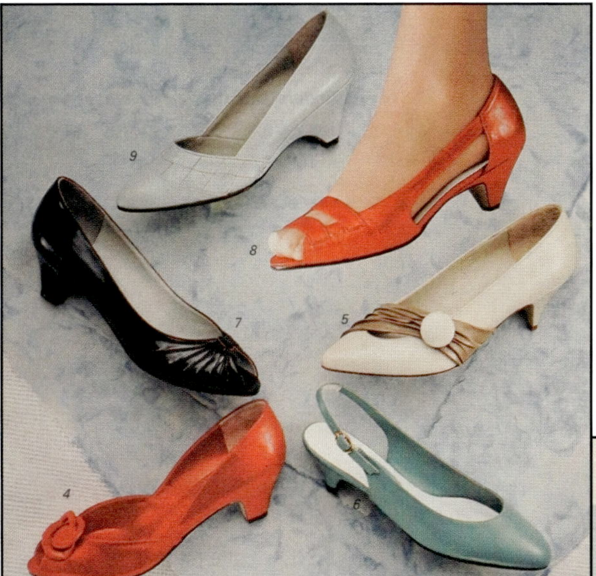

Pump and sling-back dress shoes in a variety of colors and styles. *Spring/Summer 1986*

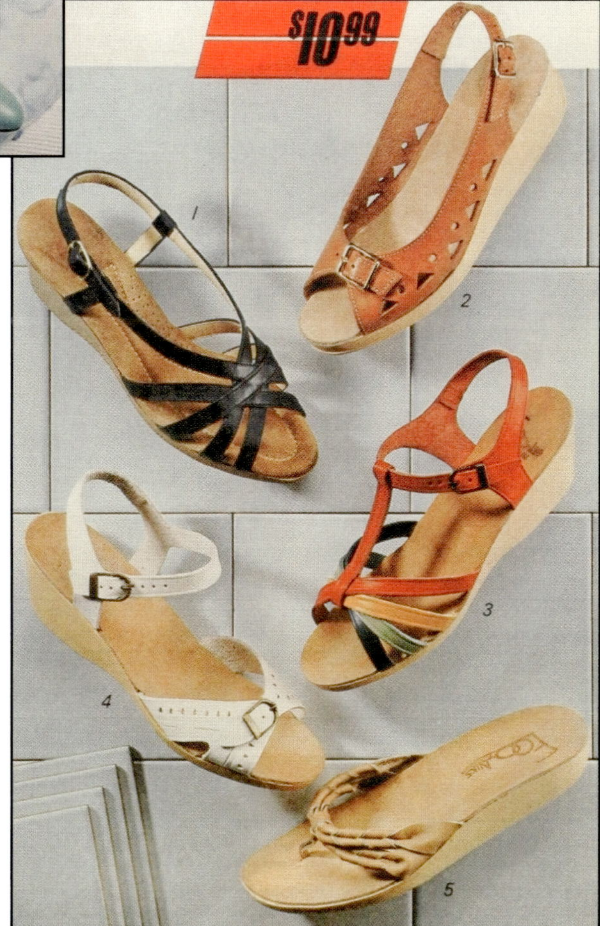

Italian leather sandals with leather uppers and cushioned sueded insoles. *Spring/Summer 1986*

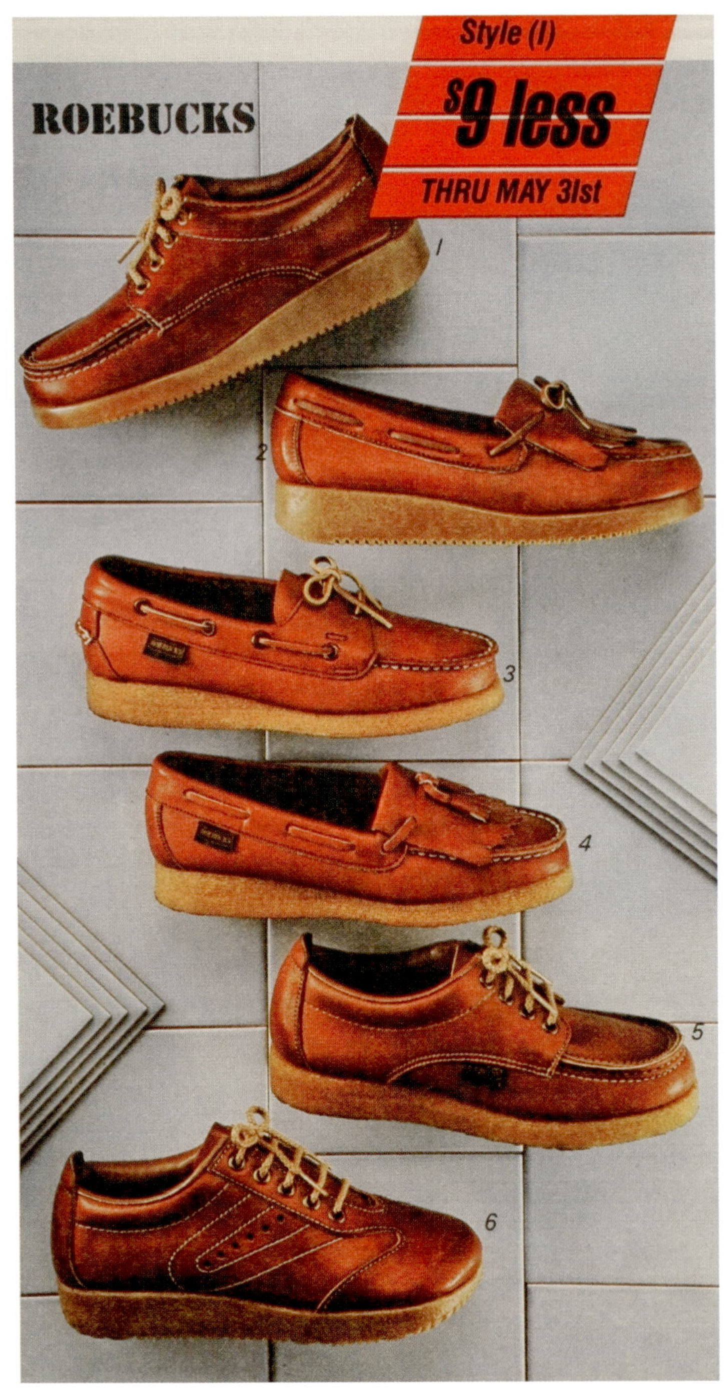

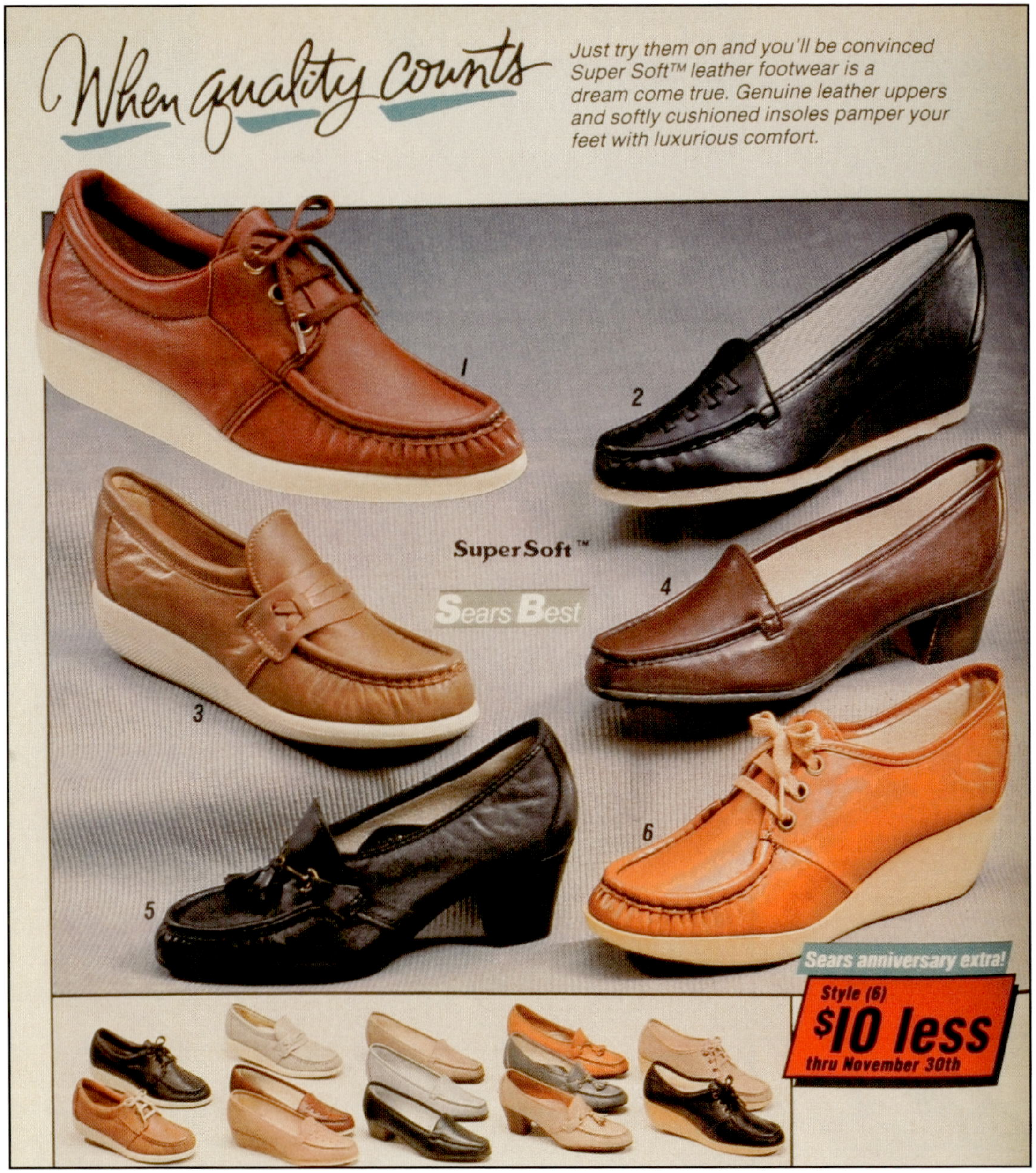

When quality counts

Just try them on and you'll be convinced Super Soft™ leather footwear is a dream come true. Genuine leather uppers and softly cushioned insoles pamper your feet with luxurious comfort.

SuperSoft™

Sears Best

Sears anniversary extra!

Style (6) $10 less thru November 30th

Super Soft leather footwear have genuine leather uppers and softly cushioned insoles. *Fall/Winter 1986*

Roebucks leather casual oxford shoes. *Spring/Summer 1986*

Coats

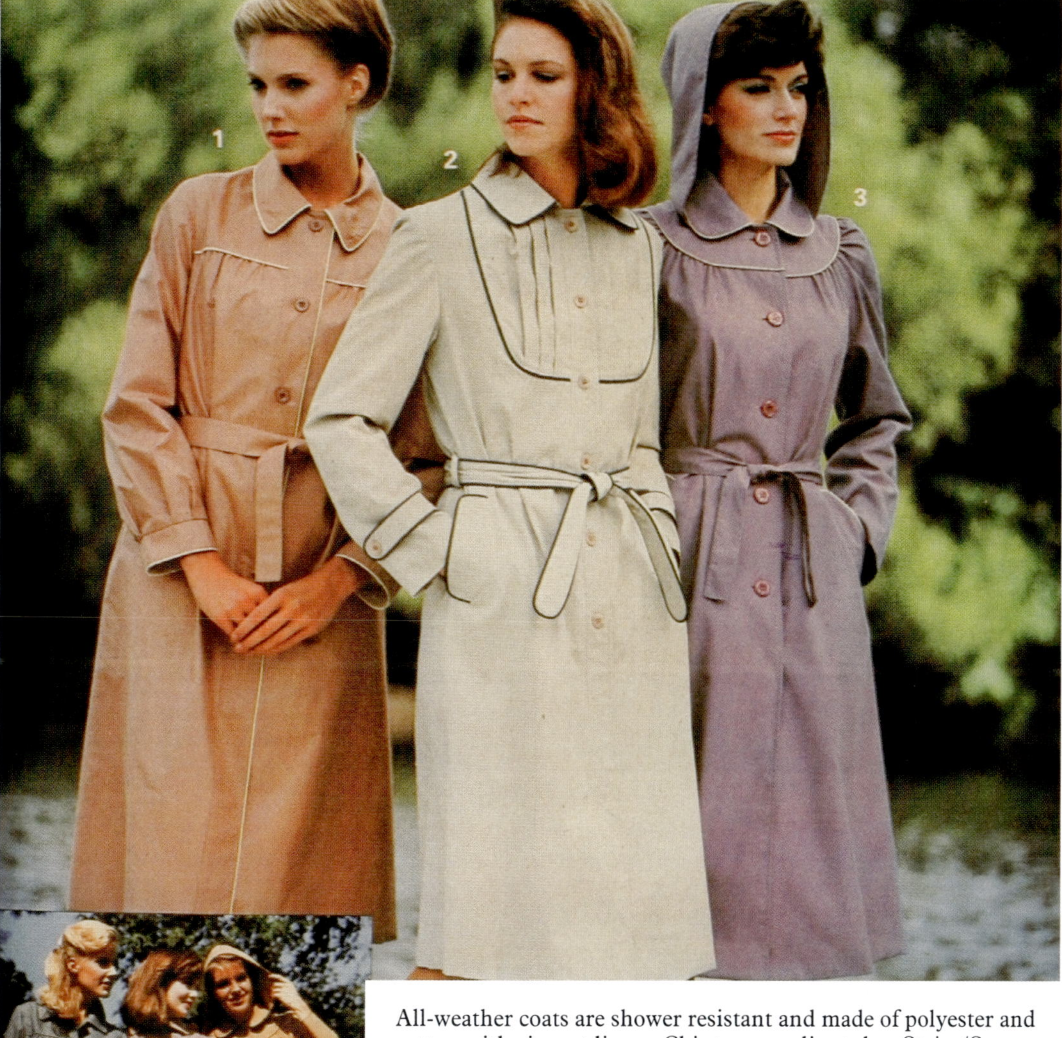

All-weather coats are shower resistant and made of polyester and cotton with zip-out liners. Chintz or poplin styles. *Spring/Summer 1984.*

Tweed coat is ¾-length with big shoulders, wide-notched collar, full dolman sleeves, slash pockets, and button-trim cuffs. Cropped coat has double-breasted look with big shoulders, deep dolman sleeves, front pockets, and turn-back cuffs. *Fall/Winter 1984.*

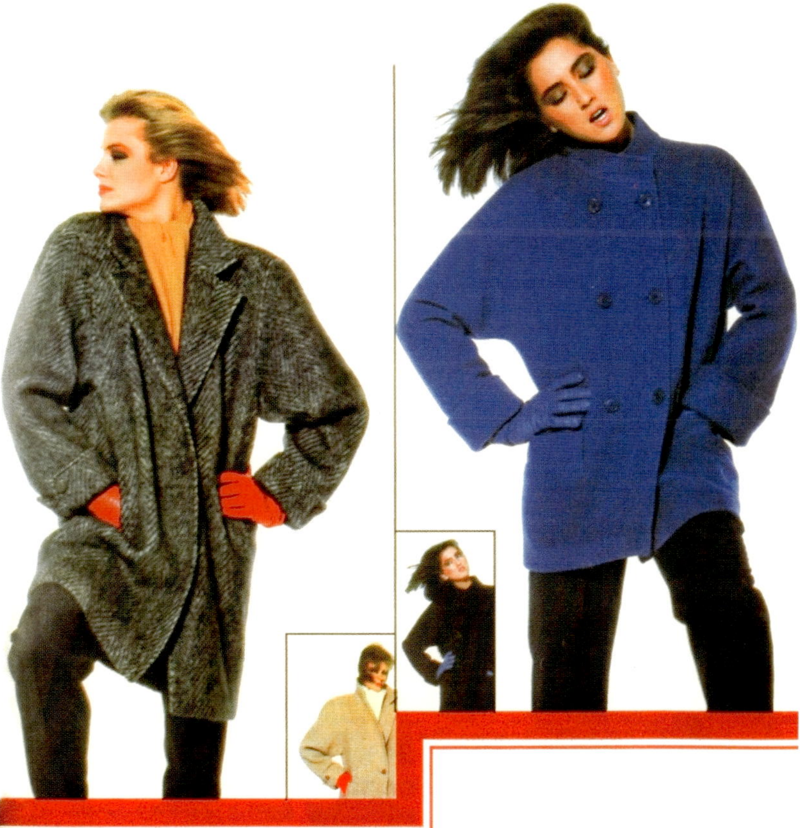

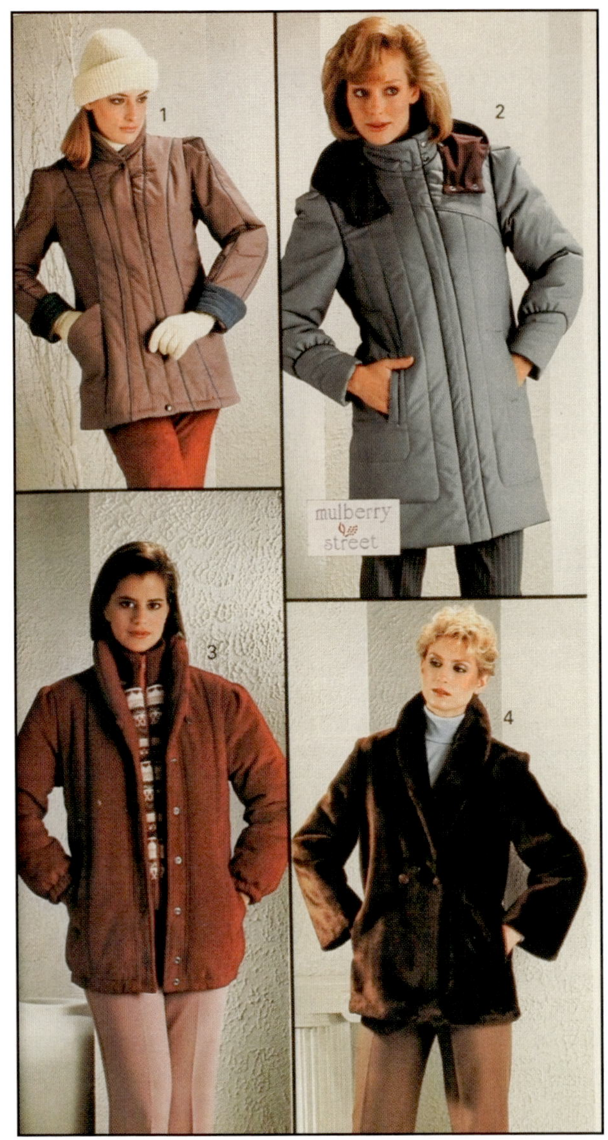

Pantcoat with contrasting body-defining piping, quilted stadium coat with detachable hood with contrasting piping, cotton corduroy blouson coat, and thick pile coat is double-breasted with single button closure. *Fall/Winter 1984.*

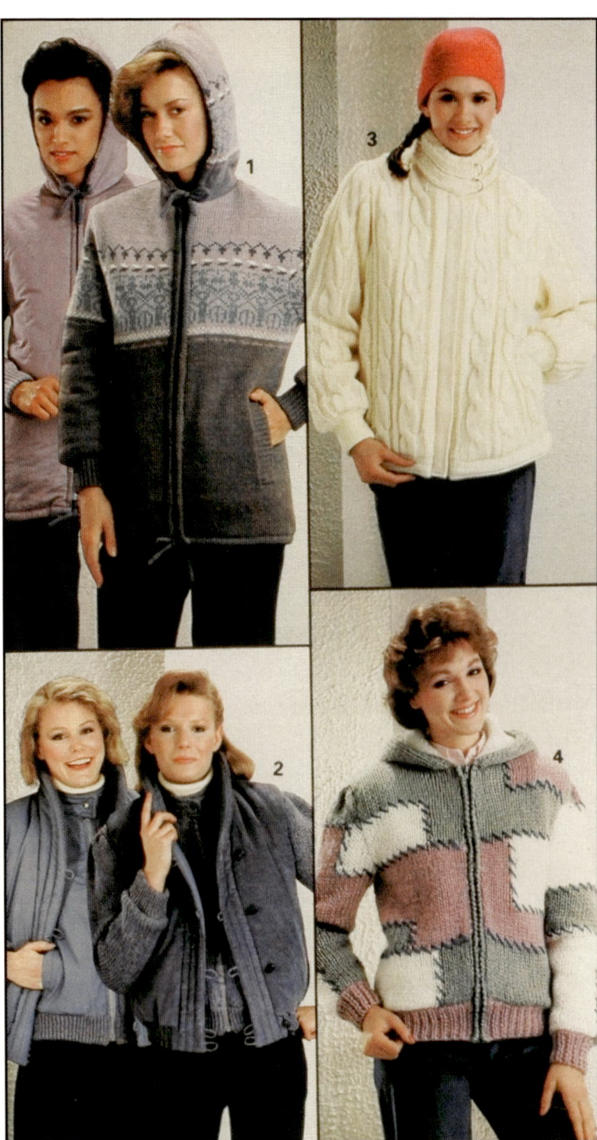

Hooded jacket has two great looks in solid or jacquard pattern. Reversible vest and jacket provide a layered look, heavy cable-knit sweater with zip-front closing, and hooded jacket with patchwork design. *Fall/Winter 1984.*

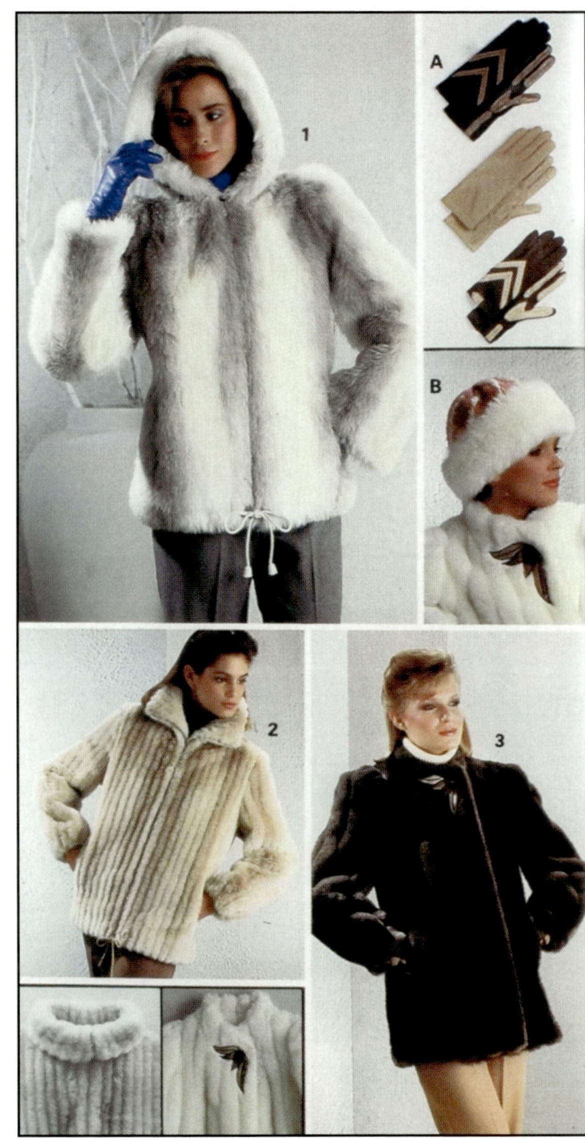

Fake furs made of acrylic and modacrylic pile. Hooded parka has the glorious look of arctic fox, jacket looks like elegant grooved mink, and the mink pretender coat has a furner's appliqué and button closure at the neck. Accessorize with Isotoner® gloves and hat with fox-look cuff. *Fall/Winter 1984.*

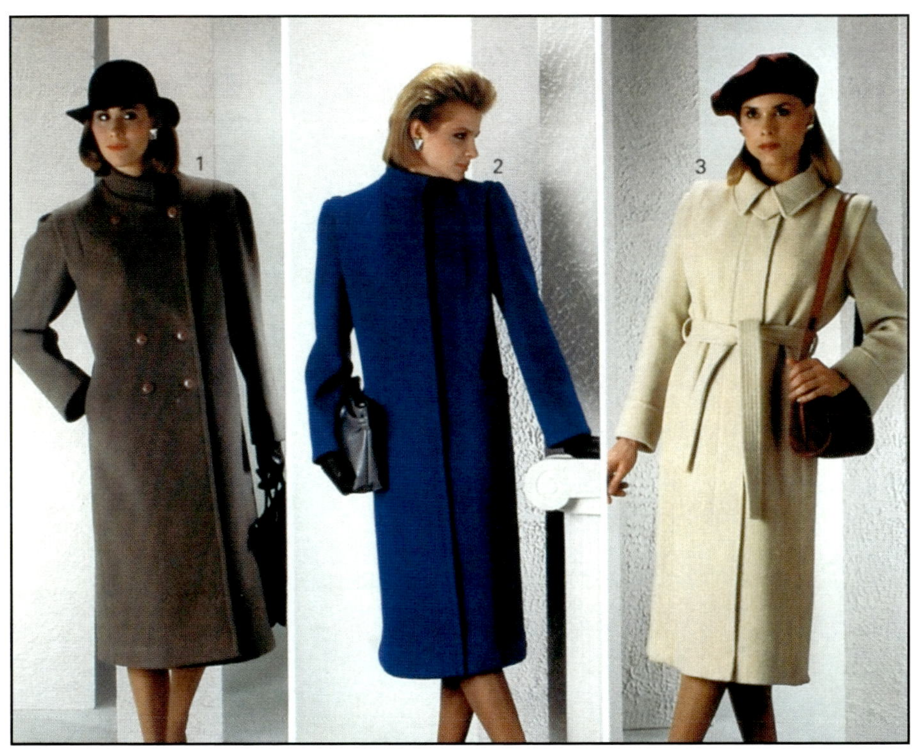

Coats with timeless fashion appeal comes in double-breasted reefer with stand-up collar, a simple coat with stitched, stand-up collar and placket with concealed button front, or a classic style with flanged shoulders club collar, and tie belt. *Fall/Winter 1984.*

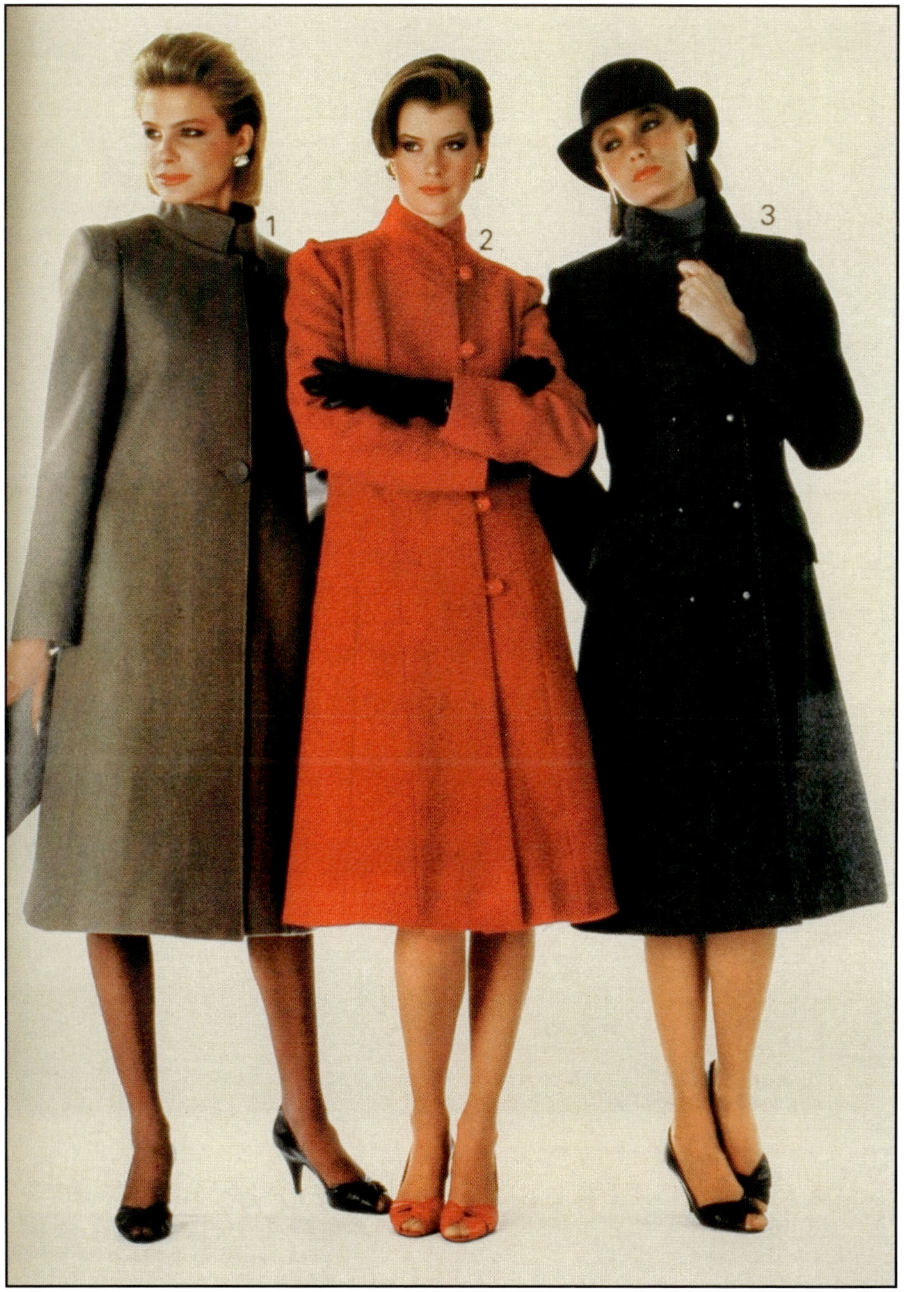

Coat with two-button closure at neck and waist, A-line coat has slightly off center buttons and stand-up collar, double-breasted reefer coat has notched collar and flap pockets. *Fall/Winter 1984.*

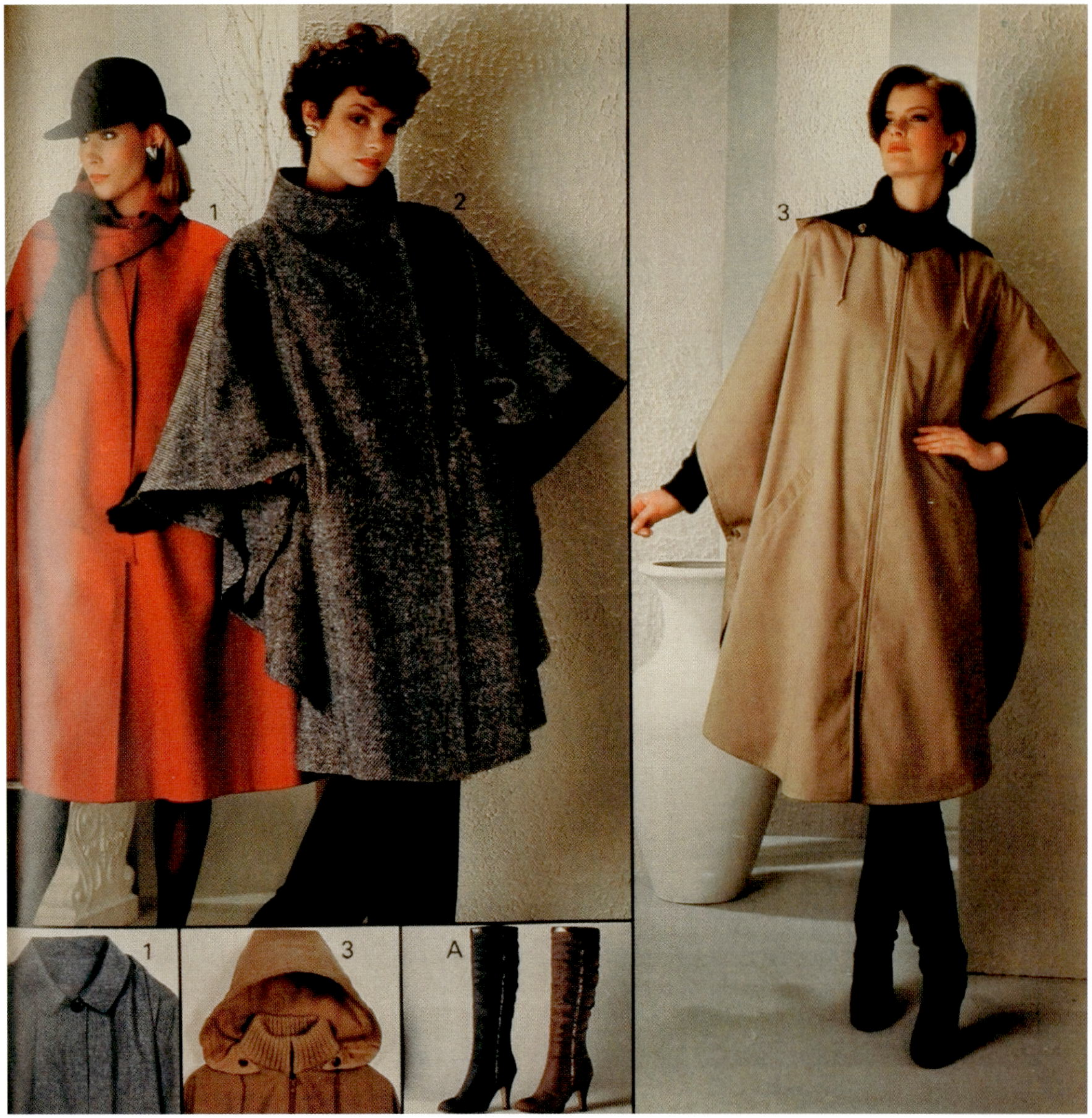

Fly-front cape in wool and nylon bonded to cotton has fly-front with concealed button closure and a detachable self scarf, cape in black and white tweed has stand-up collar and button-loop closure in a blend of wool, acrylic, rayon, polyester, and nylon. All weather cape has detachable hood, ribbed knit collar, and slash pockets in polyester and cotton poplin. *Fall/Winter 1984.*

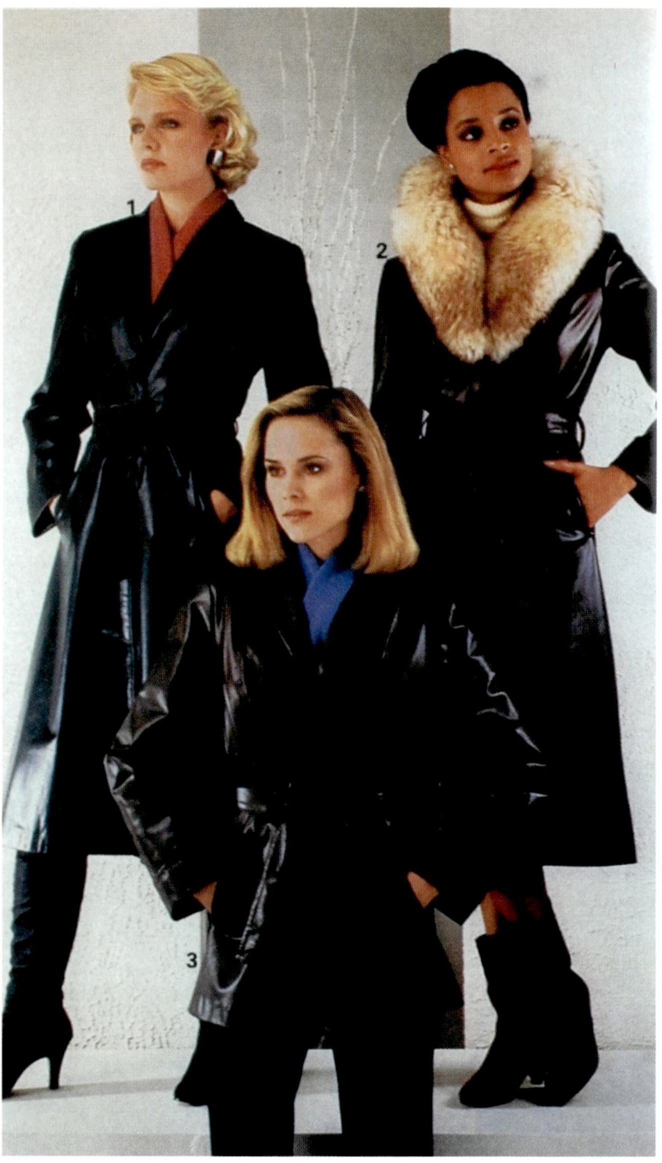

Rich leather coats and blazers. *Fall/Winter 1984.*

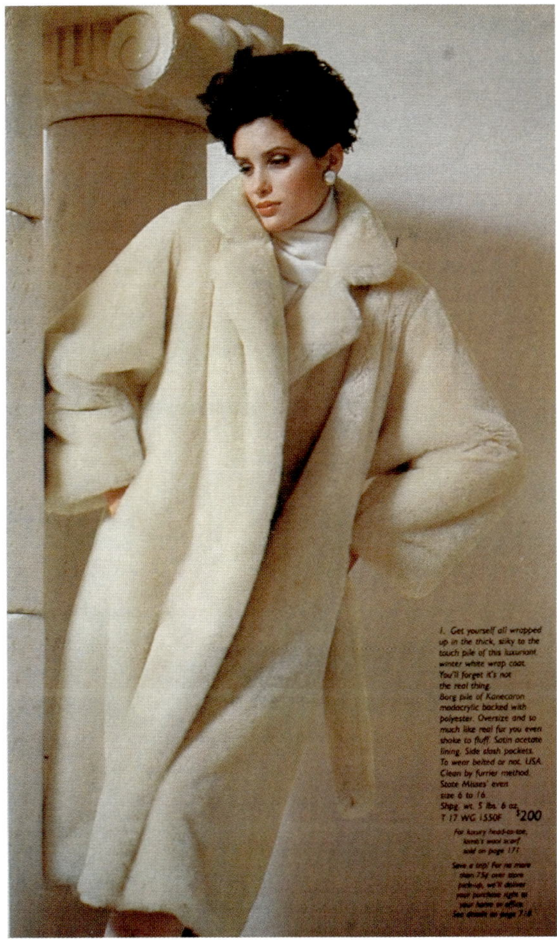

Winter white wrap coat of Borg pile of Kanecaron modacrylic backed with polyester. *Fall/Winter 1985*

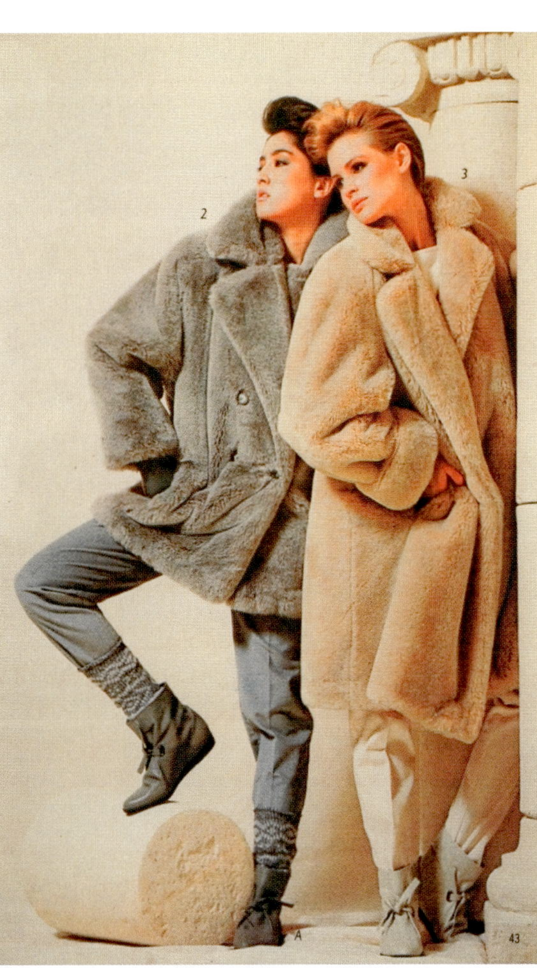

Gray coat closely imitates beaver but is made of acrylic pile. ¾-length wrap coat in honey beige color made of Kanecaron modacrylic. *Fall/Winter 1985*

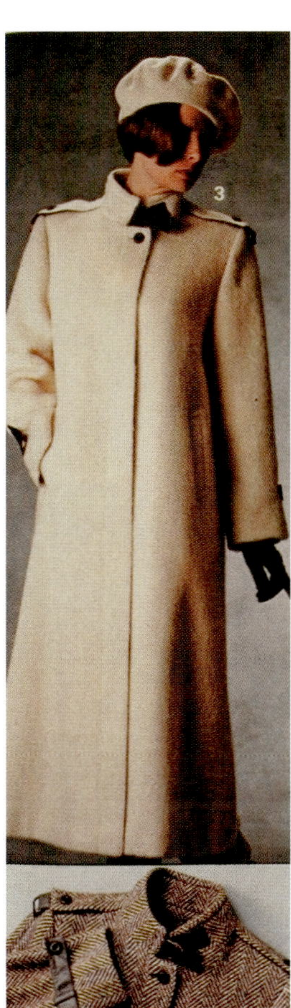

Wool fleece streamlined coat is smartly tailored with military epaulets, concealed button front and leather trim. Tweed pantcoat has dolman sleeves, button trimmed cuff and slash pockets. *Fall/Winter 1985*

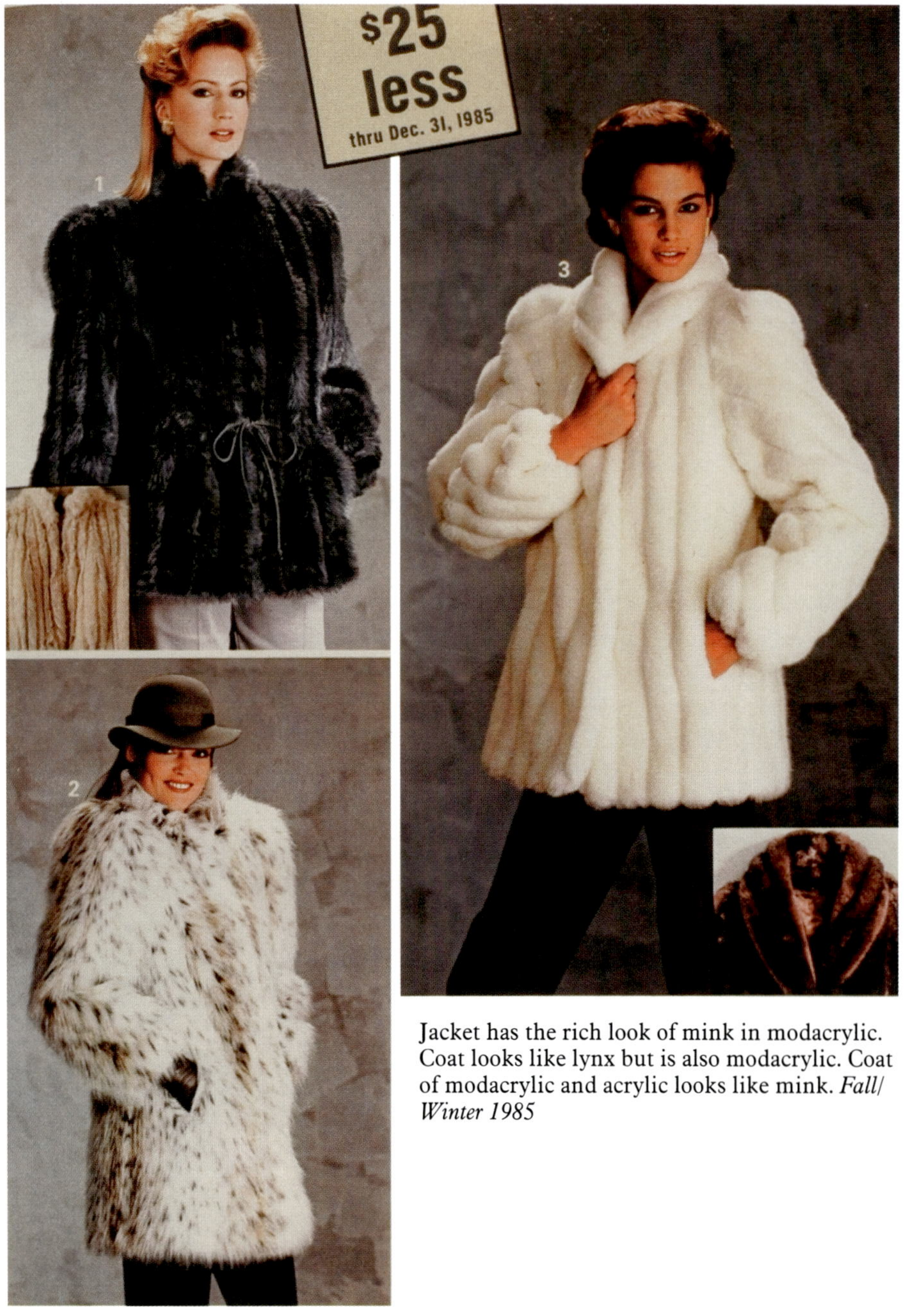

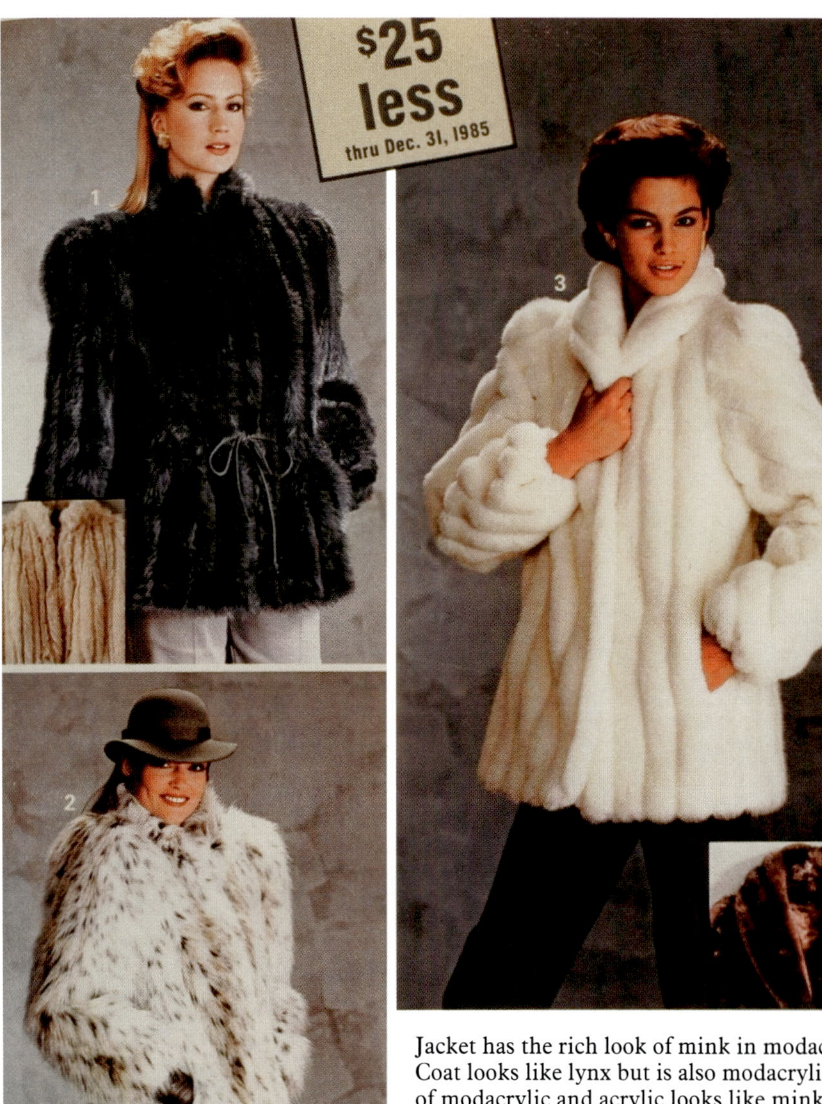

Jacket has the rich look of mink in modacrylic. Coat looks like lynx but is also modacrylic. Coat of modacrylic and acrylic looks like mink. *Fall/ Winter 1985*

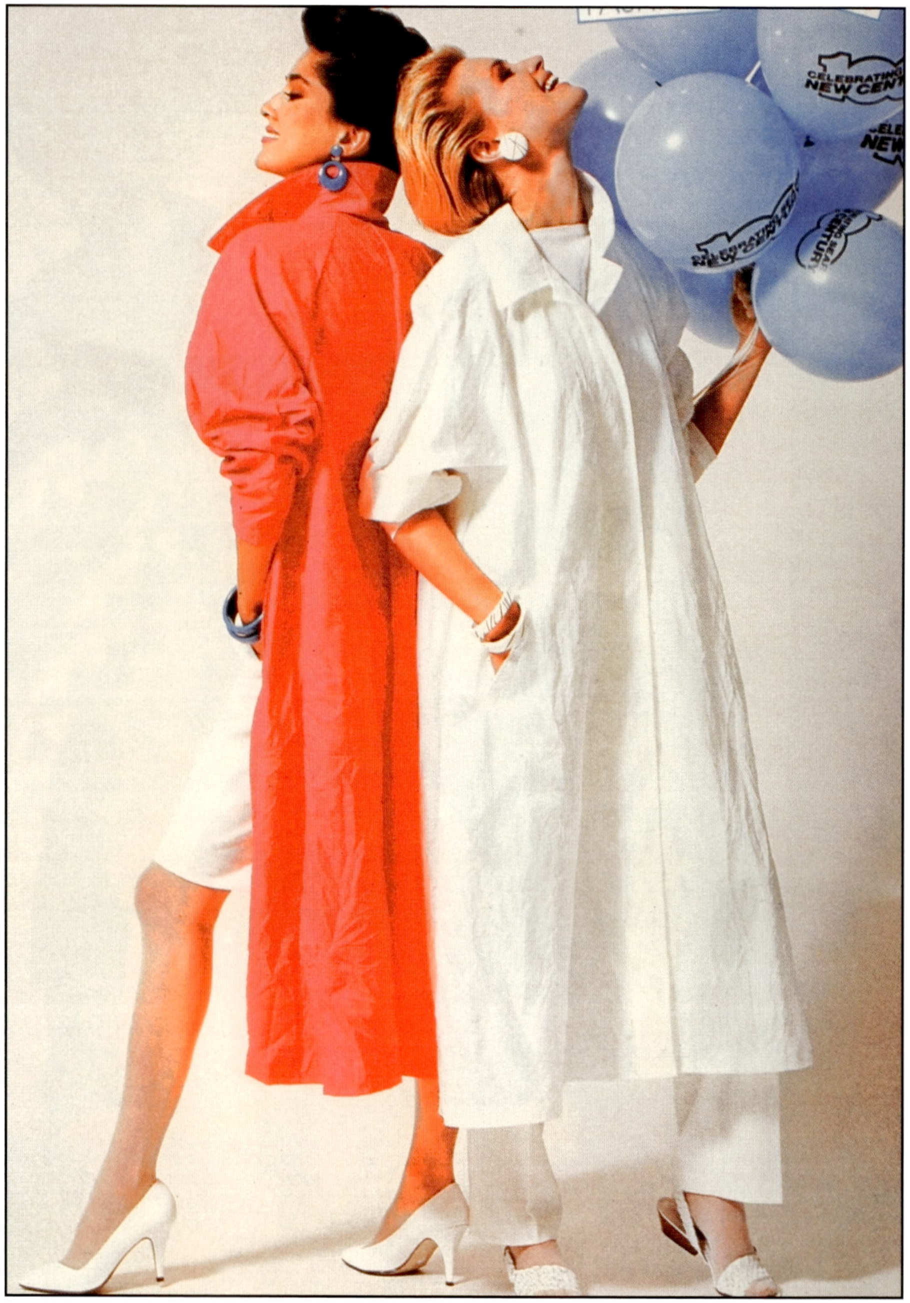

Crinkle cloth raincoats are made of nylon and feature push-up sleeves. *Spring/Summer 1986*

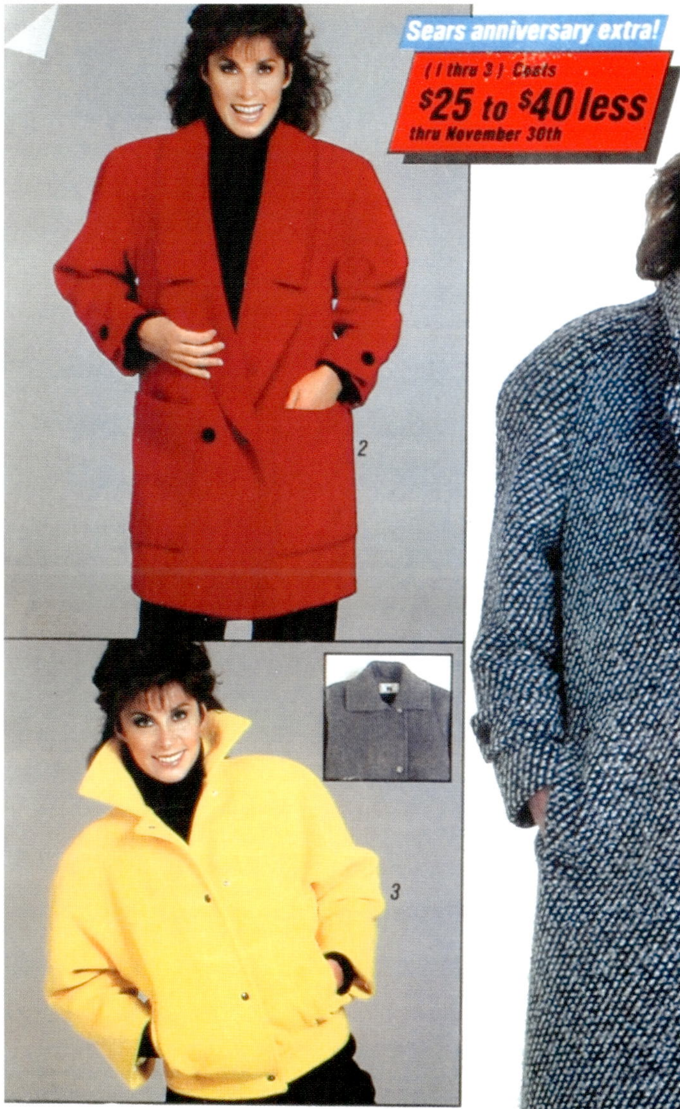

Wool and nylon coats from the Stefanie collection. *Fall/Winter 1986*

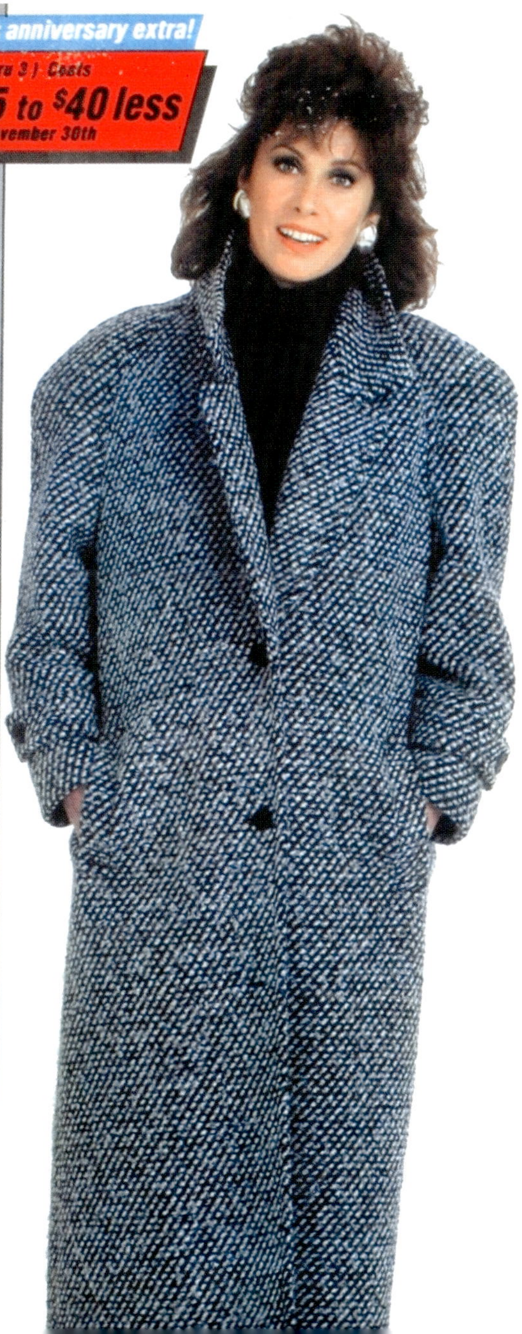

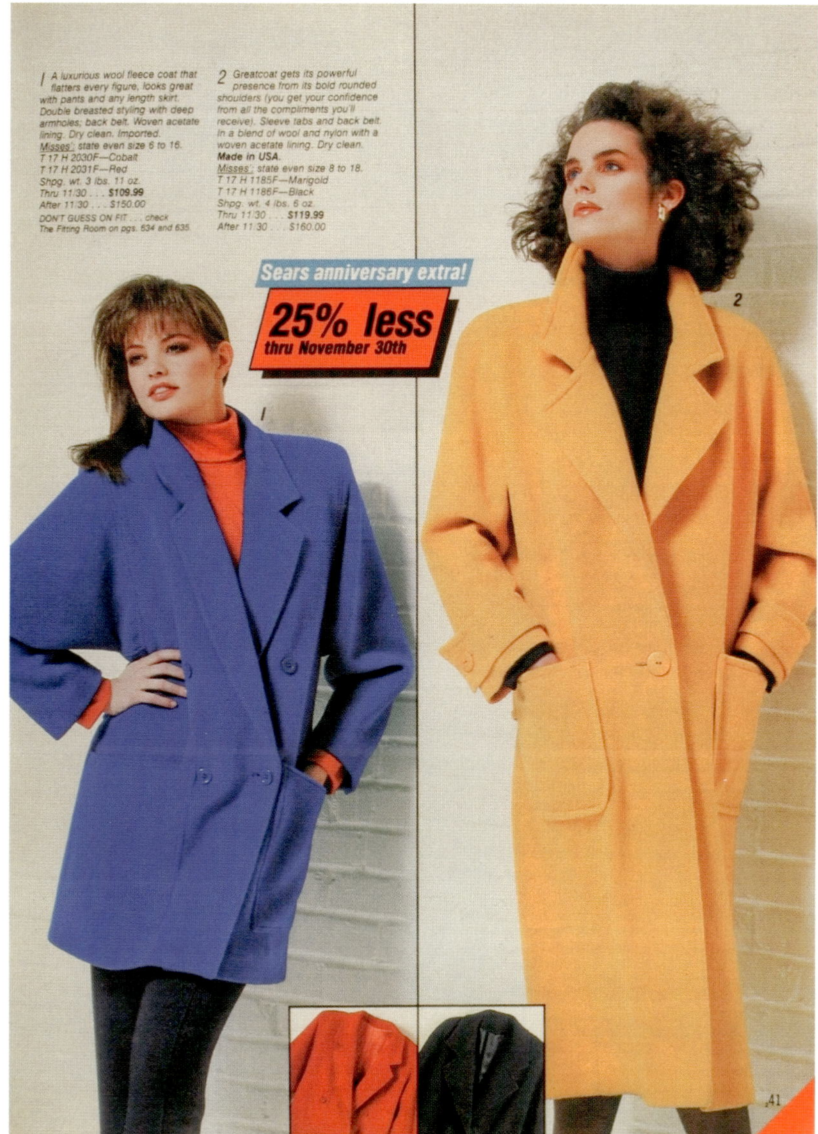

Wool fleece coat is double-breasted with deep armholes. Greatcoat has rounded shoulders, sleeve tabs, and back belt. *Fall/Winter 1986*

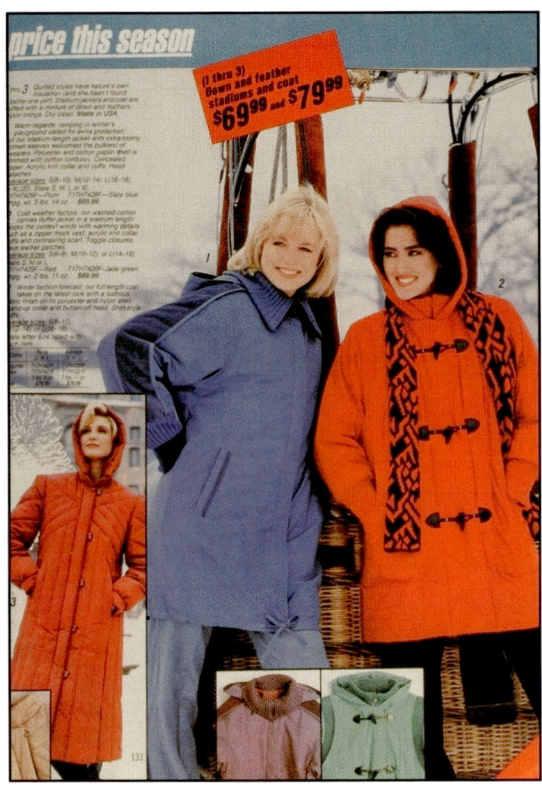

Stadium length jacket has dolman sleeves in polyester and poplin shell trimmed with cotton corduroy. Washed cotton canvas duffel jacket is stadium length with a zipper mock vest with contrasting scarf. Full length coat in a fabric finish in polyester and cotton. *Fall/Winter 1986*

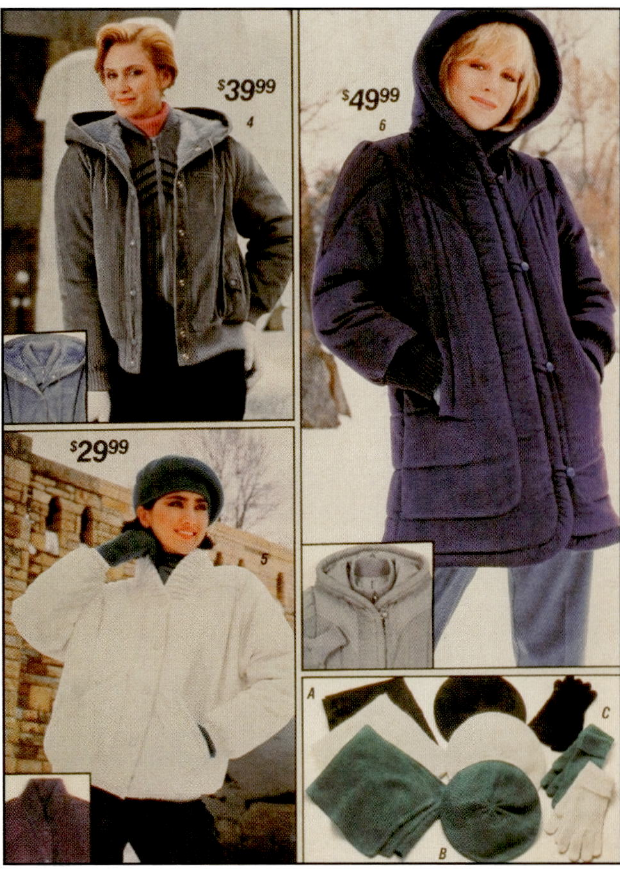

Cotton corduroy jacket has mock vest and acrylic knit cuffs. Oversized cotton corduroy jacket has room for oversized sweater underneath. Stadium length cotton corduroy coat goes great over pants or dresses. *Fall/Winter 1986*

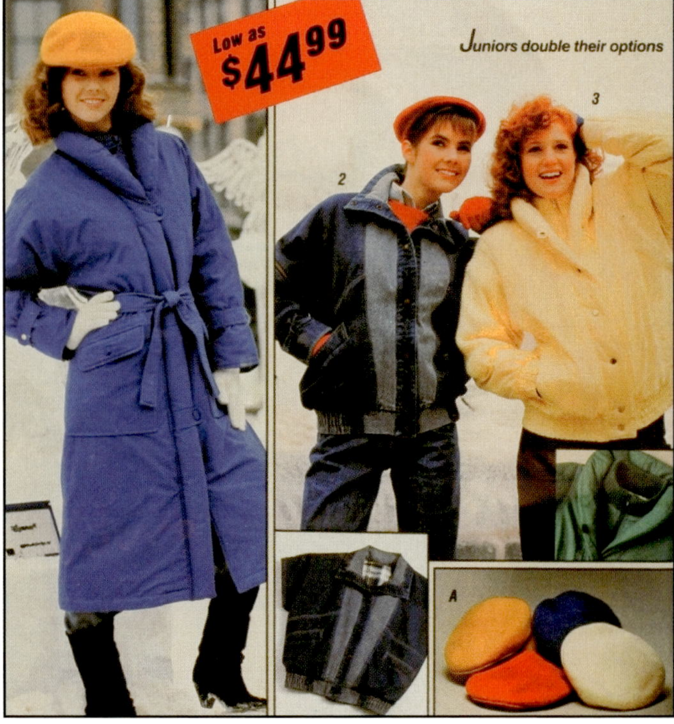

Quilted full length coat has an inside zipper, snap front closure, and self-fabric tie belt. Cotton denim jacket has a zipper on the sleeves so you can change from long to short sleeves and lined in cotton flannel. Calico jacket has mock vest and rib knit collar and snap front closure. *Fall/Winter 1986*

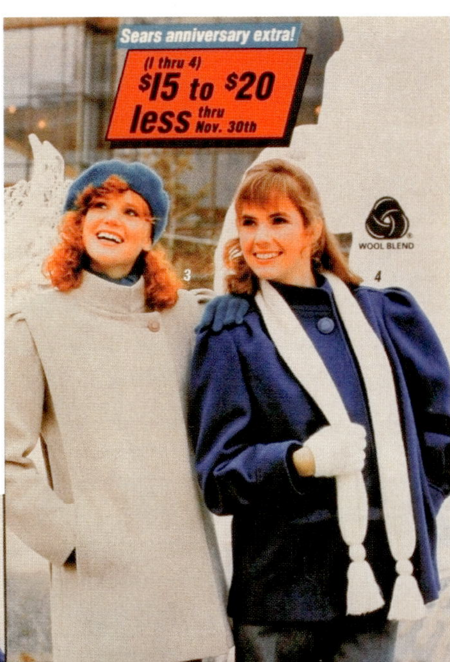

A selection of coat styles in a wool and nylon blend. *Fall/Winter 1986*

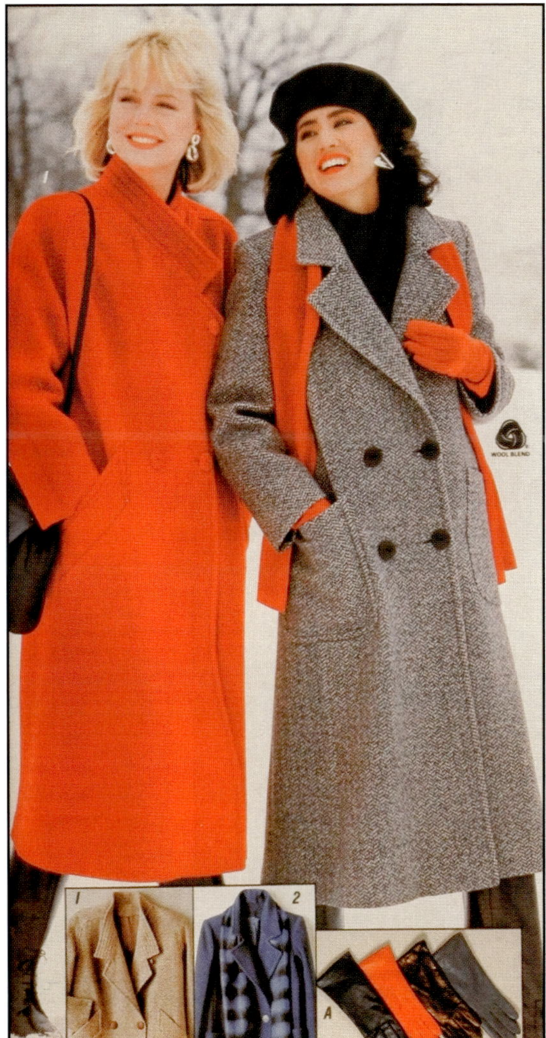

Tailored wool blend coats in a relaxed shoulder with raglan sleeves, and a double-breasted reefer with patch pockets. *Fall/Winter 1986*

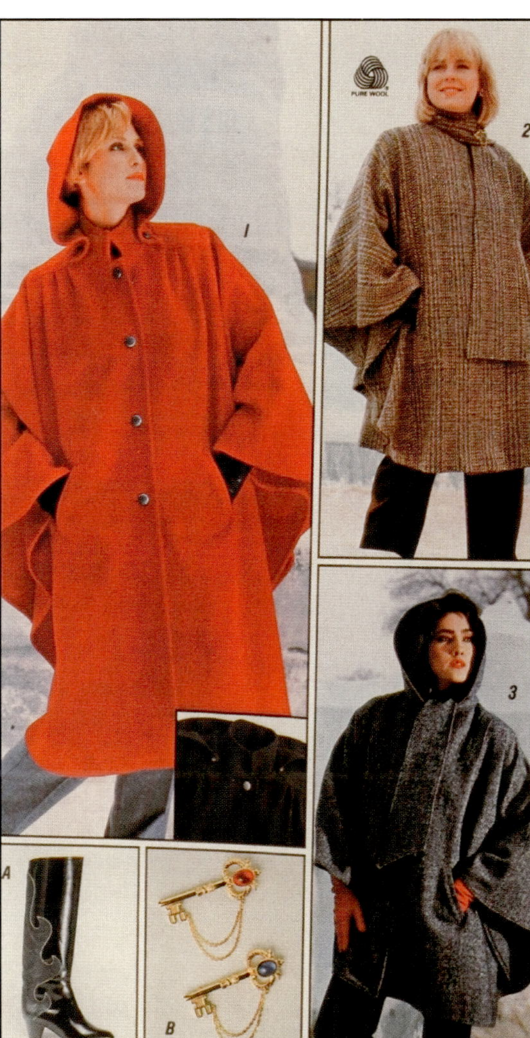

Full length cape has a stand up collar, side seam pockets, and a detachable hood. Brown tweed cape with a matching scarf. Cadet style black and white tweed cape has a special stitch to prevent raveling. *Fall/Winter 1986*

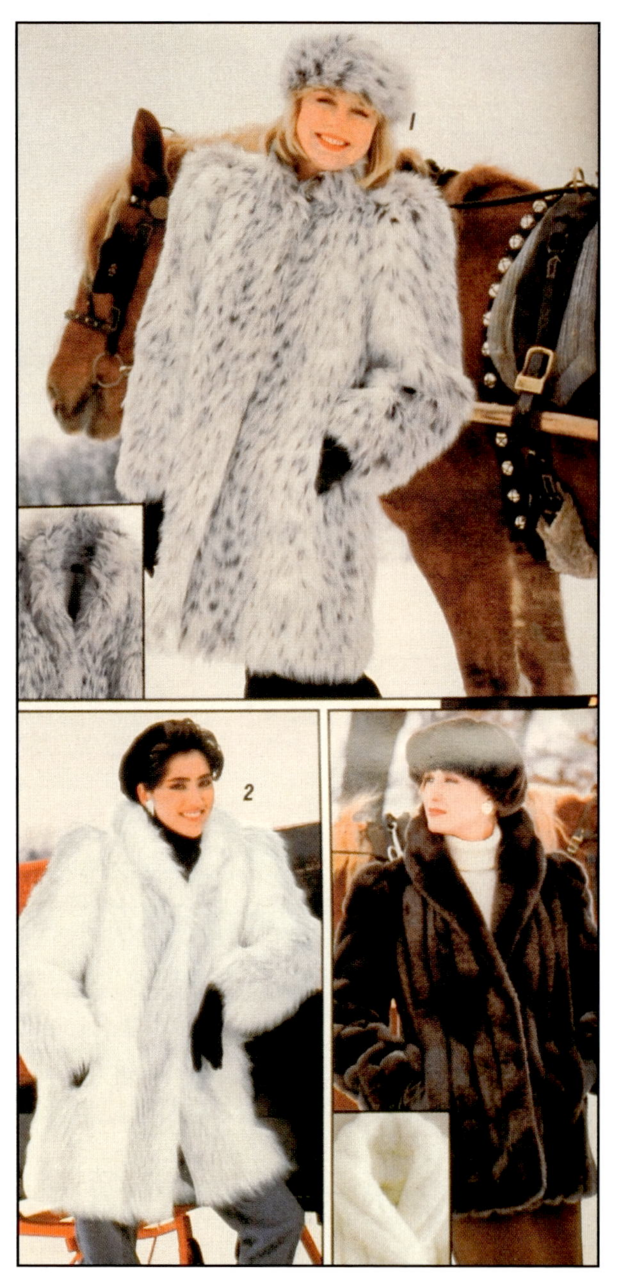

Cozy acrylic pile lined with satin acetate have the look of lynx, blue fox, and mink. *Fall/Winter 1986*

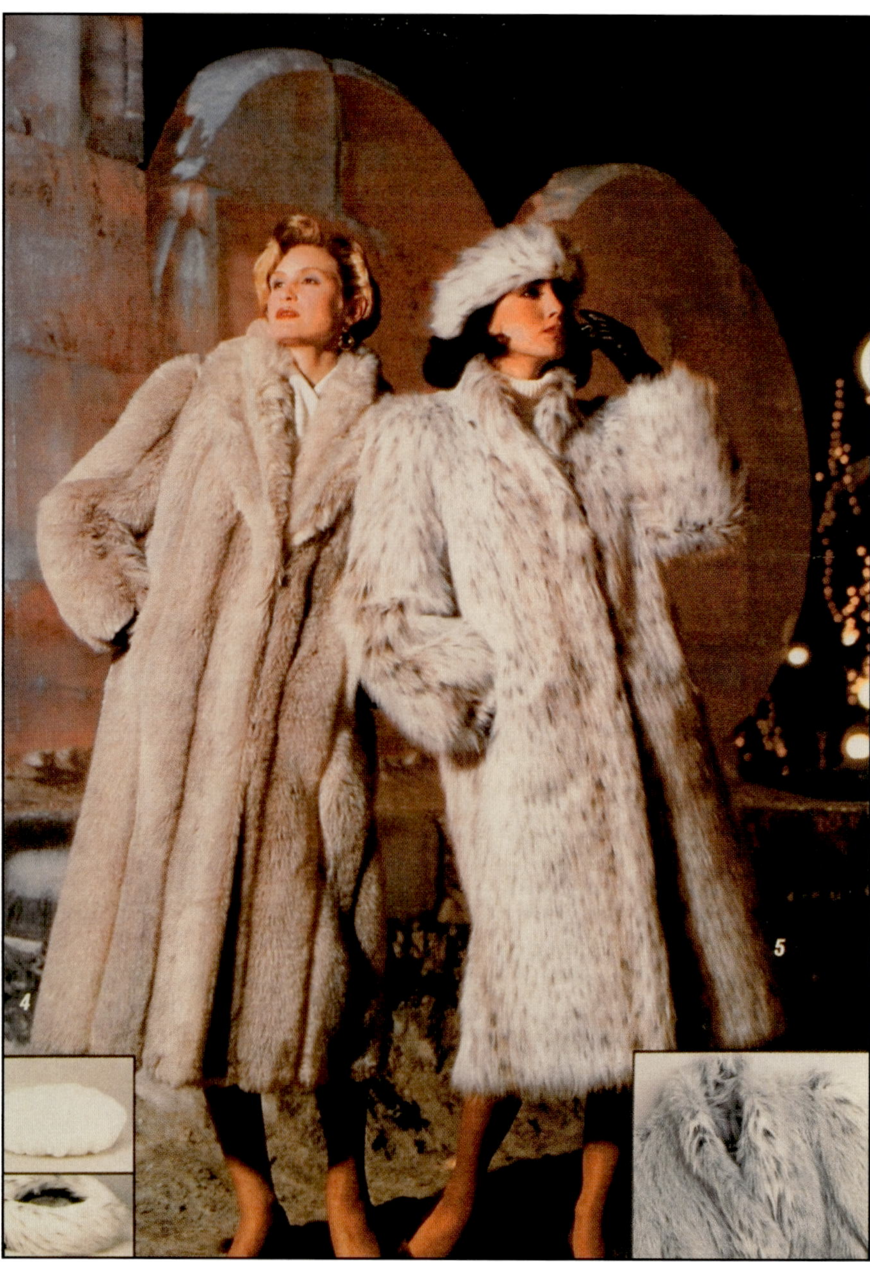

Full length fake furs imitate fox and lynx. *Fall/Winter 1986*

Men's Fashions

Career

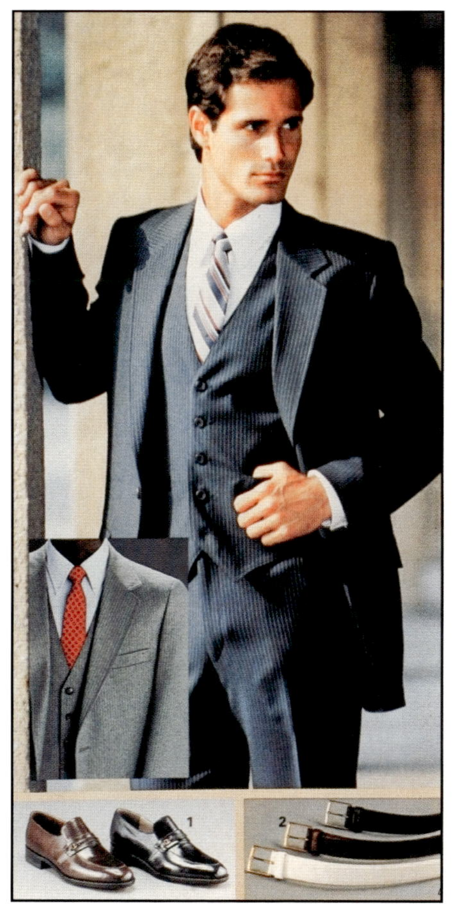

Perma-Prest® pin-stripe separates are machine washable and go right into the dryer. Made of stretch woven polyester and nylon. *Spring/Summer 1984.*

Perma-Prest® action separates resists wrinkling, puckering, snagging, or shrinking even after repeated machine washing and drying. *Spring/Summer 1984.*

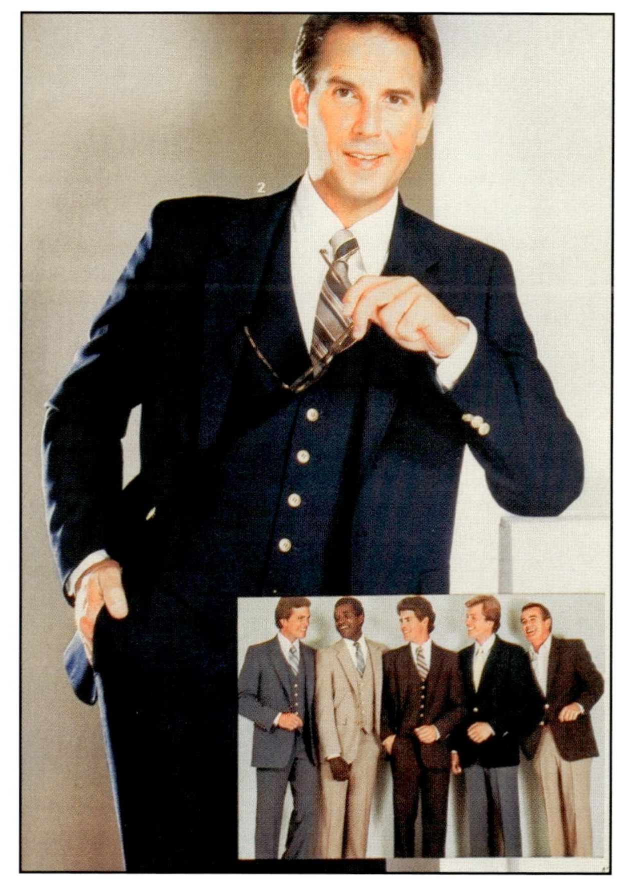

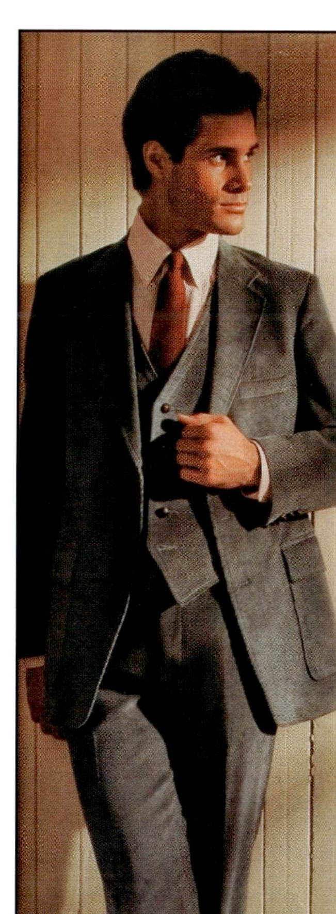

Levi's Menswear corduroy suit. *Fall/Winter 1984.*

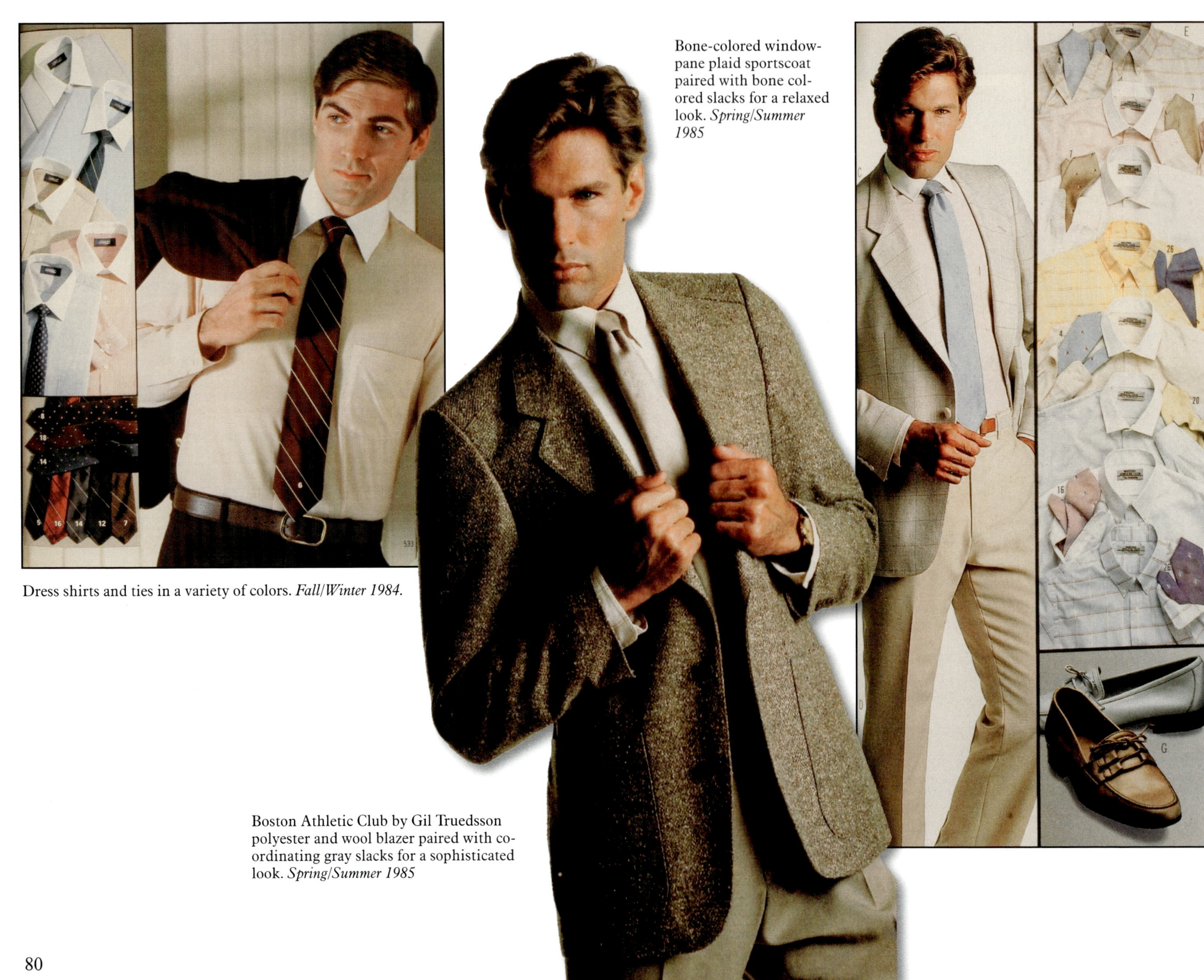

Bone-colored window-pane plaid sportscoat paired with bone colored slacks for a relaxed look. *Spring/Summer 1985*

Dress shirts and ties in a variety of colors. *Fall/Winter 1984.*

Boston Athletic Club by Gil Truedsson polyester and wool blazer paired with coordinating gray slacks for a sophisticated look. *Spring/Summer 1985*

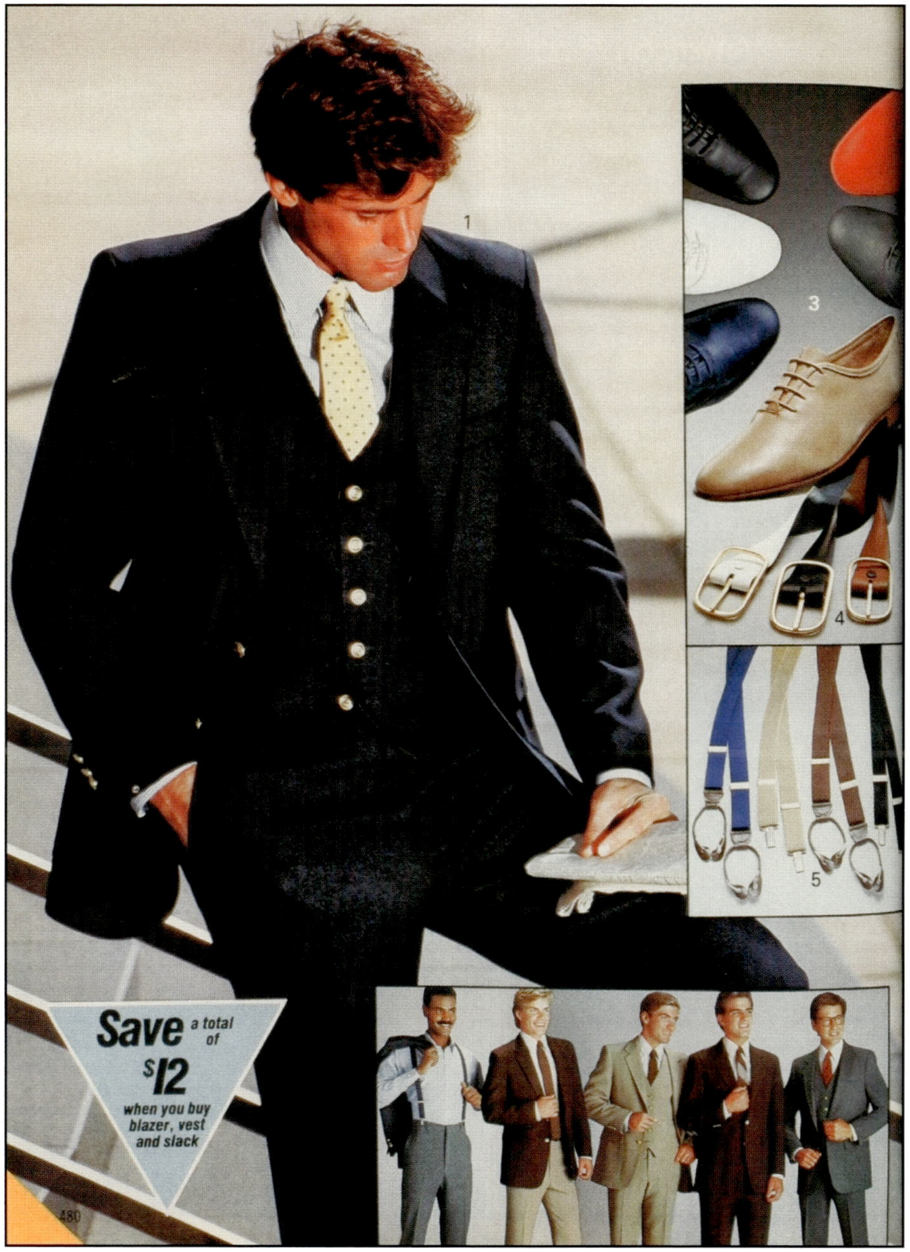

Blazers, vests, and slacks made of 100% polyester. *Spring/Summer 1985*

Mix and match separates from Classic Collection are made of stretch woven polyester for a fine fit and comfort. *Fall/Winter 1985*

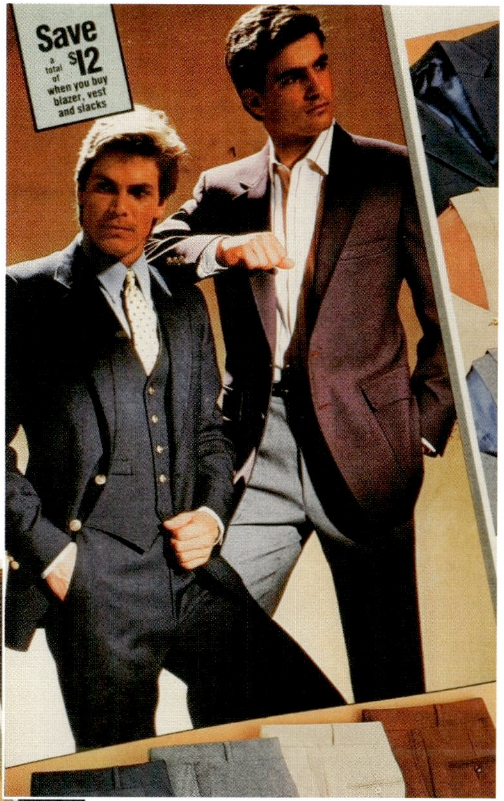

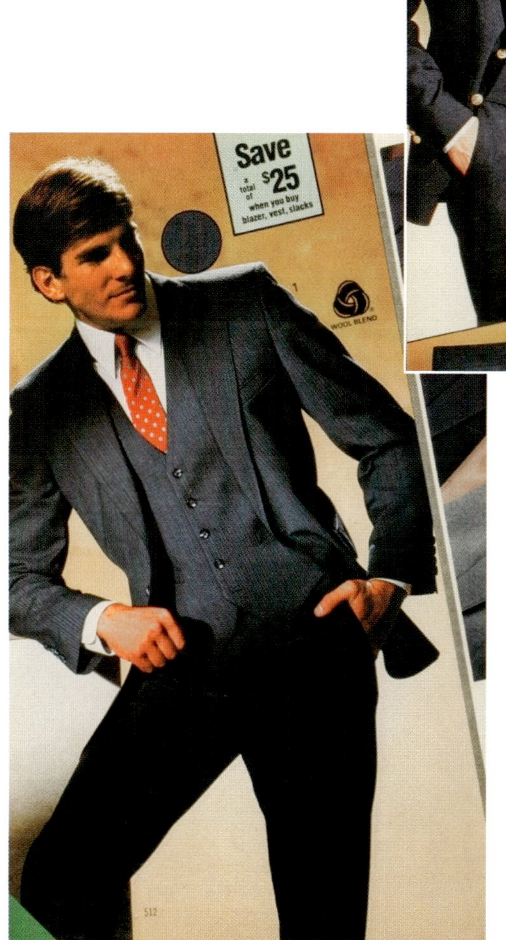

Oakton Ltd® polyester and wool blend separates in handsome solids or distinctive pinstripes. *Fall/Winter 1985*

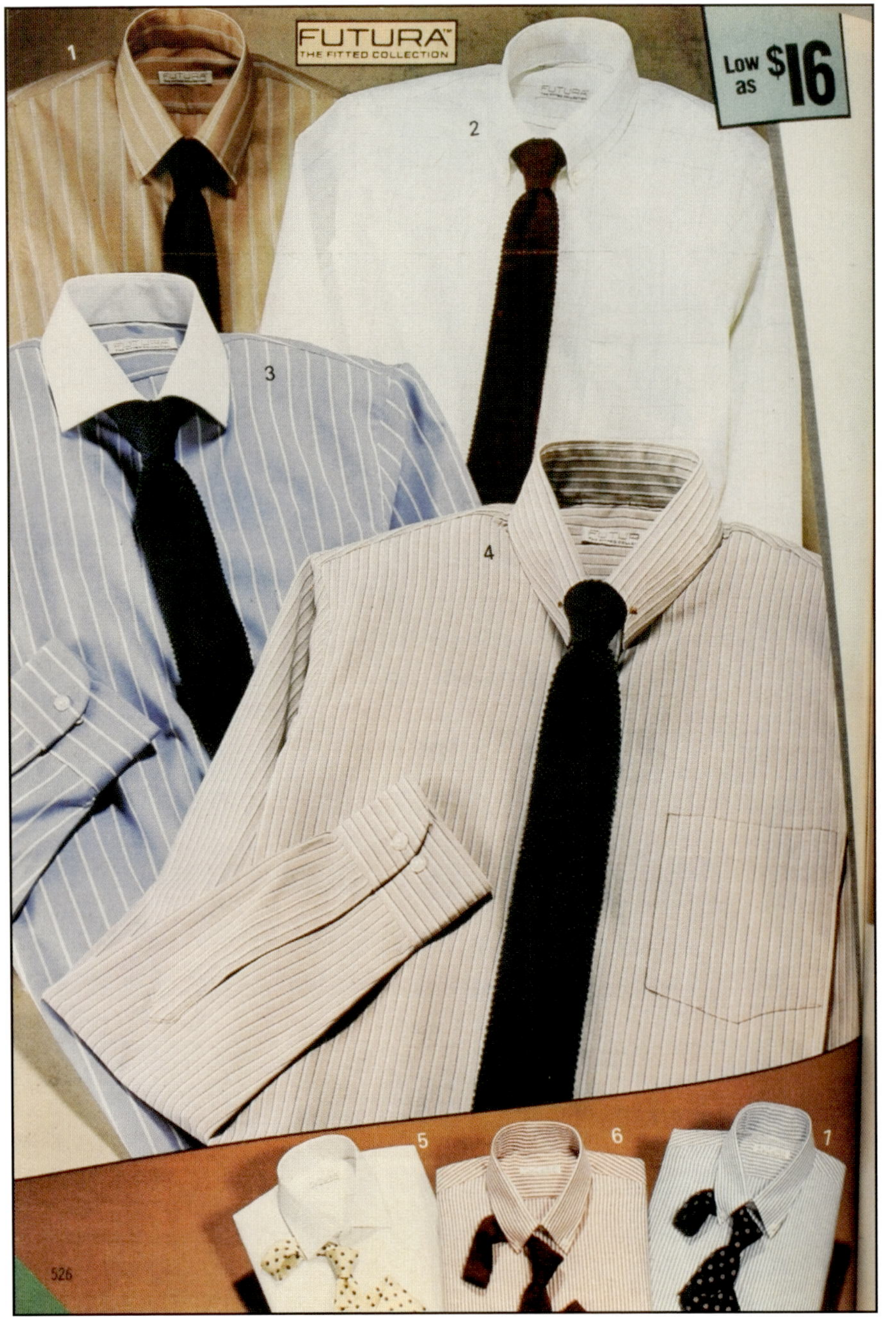

Futura tailored dress shirts in a fine blend of cotton and polyester. *Fall/Winter 1985*

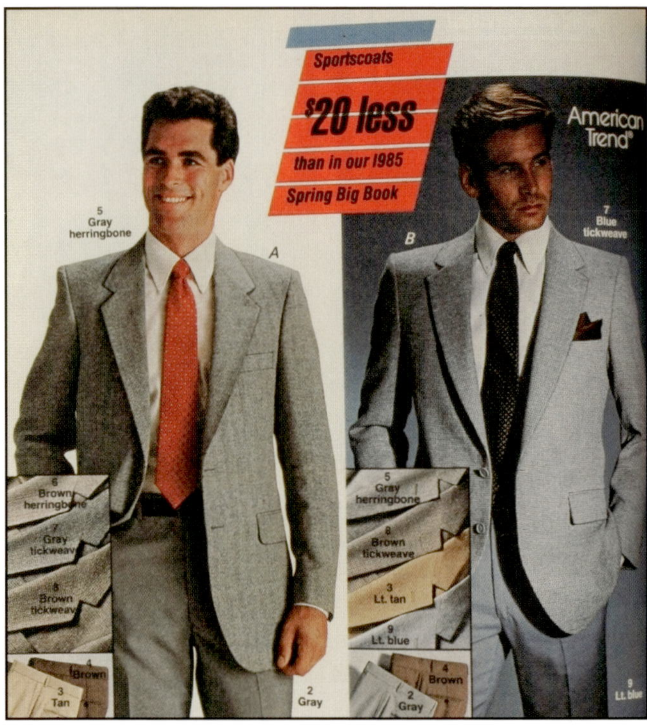

Oakton Ltd. polyester and silk sportscoat and coordinating wool blend slacks. American Trend® silk blend sportscoat and coordinating wool blend slacks. *Spring/Summer 1986*

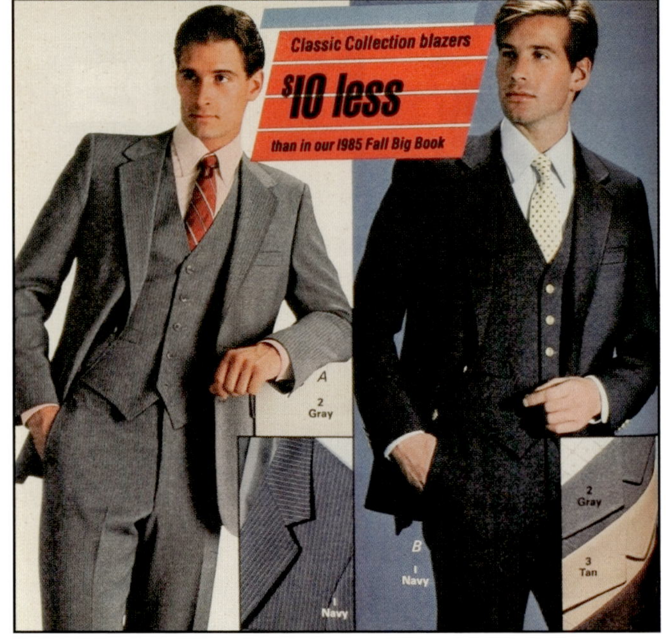

Classic pinstripe suit in polyester and nylon PERMA-PREST®. Polyester and PERMA-PREST® suit in solids or mix and match styles. *Spring/Summer 1986*

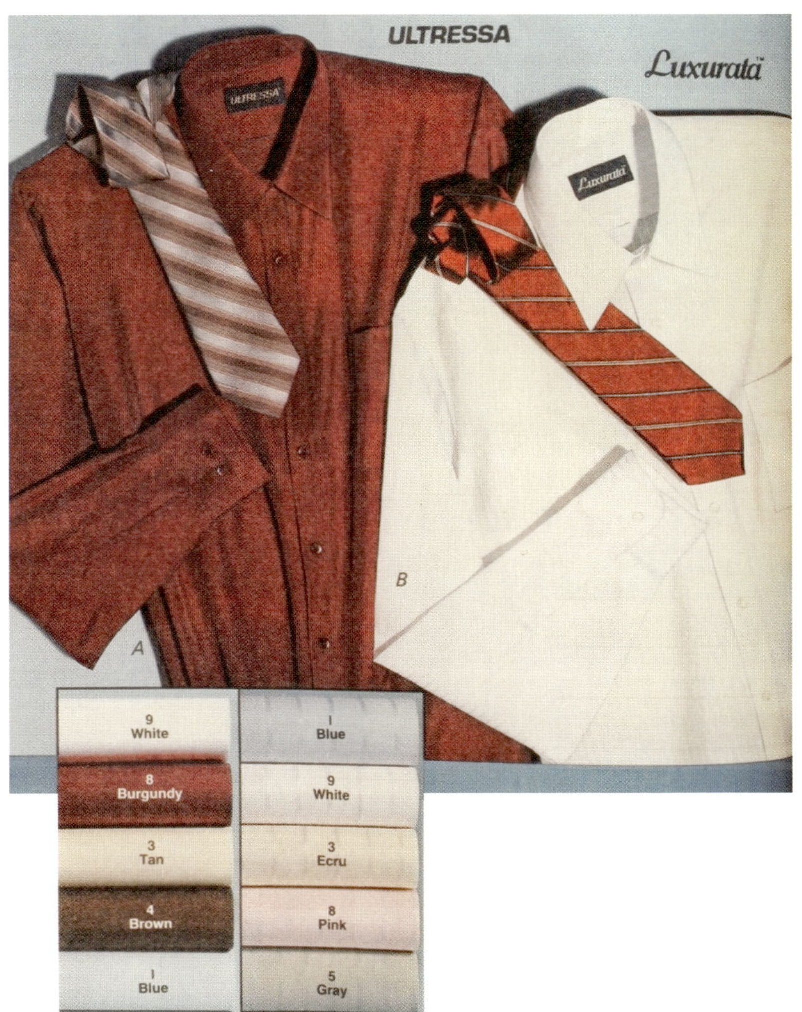

Ultressa silk-look dress shirt of 100% DuPont Dacron® polyester. Luxurata subtly striped dress shirt in polyester and cotton. *Spring/Summer 1986*

Oakton Ltd. navy pinstripe suit in polyester and wool. *Fall/Winter 1986*

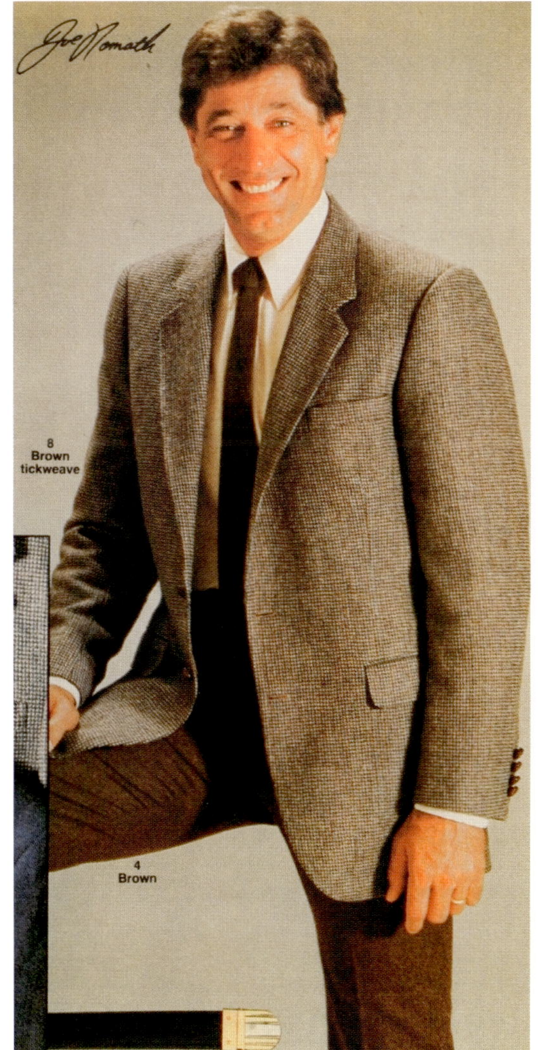

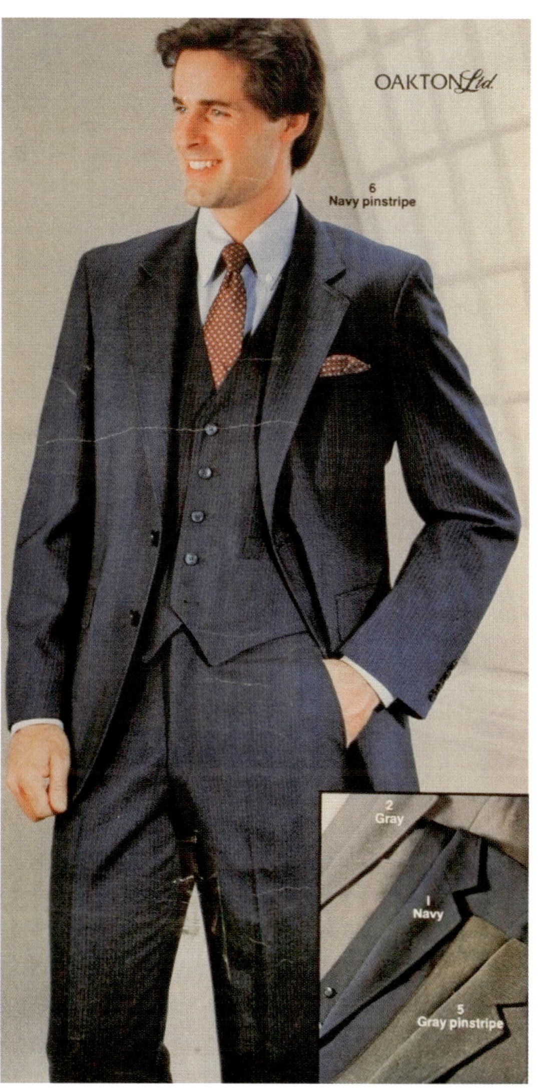

Wool blend sportscoat worn with polyester and wool slacks. *Fall/Winter 1986*

Overalls, Coveralls & Work Clothes

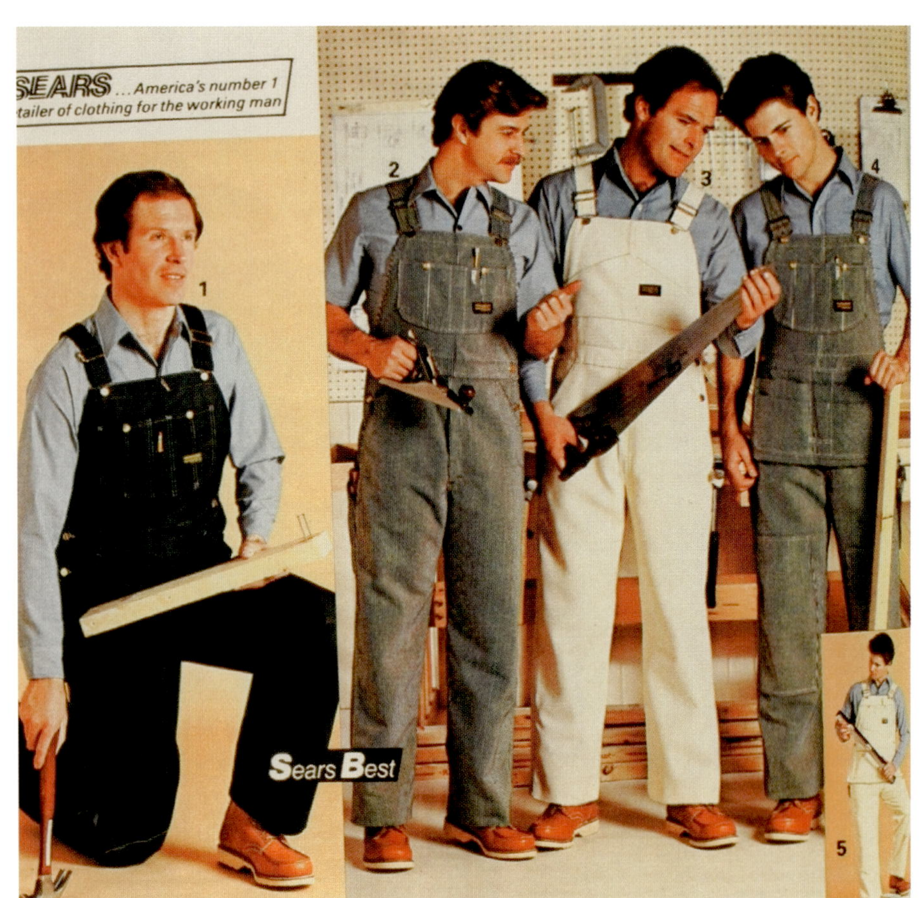

Toughskins bib overalls in cotton, polyester, and nylon fabric for durability.
Fall/Winter 1984.

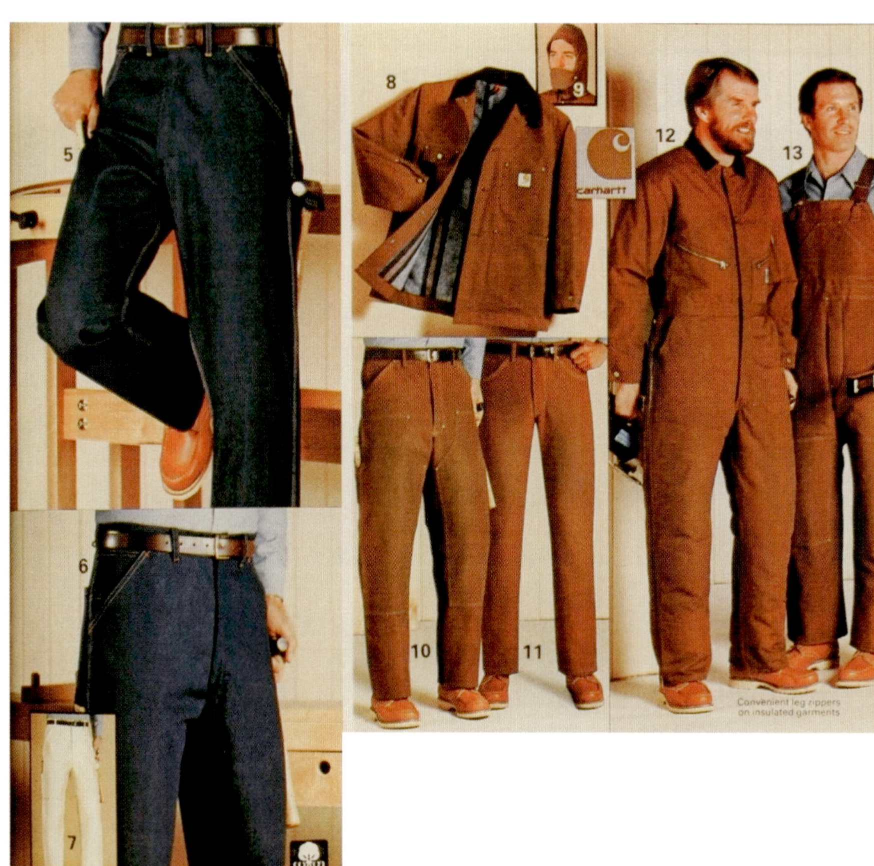

Denim work jeans in cotton and polyester. Carhartt all cotton brown duck work clothing.
Fall/Winter 1984.

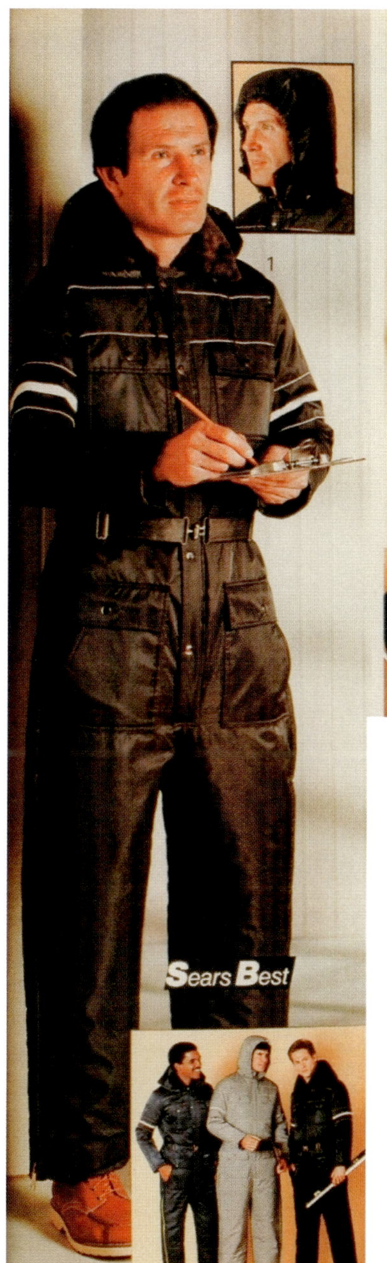

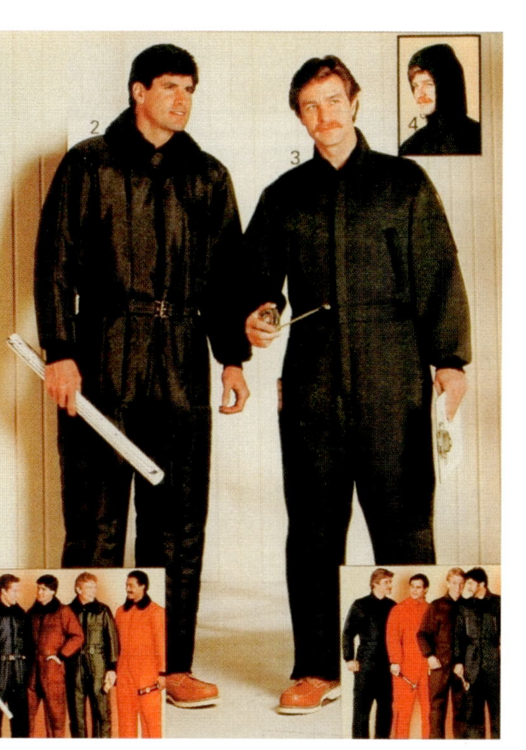

Insulated coveralls in fabrics such as satin nylon twill, heavy nylon oxford cloth, and polyester and cotton. *Fall/Winter 1984.*

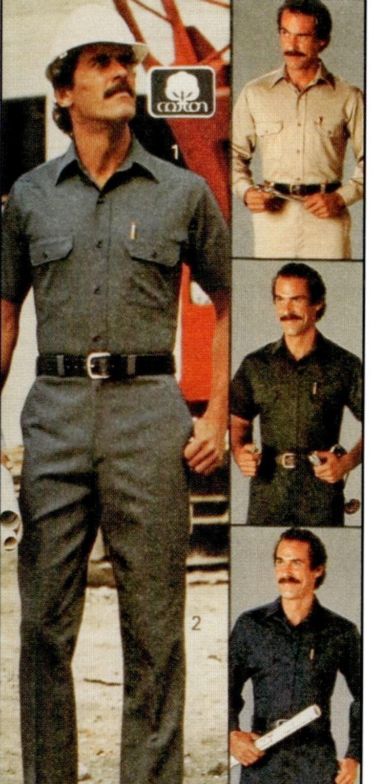

100% cotton twill work shirts and pants. *Spring/Summer 1985*

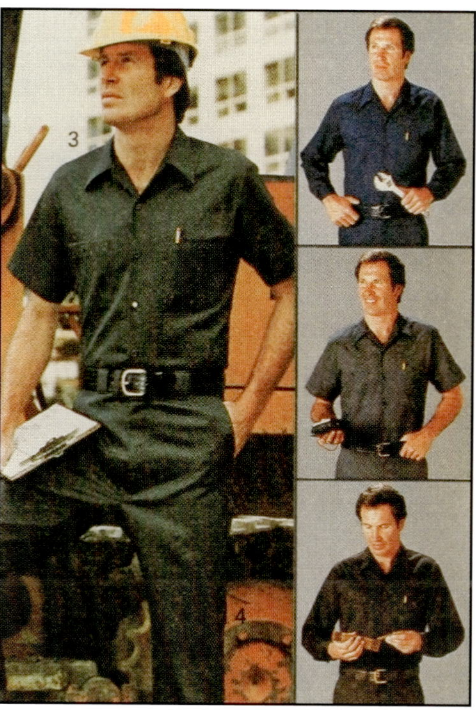

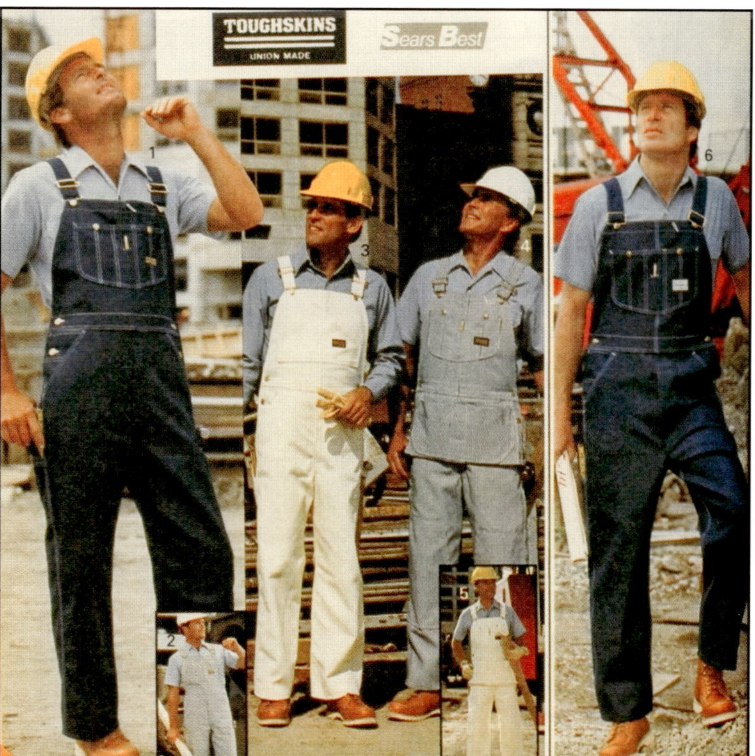

Toughskins® bib overalls are sized to wear over pants and shirt. *Spring/Summer 1985*

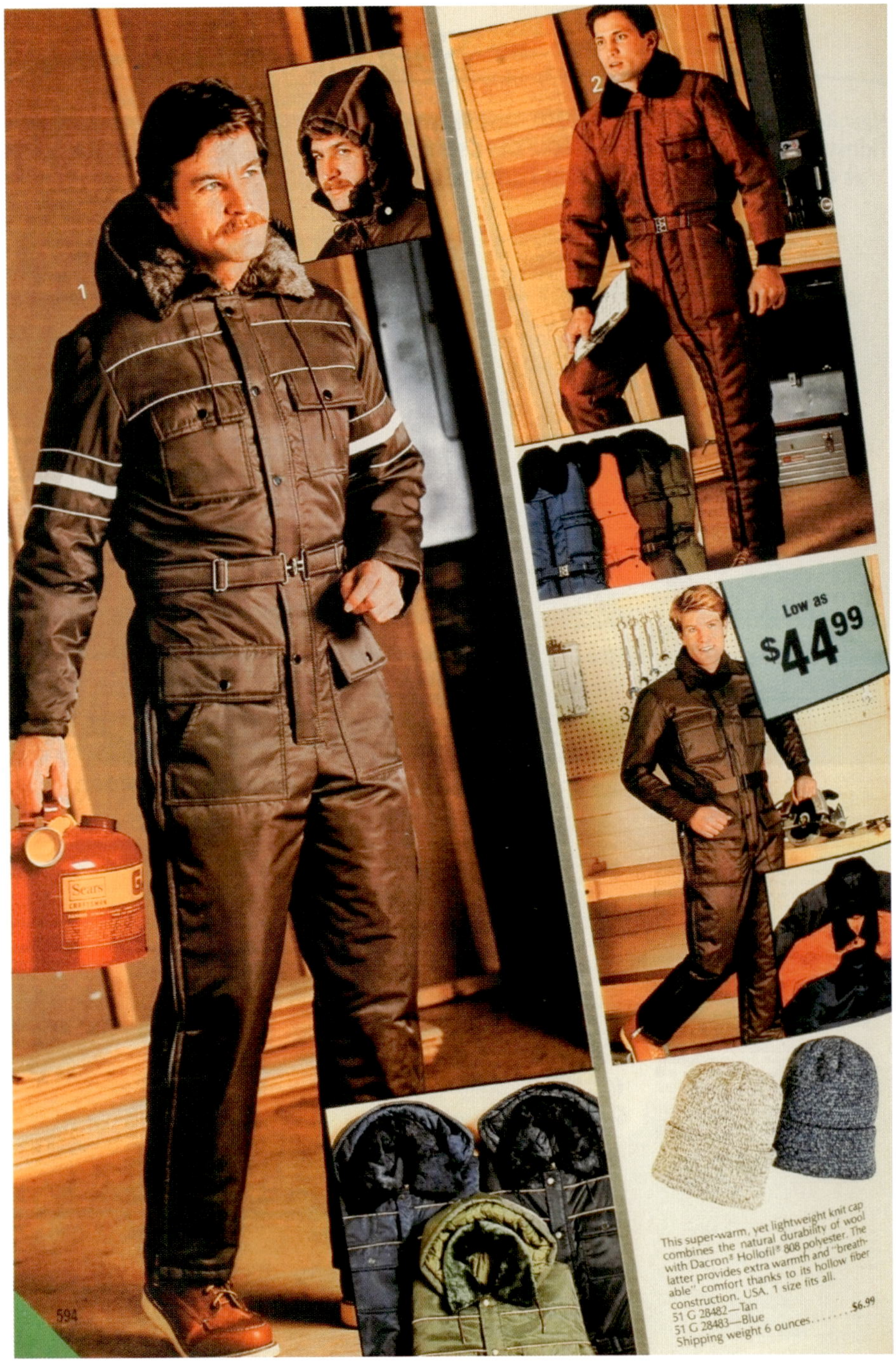

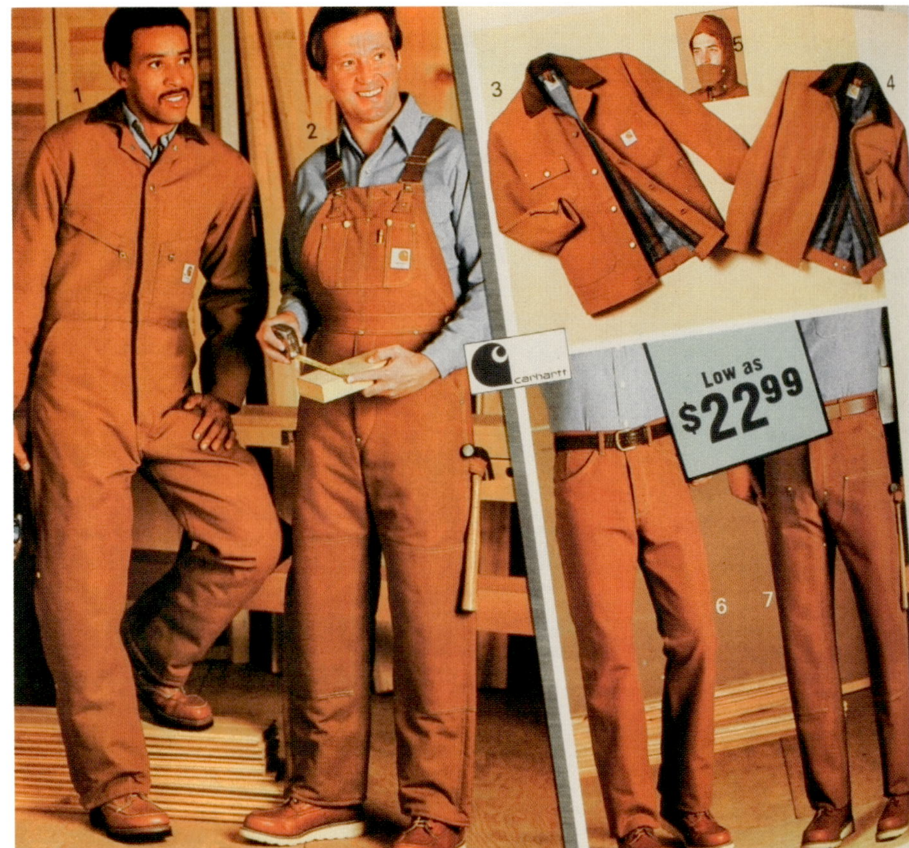

All-cotton brown duck insulated coveralls, bib overalls, coat, jacket, and work jeans. *Fall/Winter 1985*

Insulated cover-alls features leg zippers, 2-way zip front, snap storm flap, and snap-off hood. Heavy nylon oxford cloth insulated coveralls with leg zippers, pile collar, and elastic back waist. Nylon oxford cloth coveralls with leg zippers, 2-way zip front, snap storm flap, and 4 snap-flap pockets. *Fall/Winter 1985*

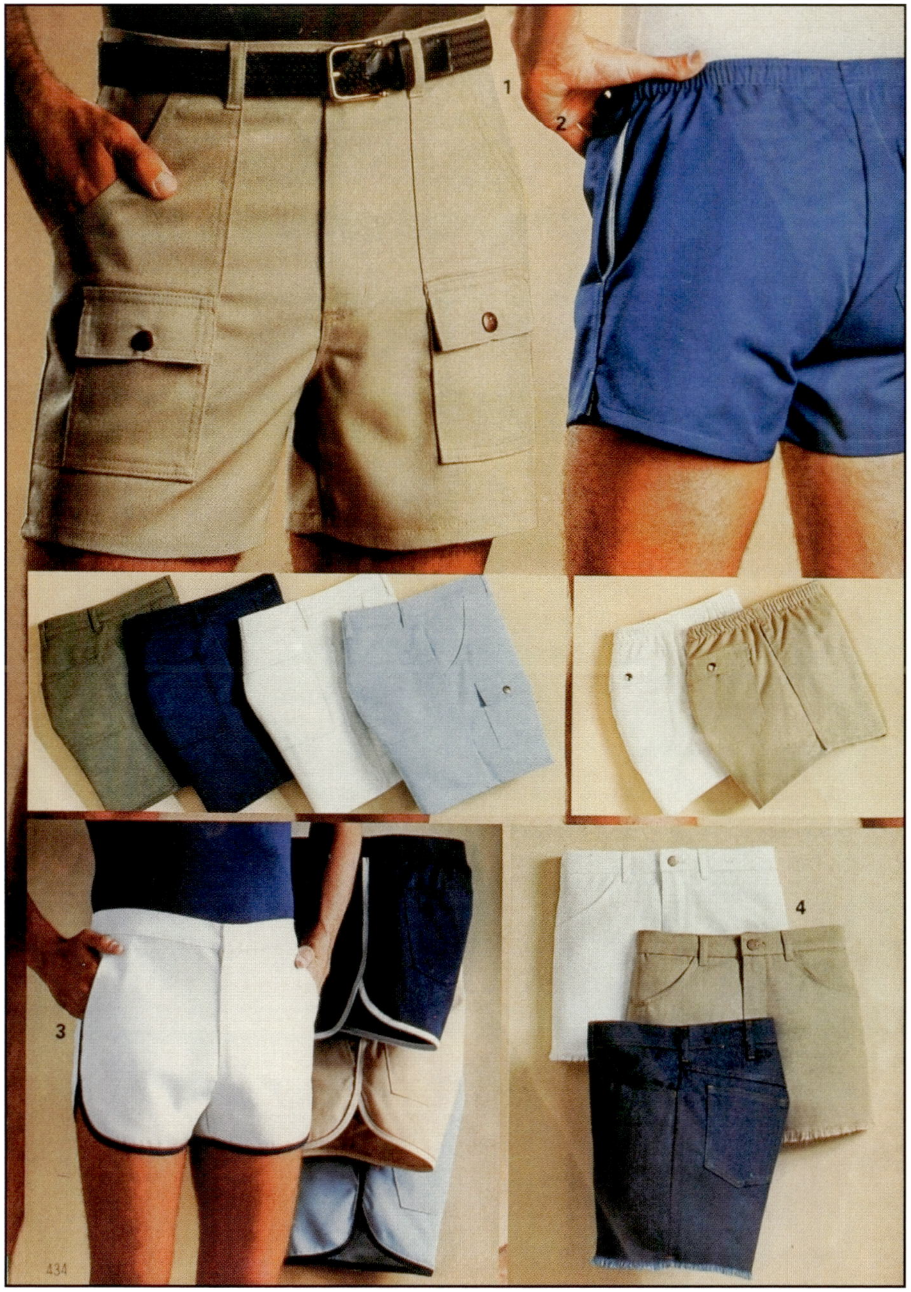

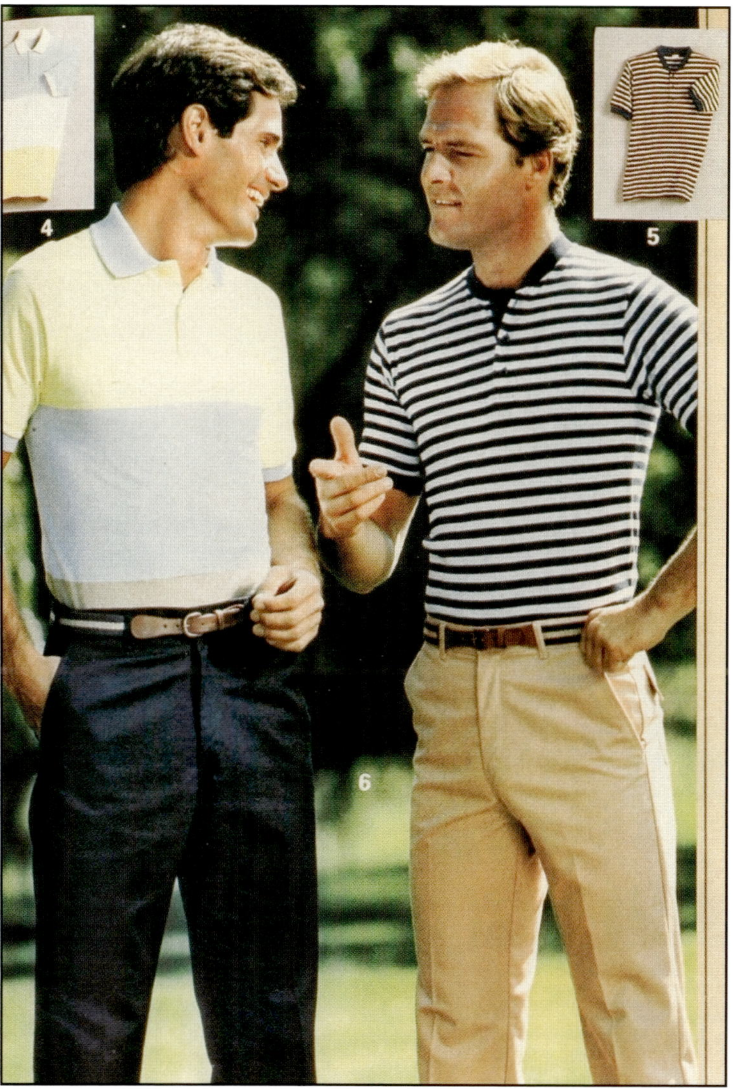

Polyester and cotton knit shirts paired with belted jean-cut pants by the Boston Athletic Club are both fashionable and practical. *Spring/Summer 1984.*

Men's shorts in denims, woven polyester and cotton blends, elastic-back, and shadow trim styles. *Spring/Summer 1984.*

Roebucks® Maxi-Blue jeans from the Western Edge collection are deeply dyed 14 oz. heavyweight cotton. Levi's® for men Two-Horse denim jeans are heavyweight 14 0z. pure cotton. *Spring/Summer 1984.*

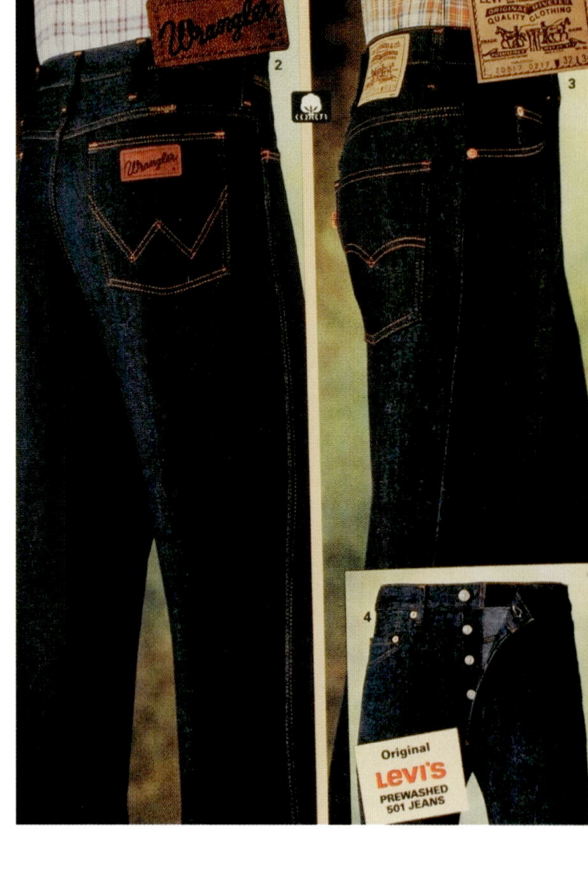

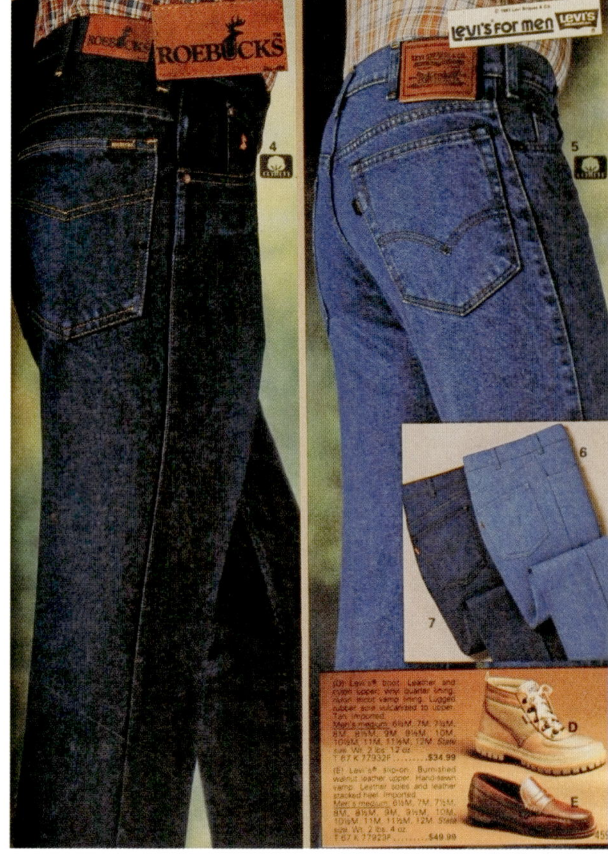

Wrangler® No-Fault® indigo-dyed jeans are made from heavy 14 oz. 100% cotton. Levi's® Western jeans are heavyweight 14 oz. all cotton denim. *Spring/Summer 1984.*

Men's Flexjeans are brushed denim with piped pocket or elastic back styles. *Spring/ Summer 1984.*

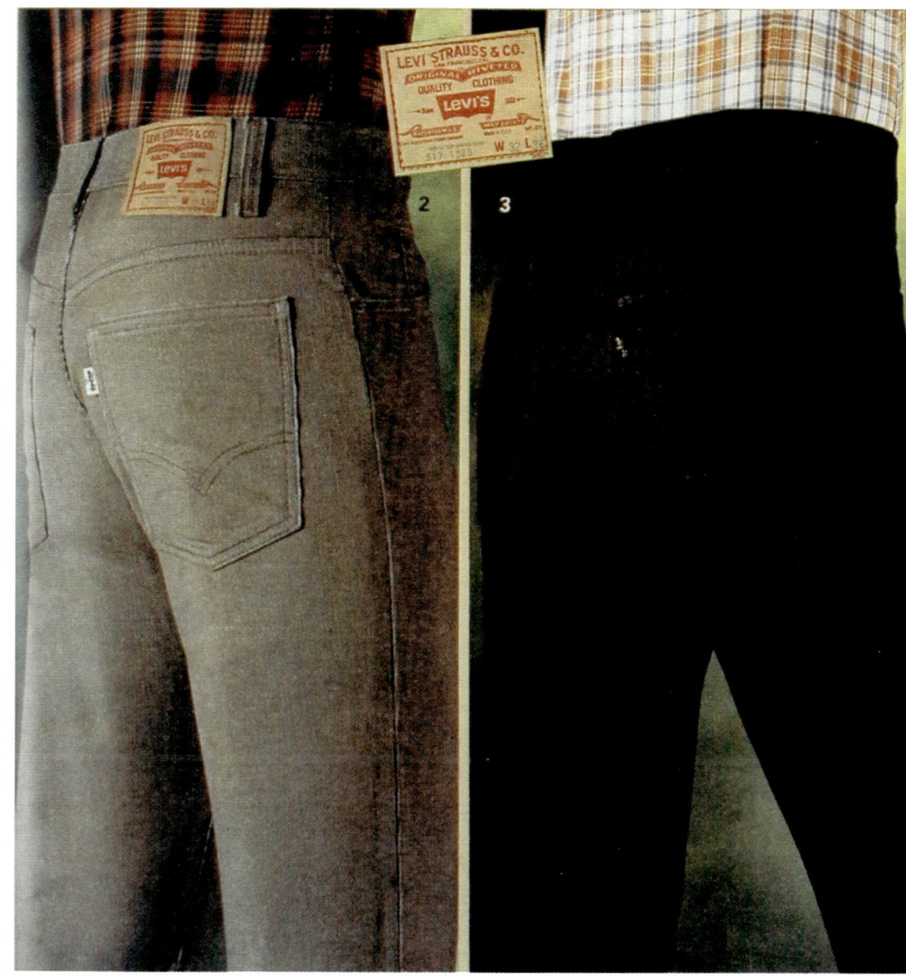

Roebucks® and Levi's® corduroy jeans. *Spring/Summer 1984.*

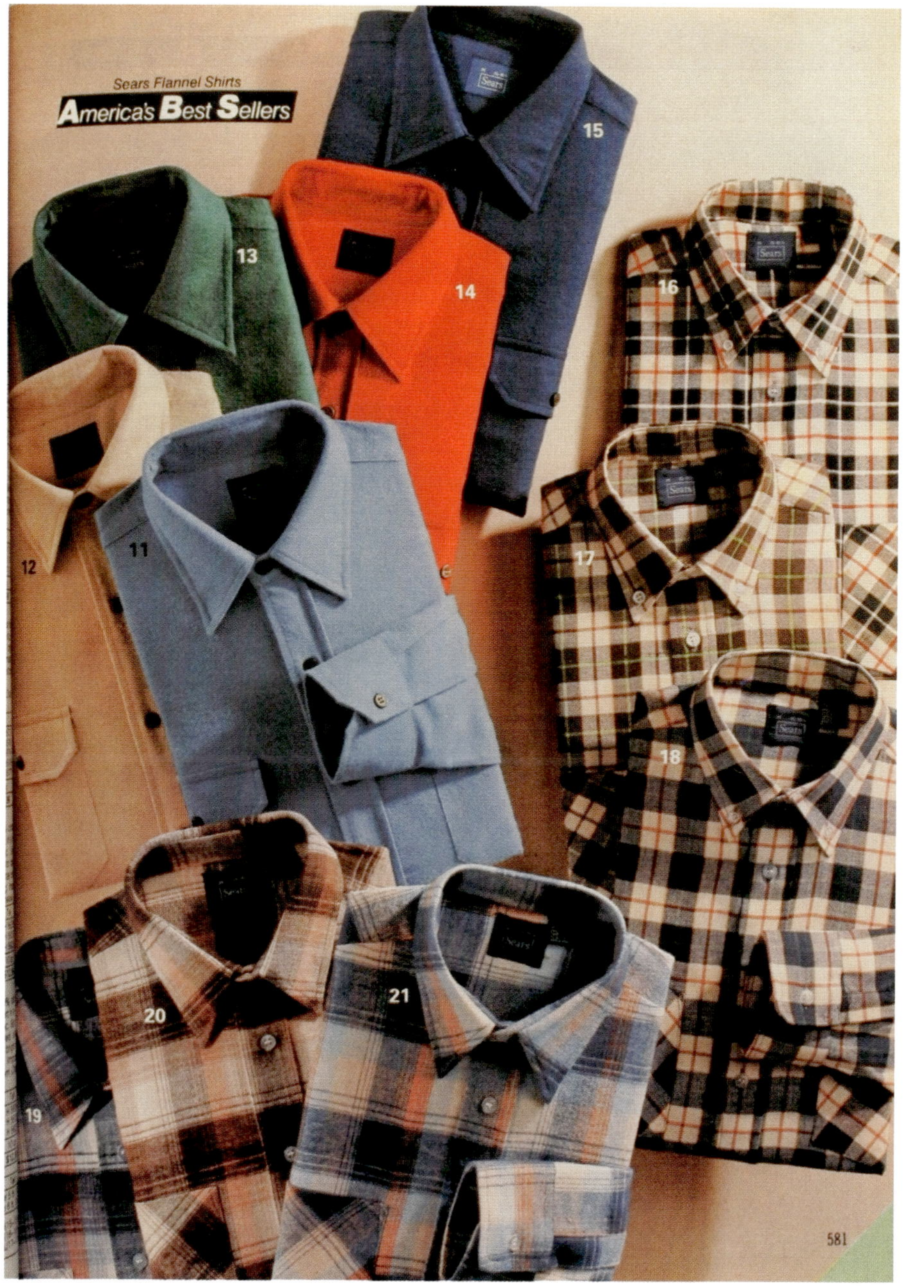

Cotton and polyester flannel shirts. *Fall/Winter 1984.*

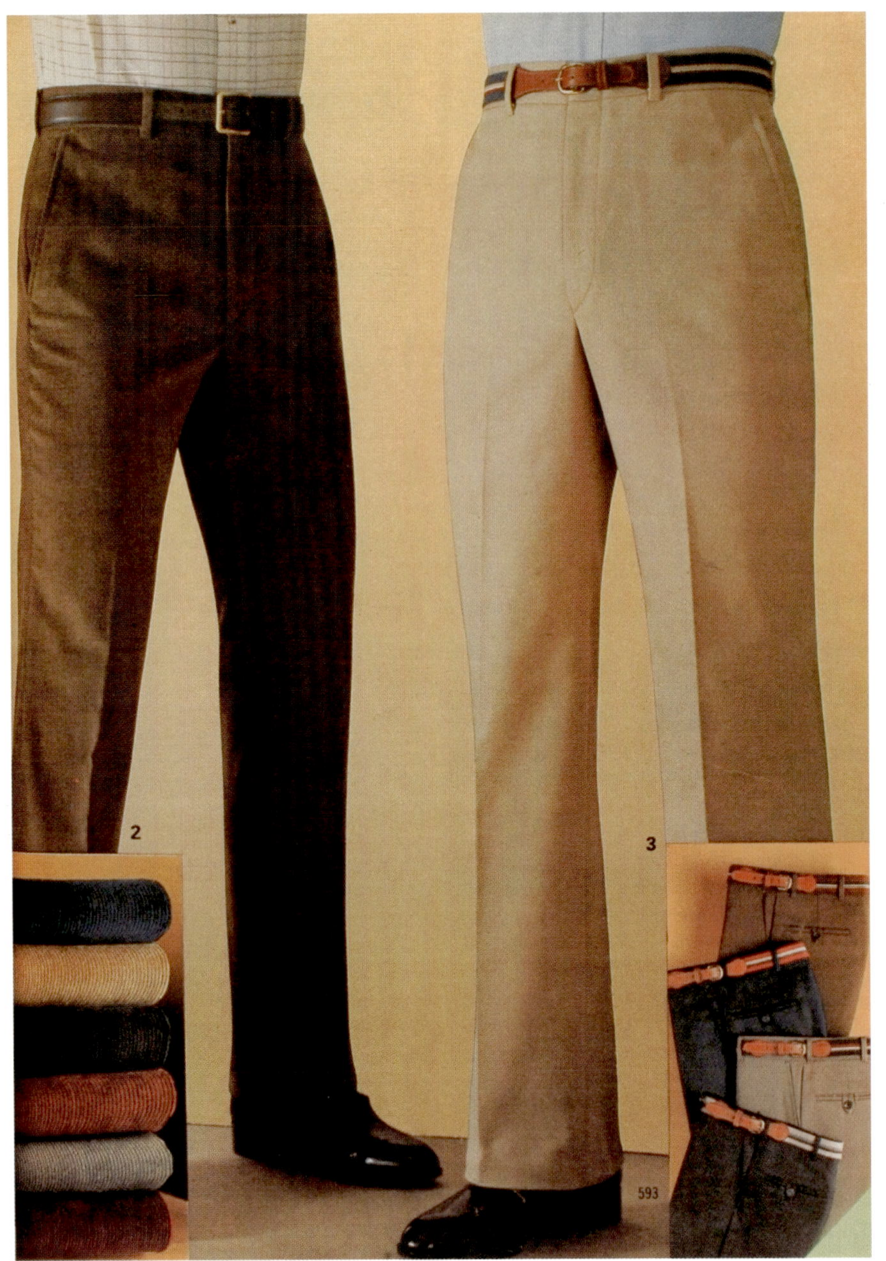

Traditional and Chino slacks in a blend of cotton and polyester. *Fall/Winter 1984.*

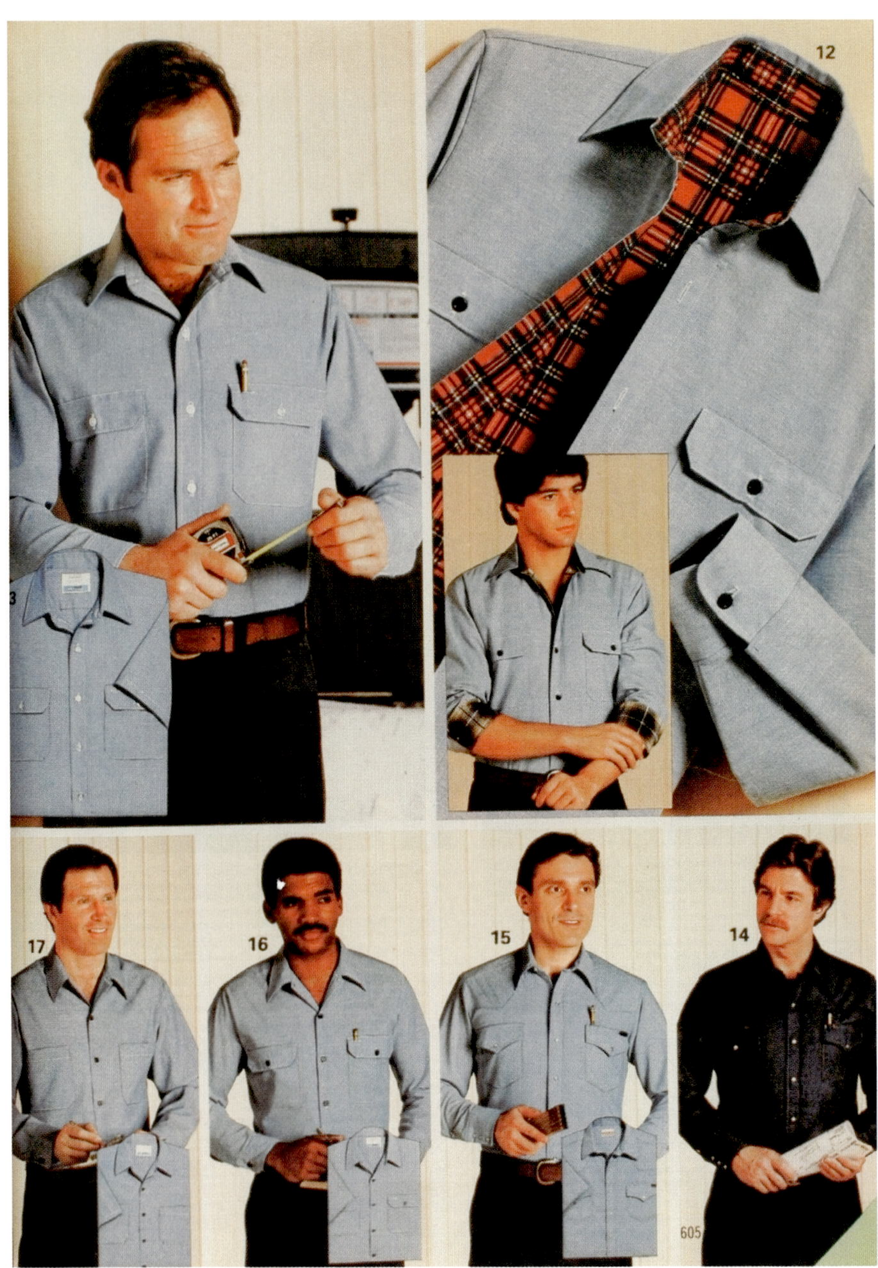

Chambray and denim shirts for work or leisure wear. *Fall/Winter 1984.*

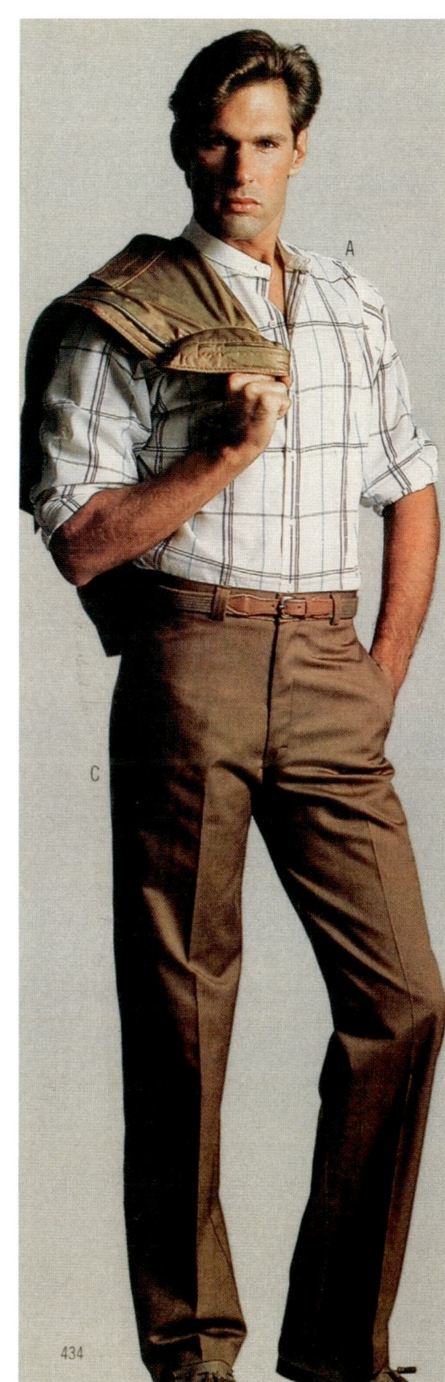

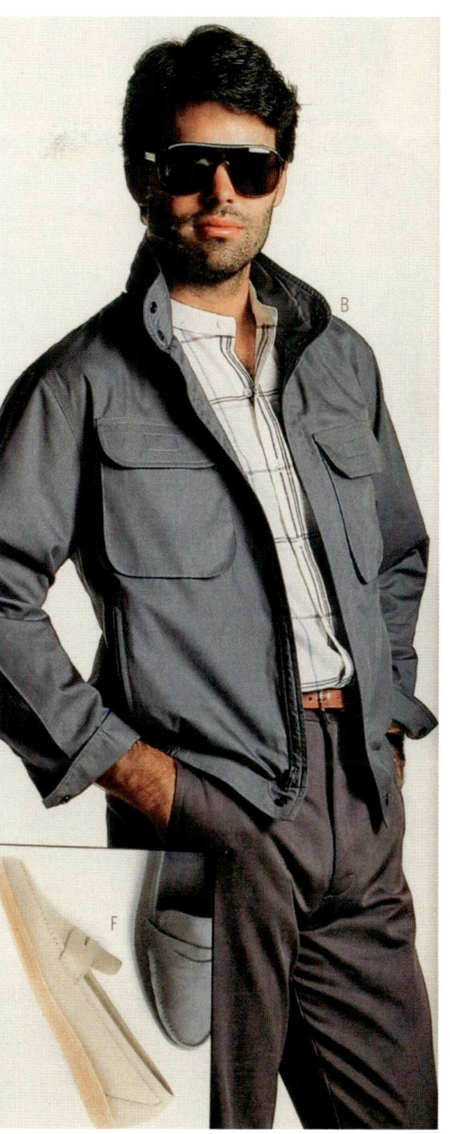

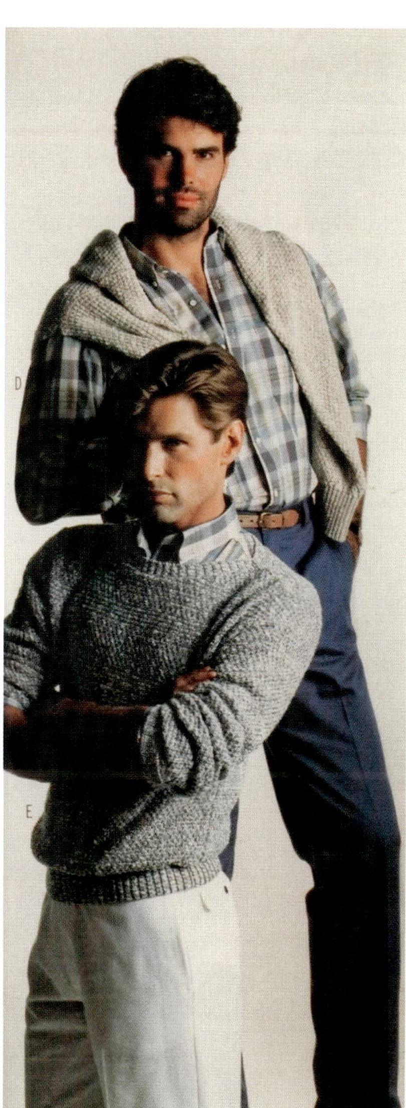

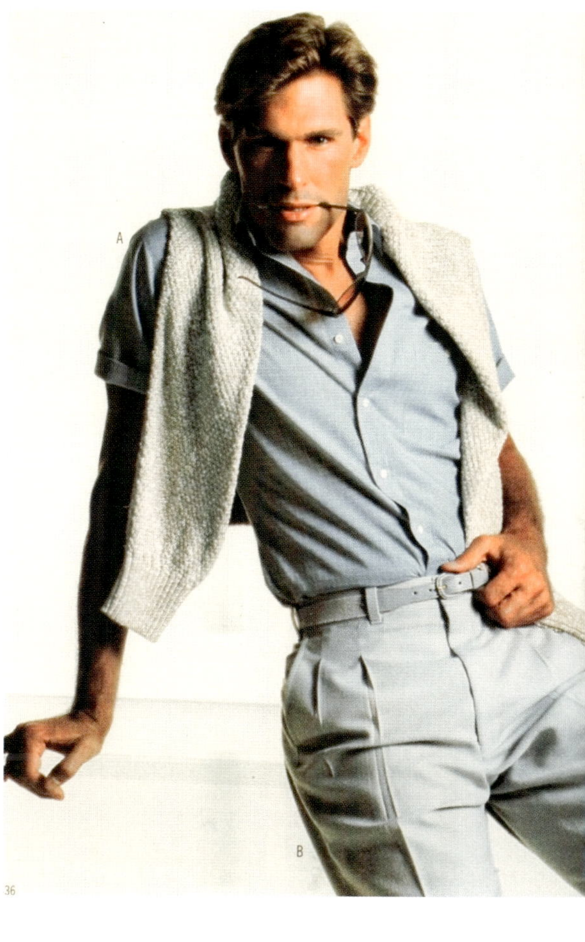

Separates from the Boston Athletic Club by Gil Truedsson for leisure hours. *Spring/Summer 1985*

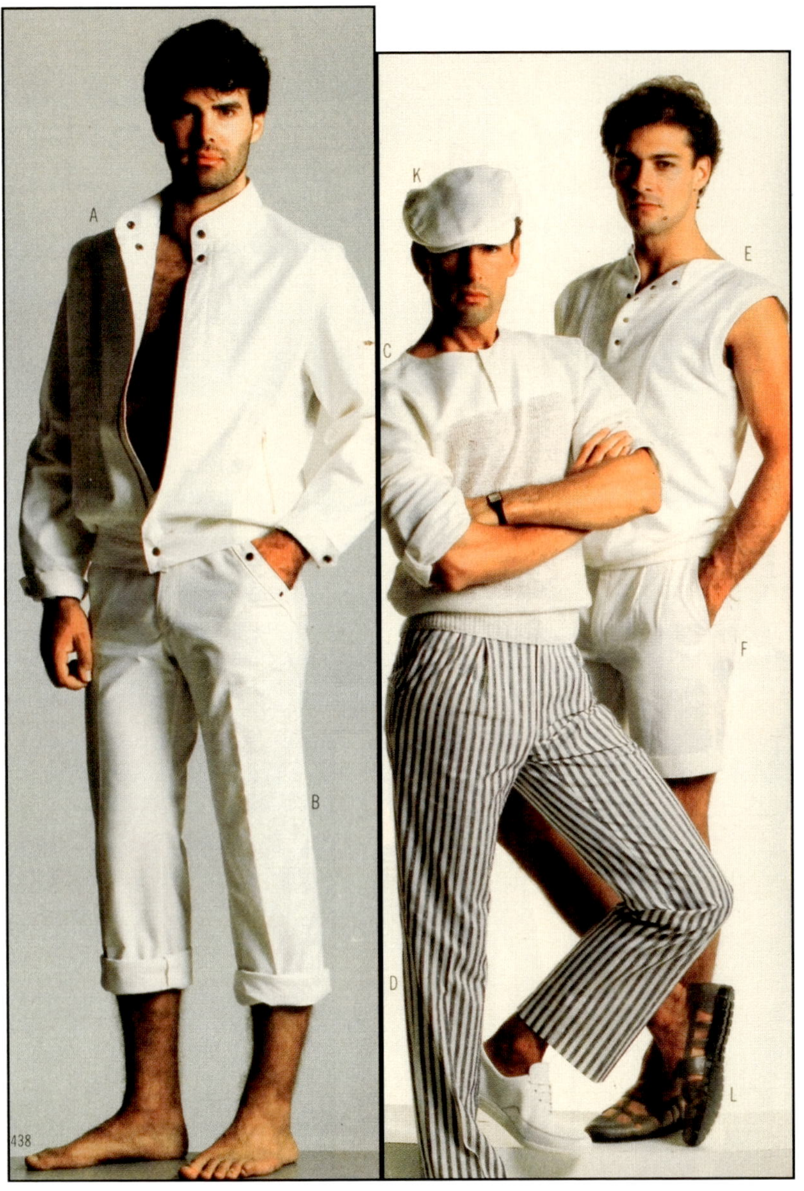

Cotton and polyester jacket and pants, linen sweater with subtly striped black on white double pleated slacks topped with an English-style brim cap, vest with a Henley collar paired with cuffed cotton shorts. *Spring/Summer 1985*

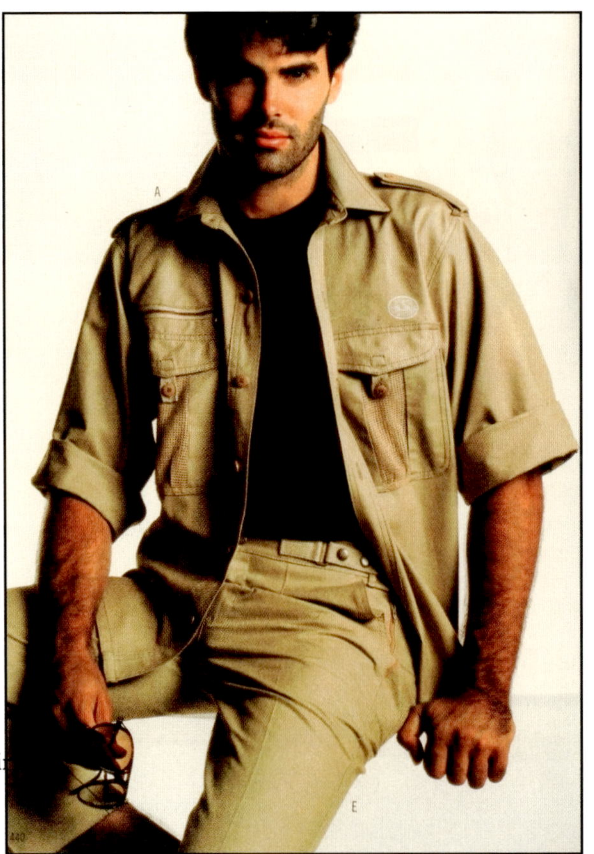

Cotter® safari style khaki shi with single-pleated pants. *Spring/Summer 1985*

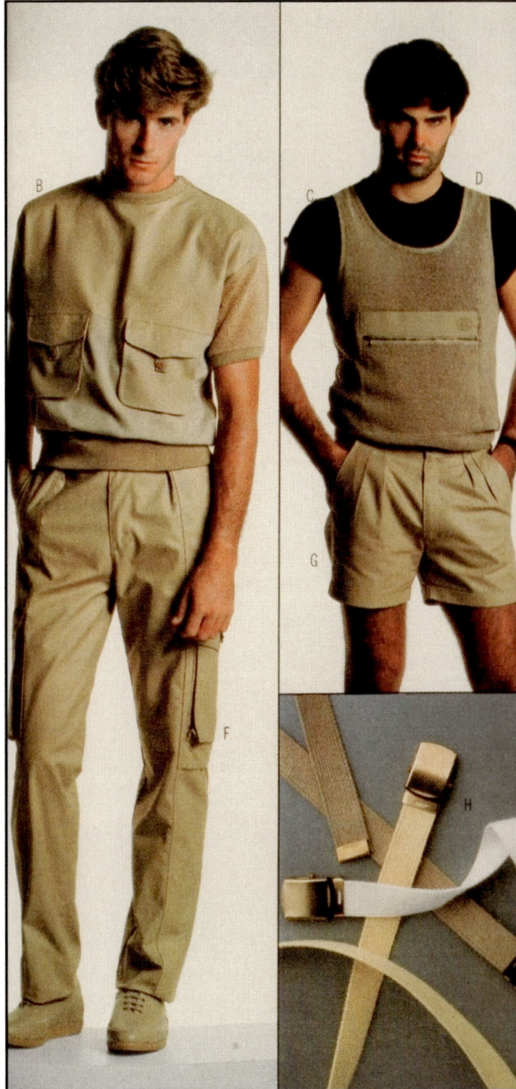

Khaki shirt with mesh sleeves and flap pockets worn with cargo pants, basic black t-shirt worn under cool khaki mesh tank top paired with ramie and cotton shorts. *Spring/ Summer 1985*

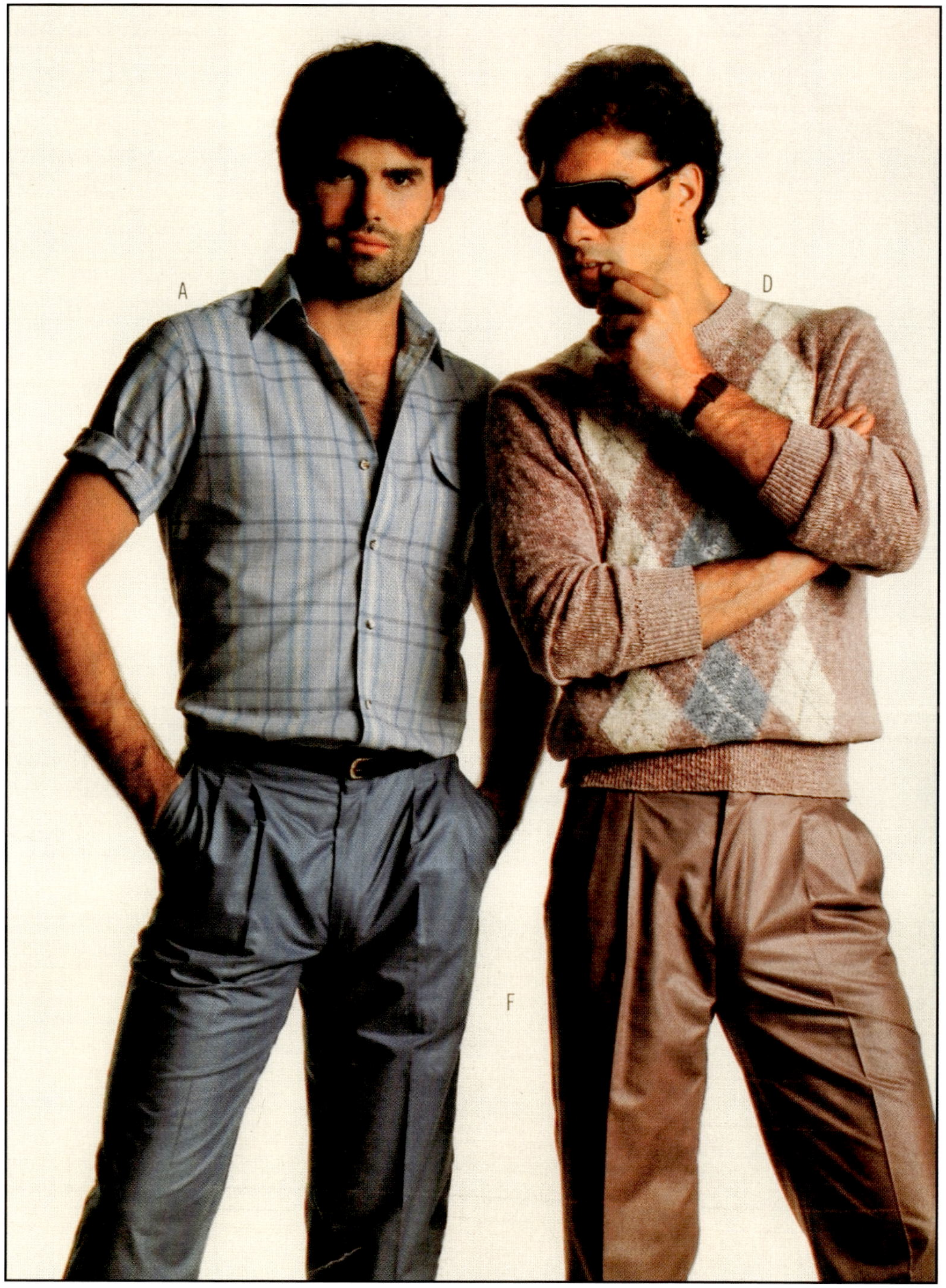

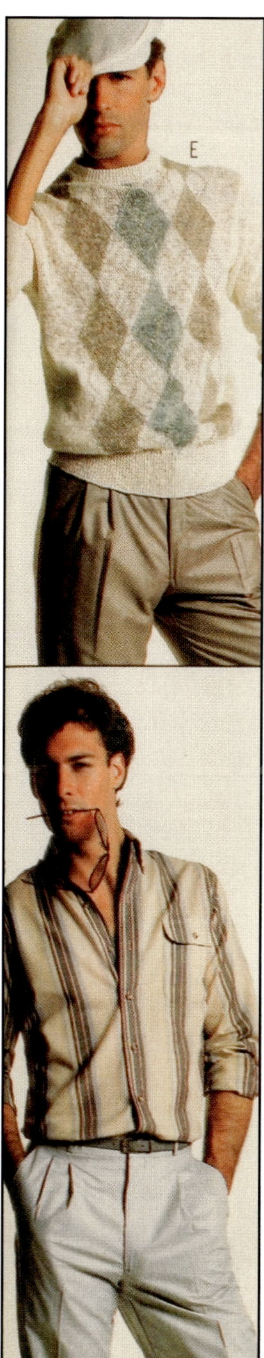

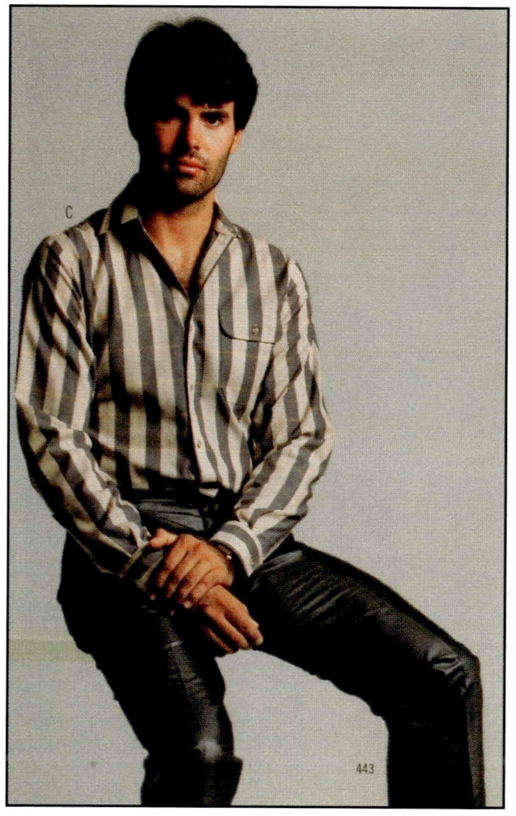

Plaid and stripe fitted shirts, argyle sweaters, and polyester and cotton chintz pants are attention getters. *Spring/Summer 1985*

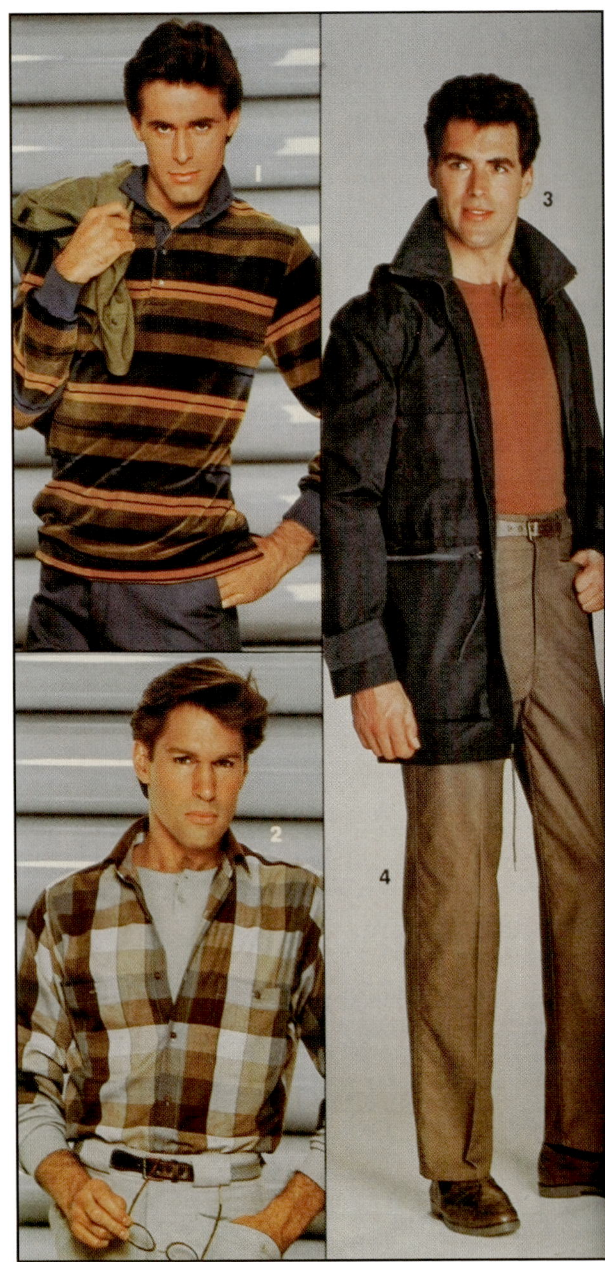

Separates from Boston Athletic Club by Gil Truedsson. *Fall/Winter 1985*

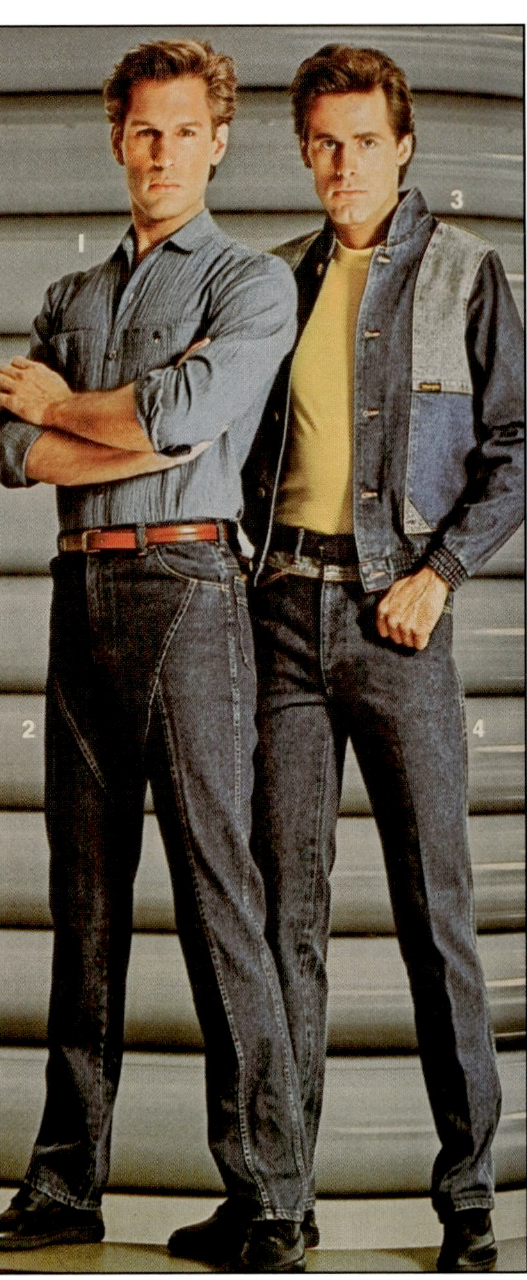

Crinkle chambray shirt in 100% cotton, denim jacket trimmed with faded gray canvas, and denim jeans from the Wrangler® Marceau® collection. *Fall/Winter 1985*

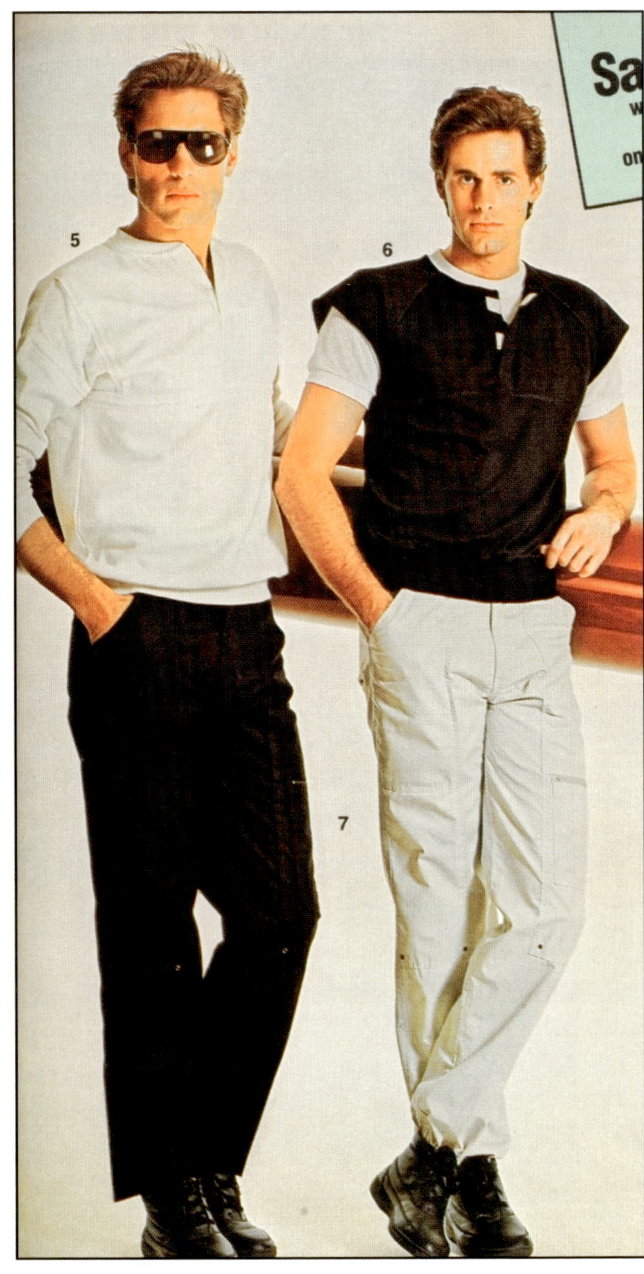

Oversized fleeced pullover, double raglan sleeve knit neck shirt, and all cotton sheeting pants from the Fizz-Ed collection. *Fall/Winter 1985*

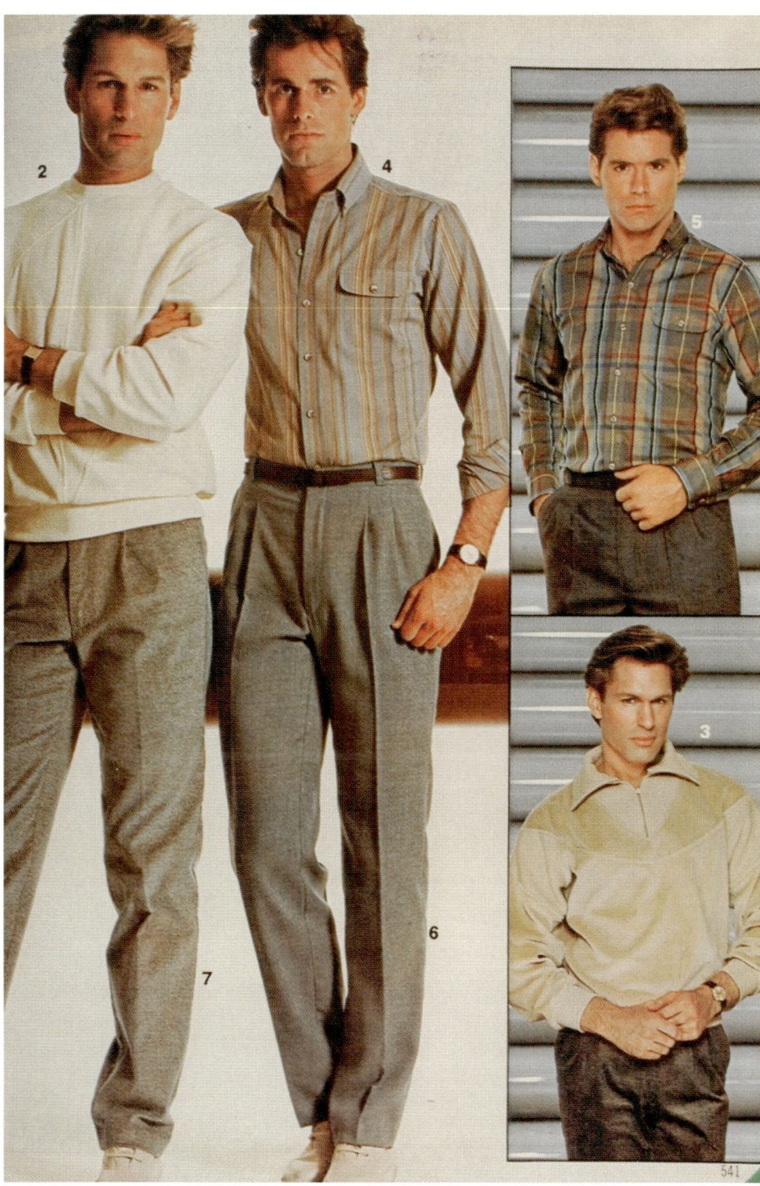

Pull-over sweaters by Oakton Ltd®, fitted sports shirts by Cavalier®, and double-pleated flannel or corduroy pants from R.P.M.®. *Fall/Winter 1985*

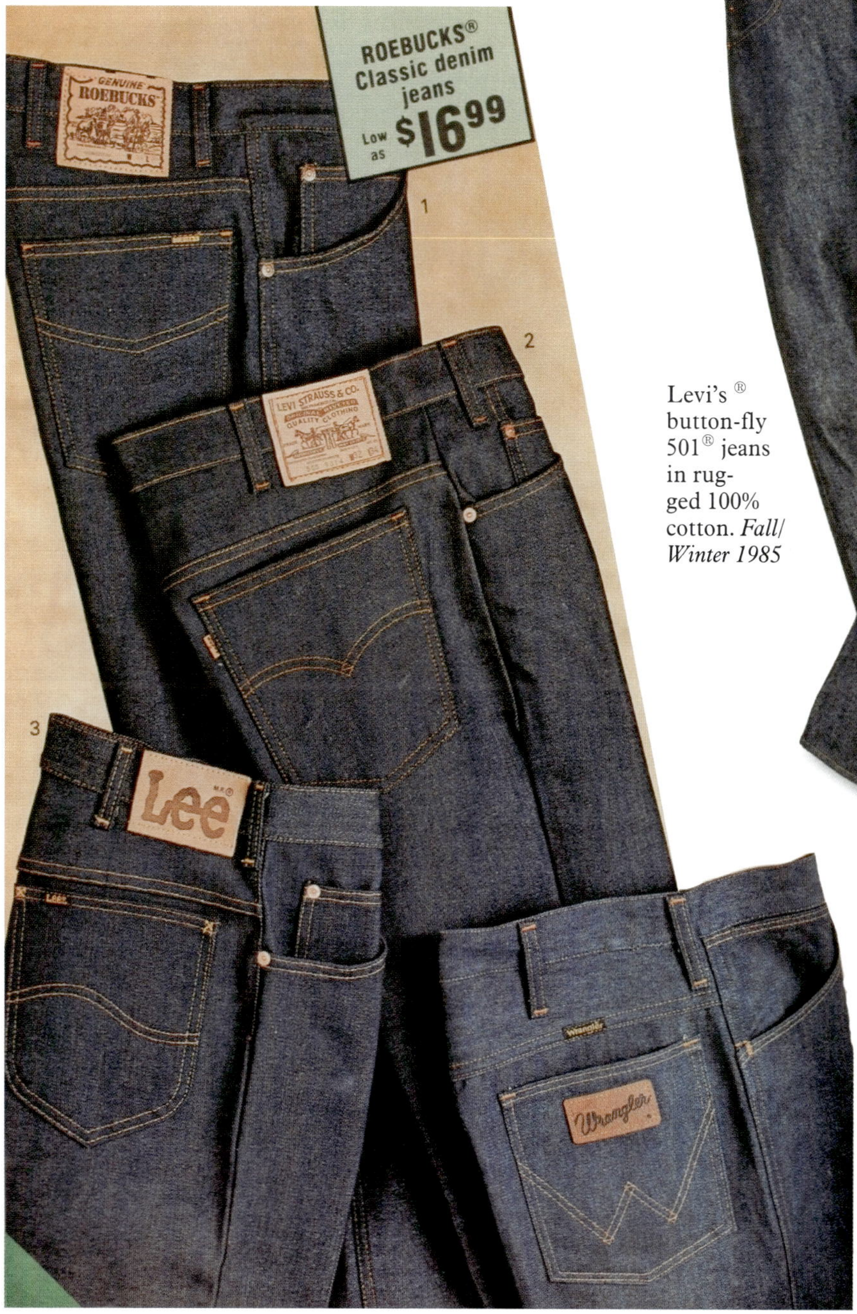

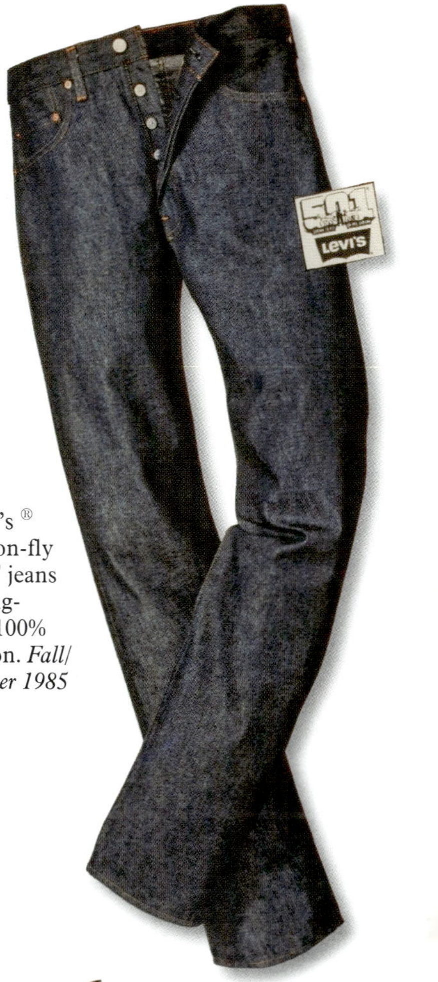

ROEBUCKS®
Classic denim jeans
Low as $16.99

Levi's® button-fly 501® jeans in rugged 100% cotton. *Fall/Winter 1985*

Denim jeans by Roebucks®, Levis's®, Lee®, and Wrangler®. *Fall/Winter 1985*

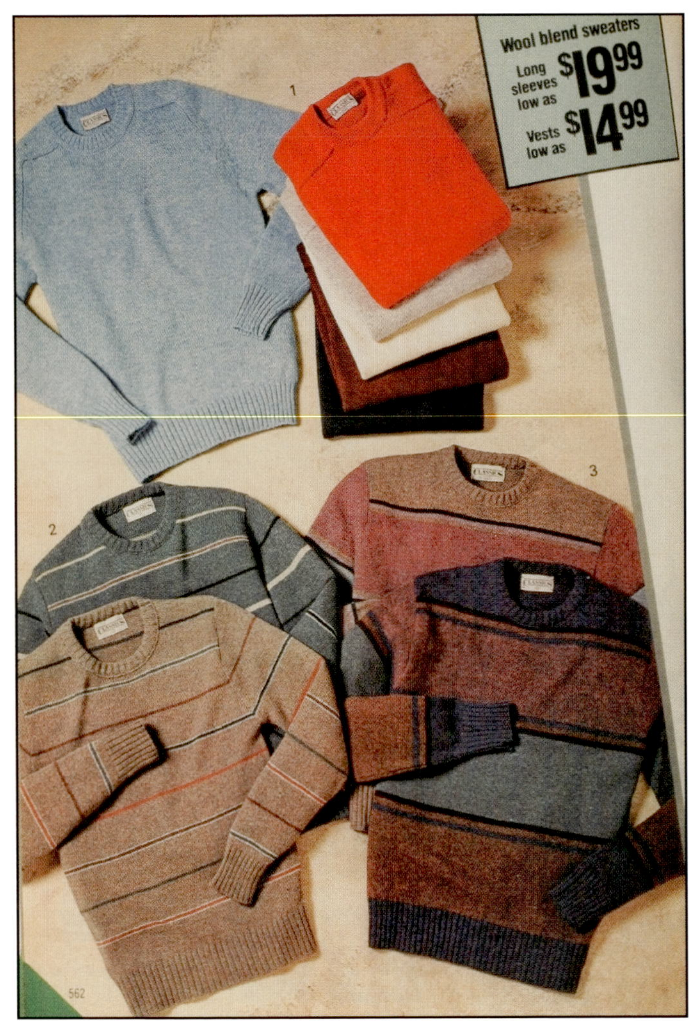

Sweaters knit of warm wool and acrylic in solids and stripes. *Fall/Winter 1985*

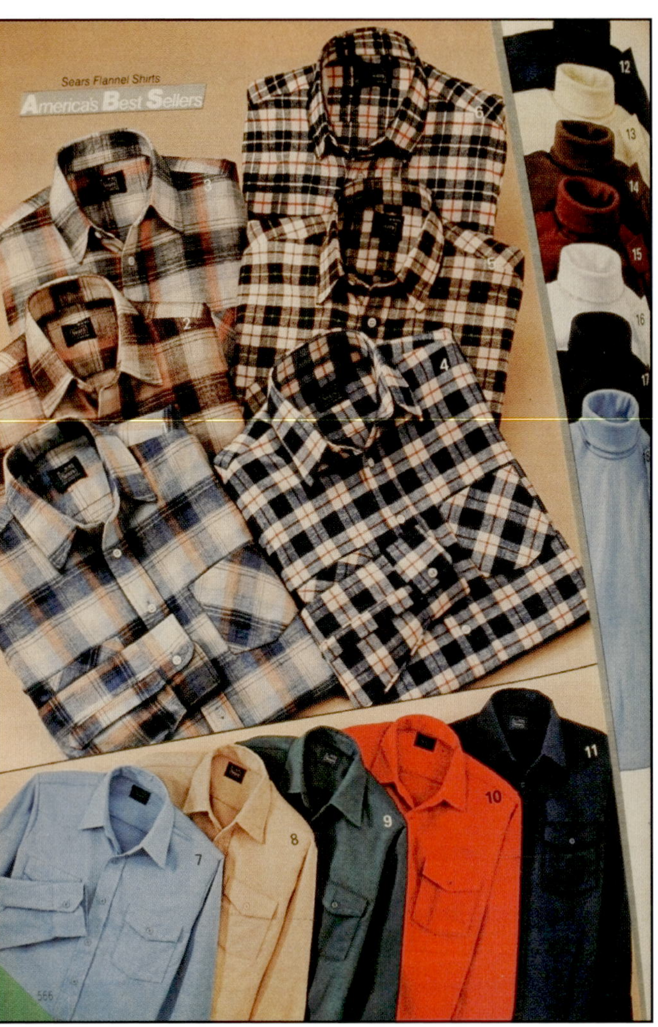

100% cotton flannel shirts, solid-colored flannels in a woven blend of cotton and polyester, and turtleneck shirts in soft cotton and polyester. *Fall/Winter 1985*

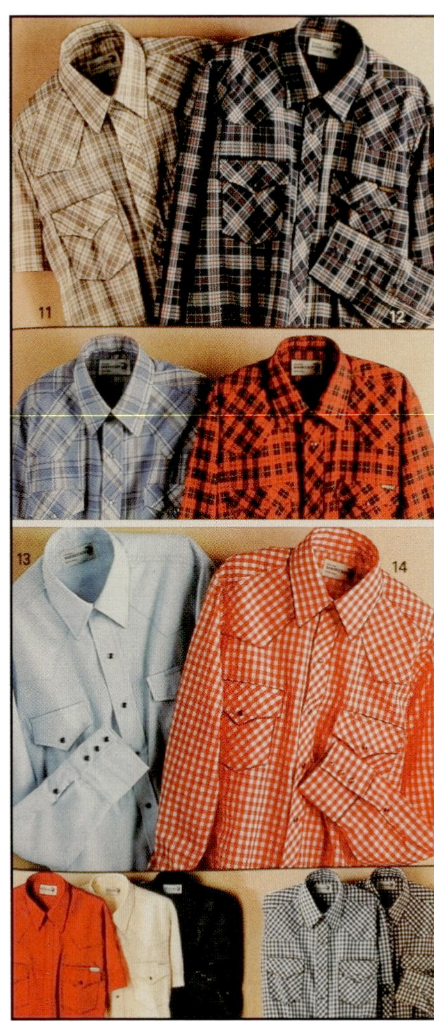

Roebucks® shirts in polyester and cotton blends, broadcloth shirt and colorful gingham shirts for a western flair. *Fall/Winter 1985*

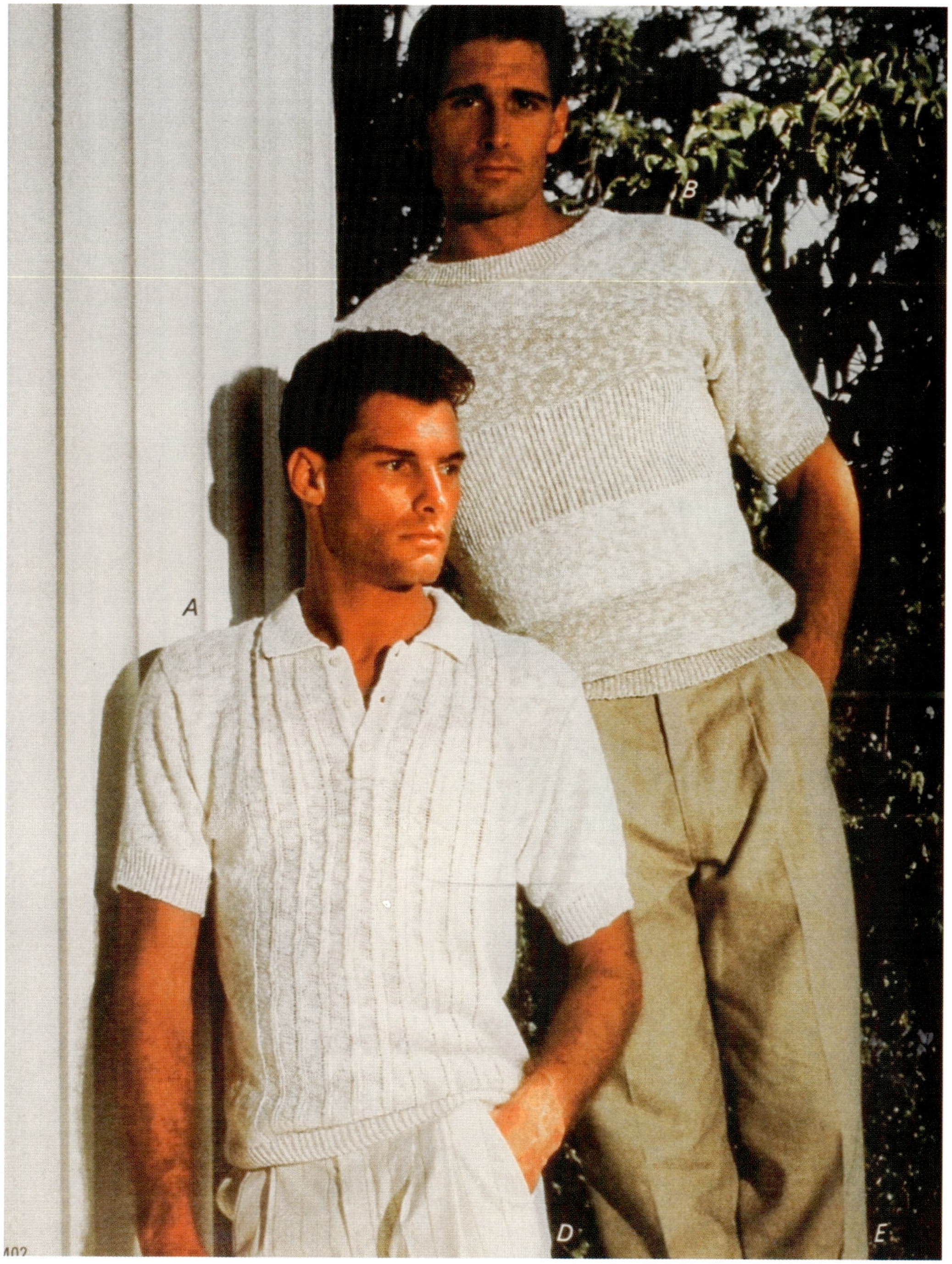

Ramie and cotton knit Billy Who? pullovers worn with ramie and cotton striped pants by Cotler and ramie and cotton slacks by Cotler. *Spring/Summer 1986*

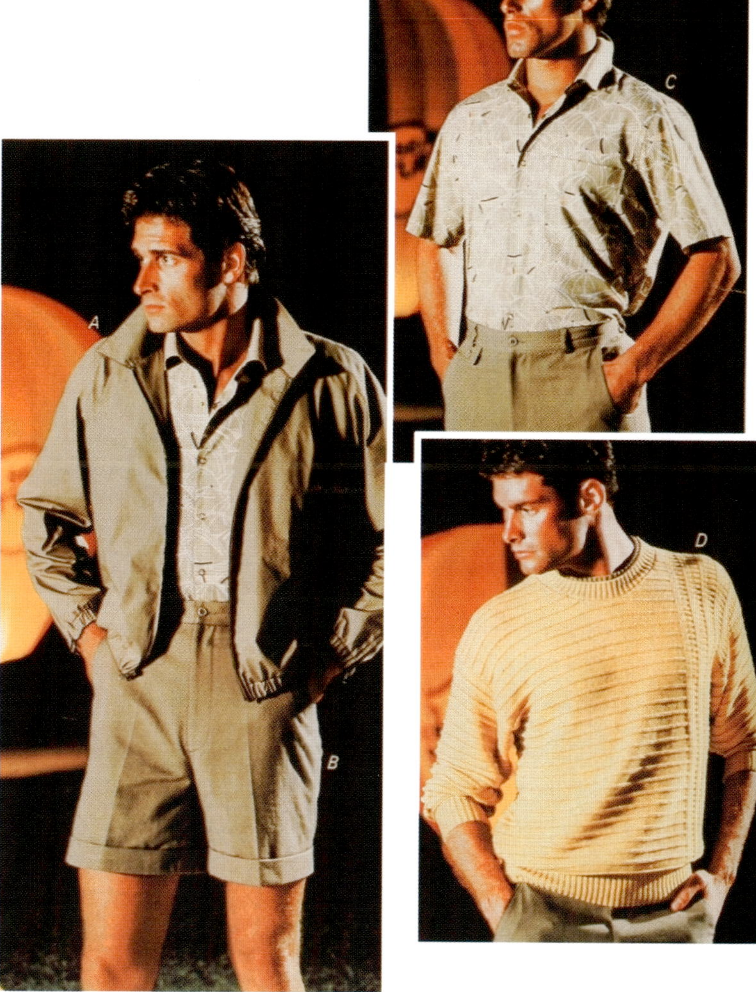

Six pieces from the Boston Athletic Club by Gil Truedsson are color, texture, and fashion compatible. *Spring/Summer 1986*

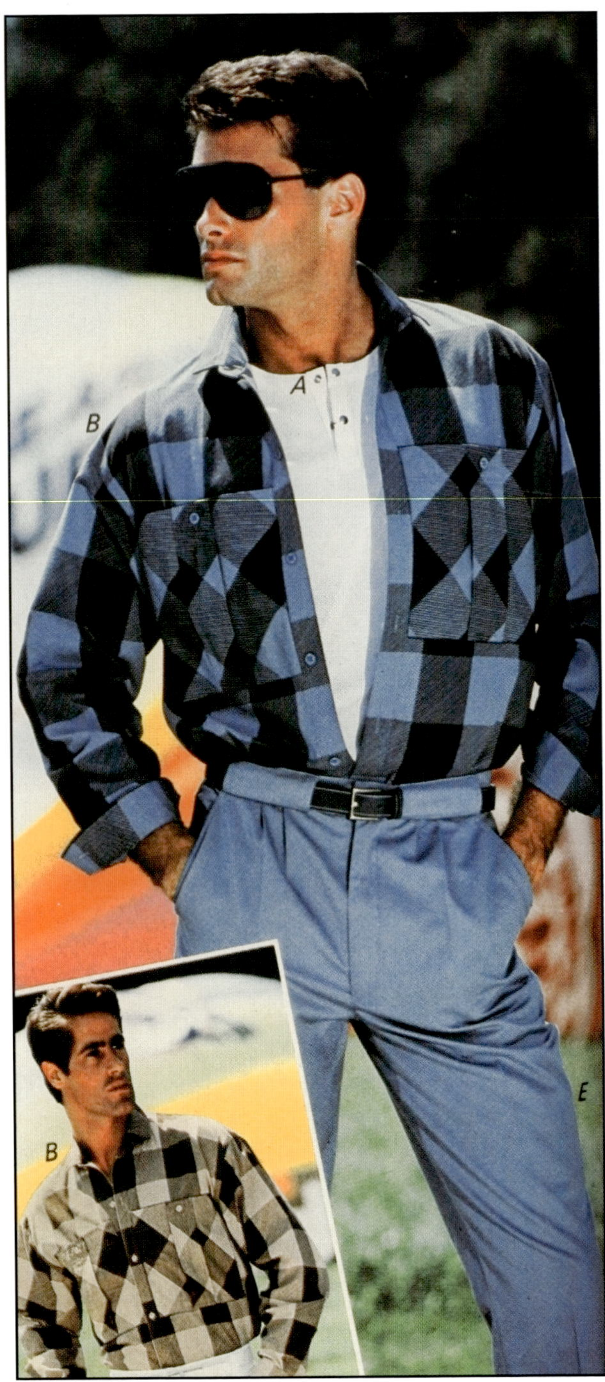

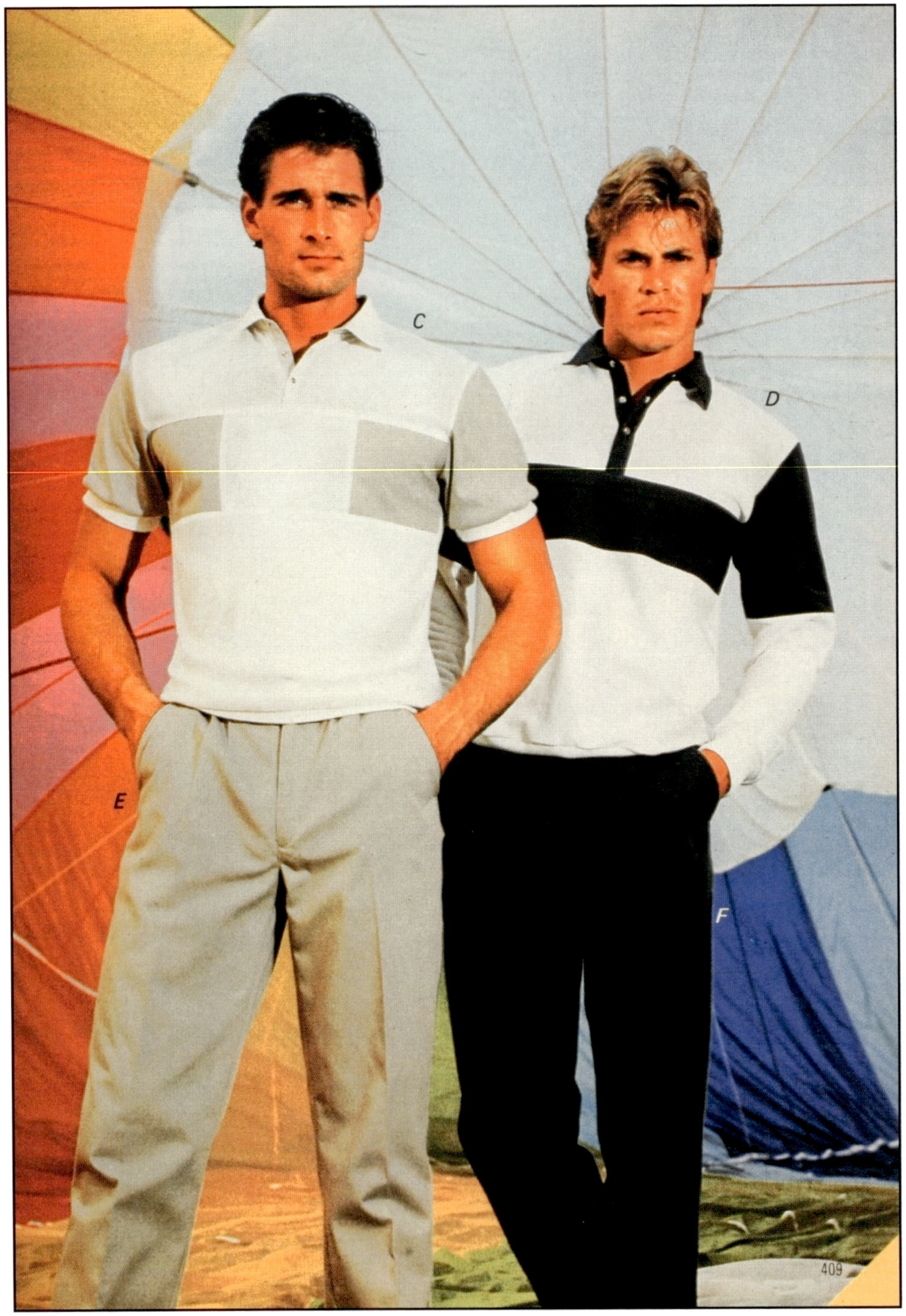

Far left:
White knit pullover has ribbed sleeves and bottom, buffalo plaid shirt has dropped shoulders and over-sized front pockets, double pleated pants have tunnel-style belt loops. *Spring/Summer 1986*

Short sleeve pullover with woven fabric detailing, knit terry shirt has woven collar and inserts on front and sleeves, and double pleated twill pants. *Spring/Summer 1986*

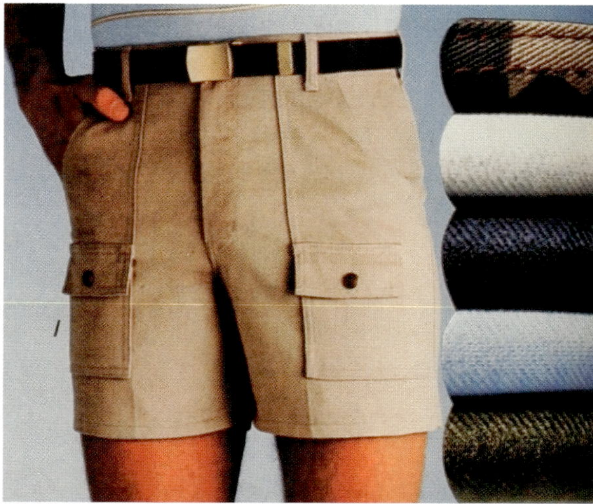

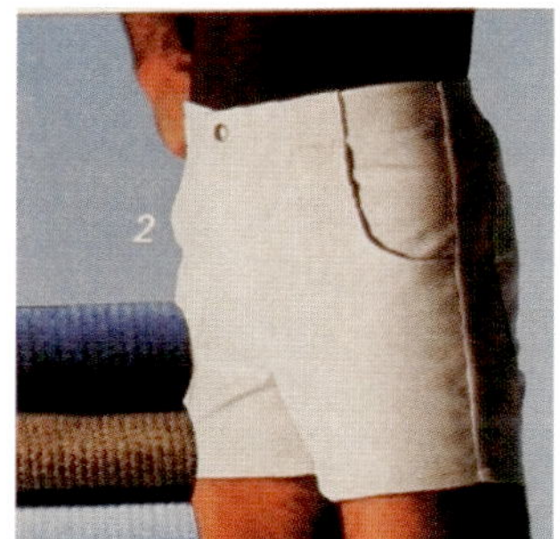

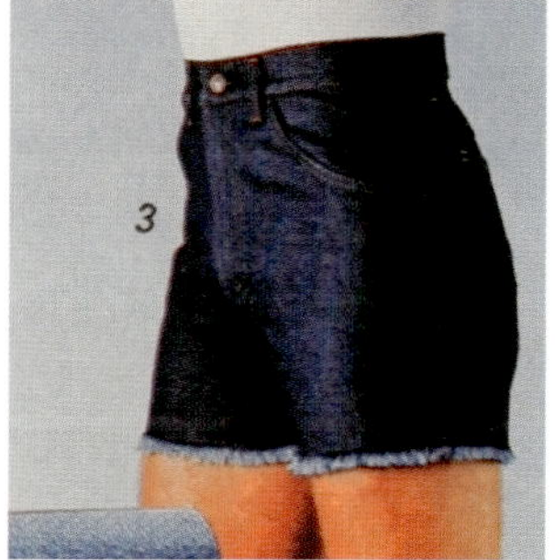

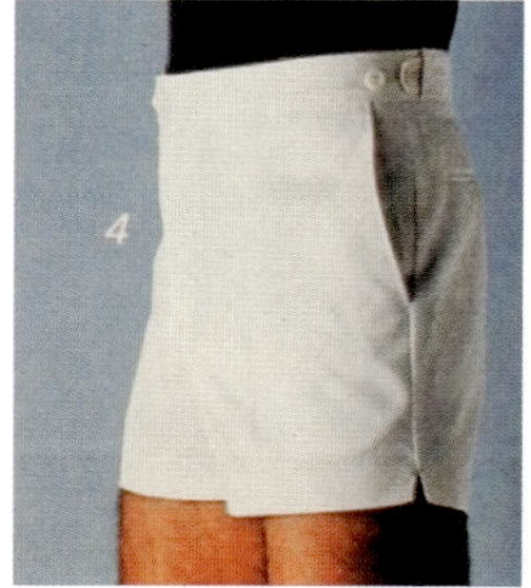

Polyester and cotton brushed denim shorts, corduroy shorts, fringed blue jean shorts, and white tennis shorts. *Spring/Summer 1986*

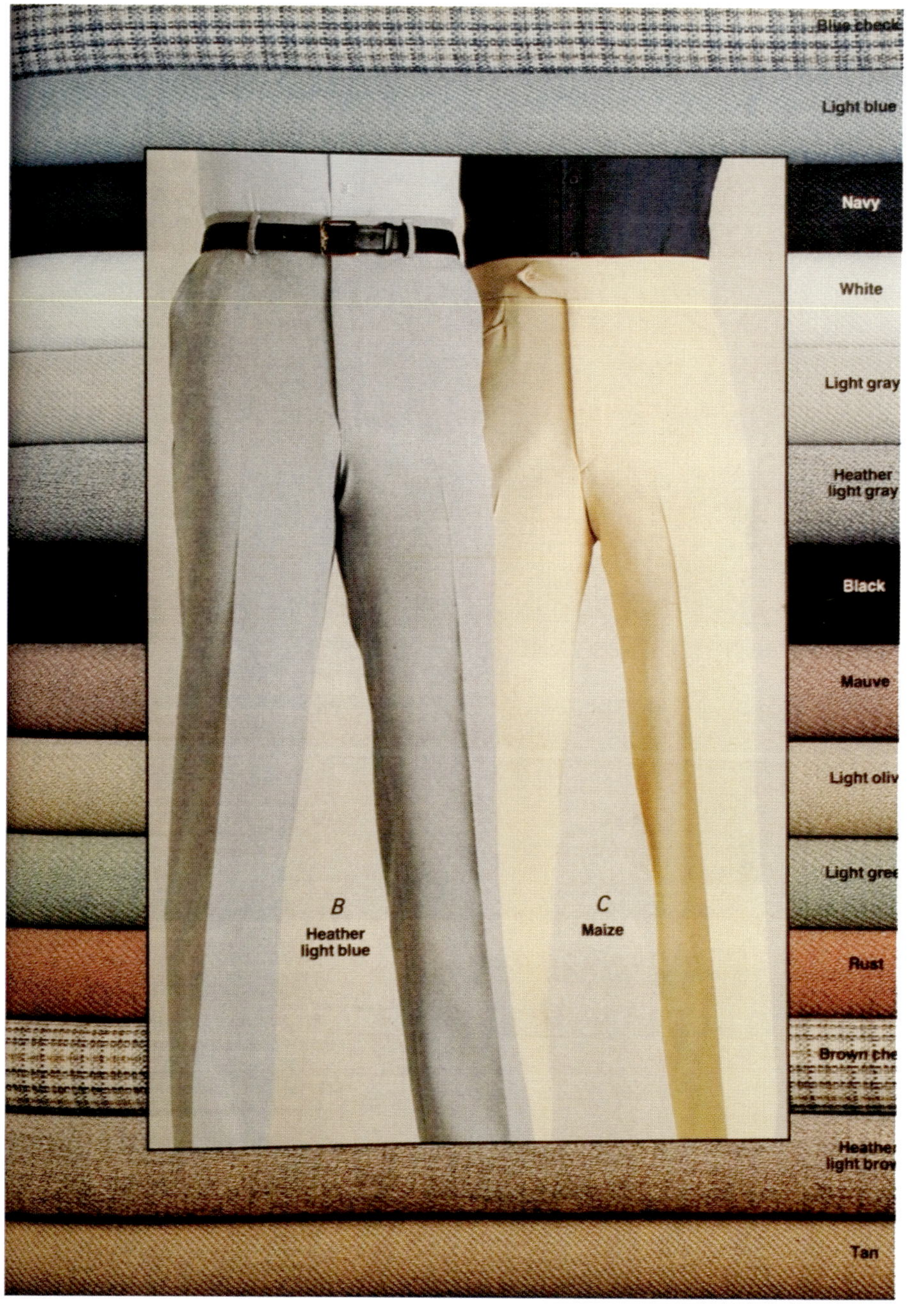

Flexslax are stretch-woven PERMA-PREST® slacks in a firmly woven gabardine with 20 colors to choose from. *Spring/Summer 1986*

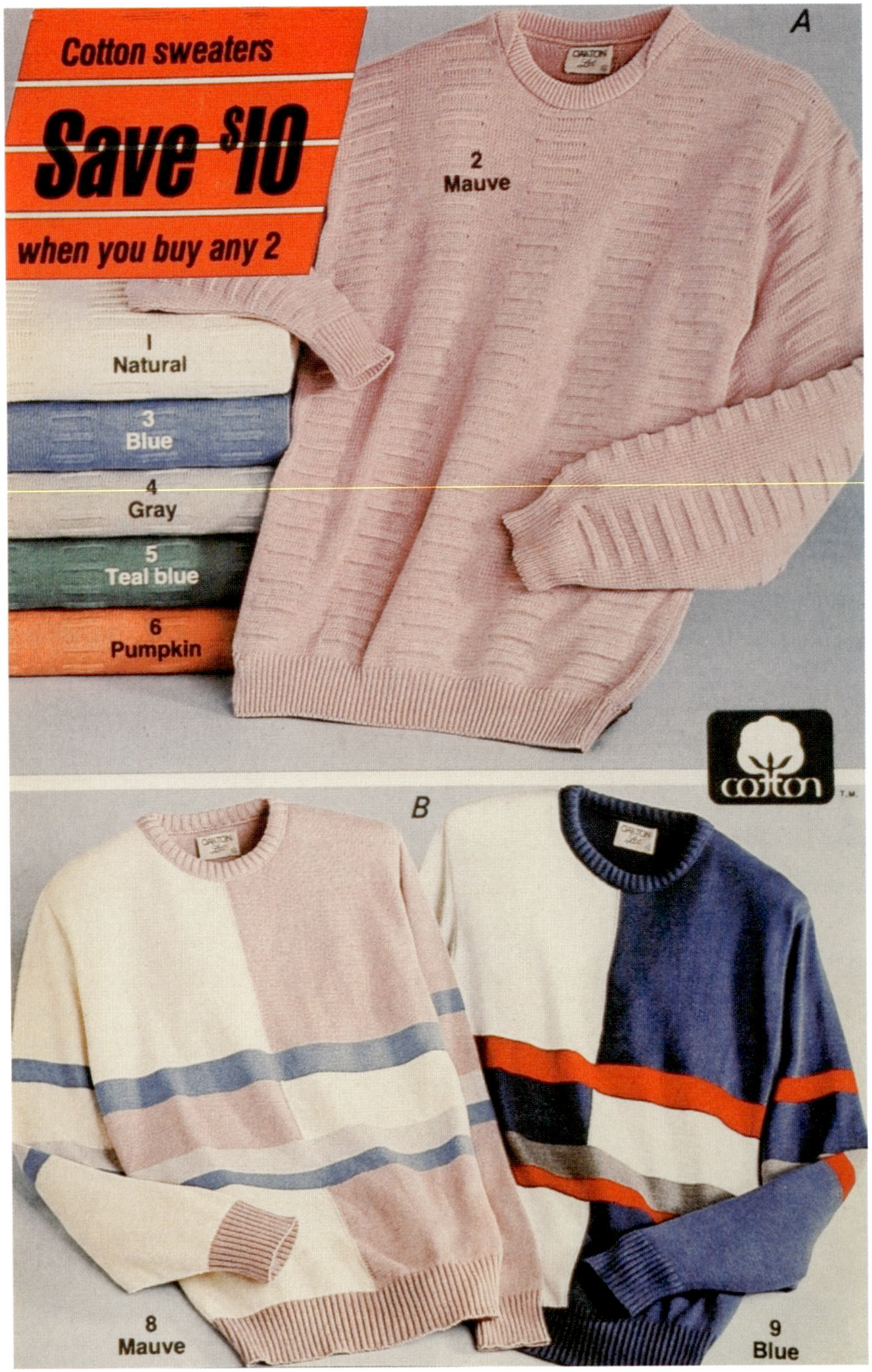

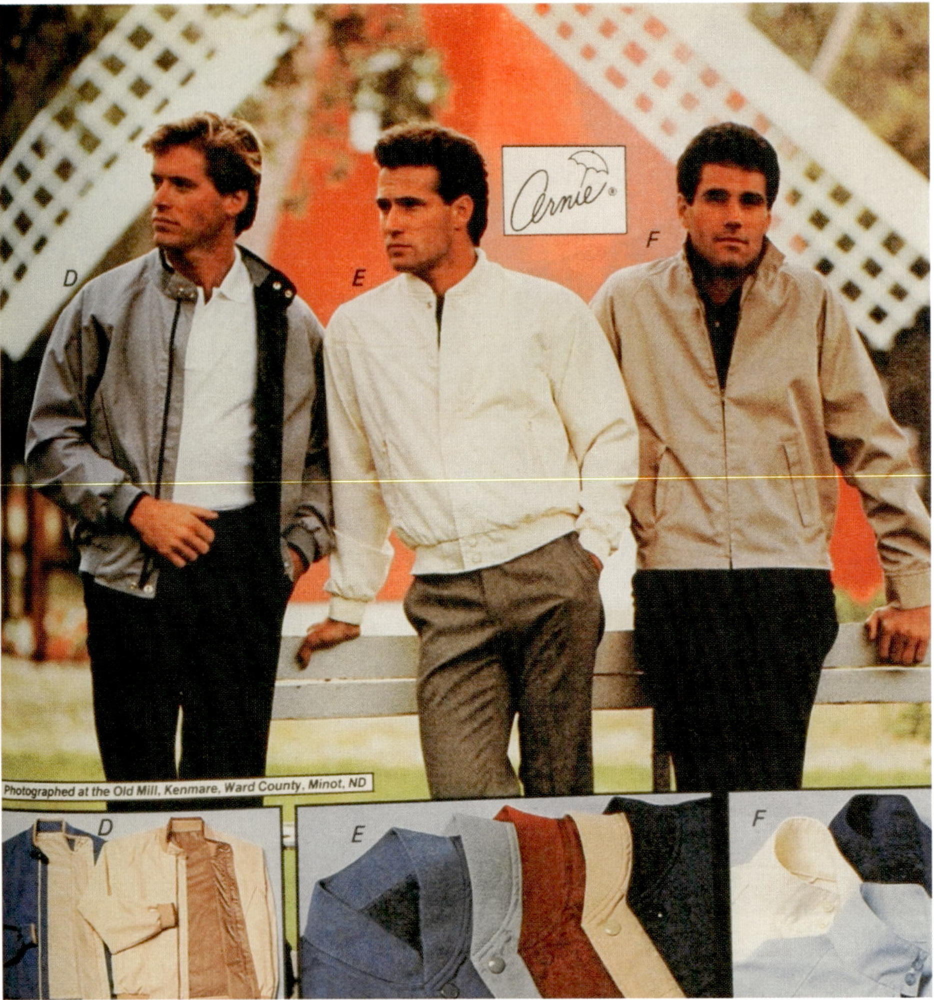

Cotton and polyester reversible jacket with stand-up collar, Arnie cotton and polyester circle-shoulder poplin jacket, and Arnie poplin golf jacket. *Spring/Summer 1986*

All cotton sweaters in solid or patterned styles. *Spring/Summer 1986*

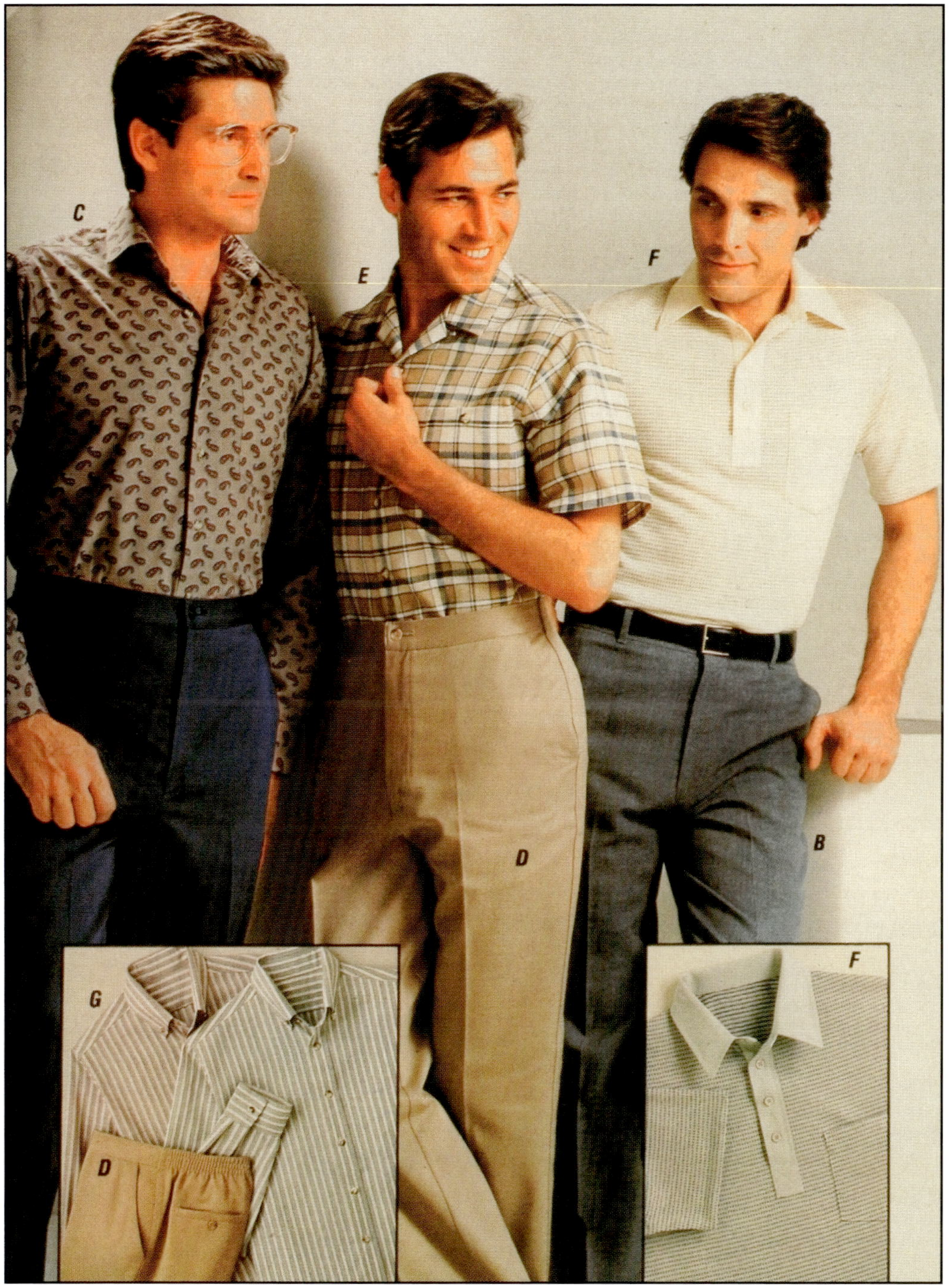

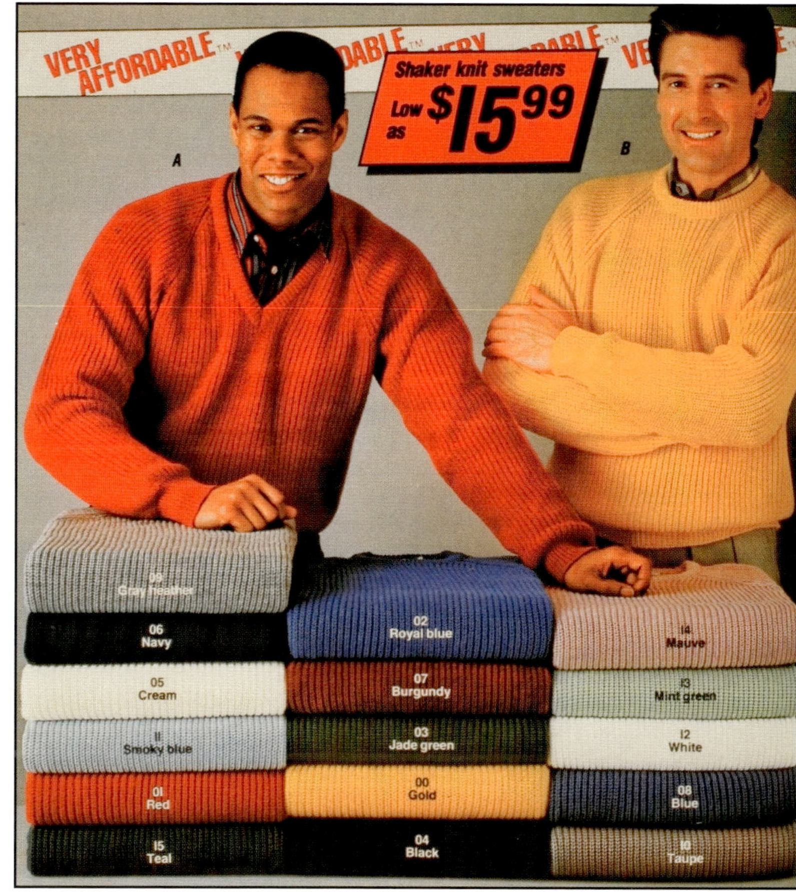

V-neck and crewneck sweaters in a variety of colors. *Fall/Winter 1986*

Gray and navy paisley shirt, khaki and teal plaid shirt, and a knit shirt are all polyester and cotton. They are worn with straight-leg twill pants and flannel slacks. *Fall/Winter 1986*

Sporty

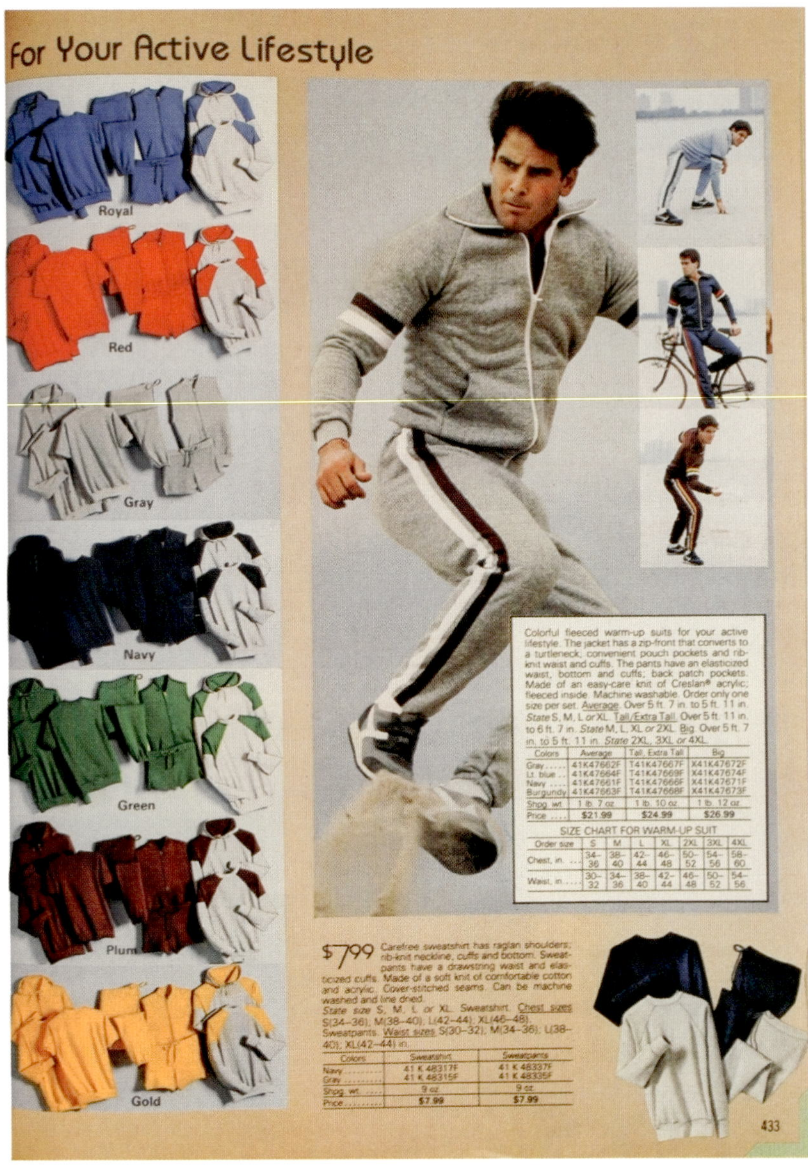

Colors	Average	Tall, Extra Tall	Big
Gray	41K47662F	T41K47667F	X41K47672F
Lt. blue	41K47664F	T41K47669F	X41K47674F
Navy	41K47661F	T41K47666F	X41K47671F
Burgundy	41K47663F	T41K47668F	X41K47673F
Shpg. wt.	1 lb. 7 oz.	1 lb. 10 oz.	1 lb. 12 oz.
Price	$21.99	$24.99	$26.99

SIZE CHART FOR WARM-UP SUIT

Order size	S	M	L	XL	2XL	3XL	4XL
Chest, in.	34–36	38–40	42–44	46–48	50–52	54–56	58–60
Waist, in.	30–32	34–36	38–40	42–44	46–48	50–52	54–56

Colors	Sweatshirt	Sweatpants
Navy	41 K 48317F	41 K 48337F
Gray	41 K 48315F	41 K 48335F
Shpg. wt.	9 oz.	9 oz.
Price	$7.99	$7.99

Colorful fleeced wear for active men on the go. *Spring/Summer 1984.*

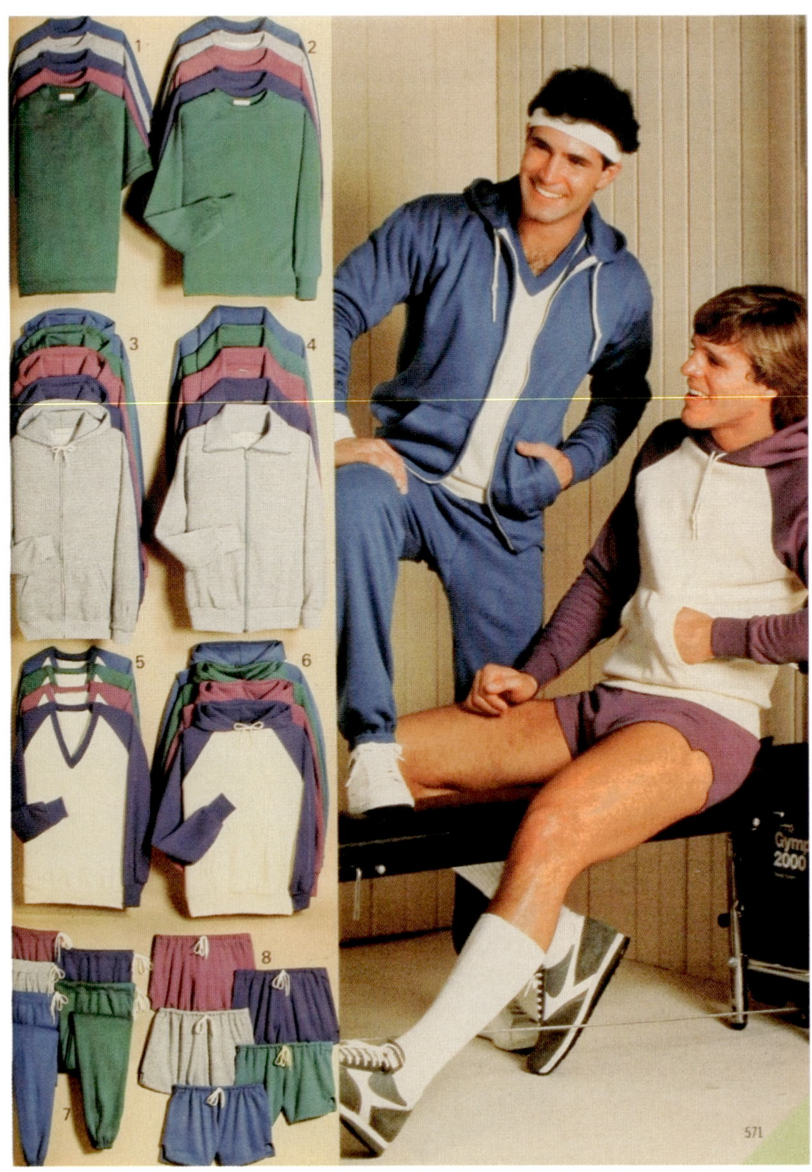

Creslan® acrylic separates from American Fleecewear for athletes. *Fall/Winter 1984.*

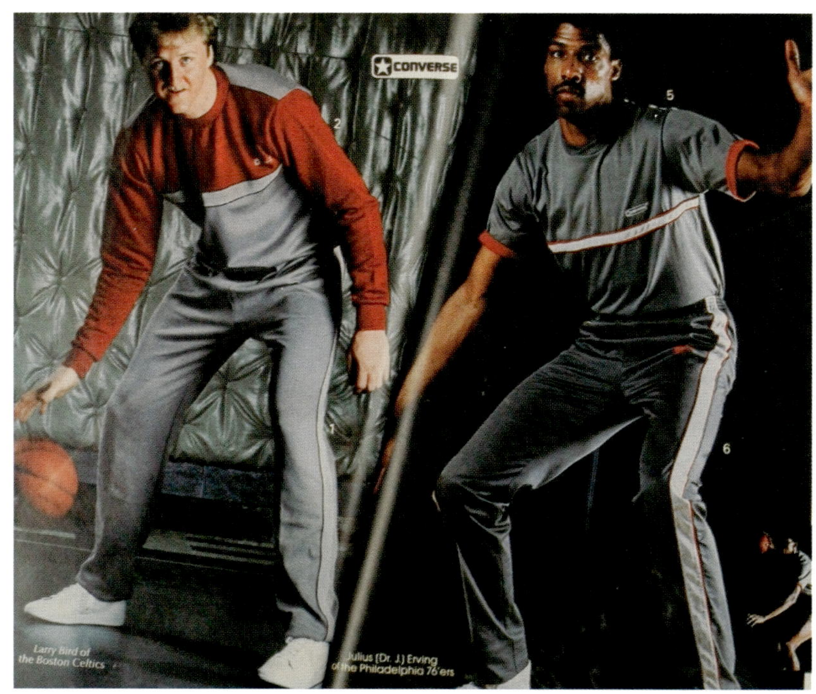

Converse® fleeced coordinates knit of machine washable acrylic or polyester and cotton blends. *Fall/Winter 1985*

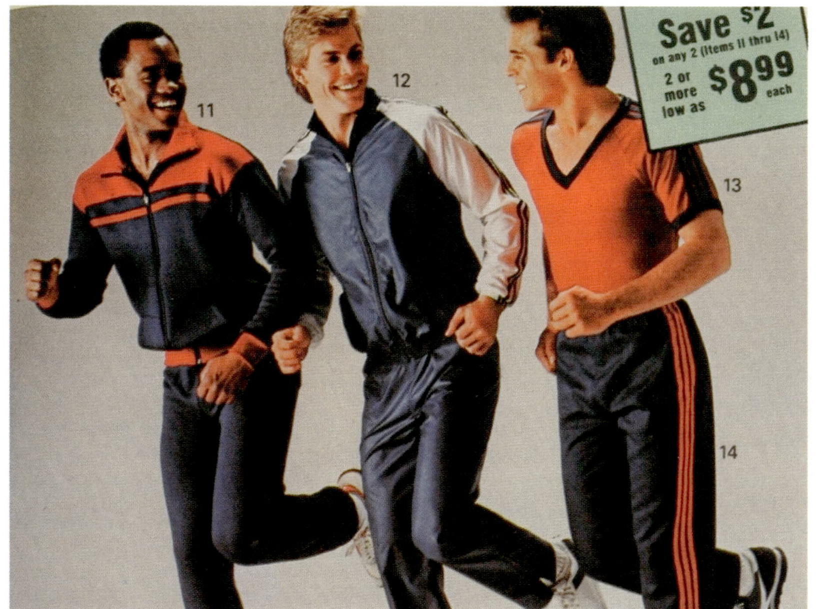

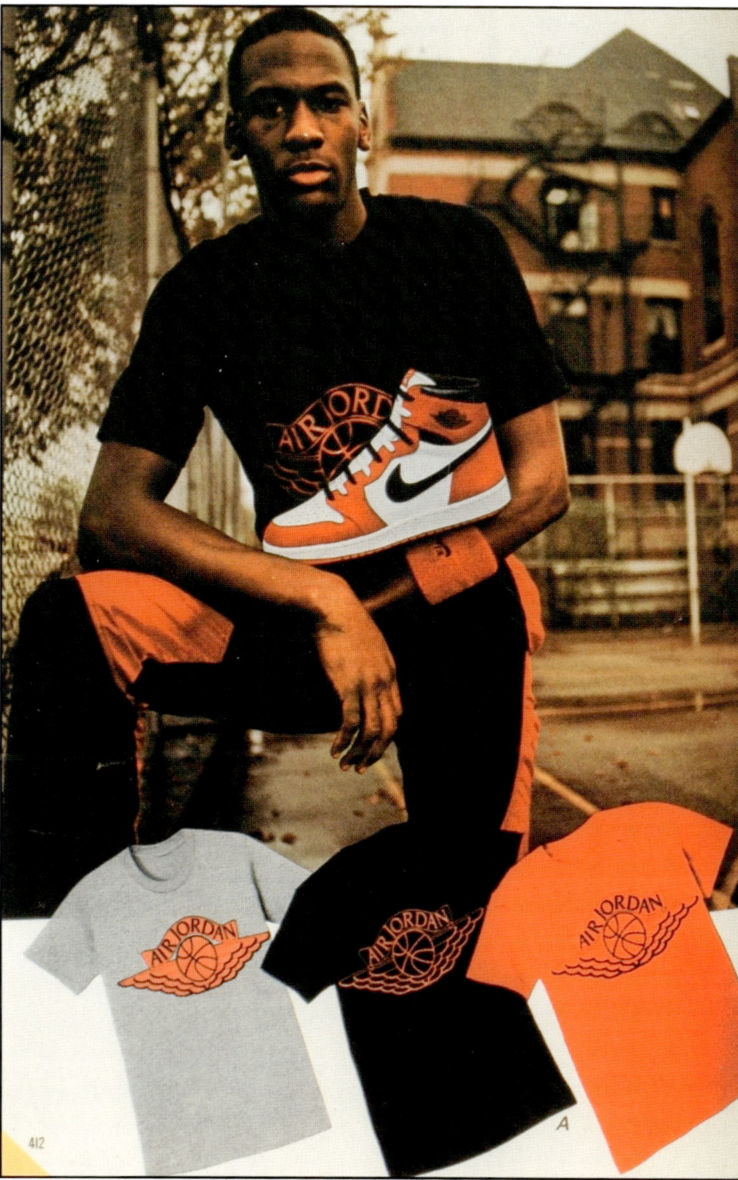

Nike Air Jordan activewear. *Spring/Summer 1986*

Versatile active-wear fleeced suit, wind suit, and v-neck jersey with twill pants. *Fall/Winter 1985*

Nightwear

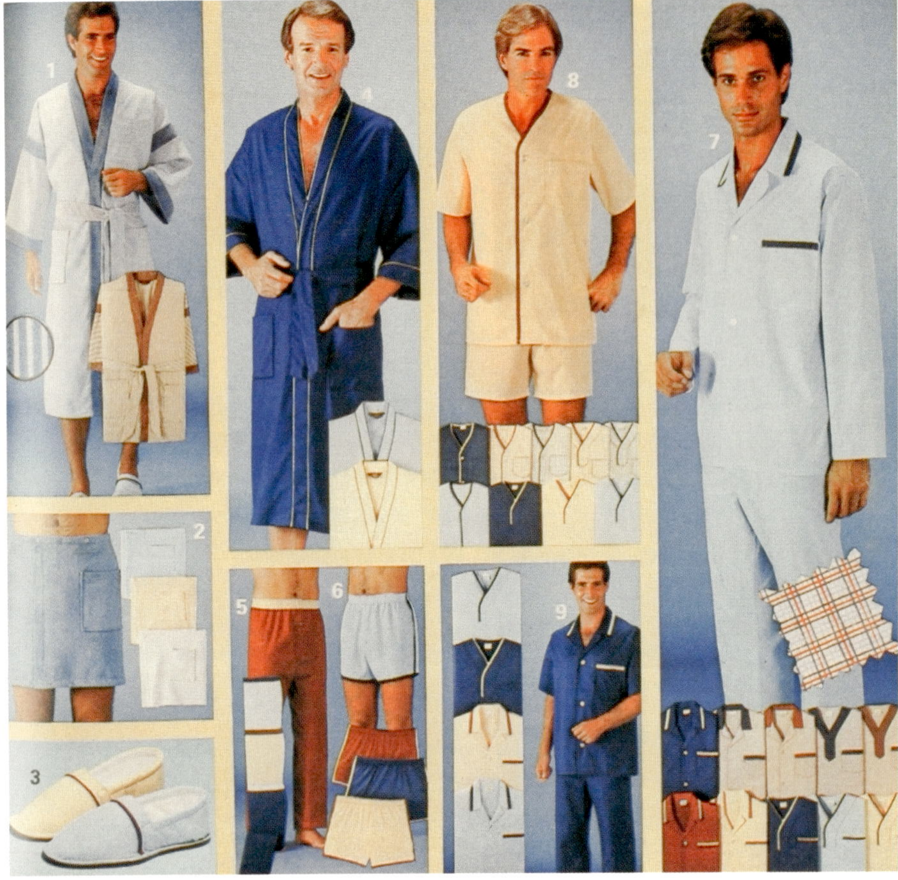

Men's Broadcloth Nightwear in assorted styles are cool and comfortable. *Spring/Summer 1984.*

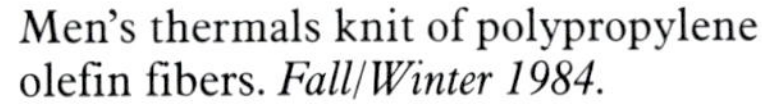

Men's thermals knit of polypropylene olefin fibers. *Fall/Winter 1984.*

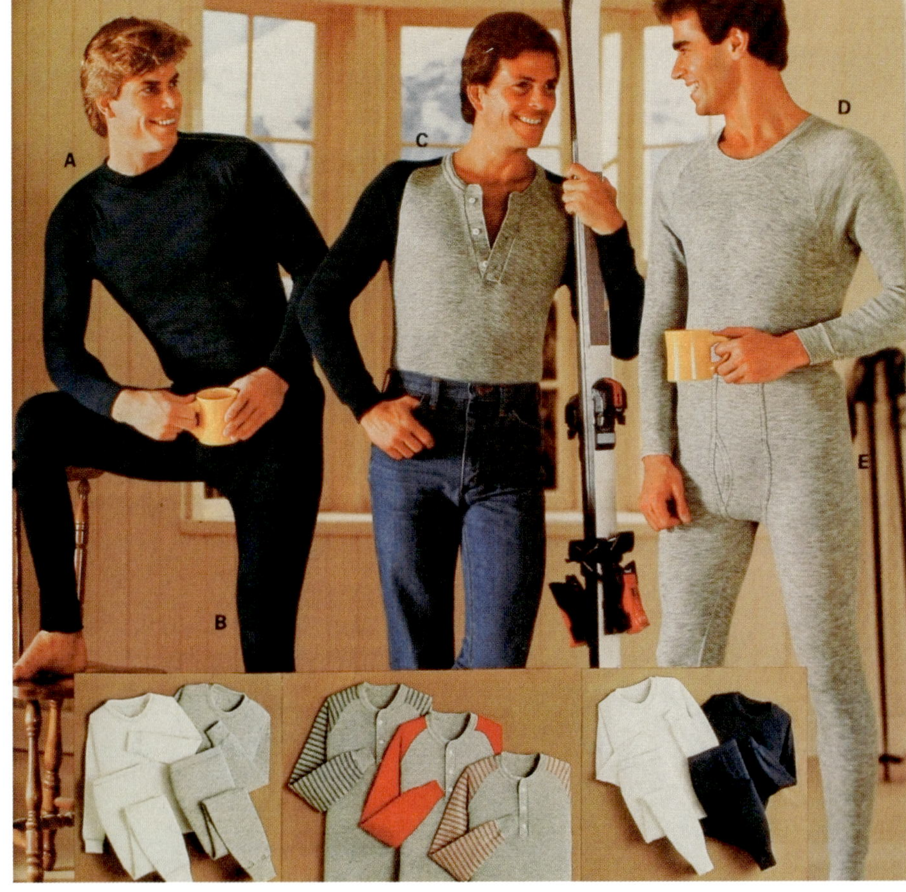

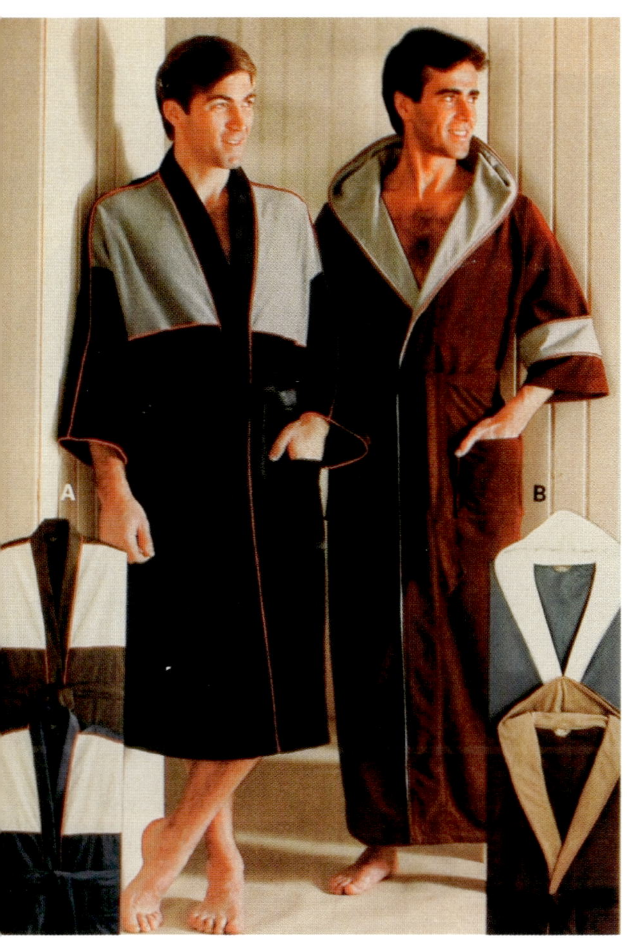

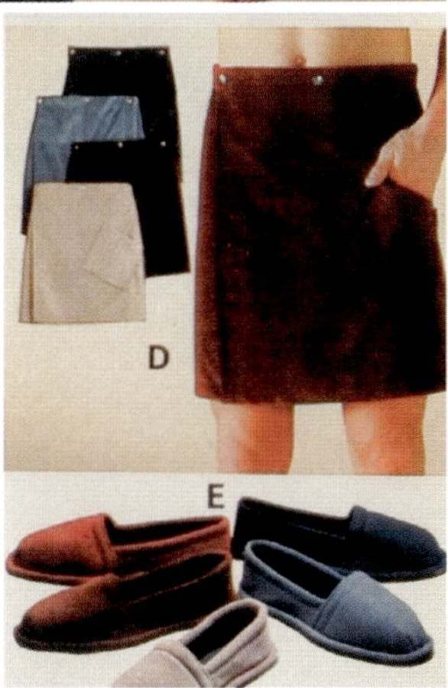

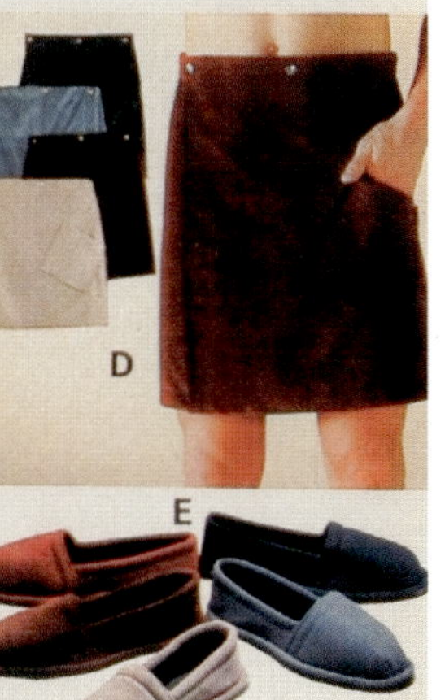

Mid and full length robes made of plush fleece velour. *Fall/Winter 1984.*

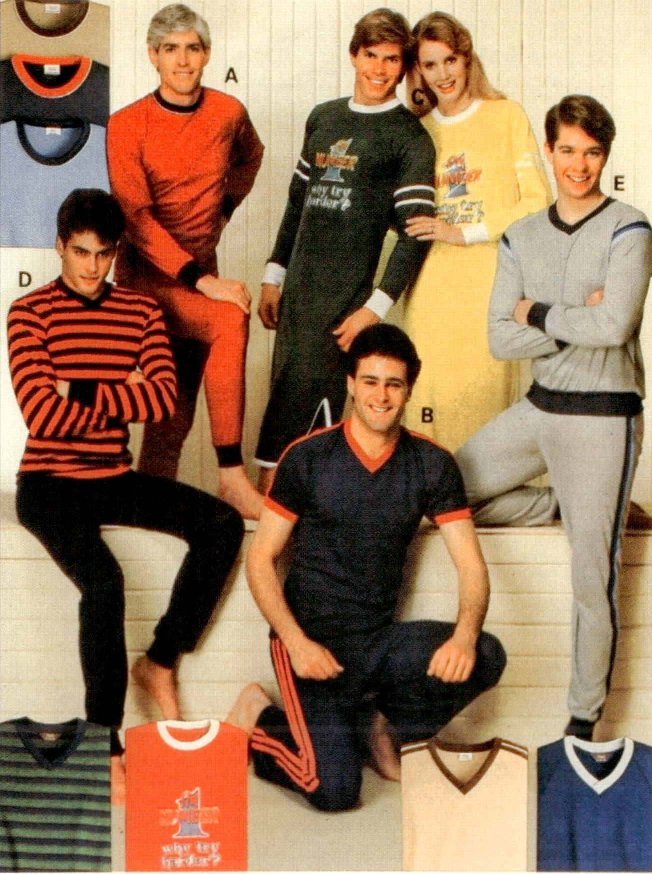

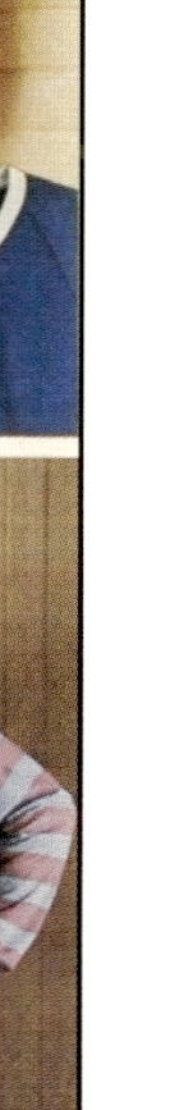

Cotton and polyester nightwear in a variety of styles are knit to stretch and move with you. *Fall/Winter 1984.*

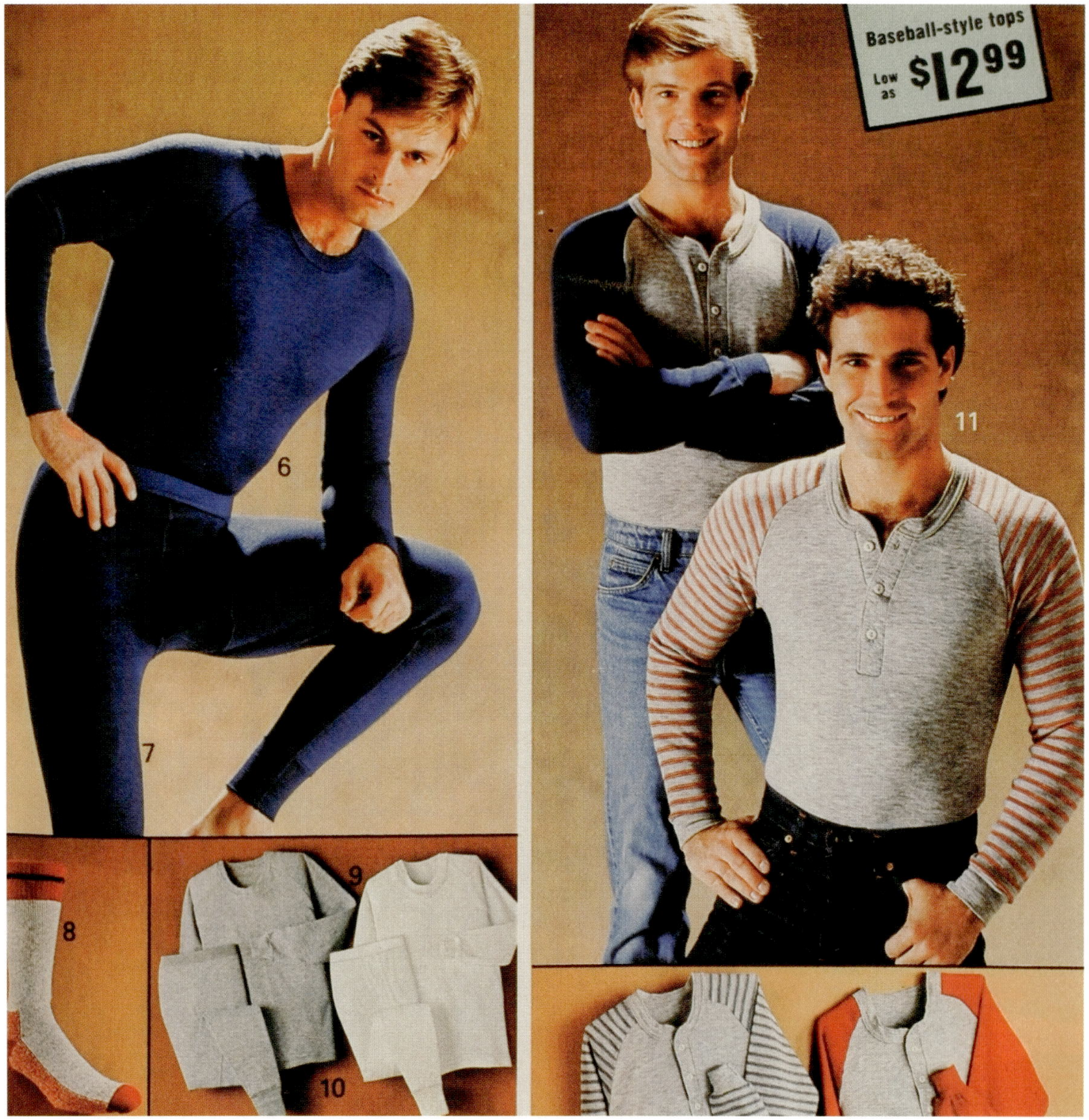

Lightweight Ameraklon® polypropylene olefin separates are perfect for winter sports or worn with jeans for a sporty look. *Fall/Winter 1985*

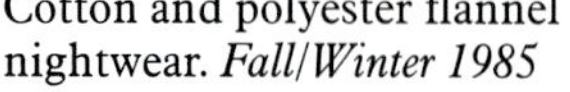

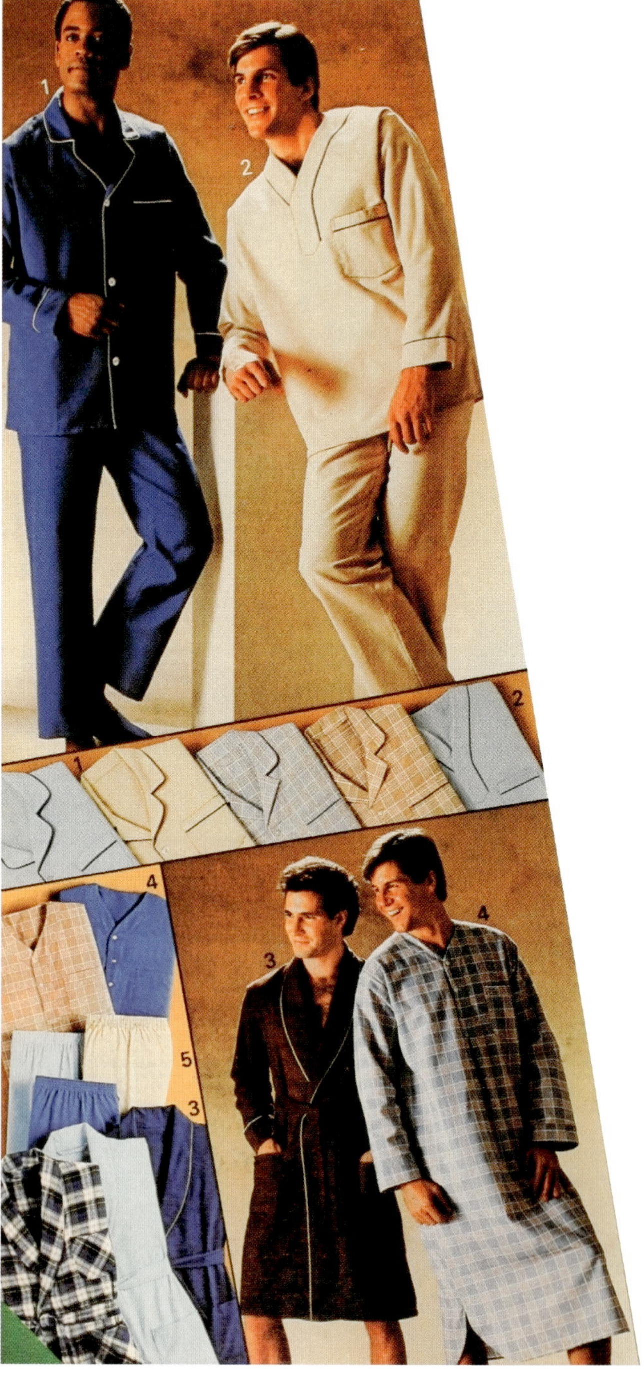

Cotton and polyester flannel nightwear. *Fall/Winter 1985*

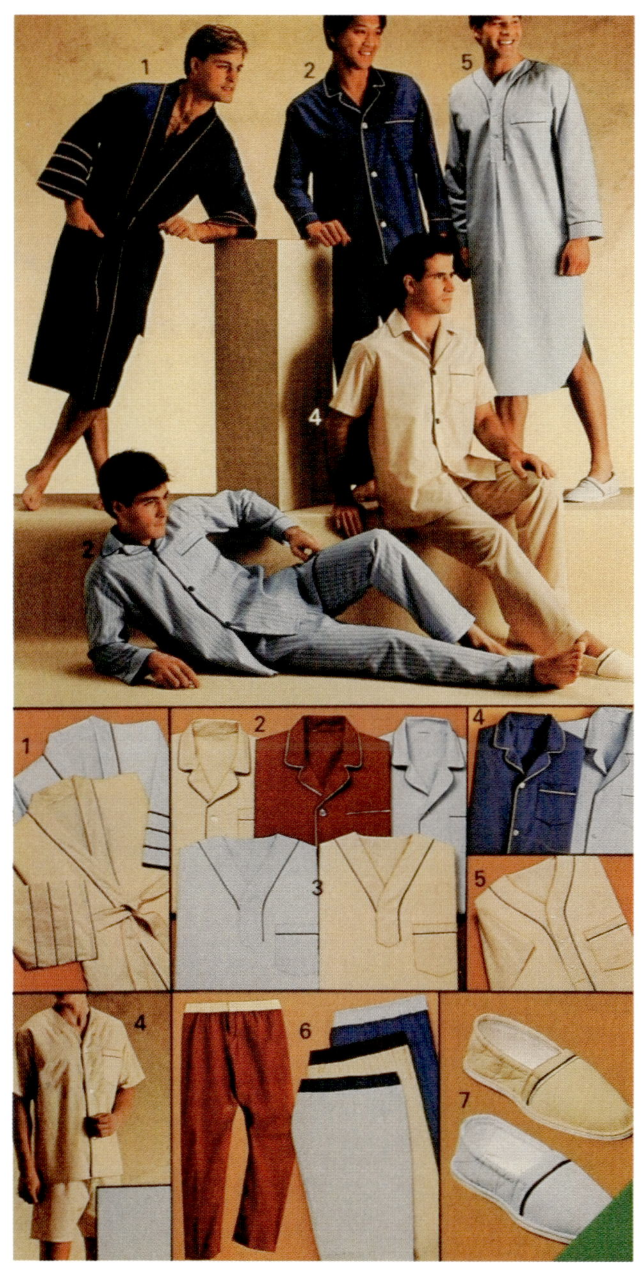

Cotton and polyester robes, pajamas, and night shirt. *Fall/Winter 1985*

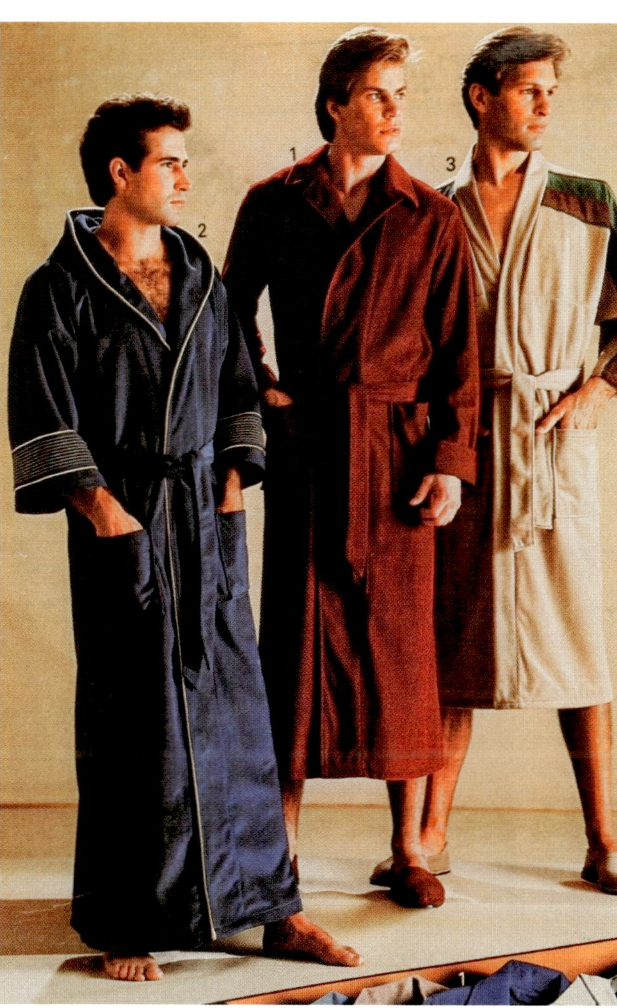

Full-length hooded robe of plush fleece velour, softly fleeced heavyweight velour robe, and mid-calf kimono. *Fall/Winter 1985*

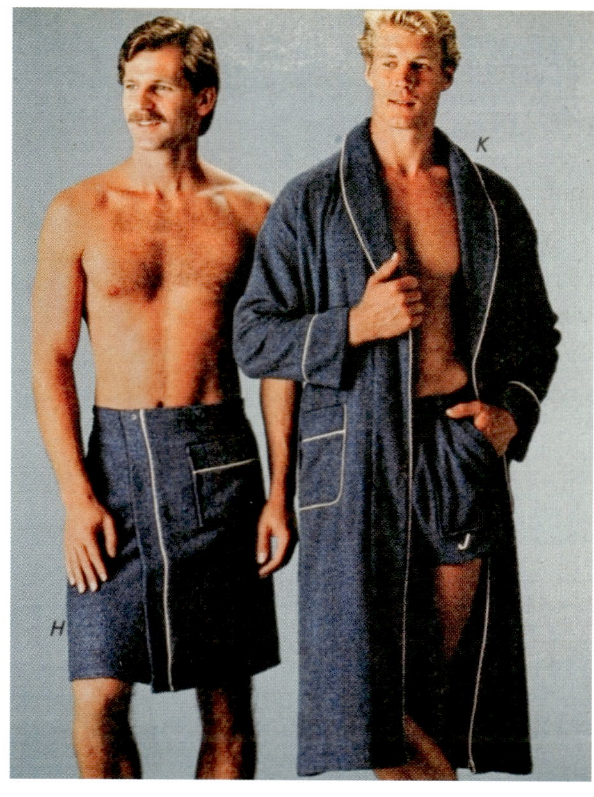

Heavyweight looped cotton terry knee-length wrap, sleep shorts, and shawl collar robe. *Spring/Summer 1986*

Swimwear

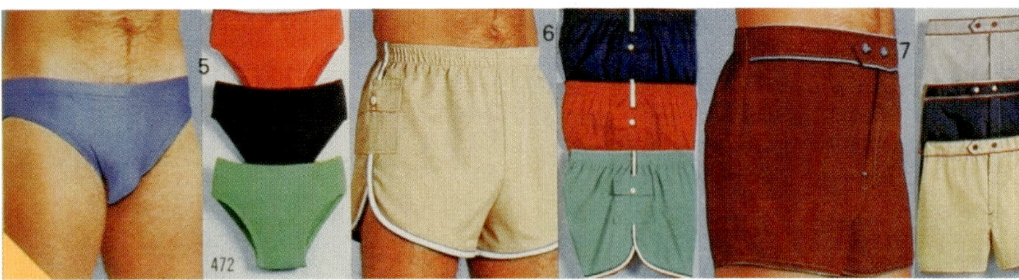

Polyester and cotton coordinated swimwear, brief and boxer style trunks. *Spring/Summer 1985*

Footwear

Athletic Shoes

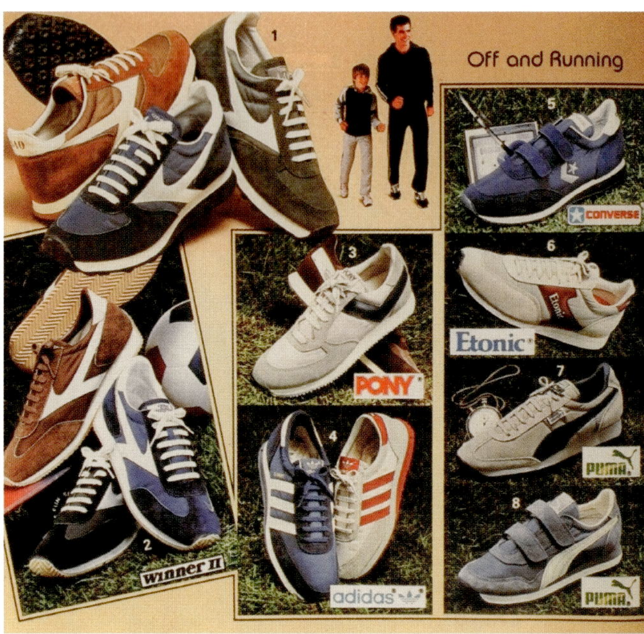

Running shoes for boys and men. Brands pictured are Winner II®, Pony®, Converse®, Etonic®, Puma®, and Adidas®. *Spring/Summer 1984.*

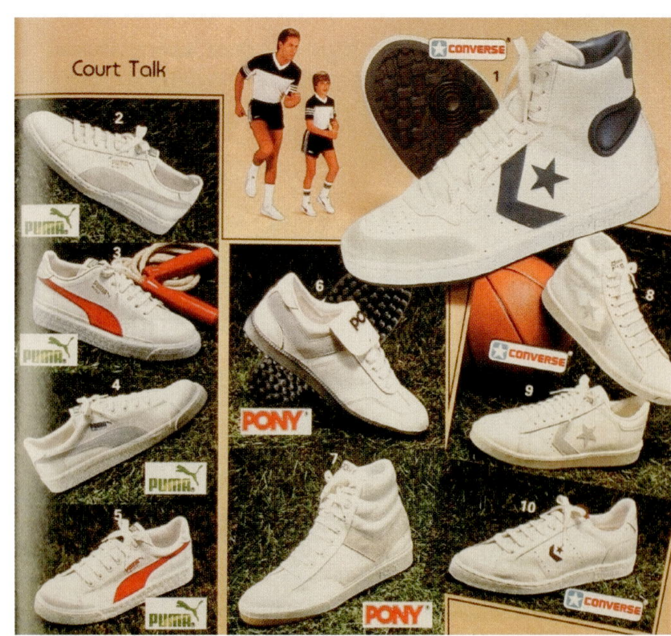

Men's basketball and sport shoes in popular brand names such as Puma®, Pony®, and Converse®. *Spring/Summer 1984.*

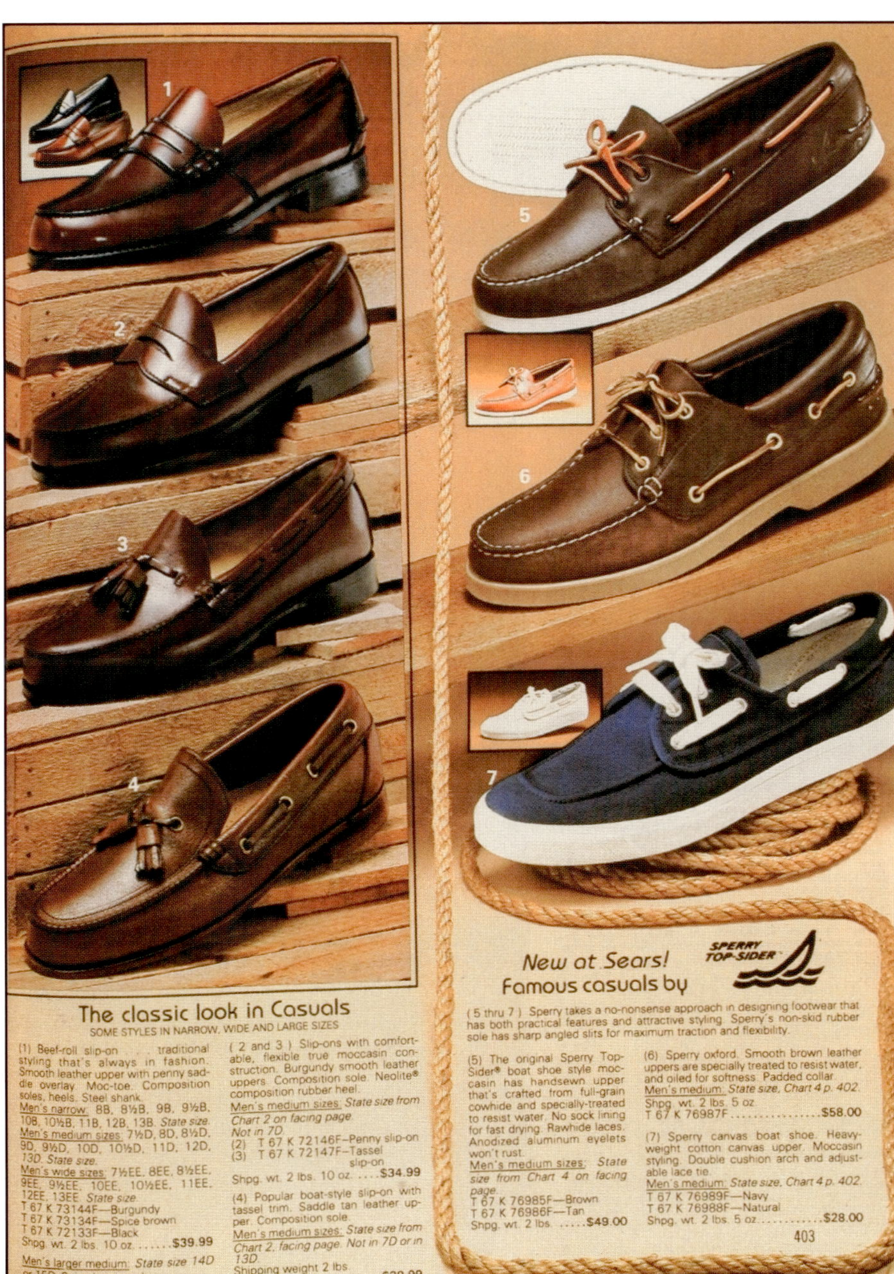

Men's casual slip-on shoes and Sperry Top-Sider® boat, leather upper, and canvas boat shoes. *Spring/Summer 1984.*

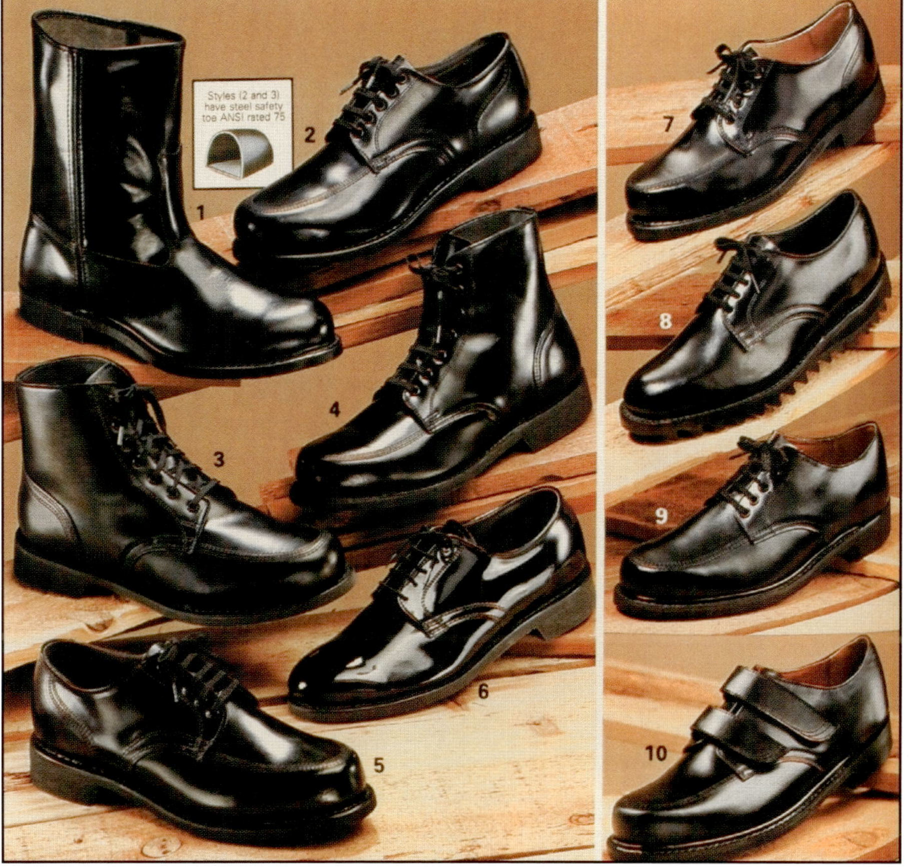

Men's leather uppers in a variety of styles. *Fall/Winter 1984.*

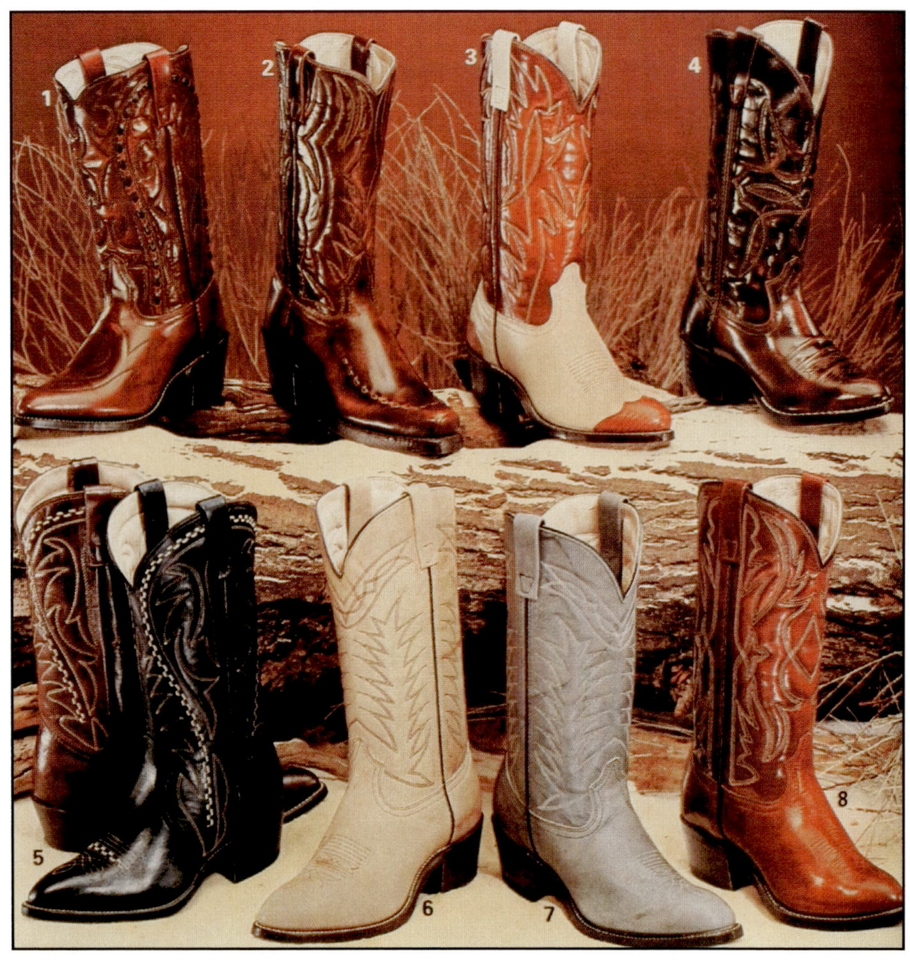

Western styled boots have composition soles, steel shanks, and Goodyear welt construction. *Fall/Winter 1984.*

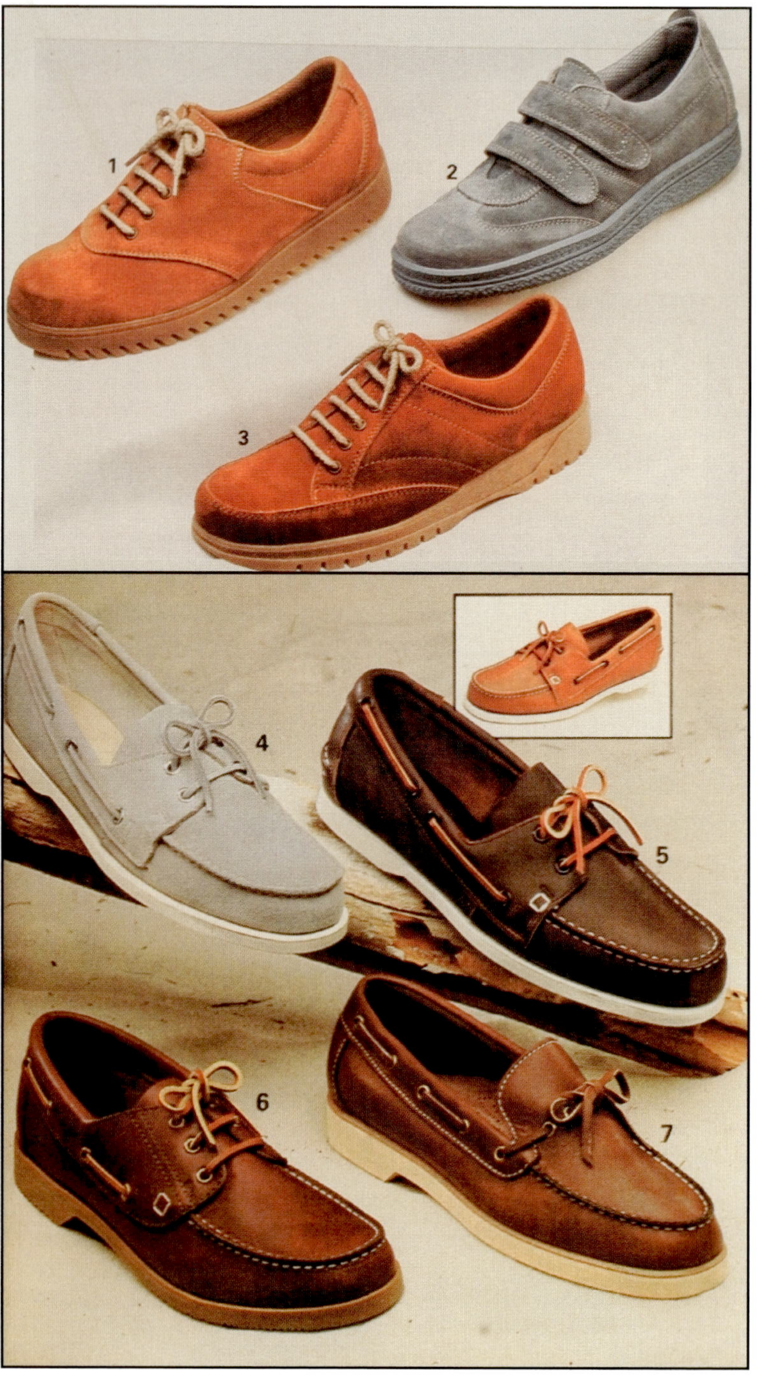

Men's casual oxfords with sueded split-leather uppers. Boat shoe in light gray sueded split-leather uppers, boat shoe with true moccasin construction, boat oxford in smooth brown leather upper, and slip-on boat shoe in brown leather upper. *Fall/Winter 1984.*

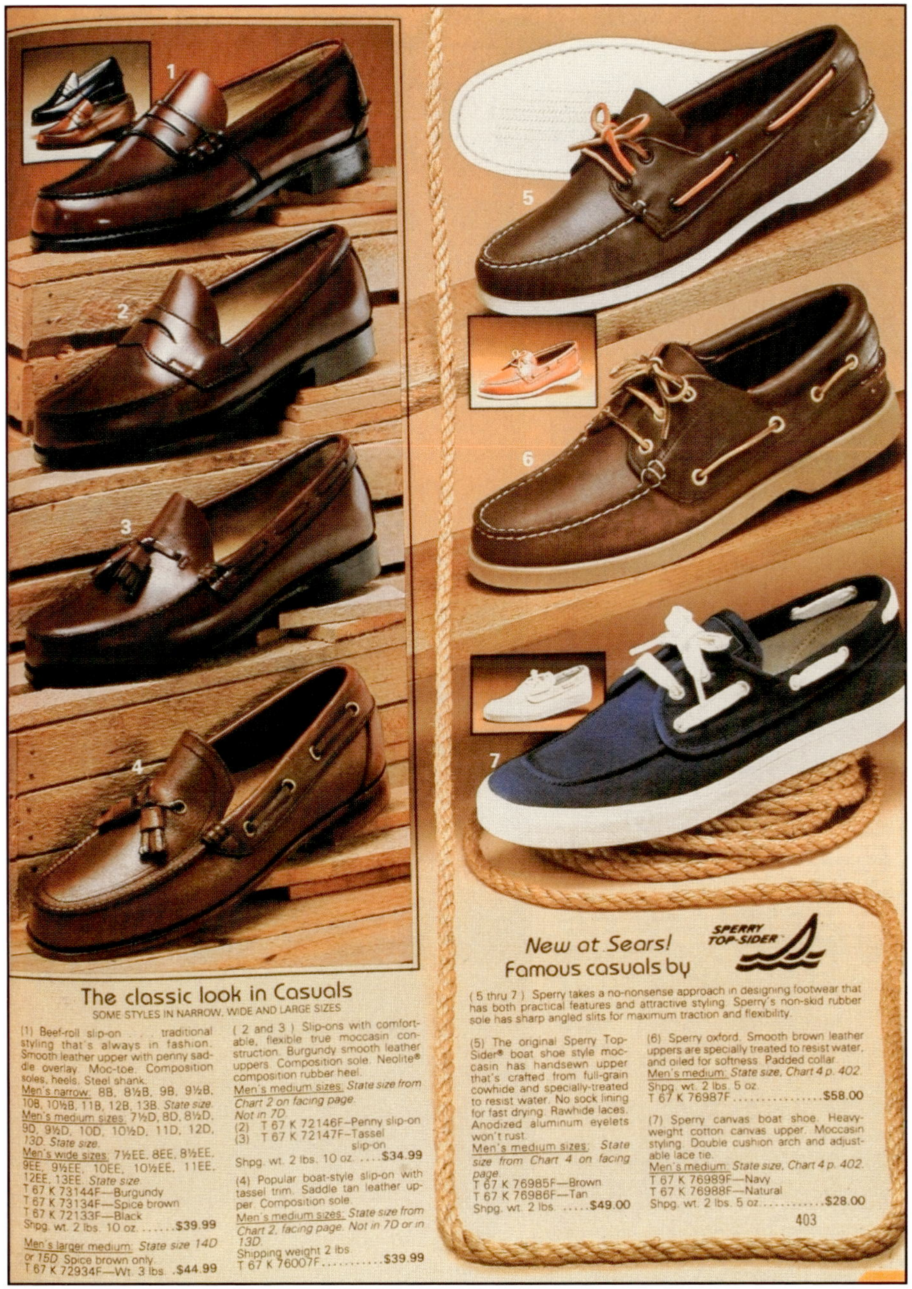

Casual/Dressy

The classic look in Casuals

SOME STYLES IN NARROW, WIDE AND LARGE SIZES

(1) Beef-roll slip-on . . . traditional styling that's always in fashion. Smooth leather upper with penny saddle overlay. Moc-toe. Composition soles, heels. Steel shank.
Men's narrow: 8B, 8½B, 9B, 9½B, 10B, 10½B, 11B, 12B, 13B. *State size.*
Men's medium sizes: 7½D, 8D, 8½D, 9D, 9½D, 10D, 10½D, 11D, 12D, 13D. *State size.*
Men's wide sizes: 7½EE, 8EE, 8½EE, 9EE, 9½EE, 10EE, 10½EE, 11EE, 12EE, 13EE. *State size.*
T 67 K 73144F—Burgundy
T 67 K 73134F—Spice brown
T 67 K 72133F—Black
Shpg. wt. 2 lbs. 10 oz. $39.99

Men's larger medium: *State size 14D or 15D.* Spice brown only.
T 67 K 72934F—Wt. 3 lbs. . $44.99

(2 and 3) Slip-ons with comfortable, flexible true moccasin construction. Burgundy smooth leather uppers. Composition sole. Neolite® composition rubber heel.
Men's medium sizes: *State size from Chart 2 on facing page. Not in 7D.*
(2) T 67 K 72146F–Penny slip-on
(3) T 67 K 72147F–Tassel slip-on
Shpg. wt. 2 lbs. 10 oz. $34.99

(4) Popular boat-style slip-on with tassel trim. Saddle tan leather upper. Composition sole.
Men's medium sizes: *State size from Chart 2, facing page. Not in 7D or in 13D.*
Shipping weight 2 lbs.
T 67 K 76007F $39.99

New at Sears!
Famous casuals by SPERRY TOP-SIDER

(5 thru 7) Sperry takes a no-nonsense approach in designing footwear that has both practical features and attractive styling. Sperry's non-skid rubber sole has sharp angled slits for maximum traction and flexibility.

(5) The original Sperry Top-Sider® boat shoe style moccasin has handsewn upper that's crafted from full-grain cowhide and specially-treated to resist water. No sock lining for fast drying. Rawhide laces. Anodized aluminum eyelets won't rust.
Men's medium sizes: *State size from Chart 4 on facing page.*
T 67 K 76985F—Brown
T 67 K 76986F—Tan
Shpg. wt. 2 lbs. $49.00

(6) Sperry oxford. Smooth brown leather uppers are specially treated to resist water, and oiled for softness. Padded collar.
Men's medium: *State size, Chart 4 p. 402.*
Shpg. wt. 2 lbs. 5 oz.
T 67 K 76987F $58.00

(7) Sperry canvas boat shoe. Heavy-weight cotton canvas upper. Moccasin styling. Double cushion arch and adjustable lace tie.
Men's medium: *State size, Chart 4 p. 402.*
T 67 K 76989F—Navy
T 67 K 76988F—Natural
Shpg. wt. 2 lbs. 5 oz. $28.00

403

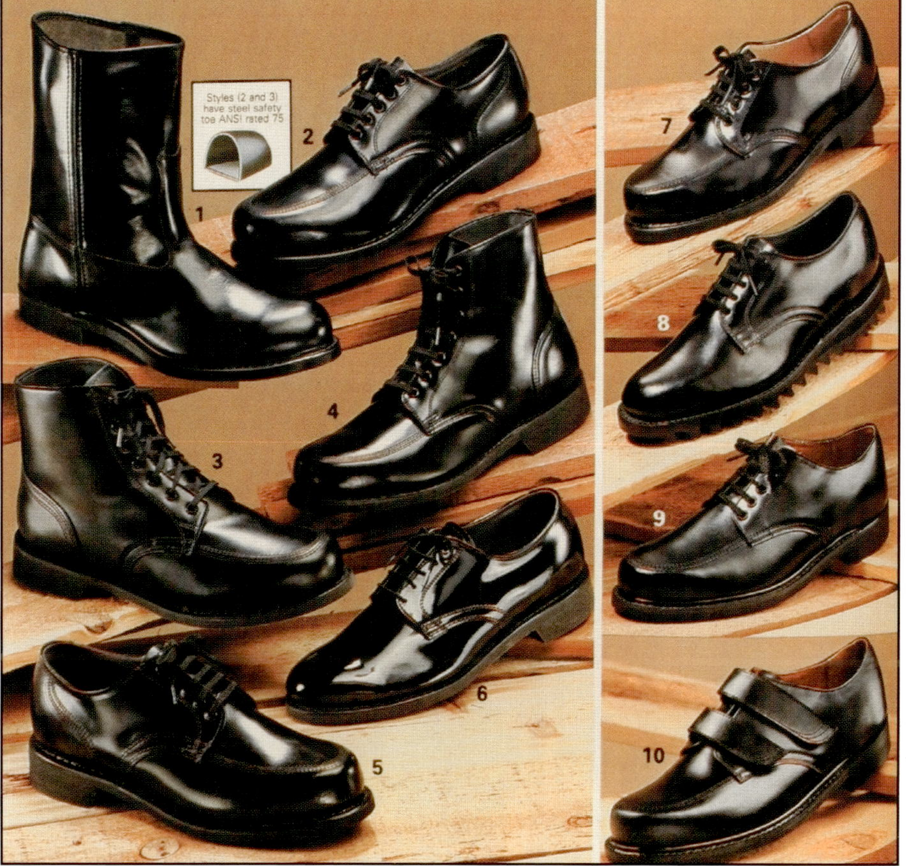

Men's leather uppers in a variety of styles. *Fall/Winter 1984.*

Men's casual slip-on shoes and Sperry Top-Sider® boat, leather upper, and canvas boat shoes. *Spring/Summer 1984.*

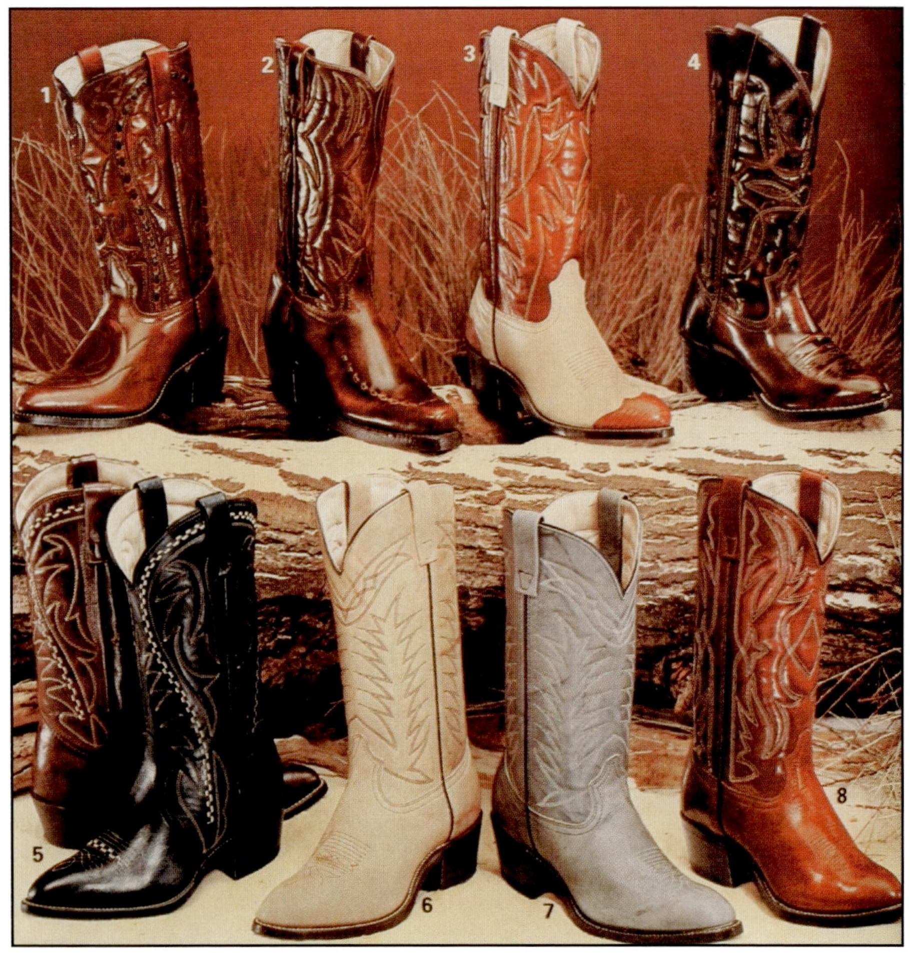

Western styled boots have composition soles, steel shanks, and Goodyear welt construction. *Fall/Winter 1984.*

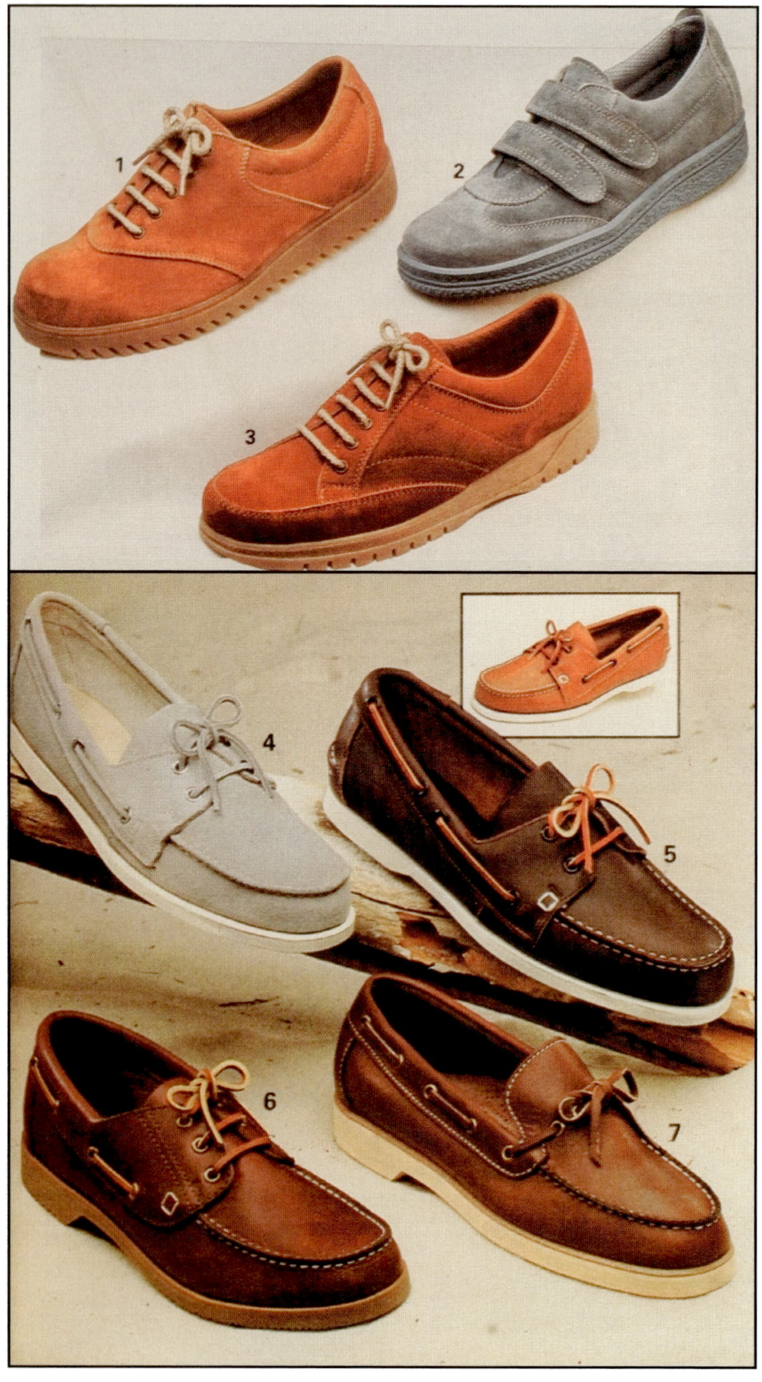

Men's casual oxfords with sueded split-leather uppers. Boat shoe in light gray sueded split-leather uppers, boat shoe with true moccasin construction, boat oxford in smooth brown leather upper, and slip-on boat shoe in brown leather upper. *Fall/Winter 1984.*

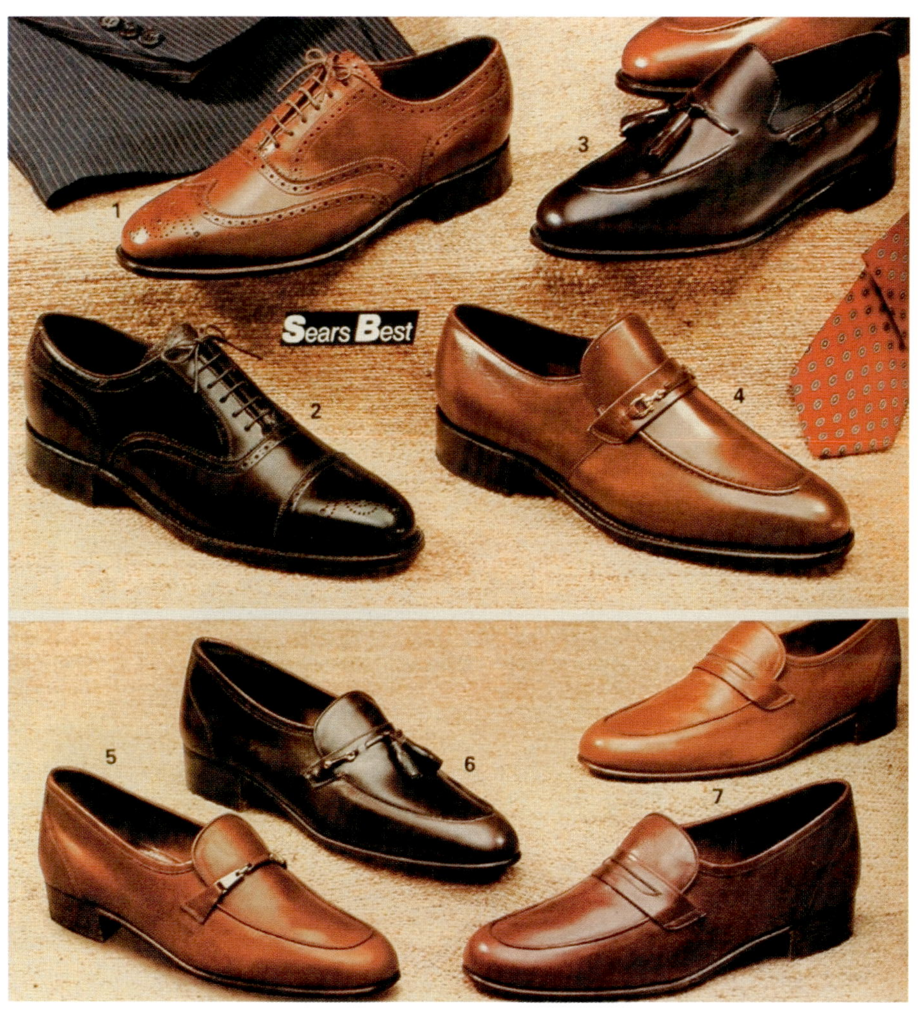

Stylish dress shoes with calfskin leather uppers. *Fall/Winter 1984.*

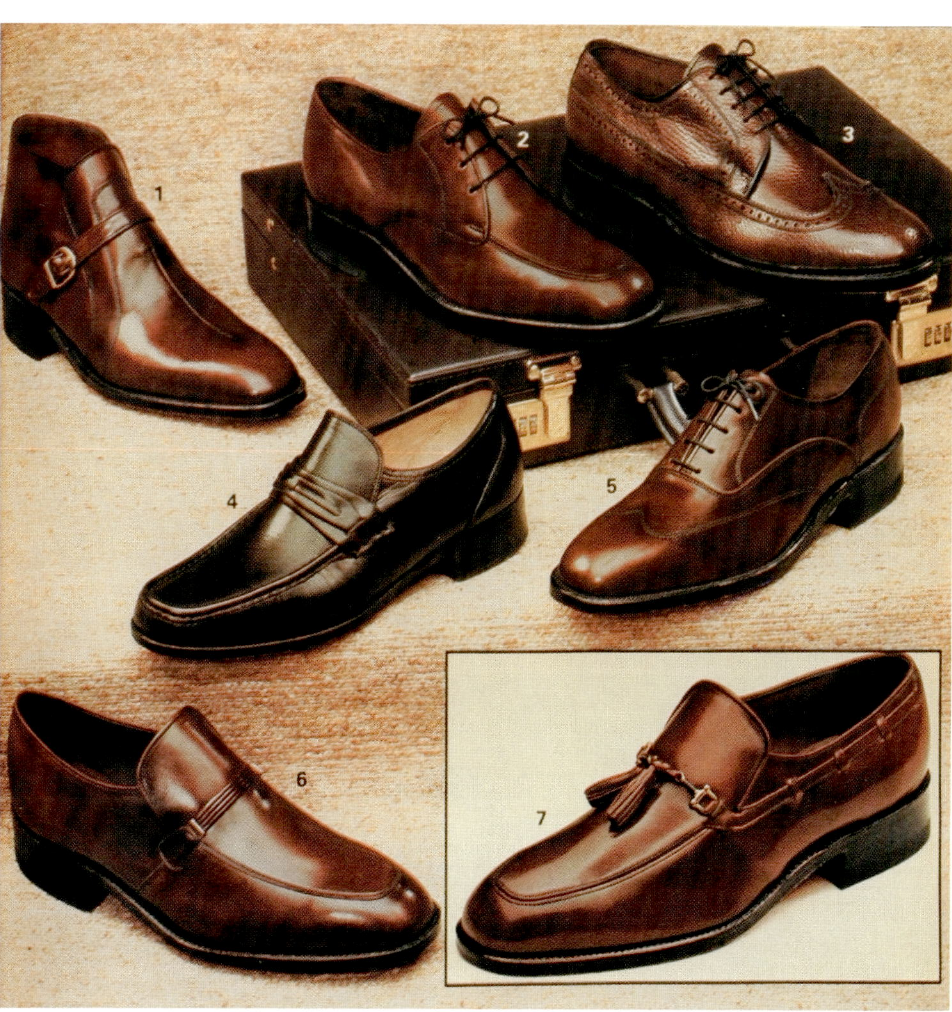

Grained leather upper dress shoes for men. *Fall/Winter 1984.*

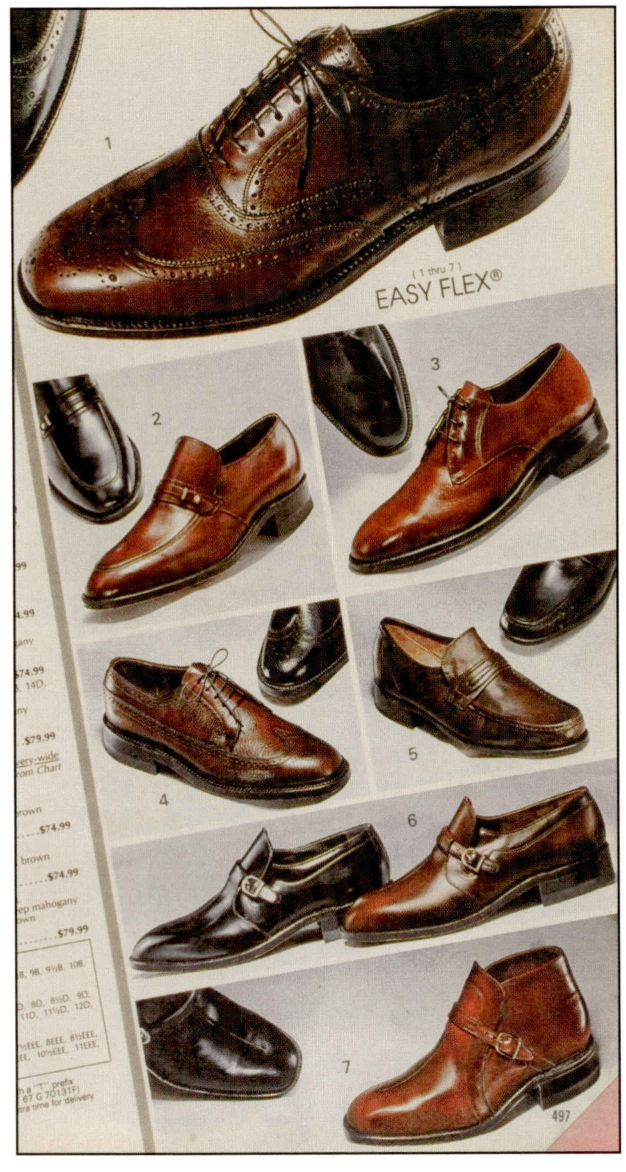

Classic styling in a wide selection of Sears Easy Flex® leather uppers. *Fall/Winter 1985*

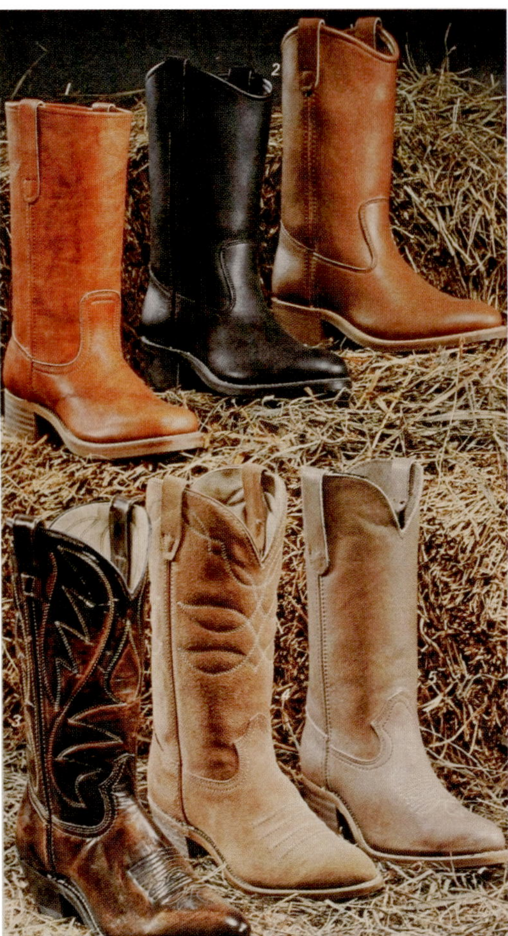

Western style boots in rich leather or sueded split leather styles. *Spring/Summer 1986*

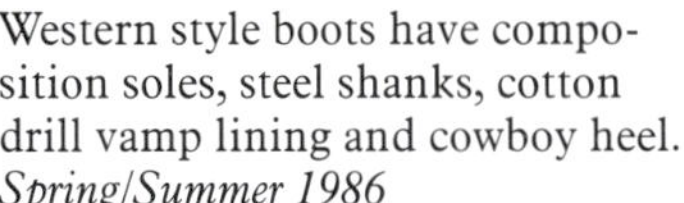

Western style boots have composition soles, steel shanks, cotton drill vamp lining and cowboy heel. *Spring/Summer 1986*

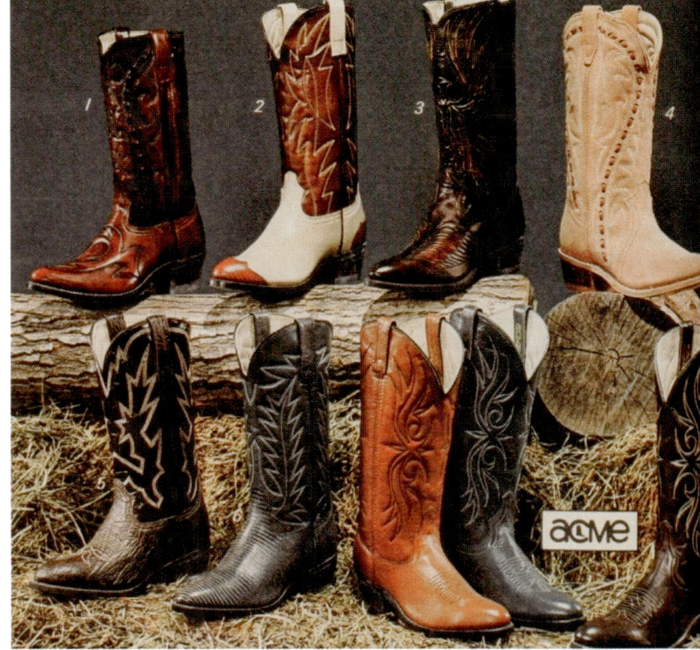

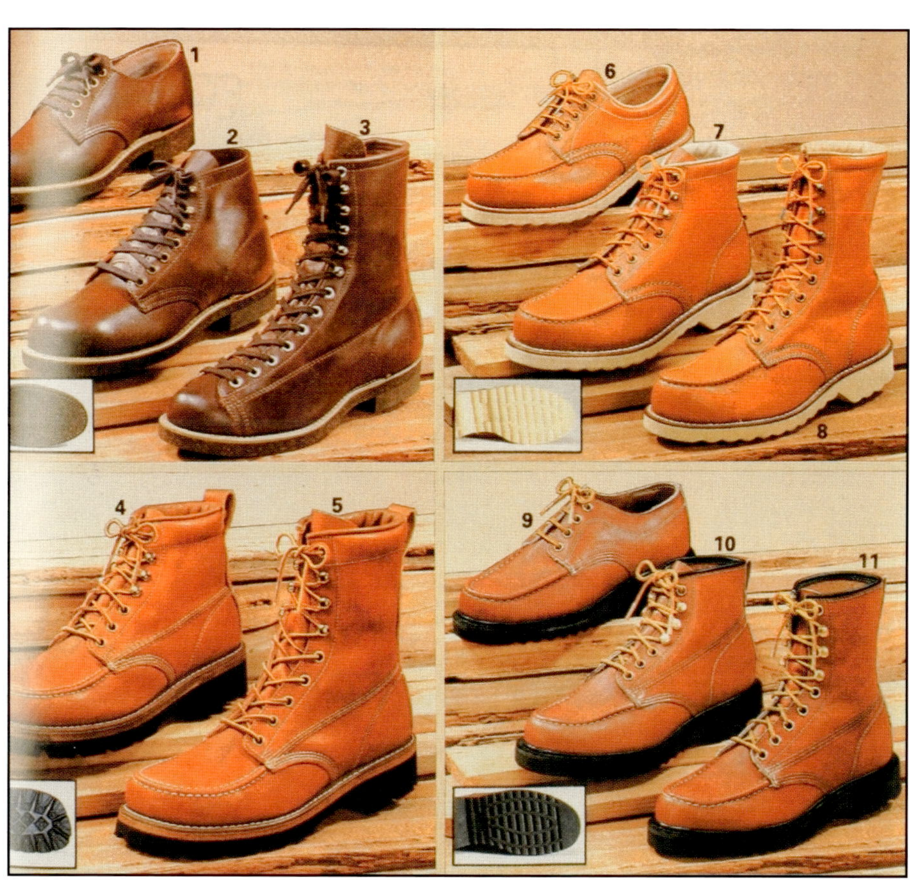

Rugged work shoes and boots have leather uppers and Goodyear's welt construction. *Spring/Summer 1984.*

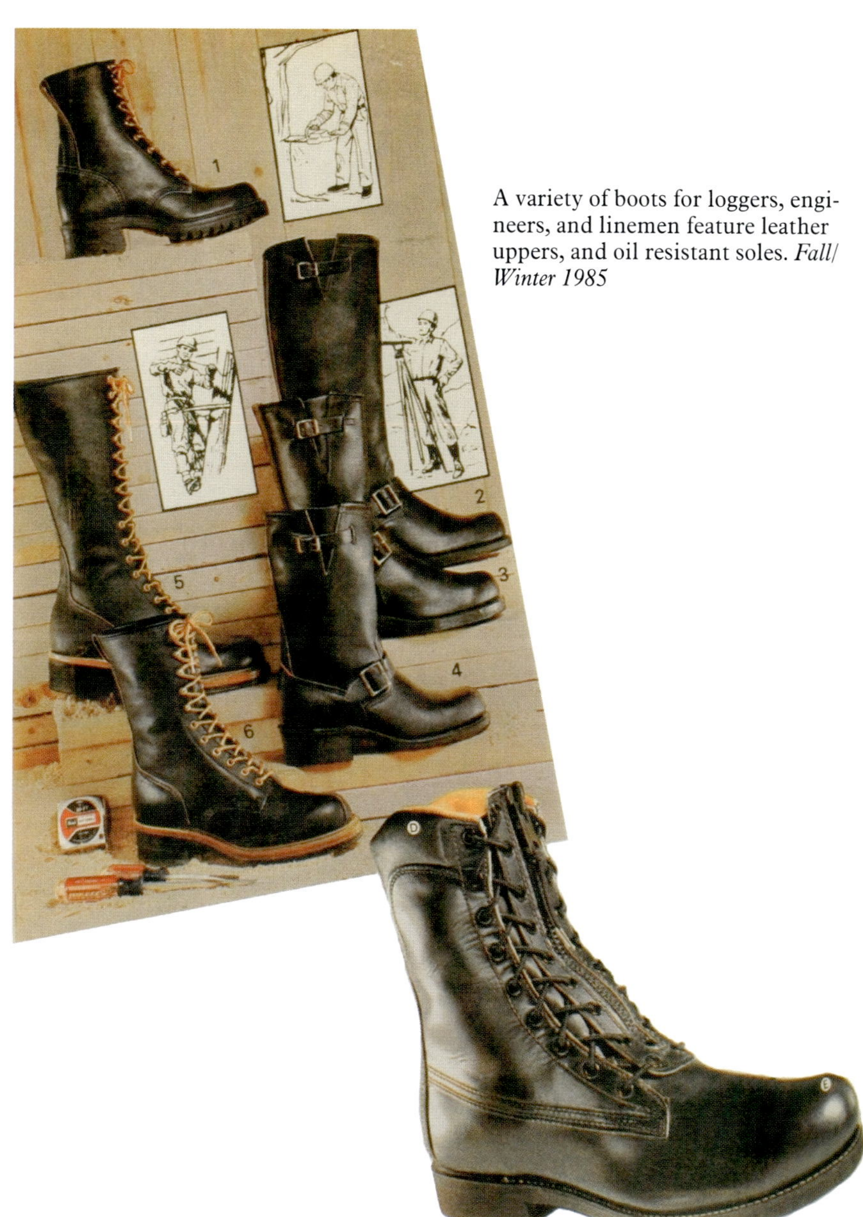

A variety of boots for loggers, engineers, and linemen feature leather uppers, and oil resistant soles. *Fall/ Winter 1985*

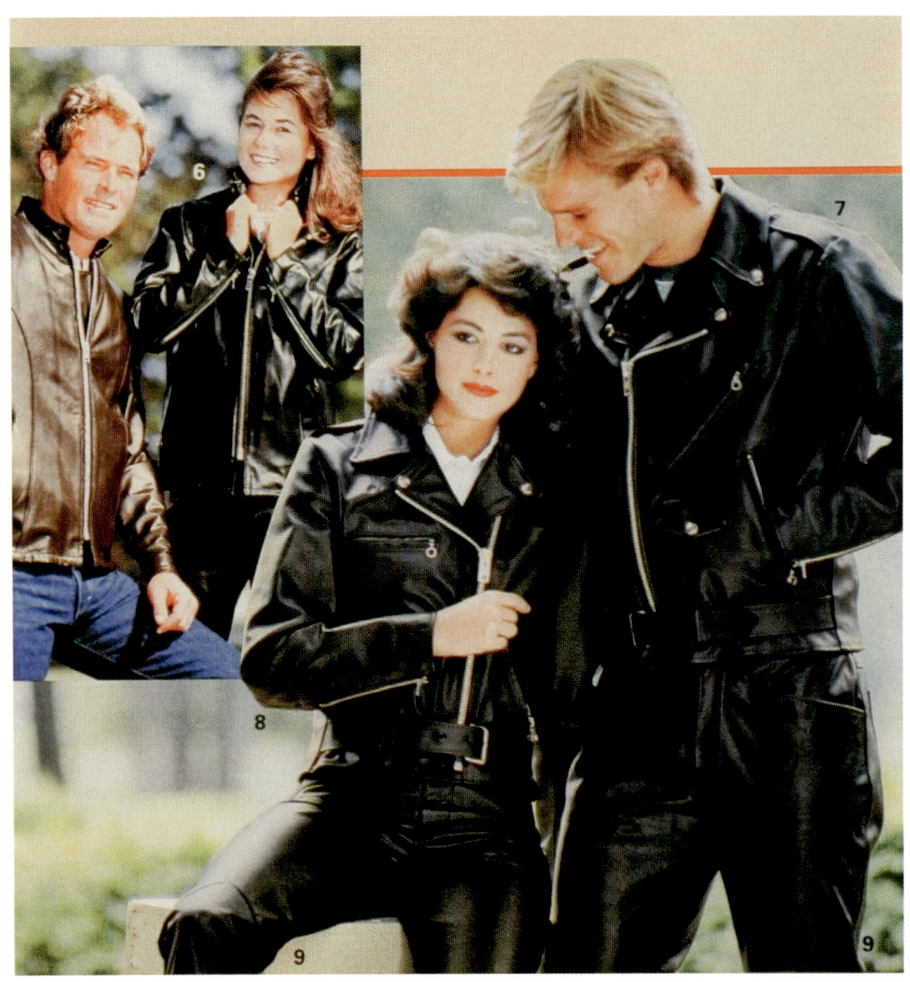

Leather motorcycle jackets and pants for men and women. *Spring/Summer 1984.*

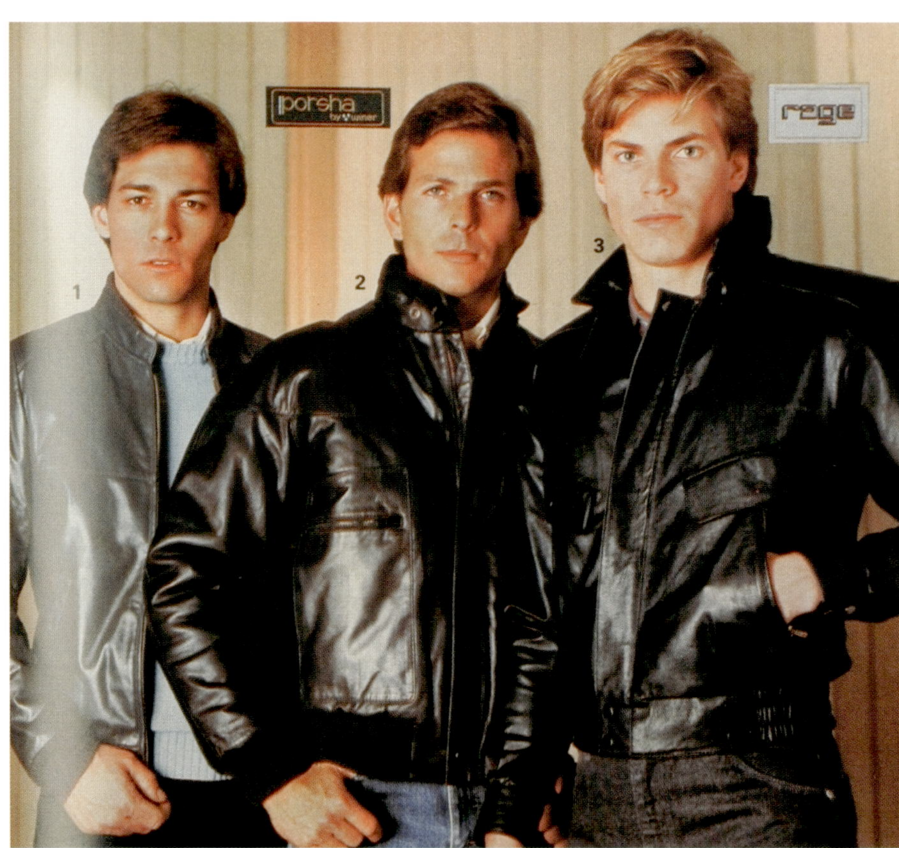

Top-grain cowhide leather jackets. *Fall/Winter 1984.*

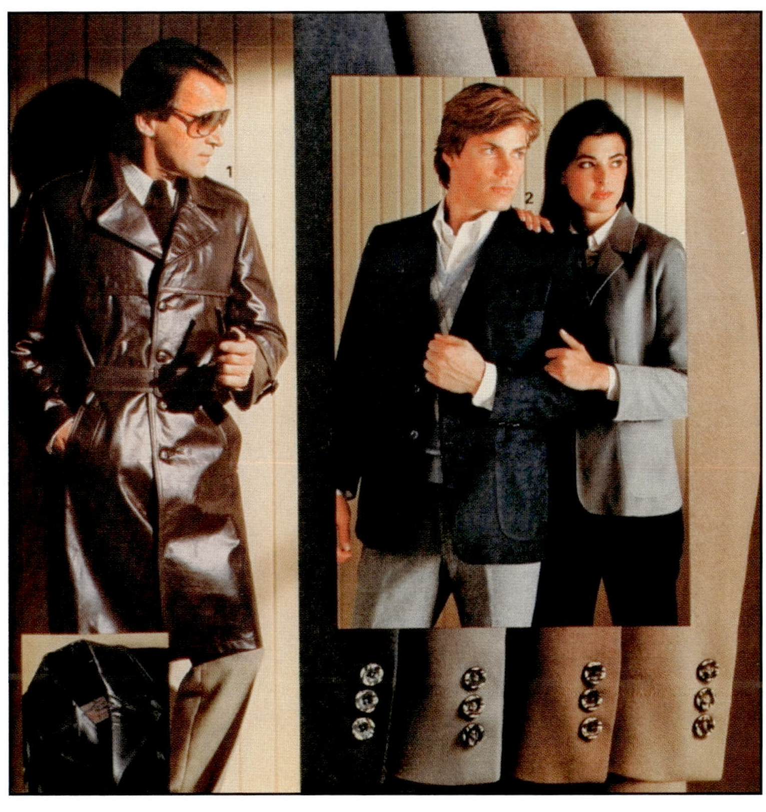

Top-grain cowhide trench coat has a zip-out liner. Golden Touch® blazers have a rich sueded texture. *Fall/Winter 1984.*

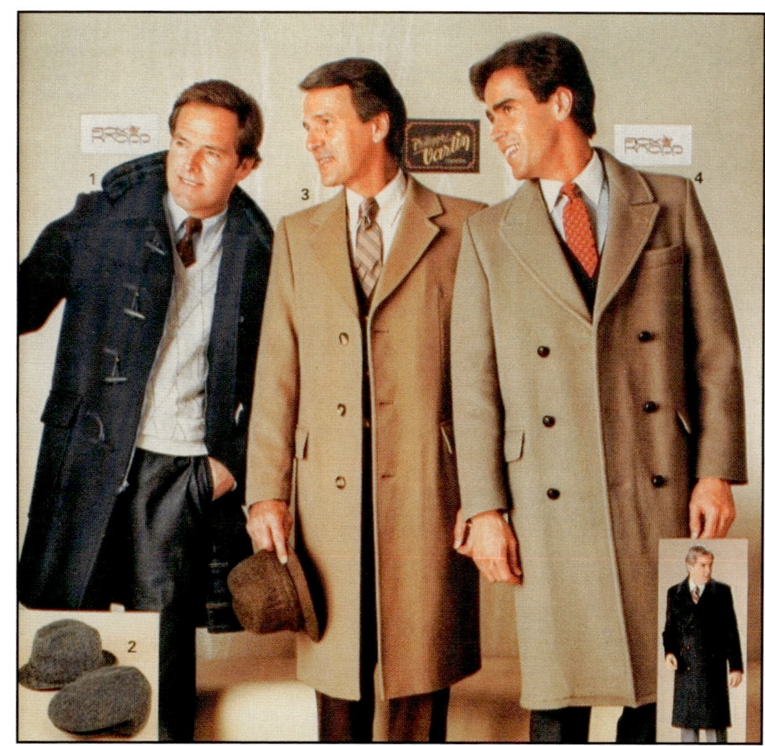

Fox Knapp wool-blend toggle coat. Phillippe Vartin single breasted top coat is 100% virgin wool. Fox Knapp 100% wool double breasted top coat. *Fall/Winter 1984.*

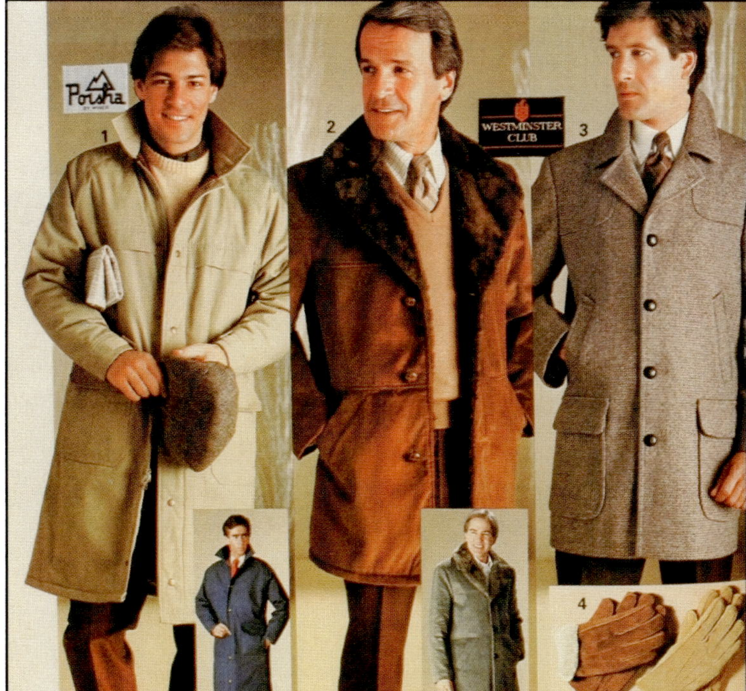

Full-length poplin coat with cotton and polyester fill. Corduroy suburban coat from Westminster Club®. Tweed suburban coat from Westminster Club® has a classic British look. *Fall/Winter 1984.*

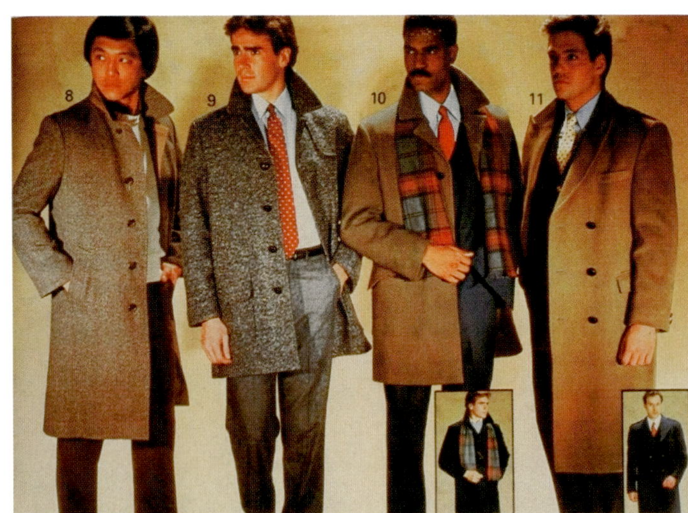

Reversible tweed coat from Cooper®, wool tweed suburban coat by Westminster Club®, wool and nylon dress coat with plaid scarf and plaid lining, classic British Warmer coat is 100% virgin wool from Egon Von Furstenberg®. *Fall/Winter 1985*

Rugged 1-piece suit has polyester insulation, elastic waist and leg zippers. Nylon-lined parka has polyester insulation and zipper/snap front. Rain parka and pants with nylon taffeta lining. *Fall/Winter 1986*

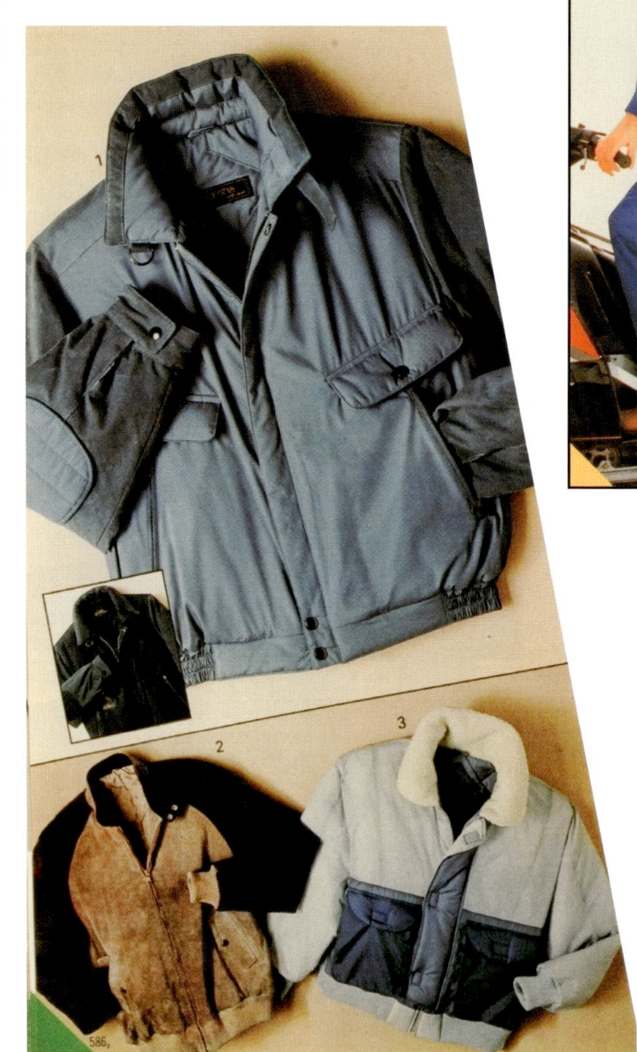

Polyester and cotton woven poplin shell coat has elbow patches, and adjustable cuffs. Split pigskin and wool blend jacket has trimmed cuffs and bottom. Jacket with acrylic shearling-look pile collar. *Fall/Winter 1985*

Teen Girls' Fashions

Dressy/Prom Dresses

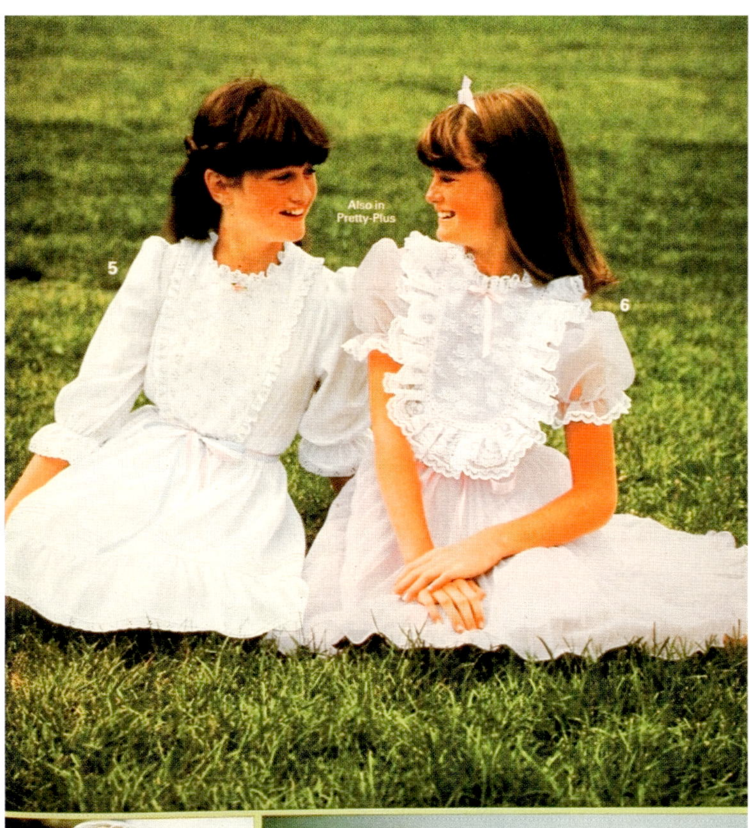

White peasant dress with multi-colored sash is trimmed with eyelet lace. Lilac dress with white lace has a ribbon waist tie and a wired hem. *Spring/Summer 1984.*

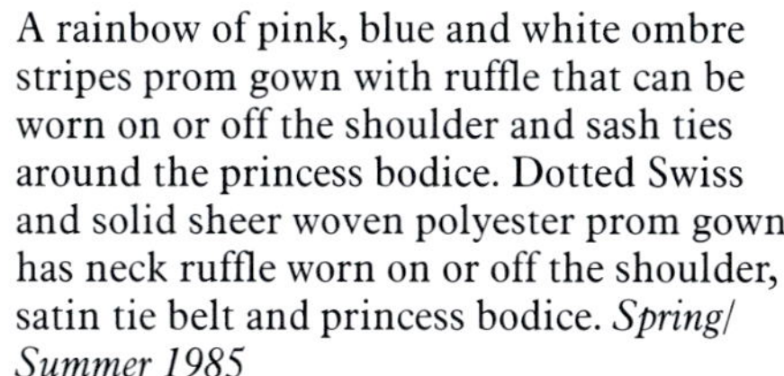

A rainbow of pink, blue and white ombre stripes prom gown with ruffle that can be worn on or off the shoulder and sash ties around the princess bodice. Dotted Swiss and solid sheer woven polyester prom gown has neck ruffle worn on or off the shoulder, satin tie belt and princess bodice. *Spring/Summer 1985*

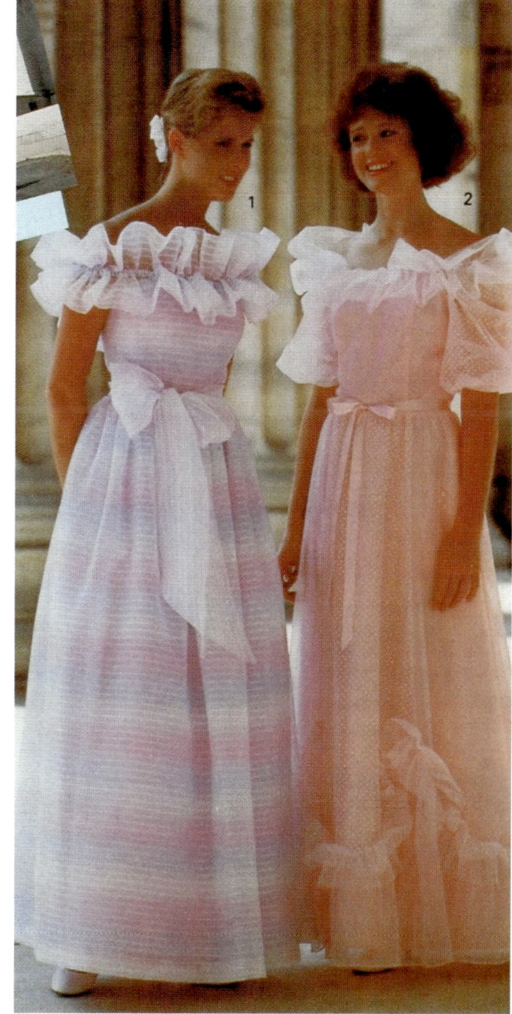

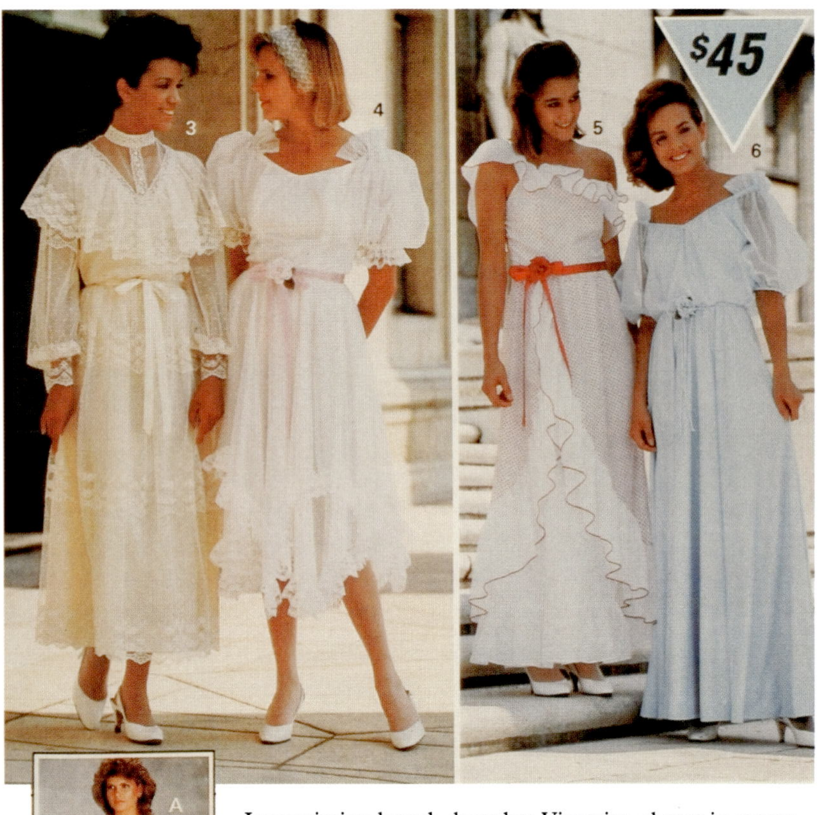

Intermission length dress has Victorian charm in cream lace. Intermission length dress with lace trimmed handkerchief-hem double skirt and ribbon belt tie with flower. Red and white sheer pin-dot dress with red satin tie belt with flower. Full-length dress in dressy chiffon blouson with shoulder ruffles and spaghetti tie belt with flower. *Spring/Summer 1985*

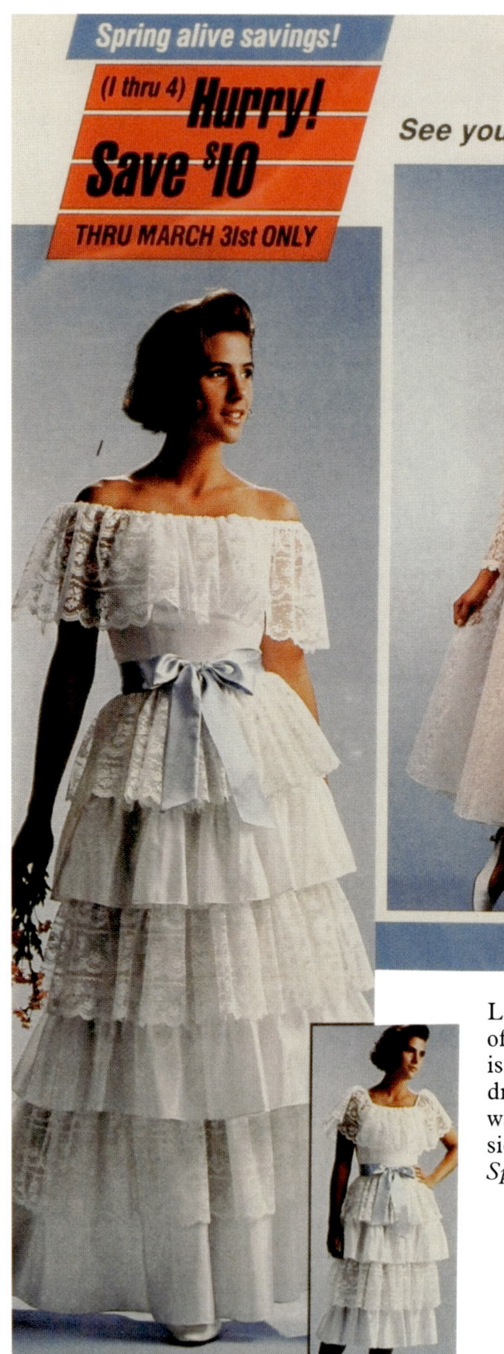

Lace and taffeta prom dress can be worn on or off the shoulder or in two different lengths and is accented by a blue satin sash. Lace over satin dress has a Princess bodice that flows into a "V" waist. Victorian style white lace gown with illusion neck and sleeves in polyester and acetate. *Spring/Summer 1986*

Casual

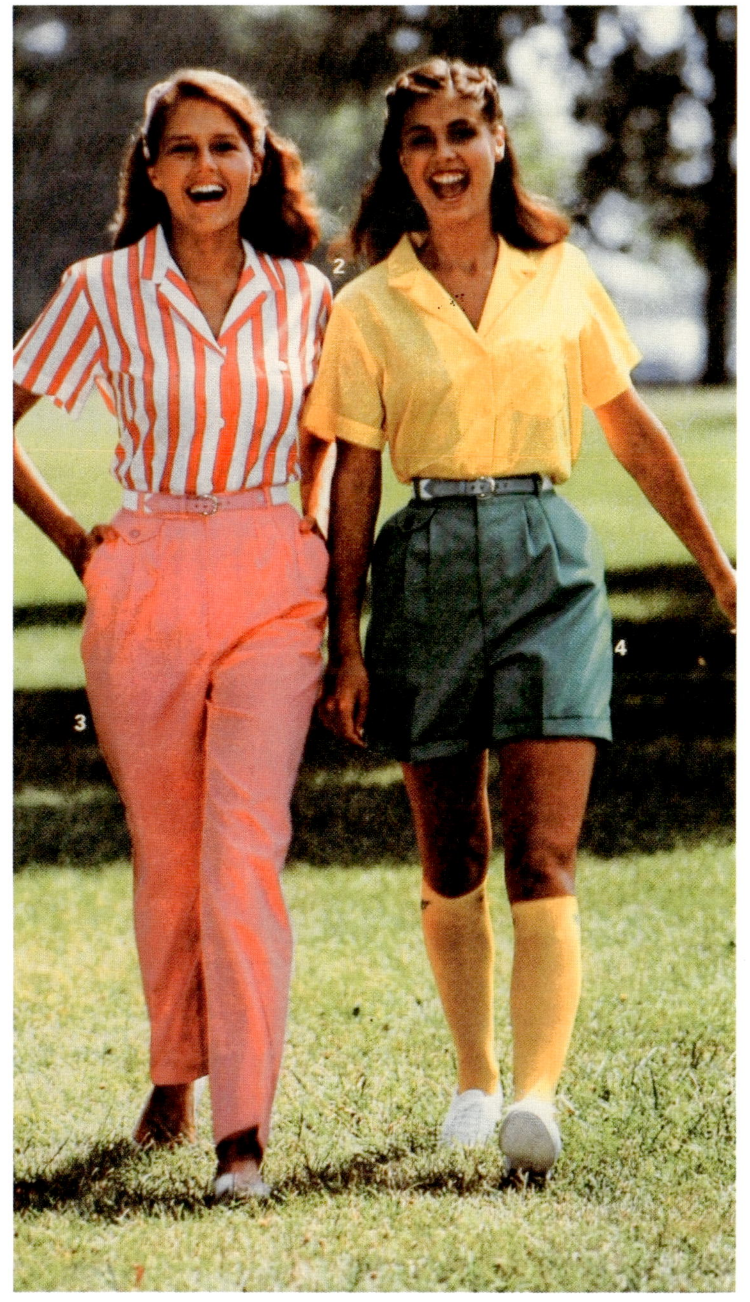

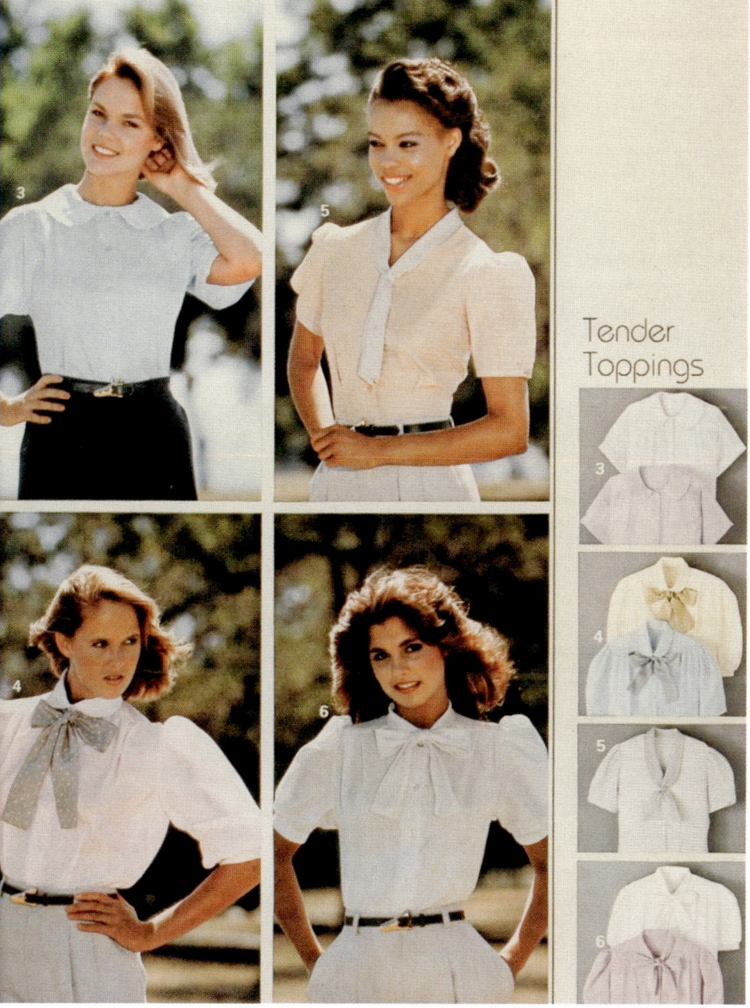

Feminine woven polyester shirts have embroidered collars, fresh print bows, attached front tie with slip-through loop, and self tie bows. *Spring/ Summer 1984.*

Color-coordinated separates in stripes and solids made of woven polyester and cotton. *Spring/Summer 1984.*

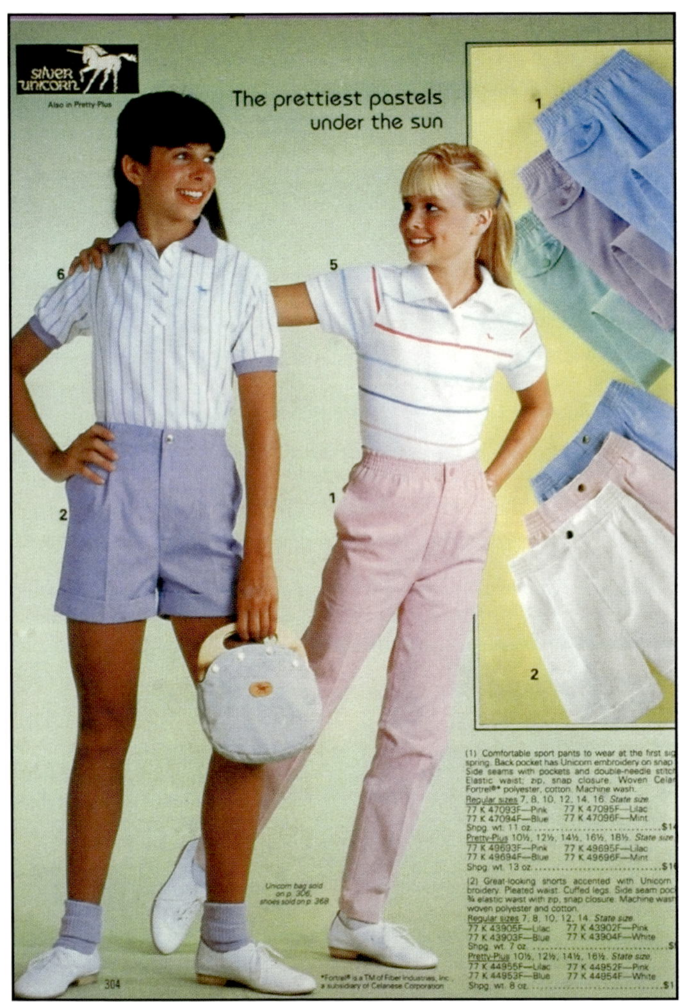

Cotton and polyester sports pants, shorts, and striped tops in pretty pastels. *Spring/Summer 1984.*

Plum color jeans in polyester and cotton, all cotton denim baggy jeans with red stripes, and all cotton denim striped skirt has 2 front pockets. *Fall/Winter 1984.*

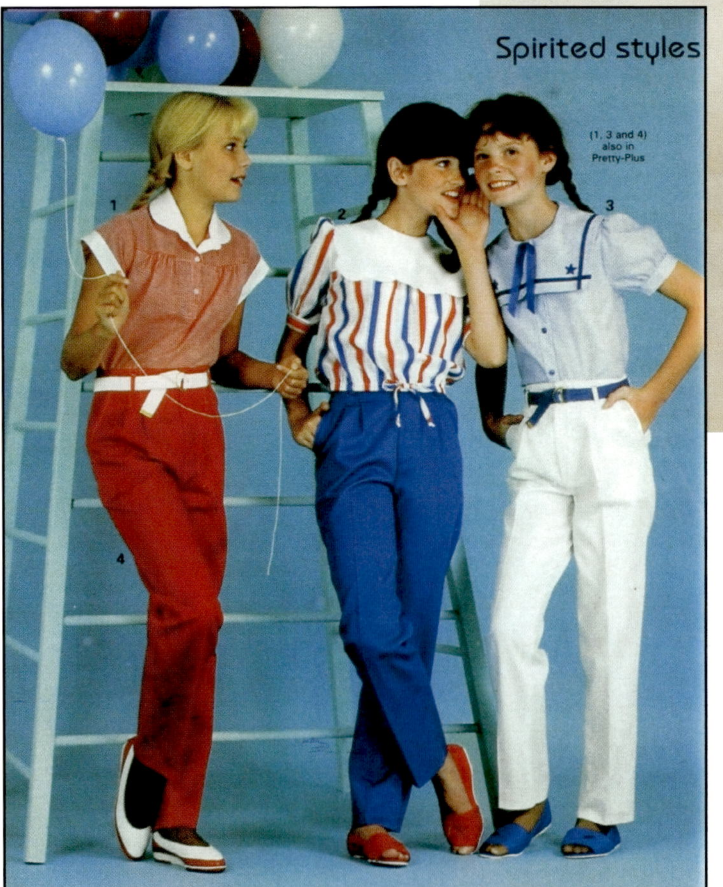

Red check blouse and pleated jeans, striped blouson blouse with scalloped edge and pleated jeans, blouse with stars and stripes has nautical collar and ribbon tie with pleated jeans. All are a cotton and polyester blend. *Spring/Summer 1984.*

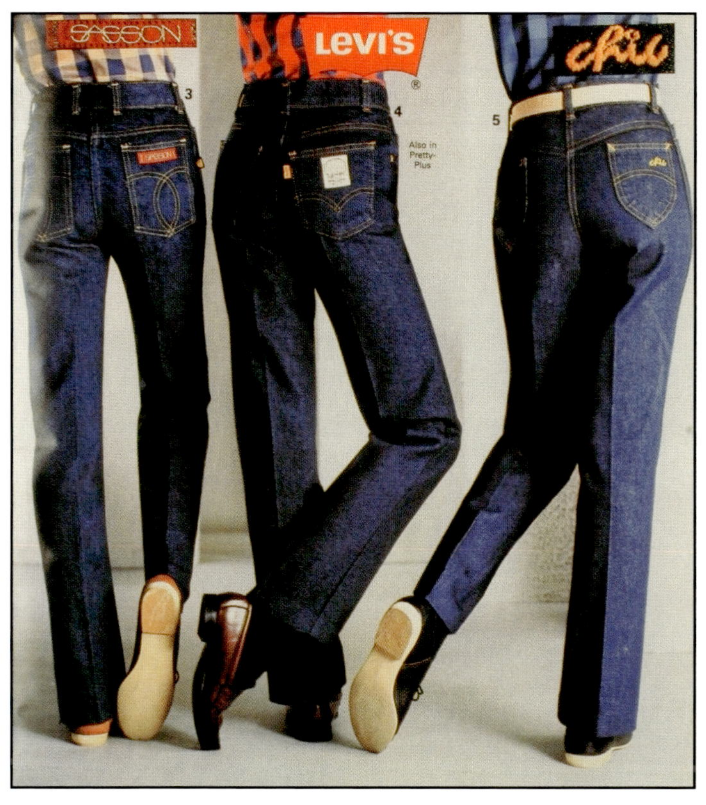

Brand name jeans that are famous for their quality and fit. *Fall/Winter 1984.*

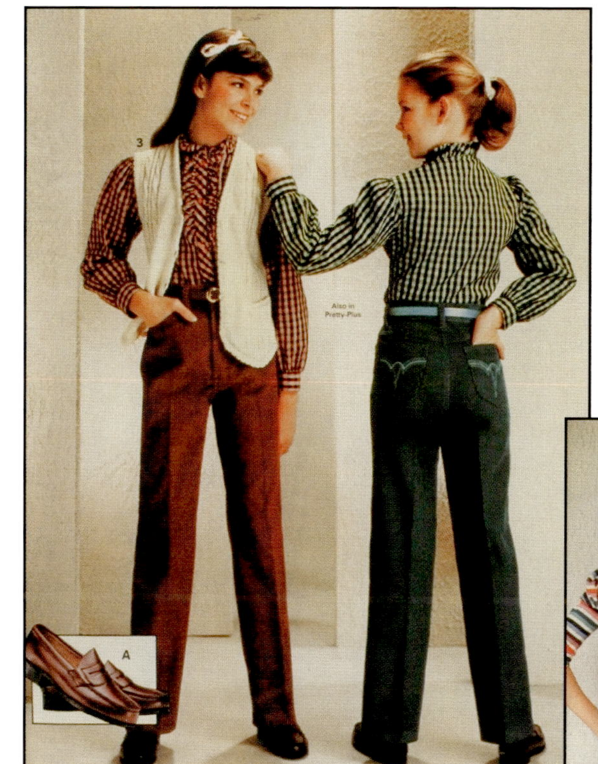

Toughskins® western corduroy jeans paired with ruffled buffalo checked shirts and creamy vest with scalloped edges. *Fall/Winter 1984.*

Tour de France twill jeans in vibrant colors paired with a striped knit top with ¾-length puffed sleeves and accessorized with a soft leather-like shoulder bag. *Fall/Winter 1984.*

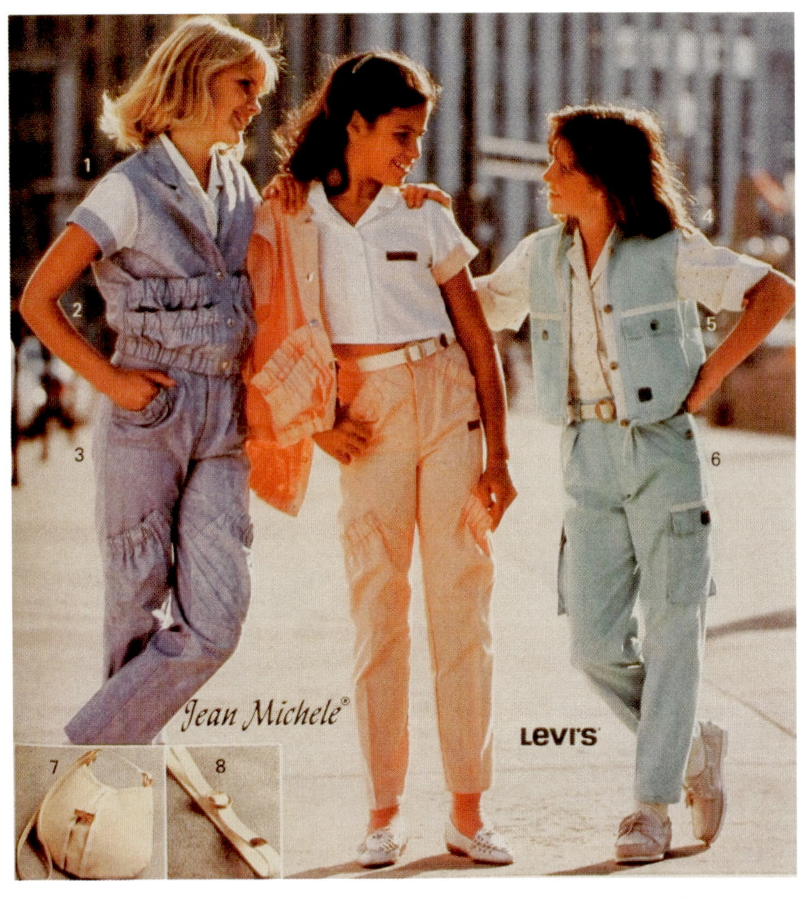

Crop tops, pants, and vests in polyester and cotton by Jean Michele® and Levi's®. *Spring/Summer 1985*

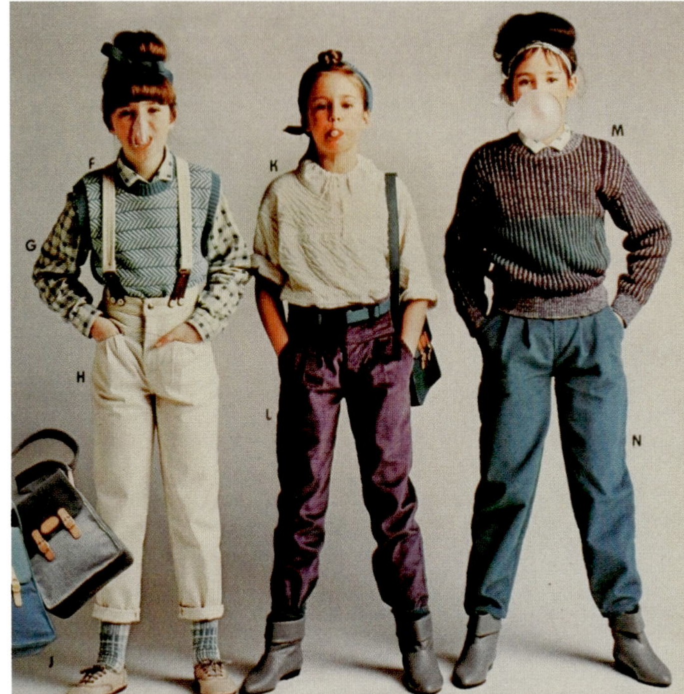

Corduroy pants in a variety of styles and colors, sweaters, flannels, and shirts that go together for a great look. *Fall/Winter 1985*

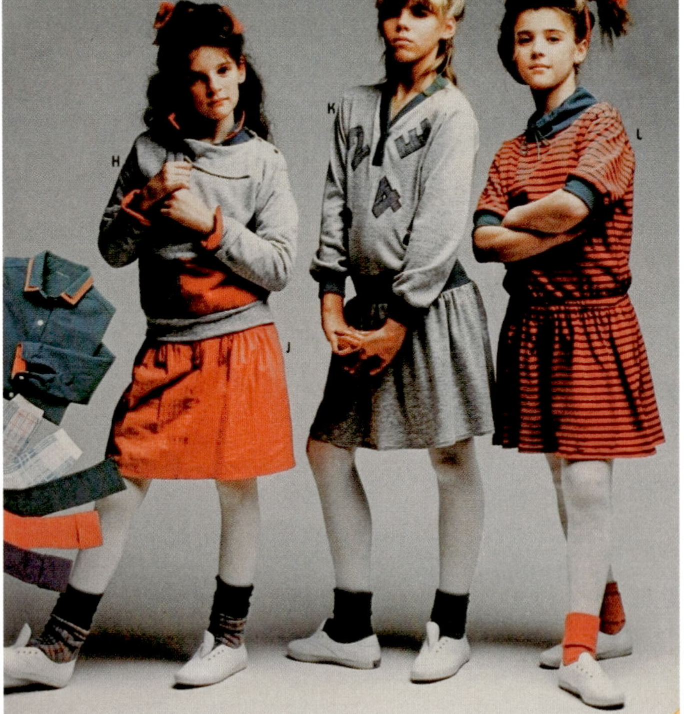

Double collar shirt worn with an abbreviated cotton canvas skirt. Sporty dress in polyester and cotton. Dress with a drawstring funnel neck in polyester and cotton. *Fall/Winter 1985*

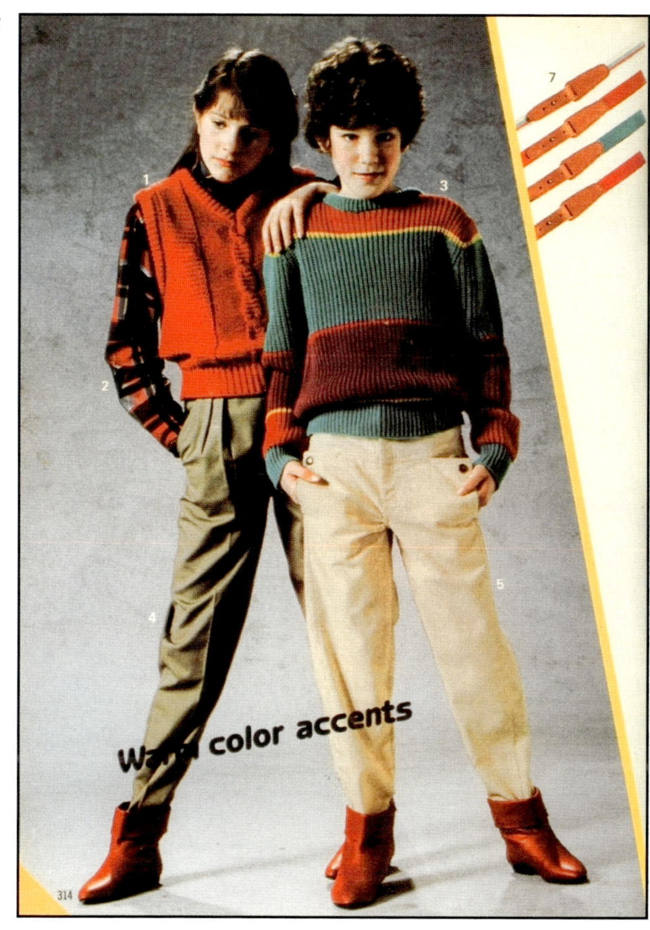

Acrylic knit vest, vivid patterned blouse, shaker-stitched sweater, cotton woven pants, and wide wale corduroy pants. *Fall/Winter 1985*

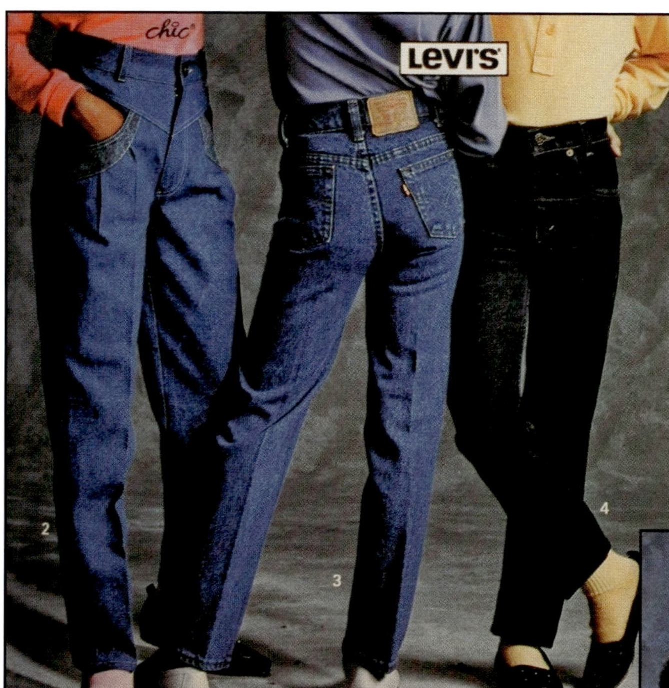

Chic® jeans with canvas detailing, and Levi's® 505® jeans. *Fall/Winter 1985*

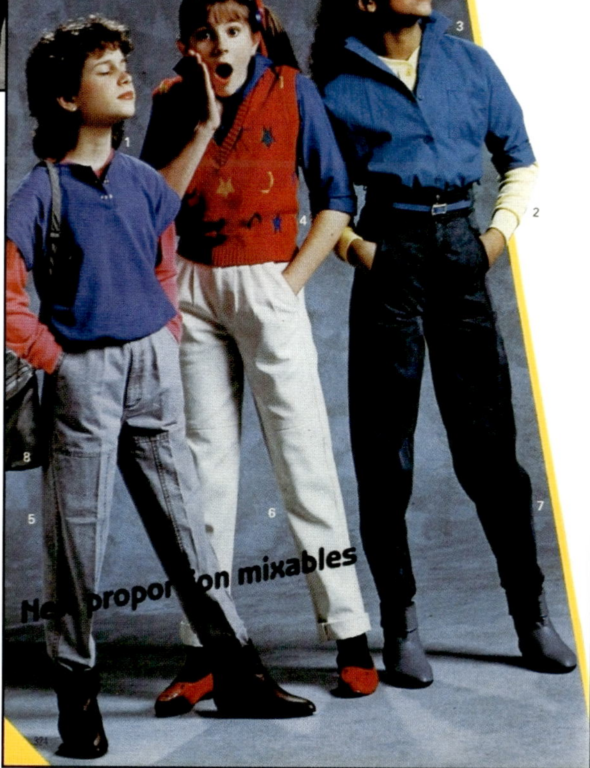

The layered look is created with mix and match colorful separates. *Fall/Winter 1985*

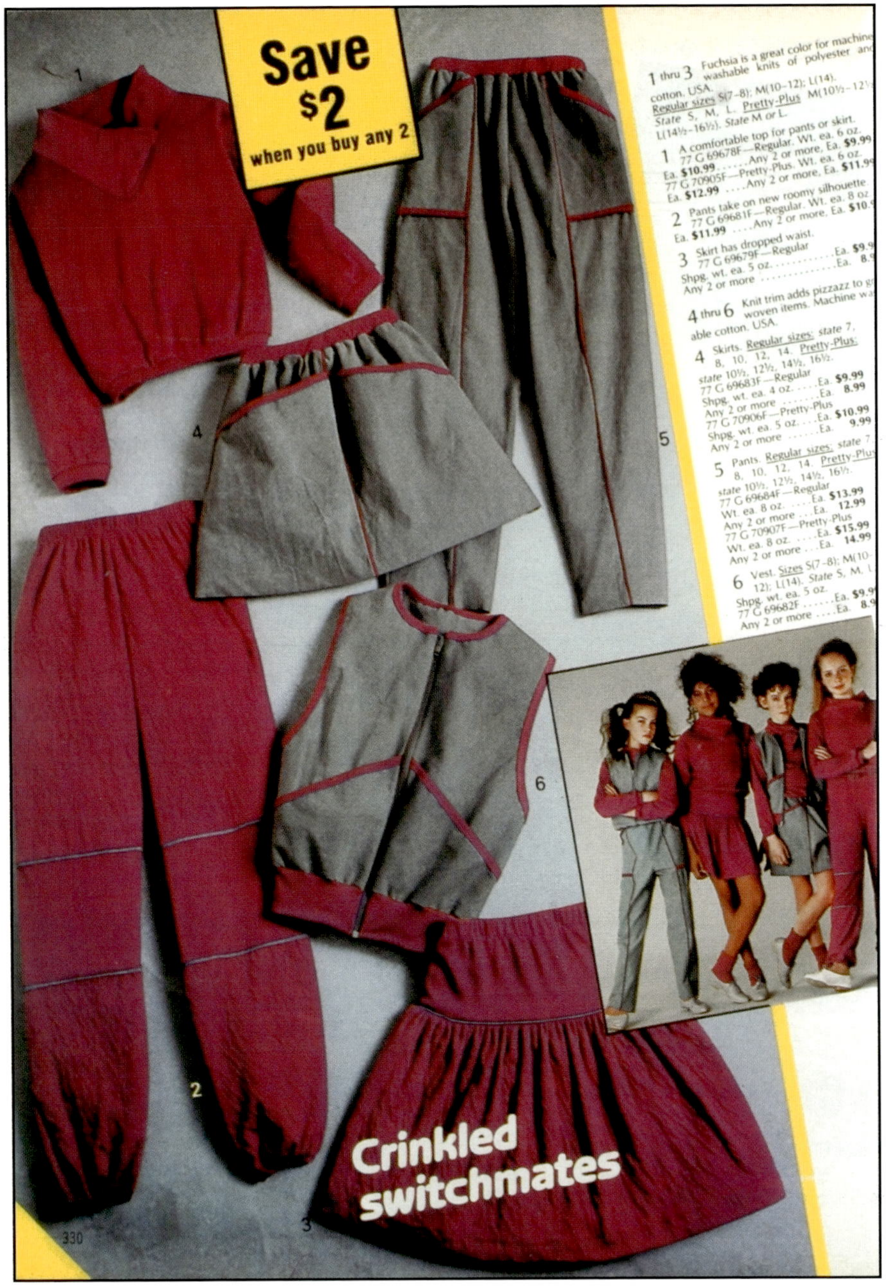

Machine wash crinkled switchmates in fuchsia and gray. Mix and match for a variety of styles. *Fall/Winter 1985*

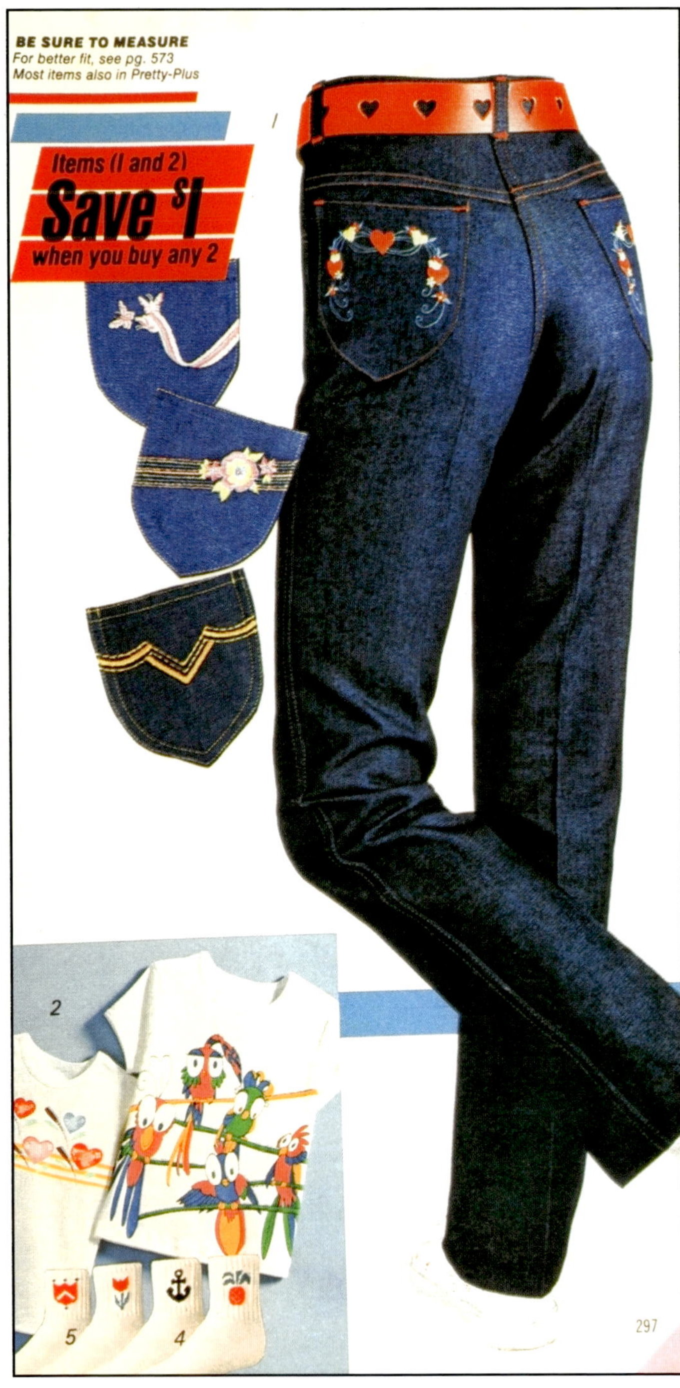

Embroidered cotton denim jeans. *Spring/Summer 1986*

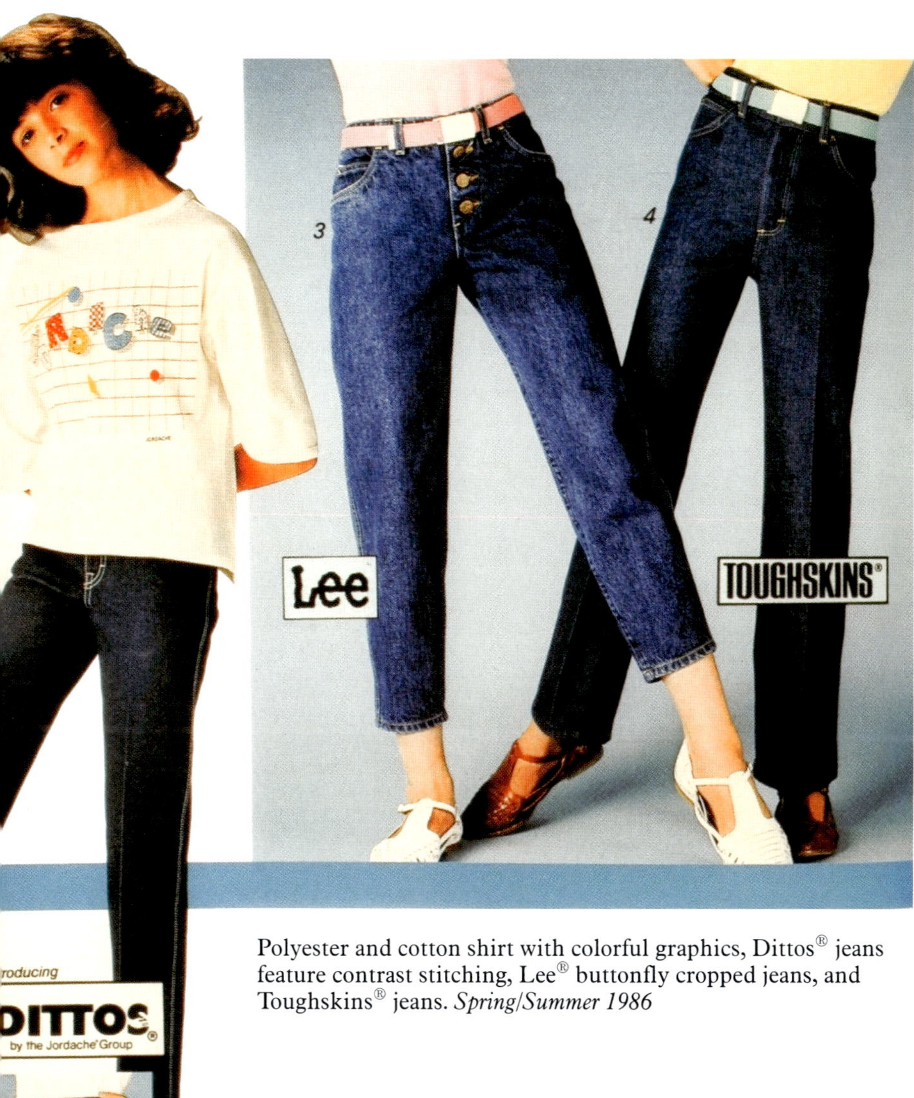

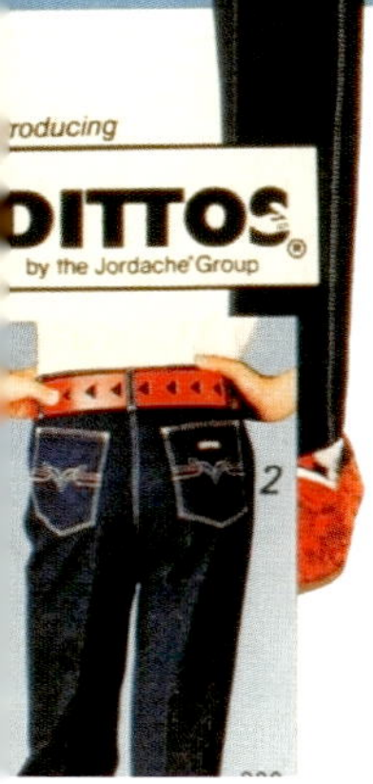

Polyester and cotton shirt with colorful graphics, Dittos® jeans feature contrast stitching, Lee® buttonfly cropped jeans, and Toughskins® jeans. *Spring/Summer 1986*

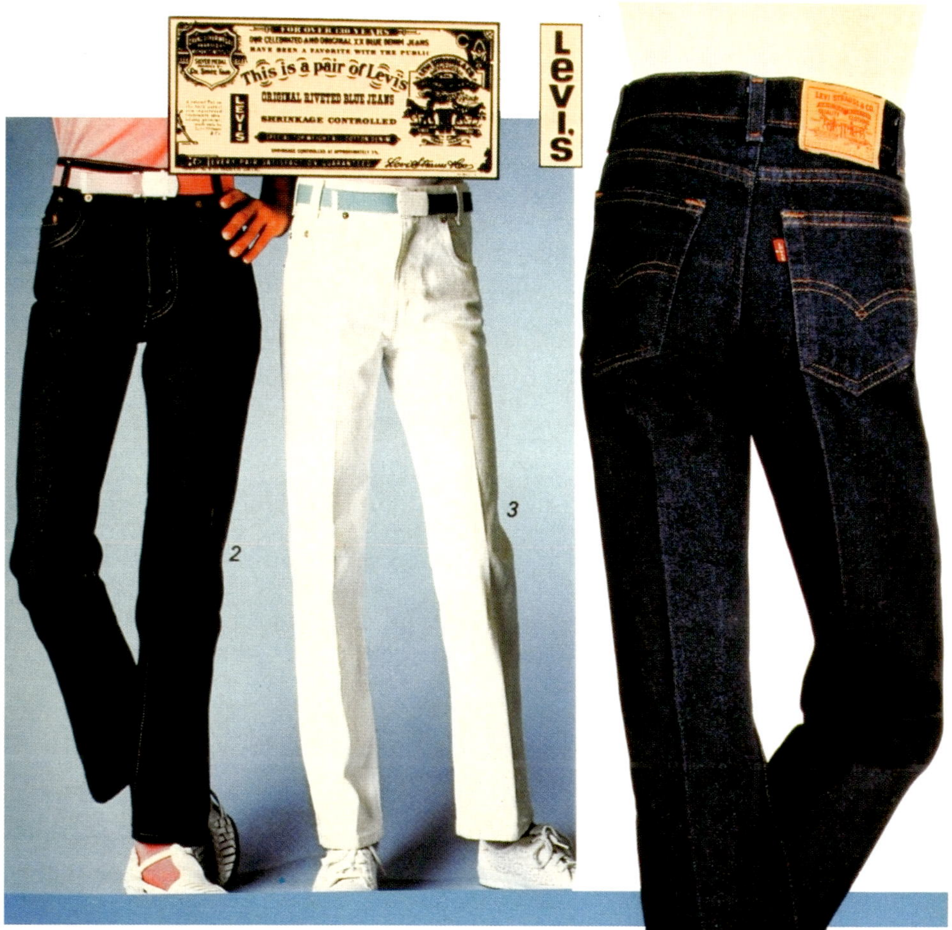

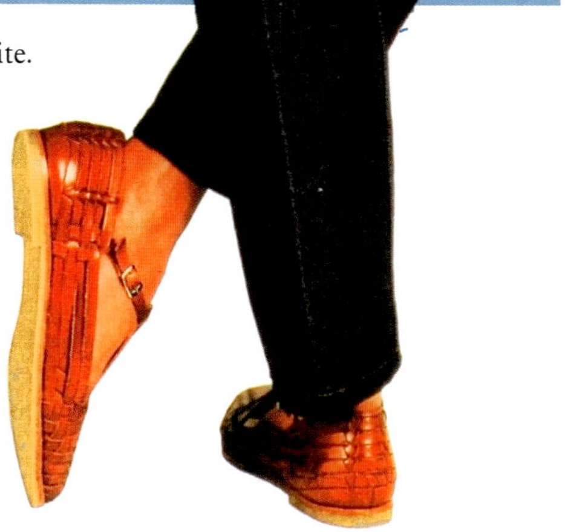

Levi's® original 505® jeans in navy, black, or white. *Spring/Summer 1986*

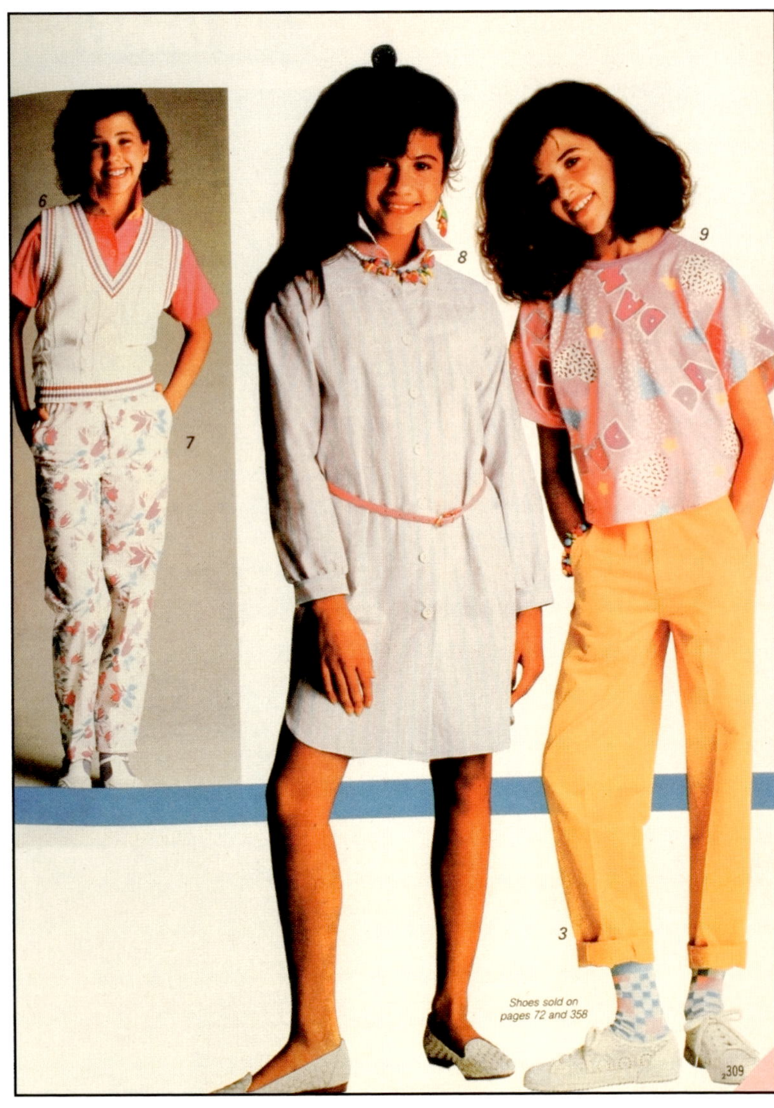

V-neck sweater with floral cotton and polyester pants, shirtdress woven of polyester and cotton worn with a jelly belt, polyester and cotton interlock knit top with soft cotton sheeting pants. *Spring/Summer 1986*

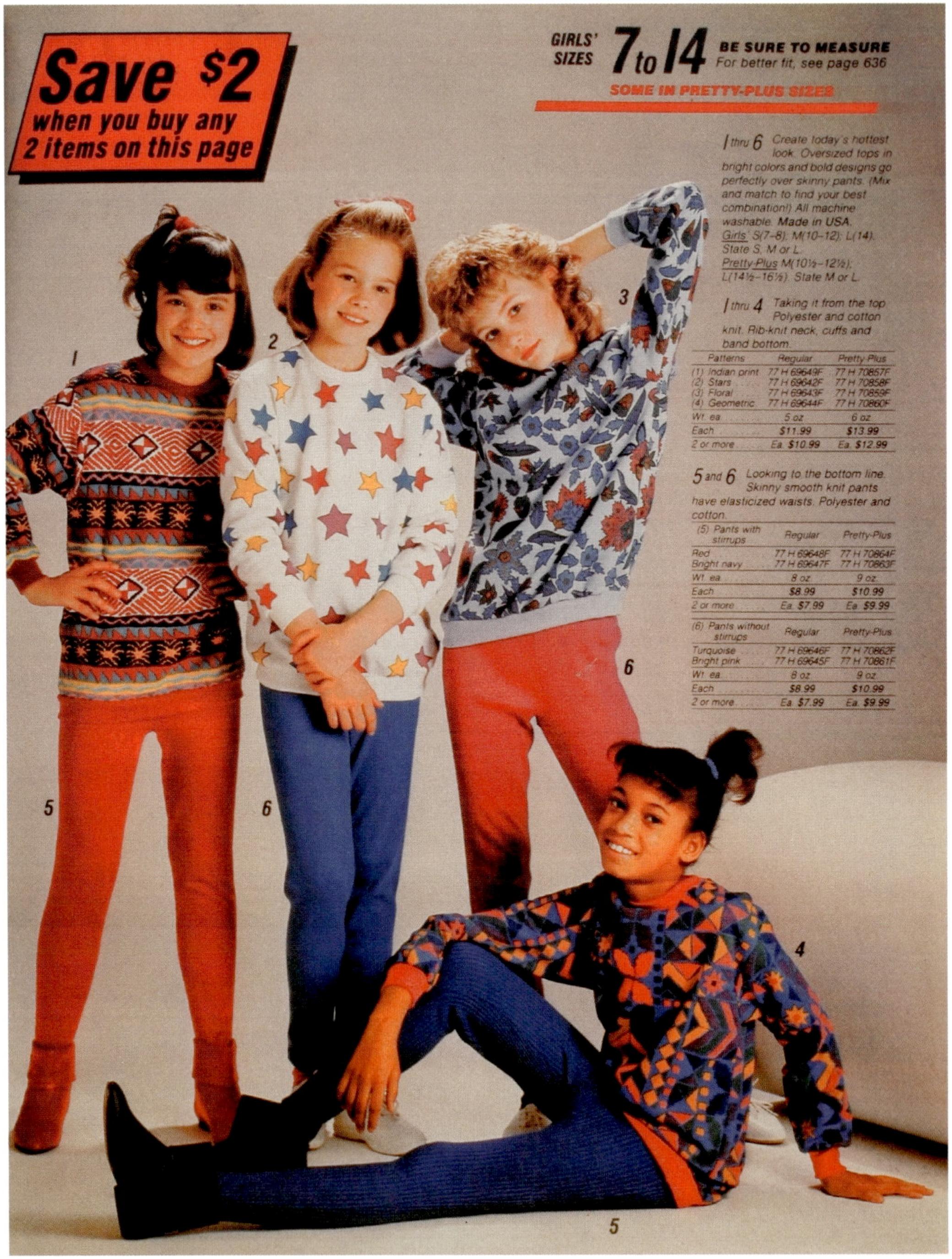

Save $2 when you buy any 2 items on this page

GIRLS' SIZES **7 to 14** **BE SURE TO MEASURE** For better fit, see page 636

SOME IN PRETTY-PLUS SIZES

1 thru 6 Create today's hottest look. Oversized tops in bright colors and bold designs go perfectly over skinny pants. (Mix and match to find your best combination!) All machine washable. Made in USA. Girls' S(7–8); M(10–12); L(14). State S, M or L. Pretty-Plus M(10½–12½); L(14½–16½). State M or L.

1 thru 4 Taking it from the top. Polyester and cotton knit. Rib-knit neck, cuffs and band bottom.

Patterns	Regular	Pretty Plus
(1) Indian print	77 H 69649F	77 H 70857F
(2) Stars	77 H 69642F	77 H 70858F
(3) Floral	77 H 69643F	77 H 70859F
(4) Geometric	77 H 69644F	77 H 70860F
Wt. ea	5 oz	6 oz
Each	$11.99	$13.99
2 or more	Ea. $10.99	Ea. $12.99

5 and 6 Looking to the bottom line. Skinny smooth knit pants have elasticized waists. Polyester and cotton.

(5) Pants with stirrups	Regular	Pretty-Plus
Red	77 H 69648F	77 H 70864F
Bright navy	77 H 69647F	77 H 70863F
Wt. ea	8 oz	9 oz
Each	$8.99	$10.99
2 or more	Ea. $7.99	Ea. $9.99

(6) Pants without stirrups	Regular	Pretty-Plus
Turquoise	77 H 69646F	77 H 70862F
Bright pink	77 H 69645F	77 H 70861F
Wt. ea	8 oz	9 oz
Each	$8.99	$10.99
2 or more	Ea. $7.99	Ea. $9.99

Bold and bright oversized tops paired with skinny pants in polyester and cotton fabrics. *Fall/Winter 1986*

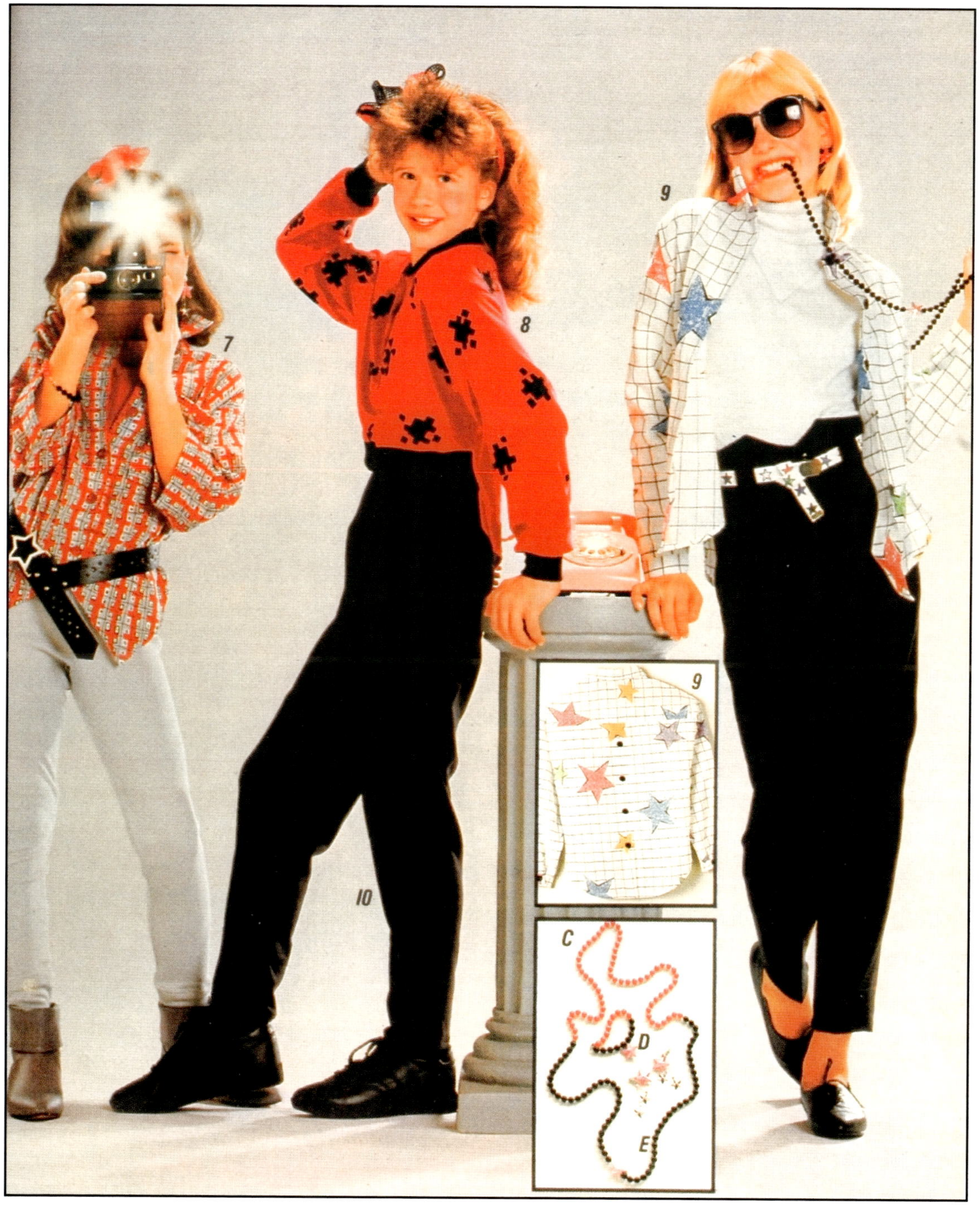

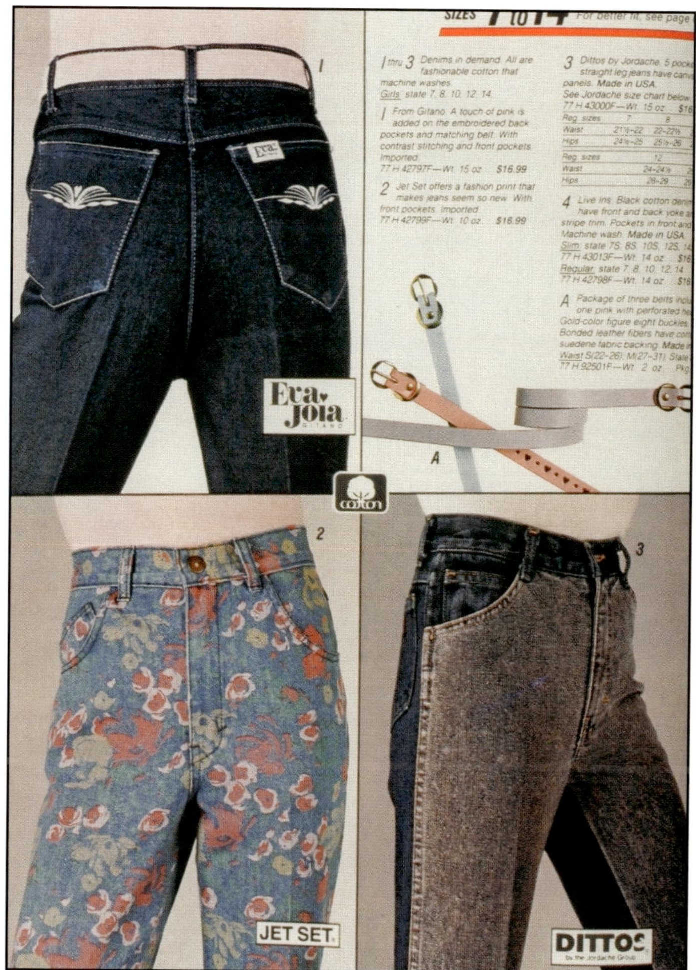

Gitano, Jet Set, and Dittos cotton jeans. *Fall/Winter 1986*

Tuxedo styled print shirt, High-low top, big shirt with stars, all worn with full and comfortable pants. Polyester and cotton fabrics. *Fall/Winter 1986*

Sporty & Exercise Wear

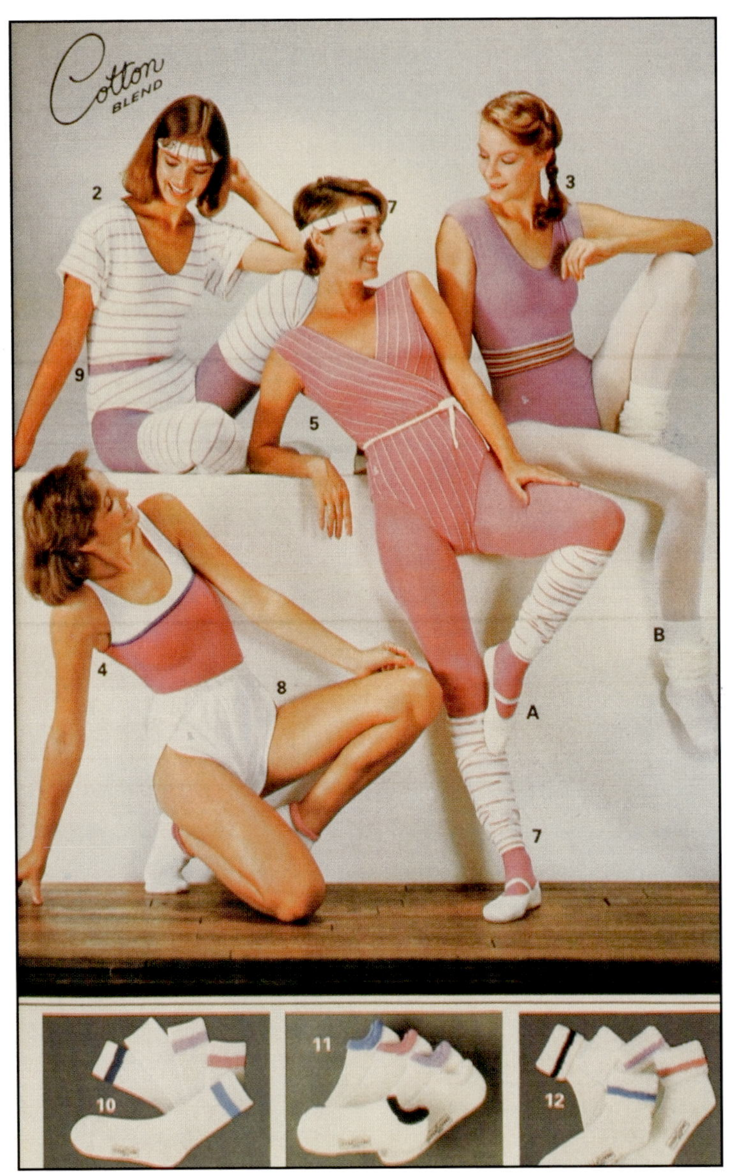

Getting physical takes the right kind of gear! Goolagong's cotton blend* "works out." *Spring/Summer 1984.*

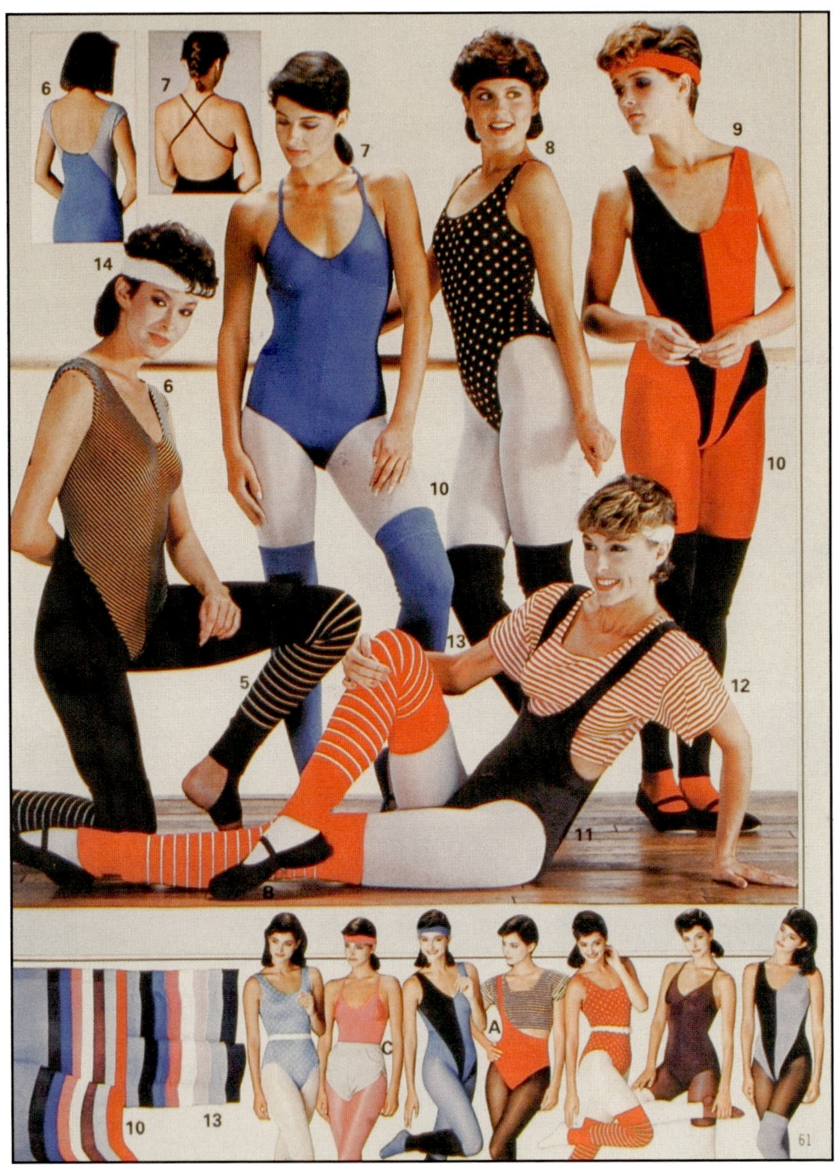

Assorted headbands, leg warmers, body trunk suits, leotards and tights. *Spring/Summer 1984.*

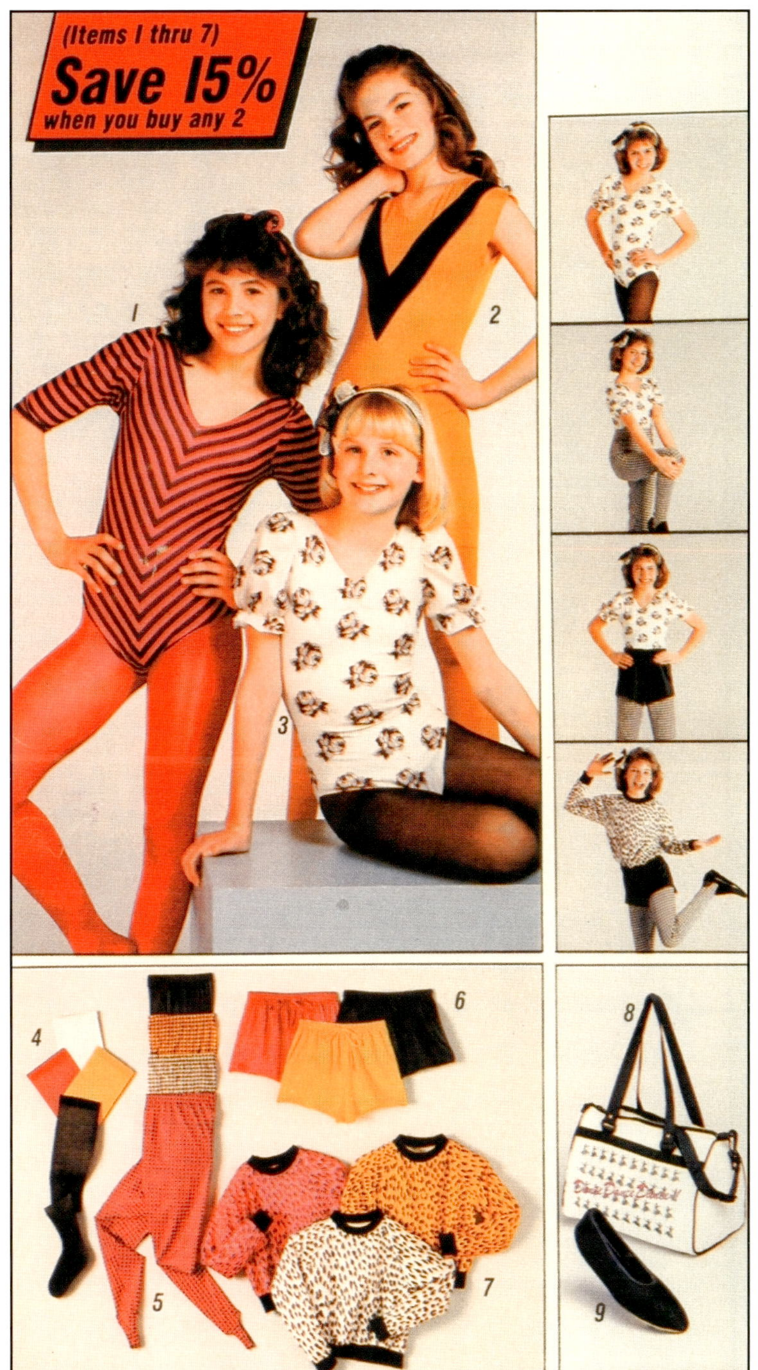

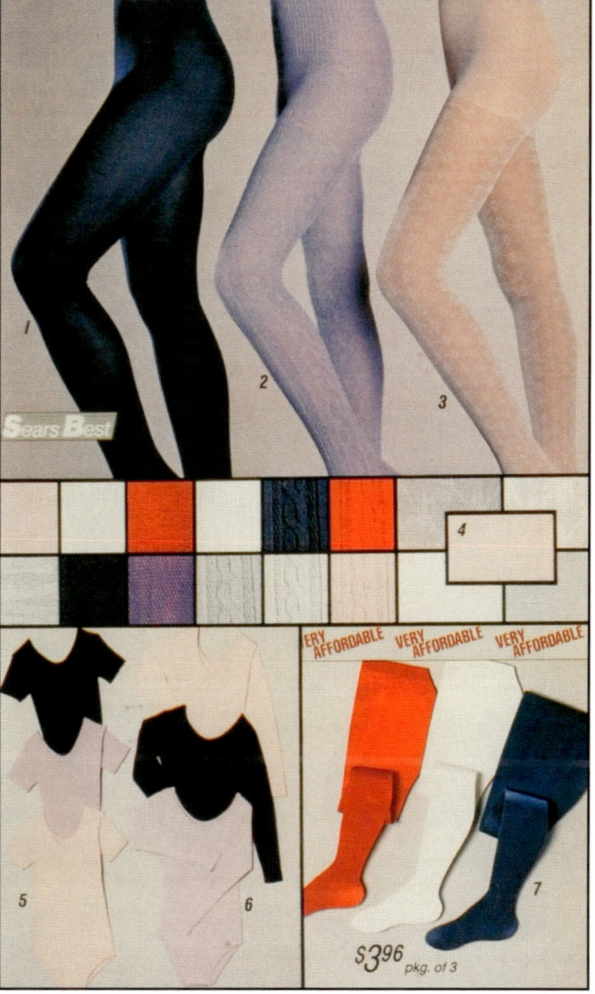

Tights from warm sweater knit to sheer lace. Basic leotards knit of nylon in short or long sleeves. Colorful nylon tights. *Fall/Winter 1986*

Dancewear in lively colors and styles to get your groove on. *Fall/Winter 1986*

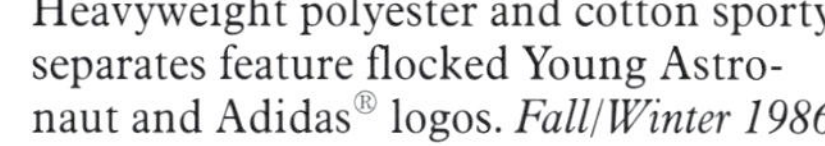

Heavyweight polyester and cotton sporty separates feature flocked Young Astronaut and Adidas® logos. *Fall/Winter 1986*

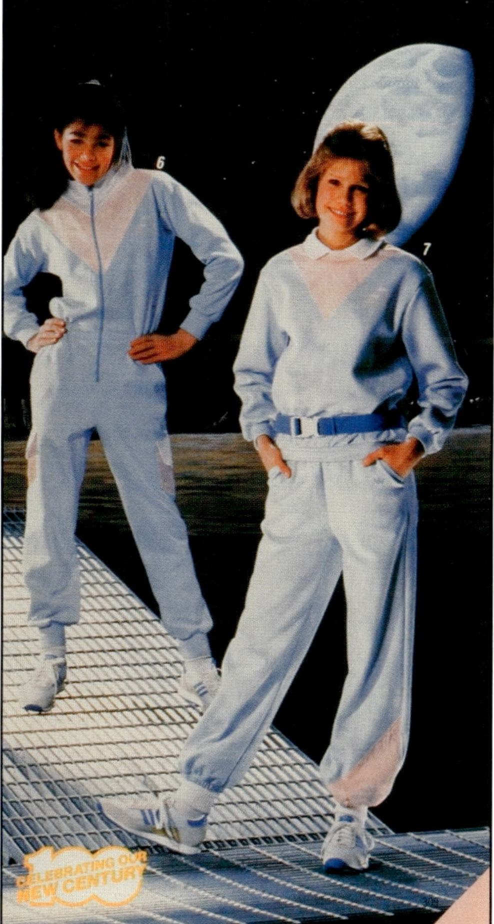

Swimwear

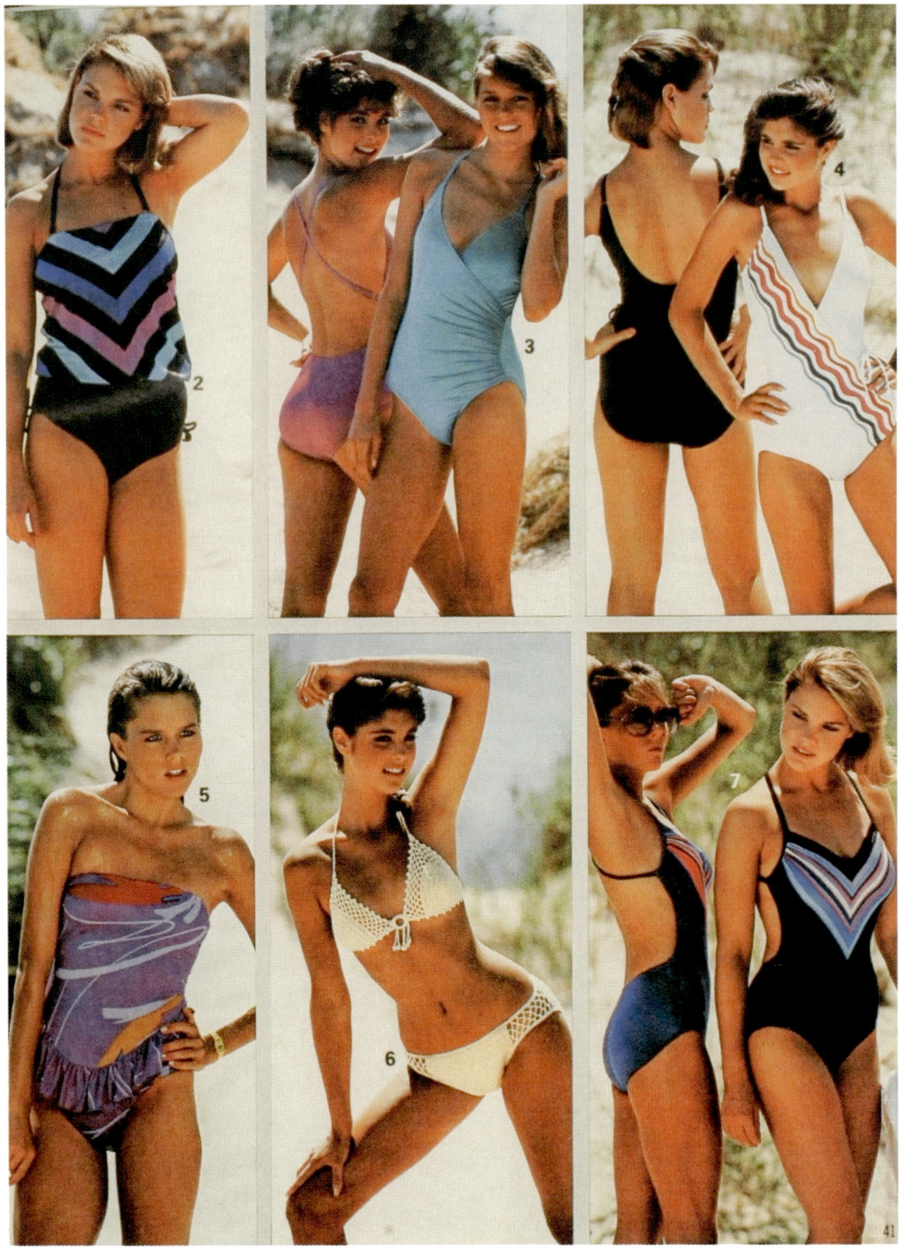

Swimsuits and bikini in Biouson, maillot, and hand crocheted styles. *Spring/Summer 1984.*

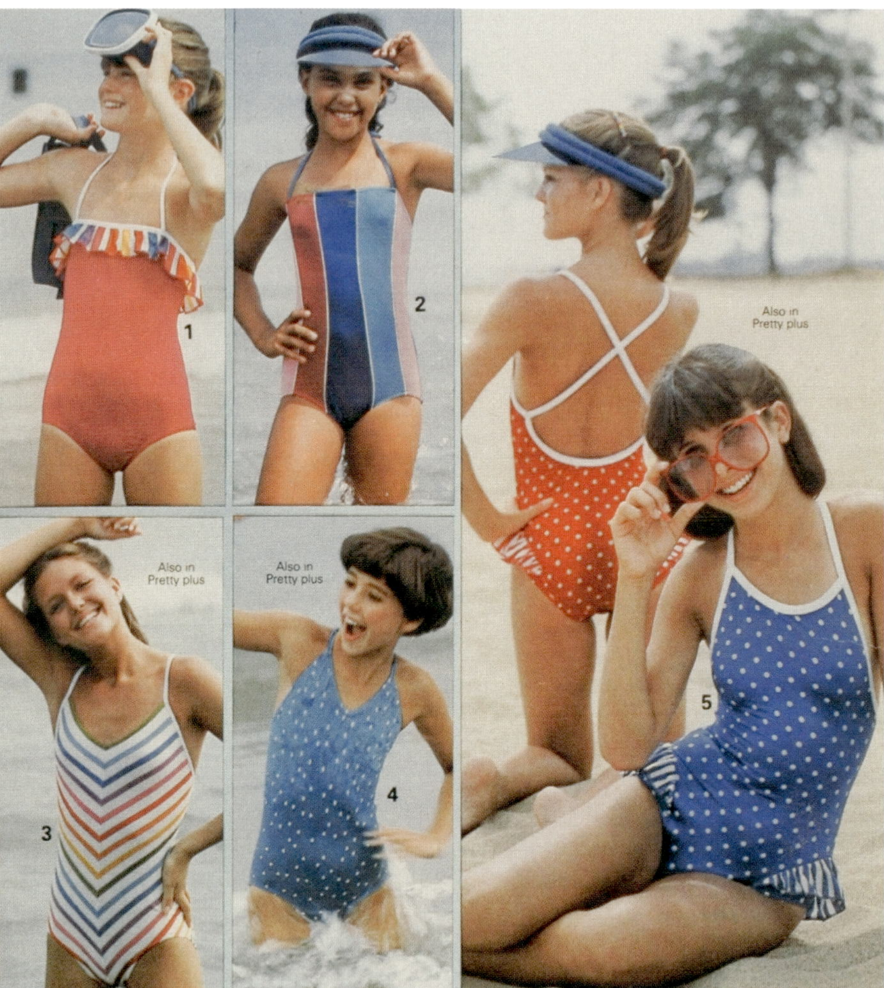

An assortment of Lycra® swimsuits for girls. *Spring/Summer 1984.*

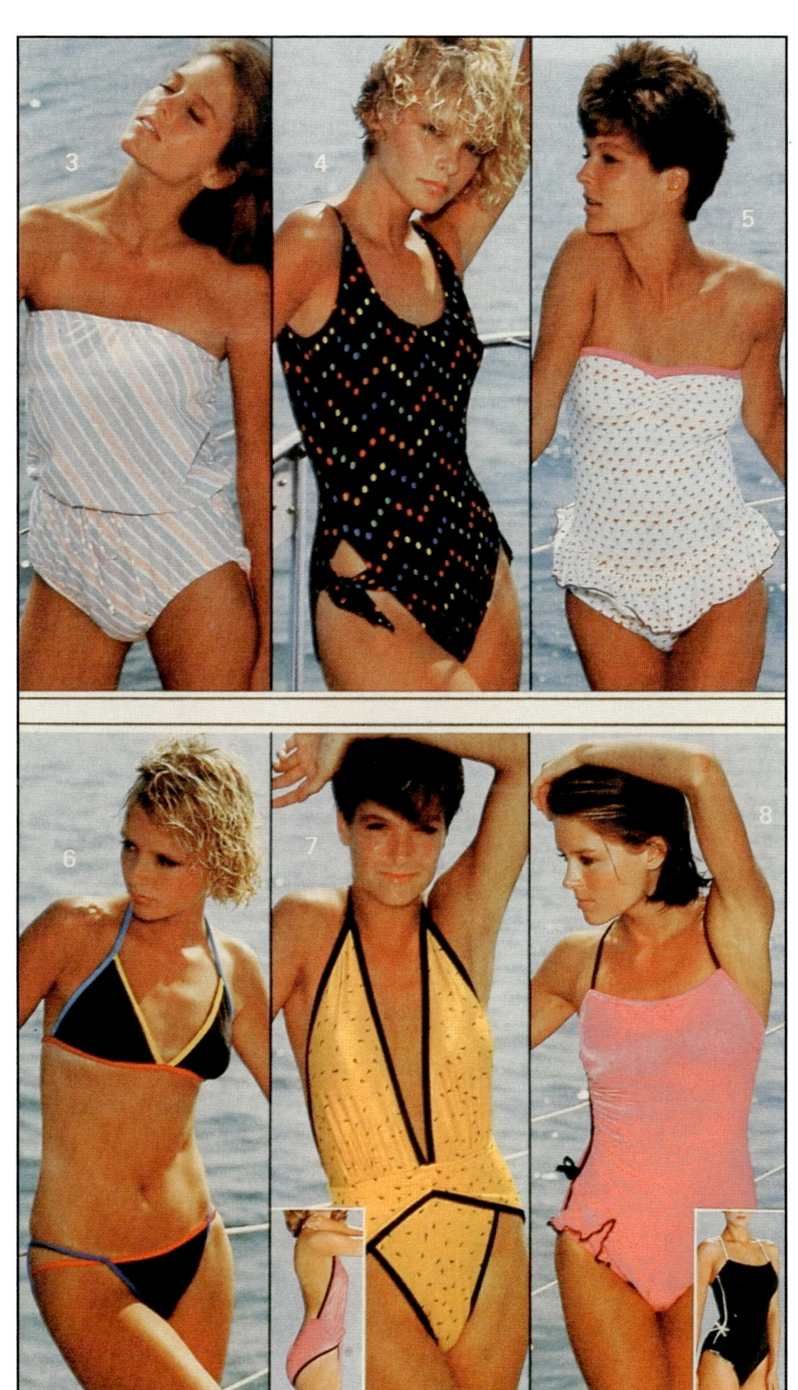

A sample of options for swimwear. *Spring/Summer 1985*

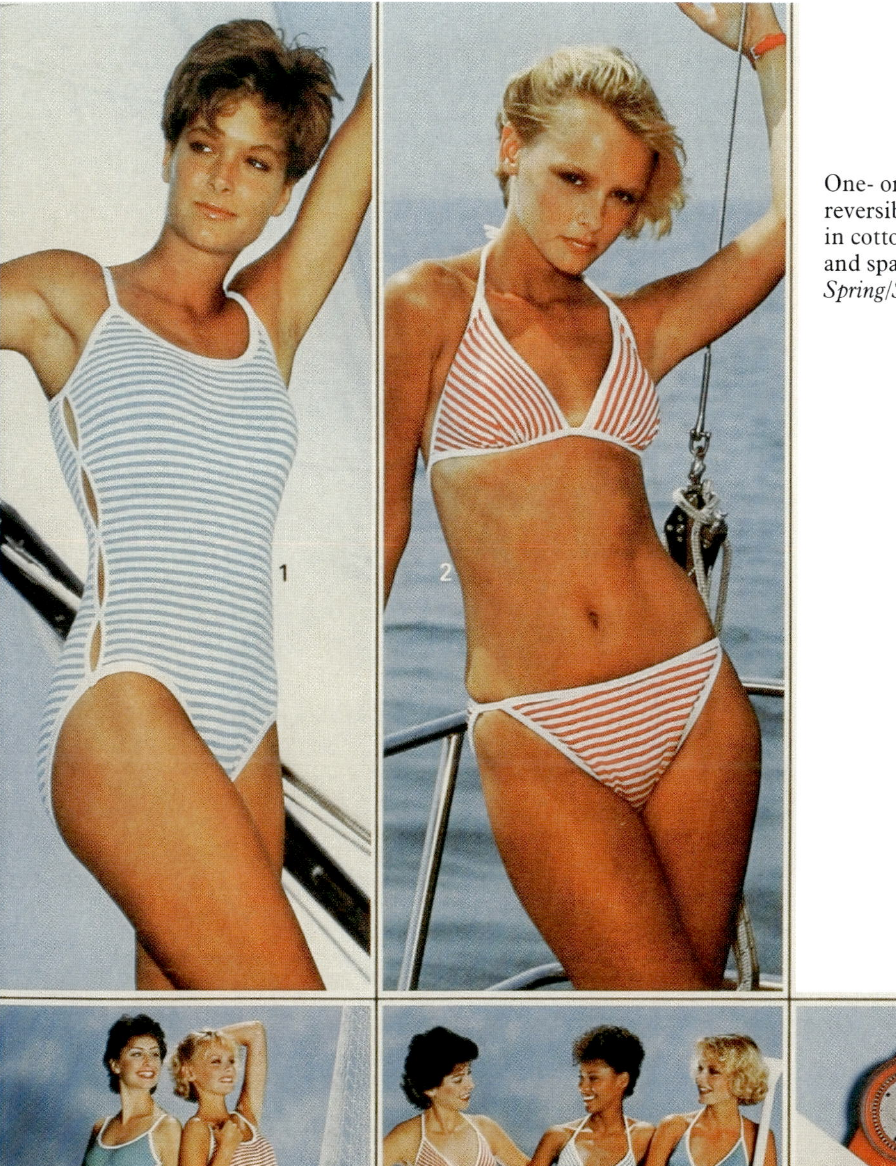

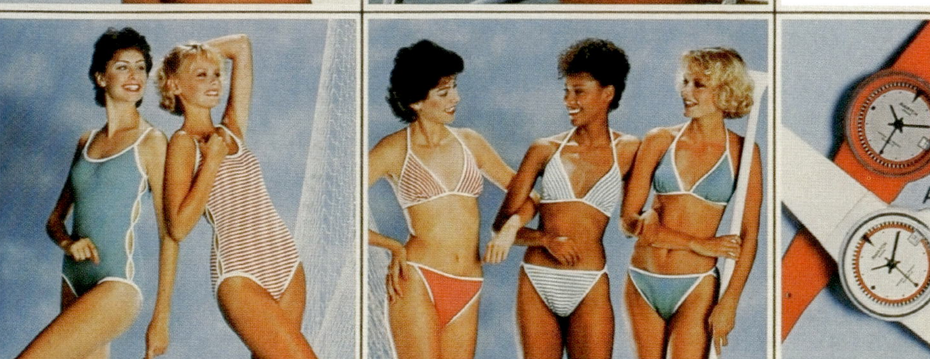

One- or two-piece reversible swimsuits in cotton, polyester, and spandex fabric. *Spring/Summer 1985*

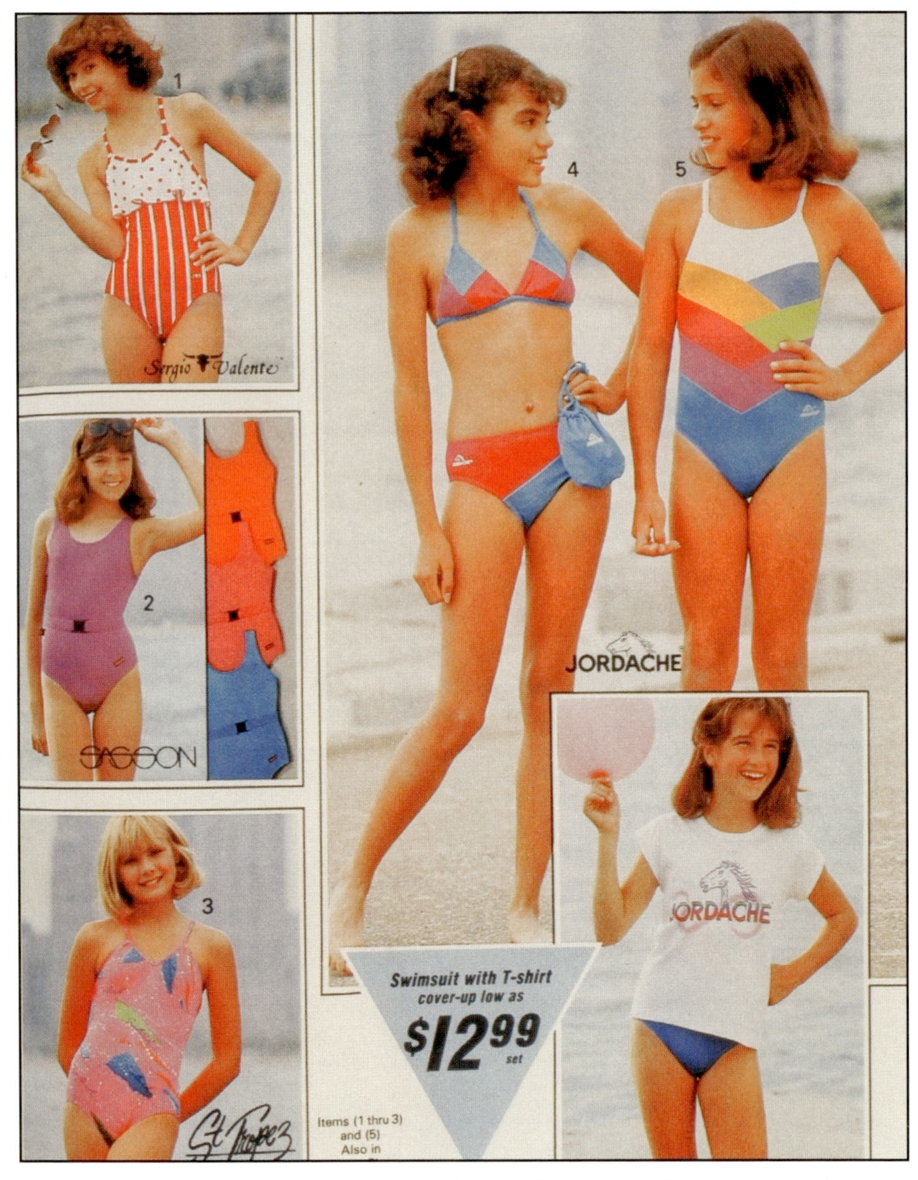

Brand name swimsuits from Sergio Valente®, Sasson®, St. Tropez®, and Jordache®. *Spring/Summer 1985*

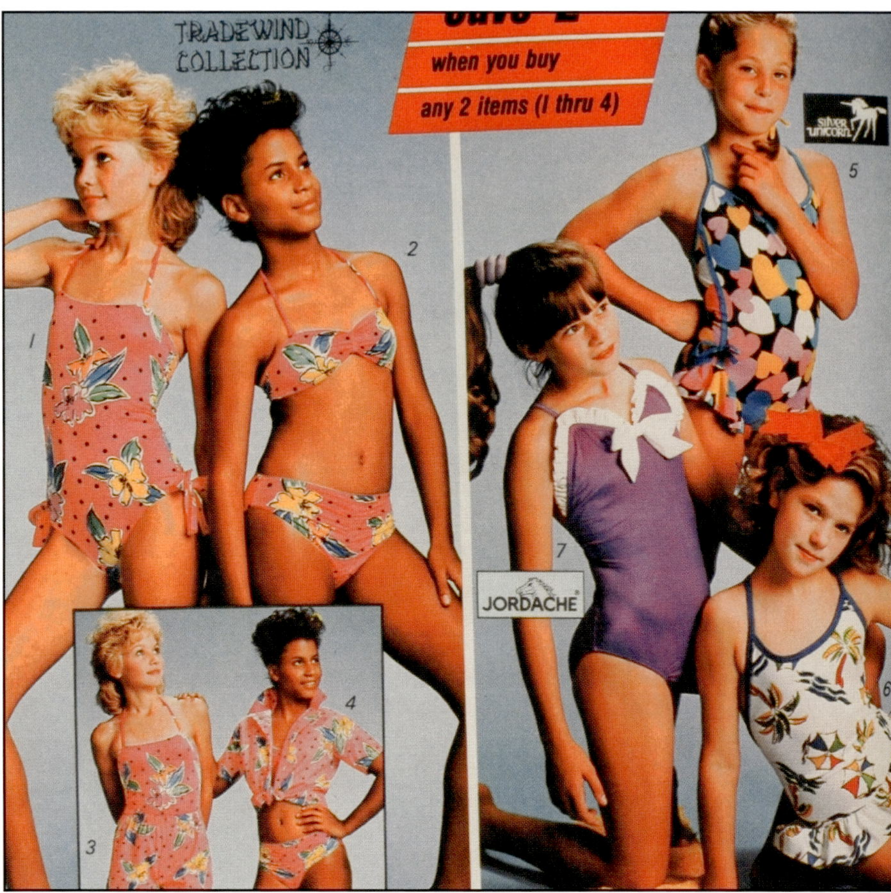

Swimwear coordinates from the Tradewind collection. Silver Unicorn heart print suit, beach print skirted suit, and Jordache® ruffle and bow trim suit. *Spring/Summer 1986*

Coats

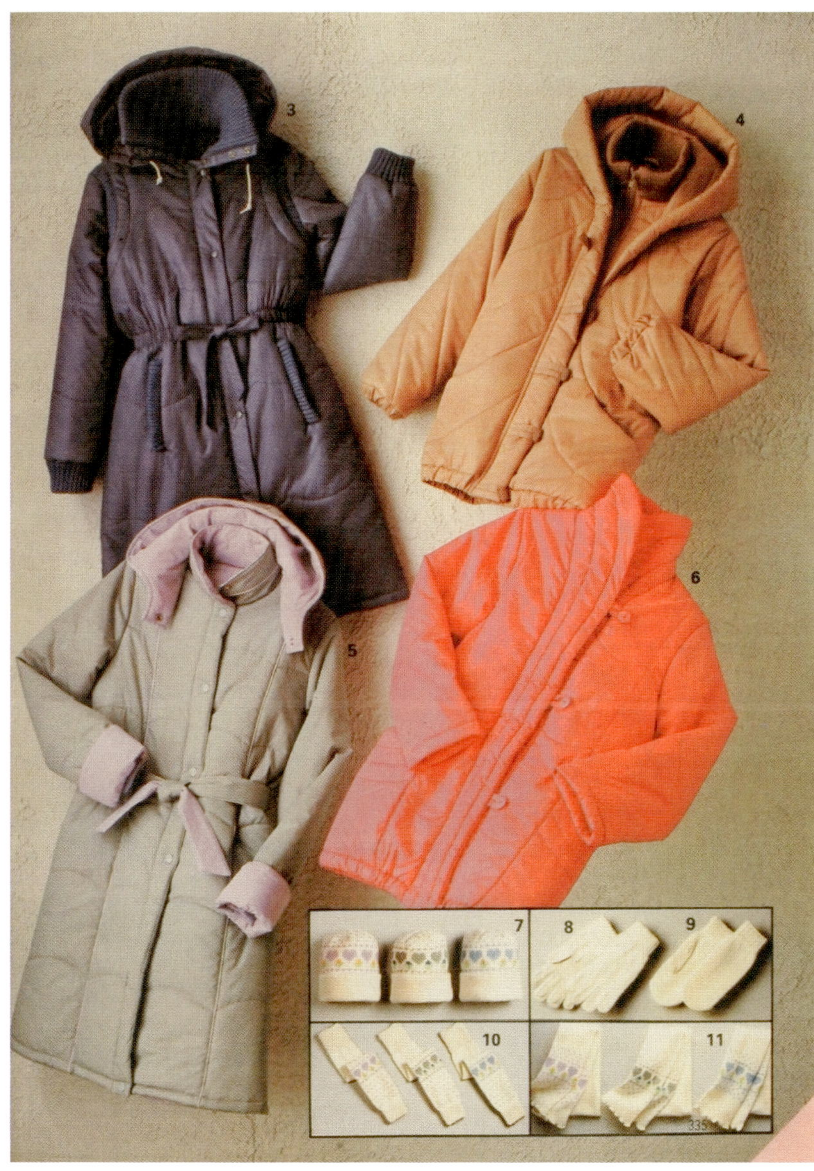

Violet boot-length hooded coat in quilted water-repellant polyester and cotton chintz. Tan stadium coat has mock vestee and is made of polyester and cotton chintz shell. Gray and lilac boot length coat has zip on/off hood and piping on princess seams. Hot pink stadium coat in chintz shell of polyester and cotton. *Fall/Winter 1984.*

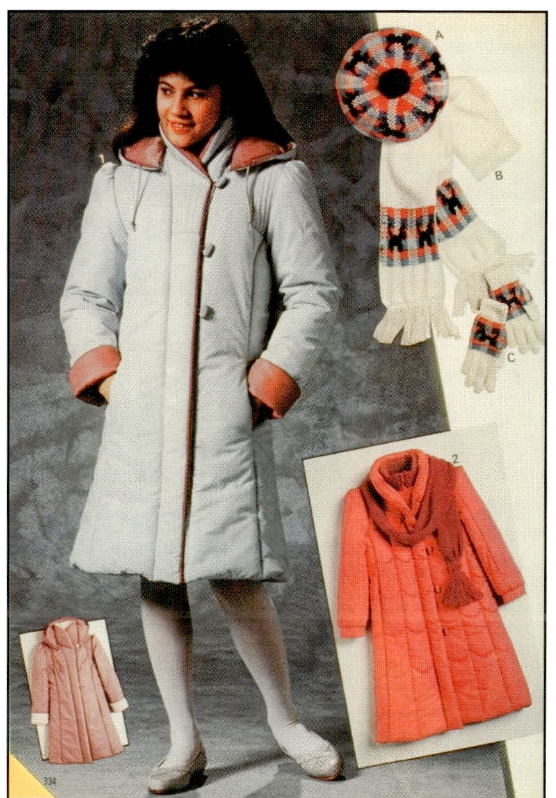

Quilted coat has a triple row of quilting accents on the standup collar, and front and back shoulders. Made of polyester and nylon. *Fall/Winter 1985*

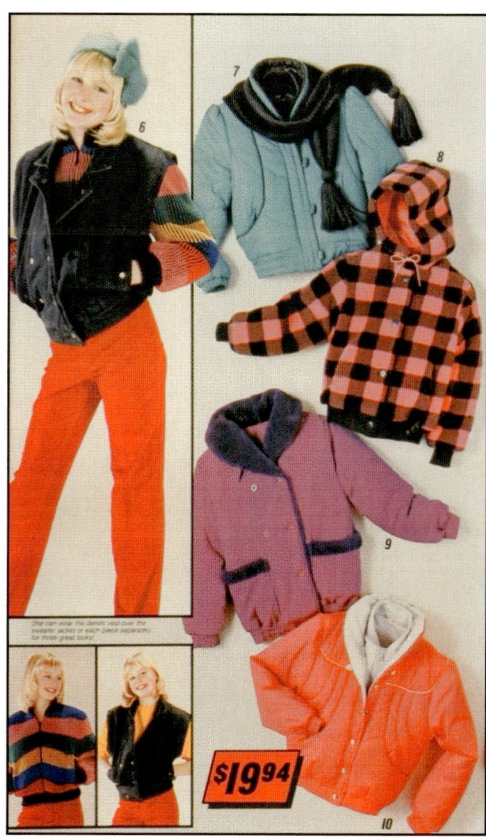

Black denim vest, bright turquoise jacket with black vestee, check pattern jacket, bright purple jacket, and hot pink jacket for stylish warmth. *Fall/Winter 1986*

Teen Boys' Fashions

Dressy

Mix-n-match PERMA-PREST® separates. *Spring/Summer 1984.*

Michael Giraud 3-piece suits are made of texturized woven polyester with an assortment of Michael Giraud ties to accessorize. *Fall/Winter 1984.*

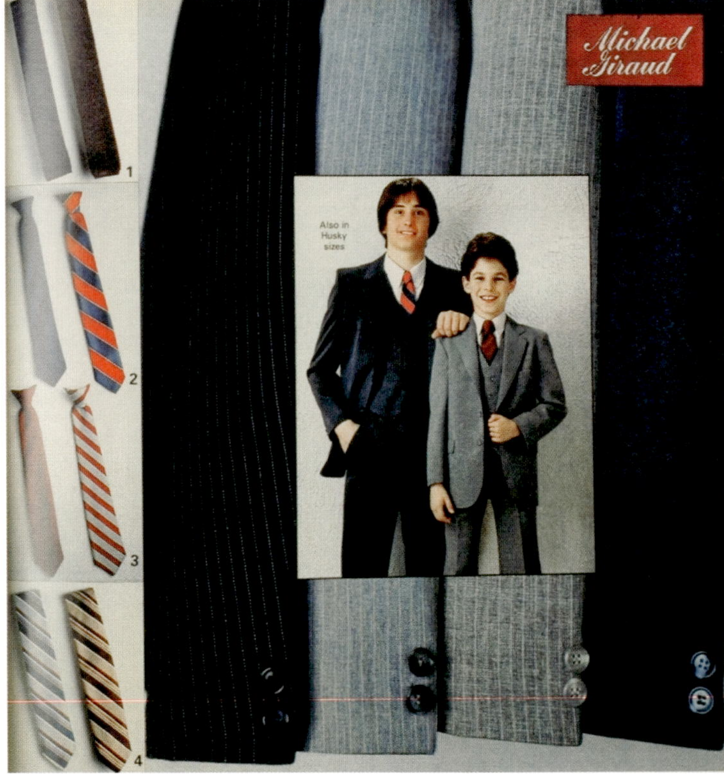

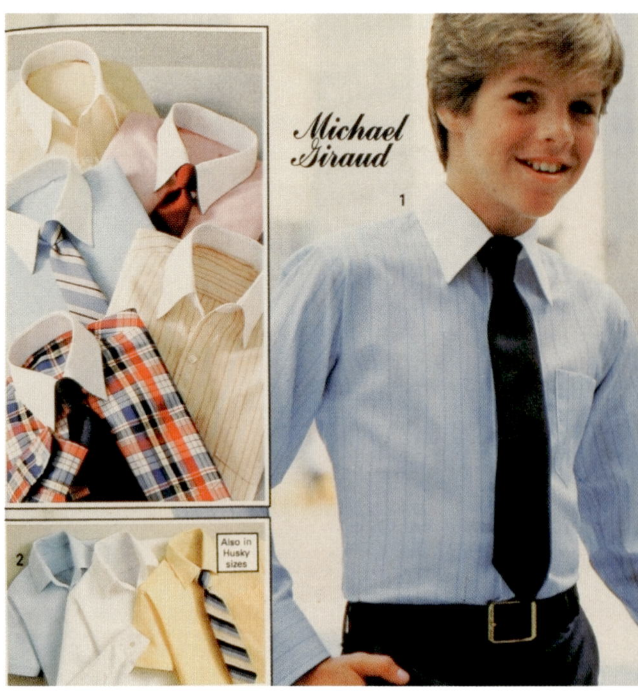

Classic oxford shirts in a variety of colors and patterns. Woven polyester and cotton. *Spring/Summer 1985*

Casual

Khaki shirts and camouflage shorts and pants to mix and match. *Spring/Summer 1984.*

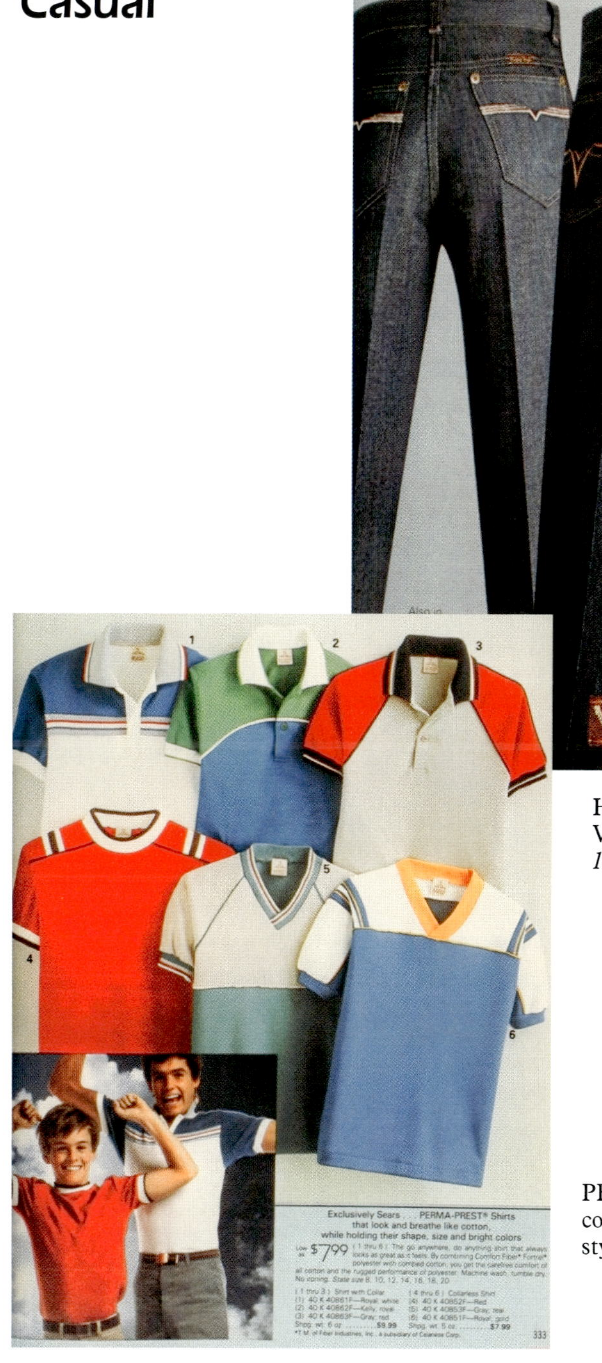

Hanging Tough, Wrangler, and Sergio Valente denim jeans for men. *Spring/Summer 1984.*

PERMA-PREST® shirts with collars, v-necks, or no collar style. *Spring/Summer 1984.*

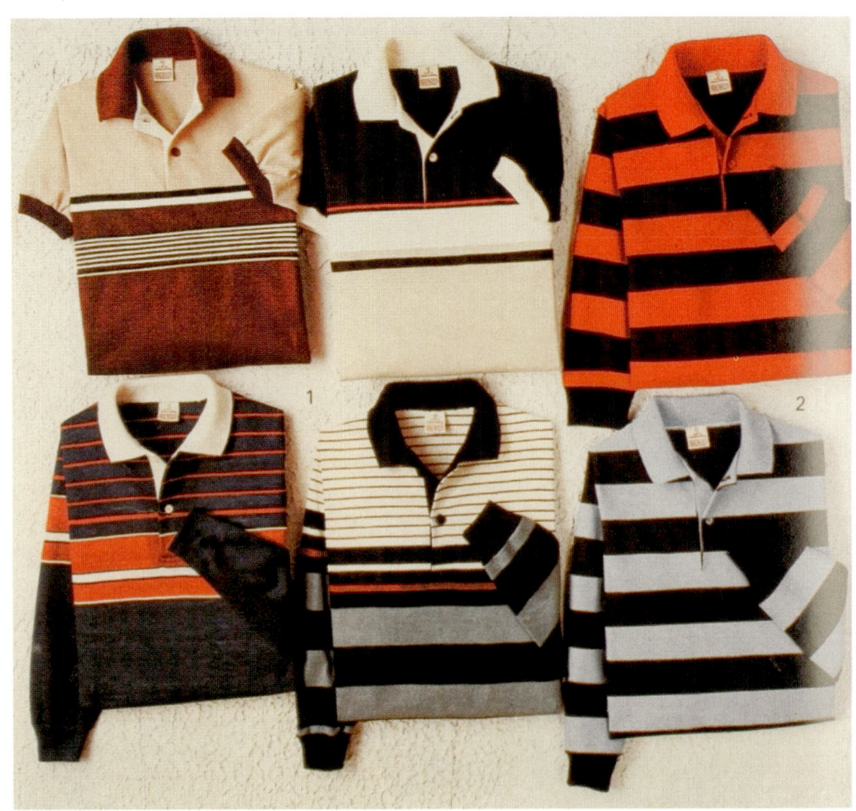

PERMA-PREST® striped shirts for boys and teens. *Fall/Winter 1984.*

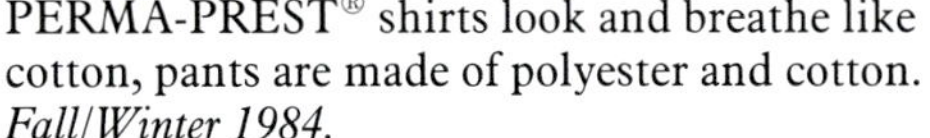
PERMA-PREST® shirts look and breathe like cotton, pants are made of polyester and cotton. *Fall/Winter 1984.*

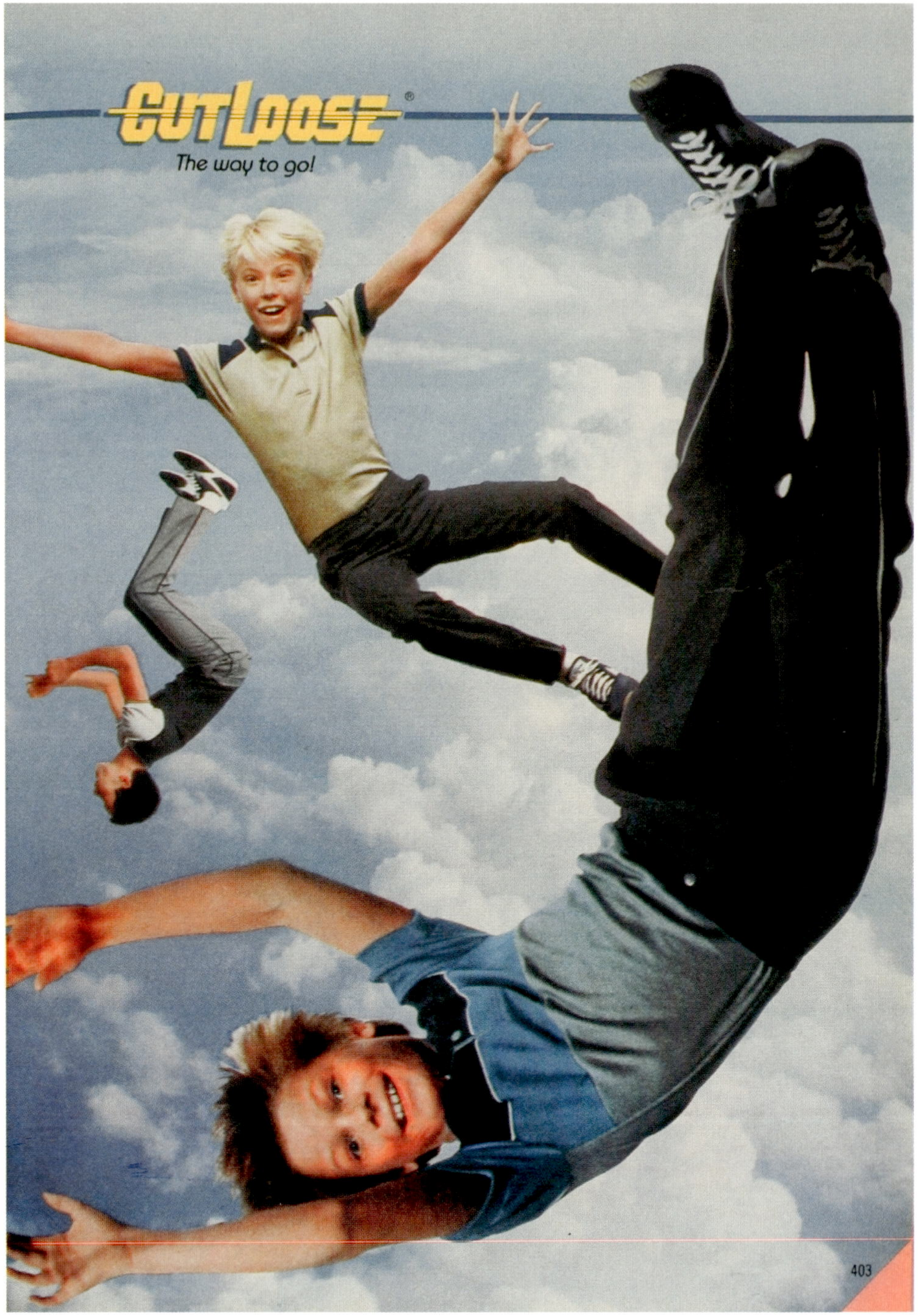

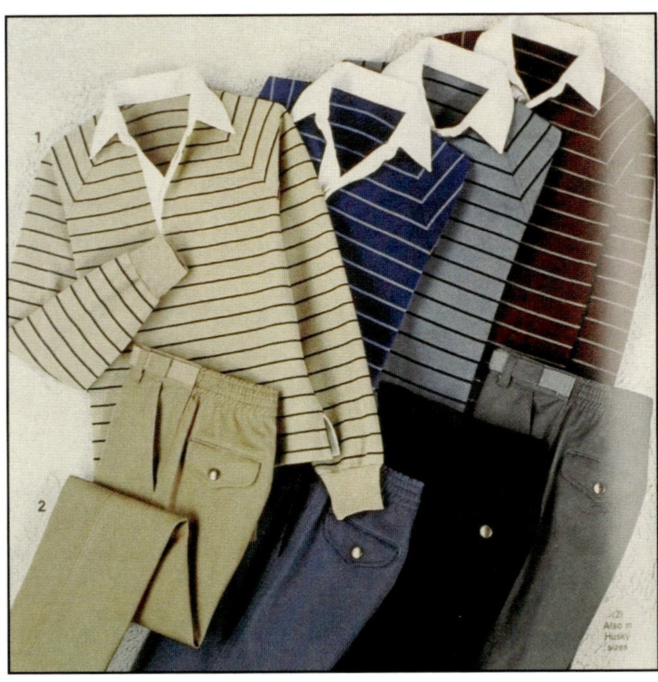

Striped cotton and polyester shirts paired with twill polyester and cotton pants. *Fall/Winter 1984.*

14 ¾ oz. denim jeans by Roebucks® and Wrangler®. *Fall/Winter 1984.*

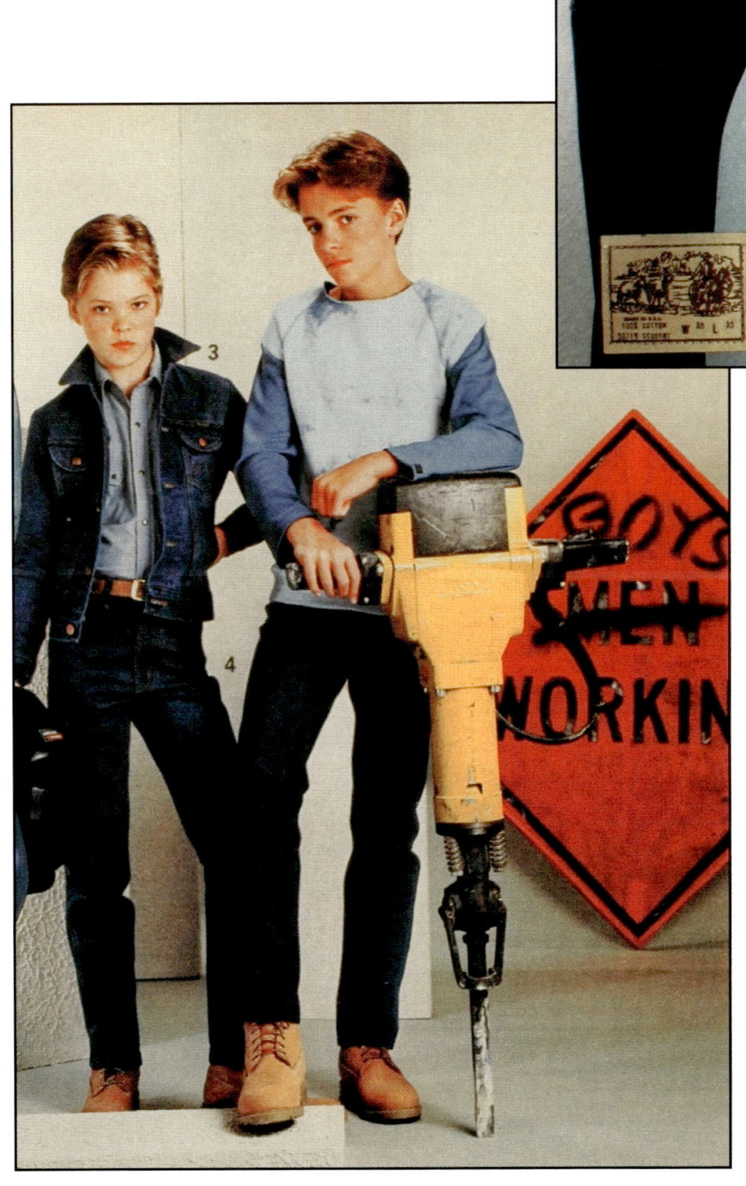

Chambray shirt fits in with the new urban look, tie-dyed fleece shirt has popular layered look, and cotton denim jeans. All are made by Wrangler®. *Fall/Winter 1984.*

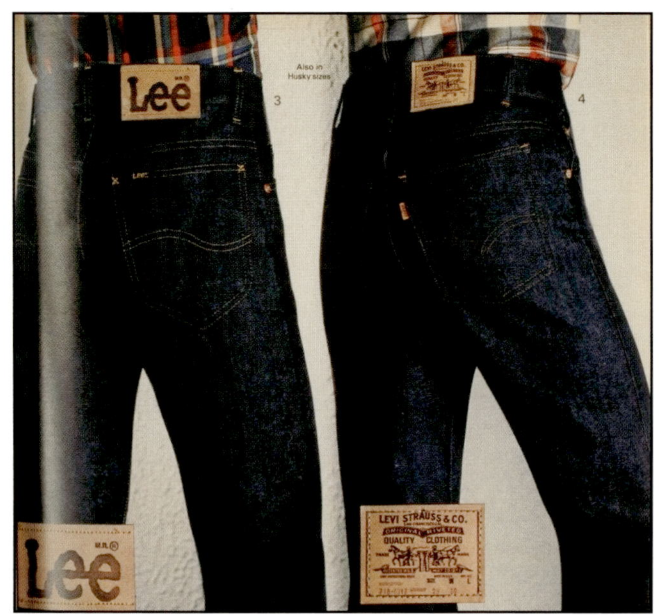

14 ¾ oz. denim jeans by Lee® and Levi's®. *Fall/Winter 1984.*

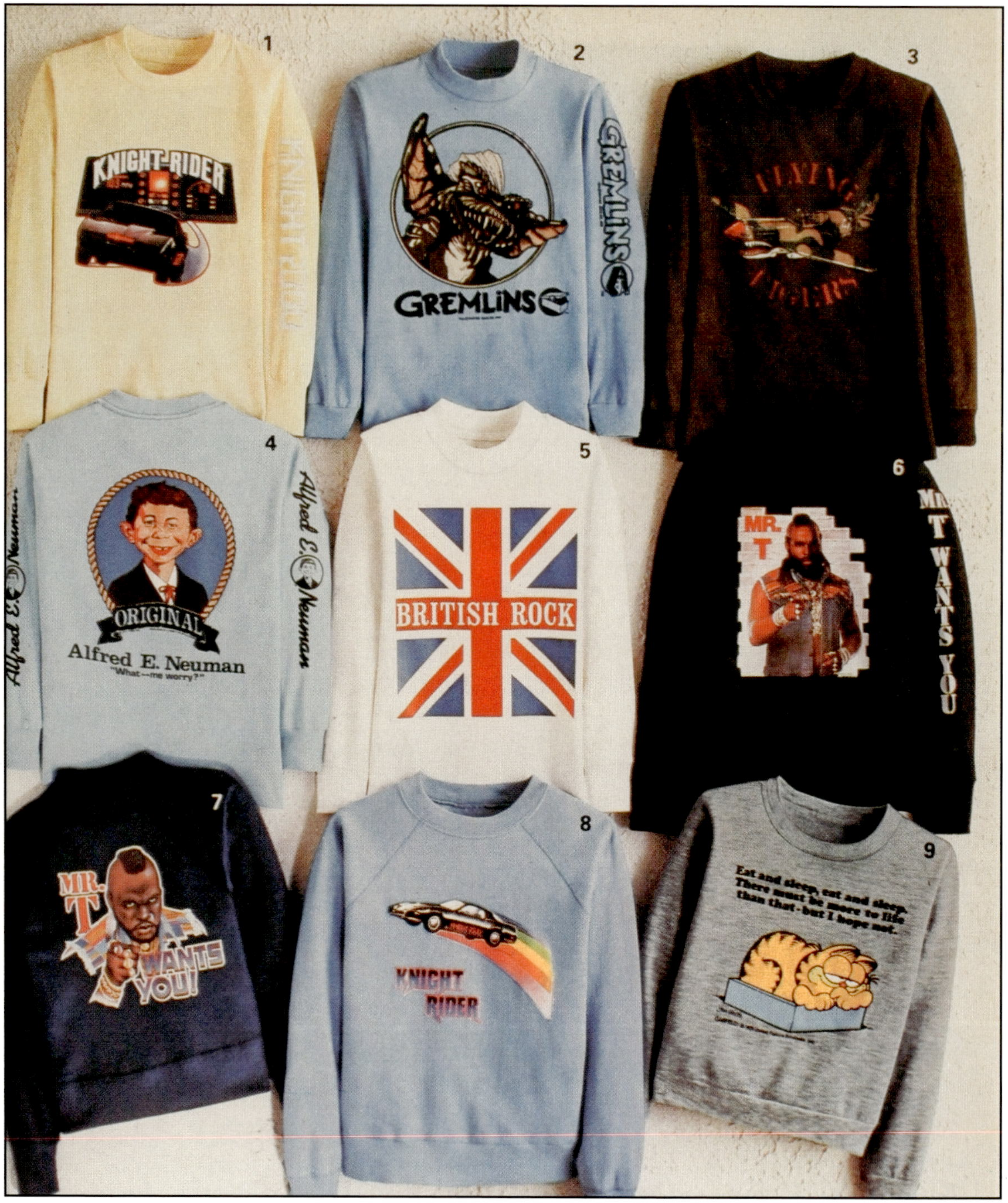

Knit shirts in popular prints. *Fall/Winter 1984.*

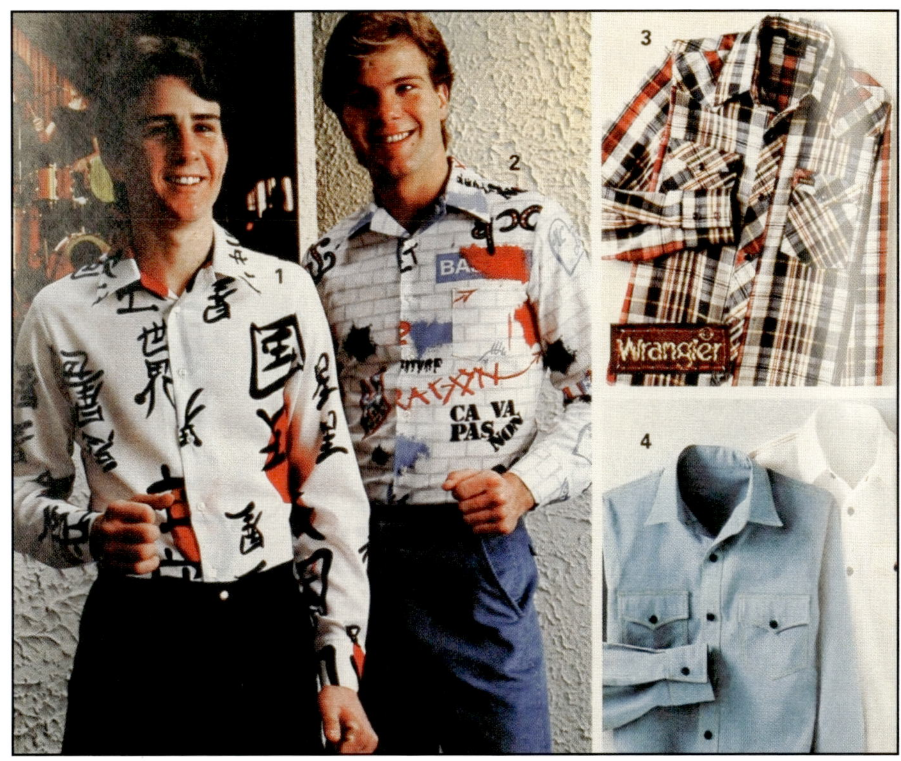

Woven polyester and rayon print shirts. Wrangler® blue and red plaid shirt and has authentic western details such as front and back yoke, snap plackets, pockets, and cuffs. PERMA-PREST® shirt has chambray look. *Fall/Winter 1984.*

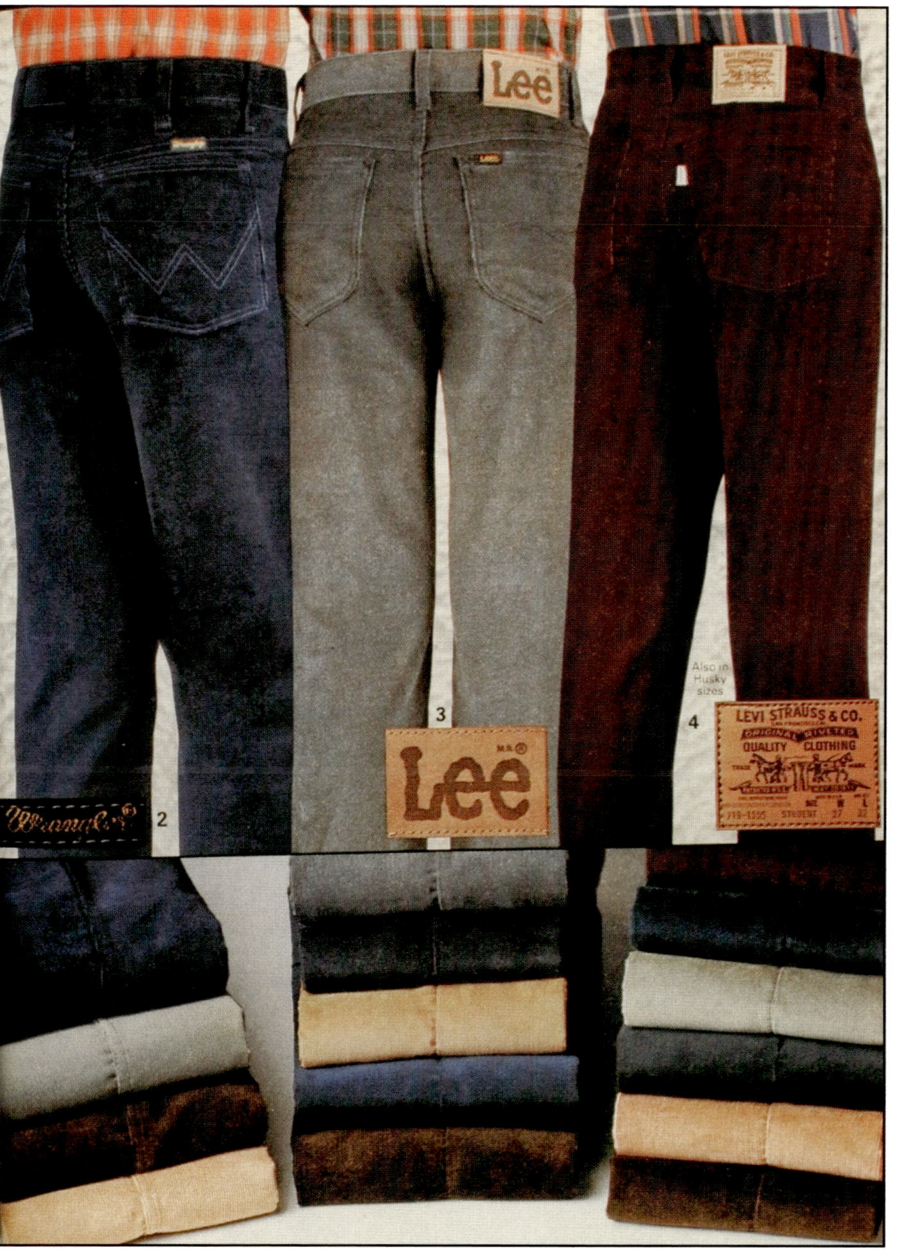

Brand name cords from Wrangler®, Lee®, and Levi's®. *Fall/Winter 1984.*

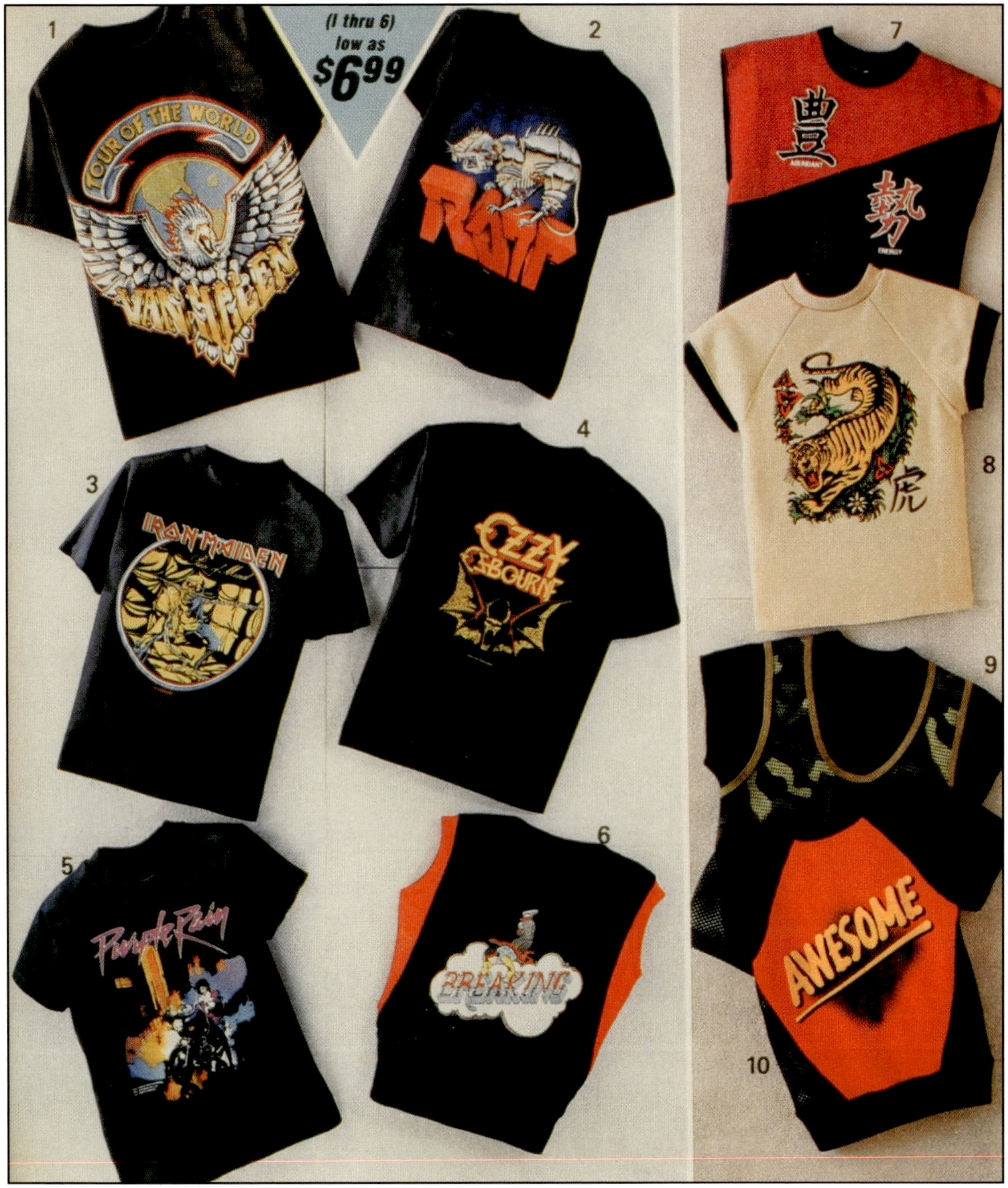

Heavy metal t-shirts and street-wise sweatshirt fleeces. *Spring/Summer 1985*

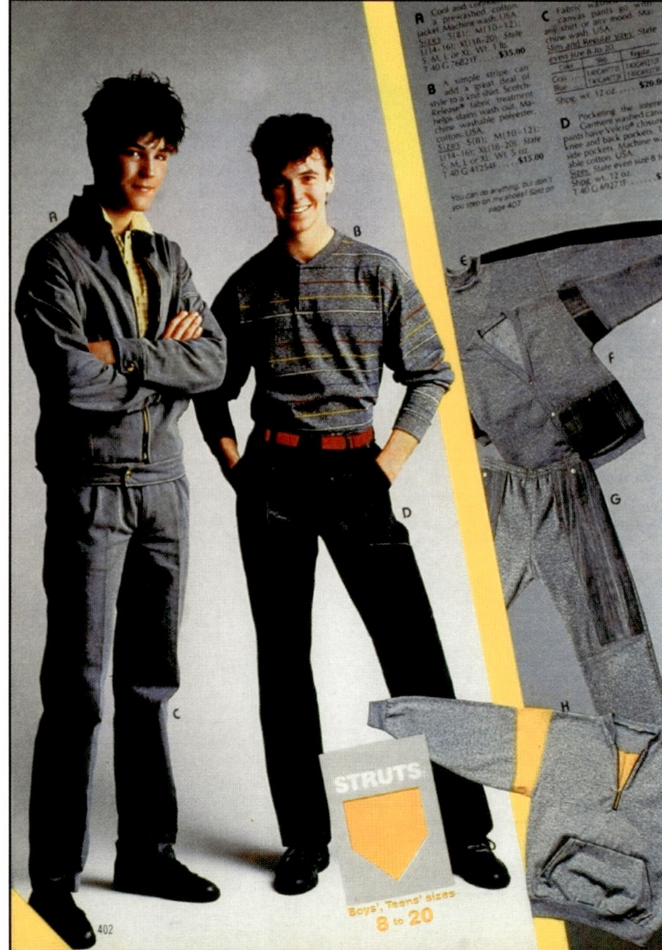

Cotton jacket, striped knit shirt, and cotton canvas pants in fabric and garment wash. *Fall/Winter 1985*

Polyester and cotton tropical print shirt worn with all cotton jeans. Jacket is woven of crinkled cotton and has push up sleeves, worn with all cotton sheeting pants. Polyester and cotton knit shirt worn with all cotton sheeting pants. *Spring/Summer 1986*

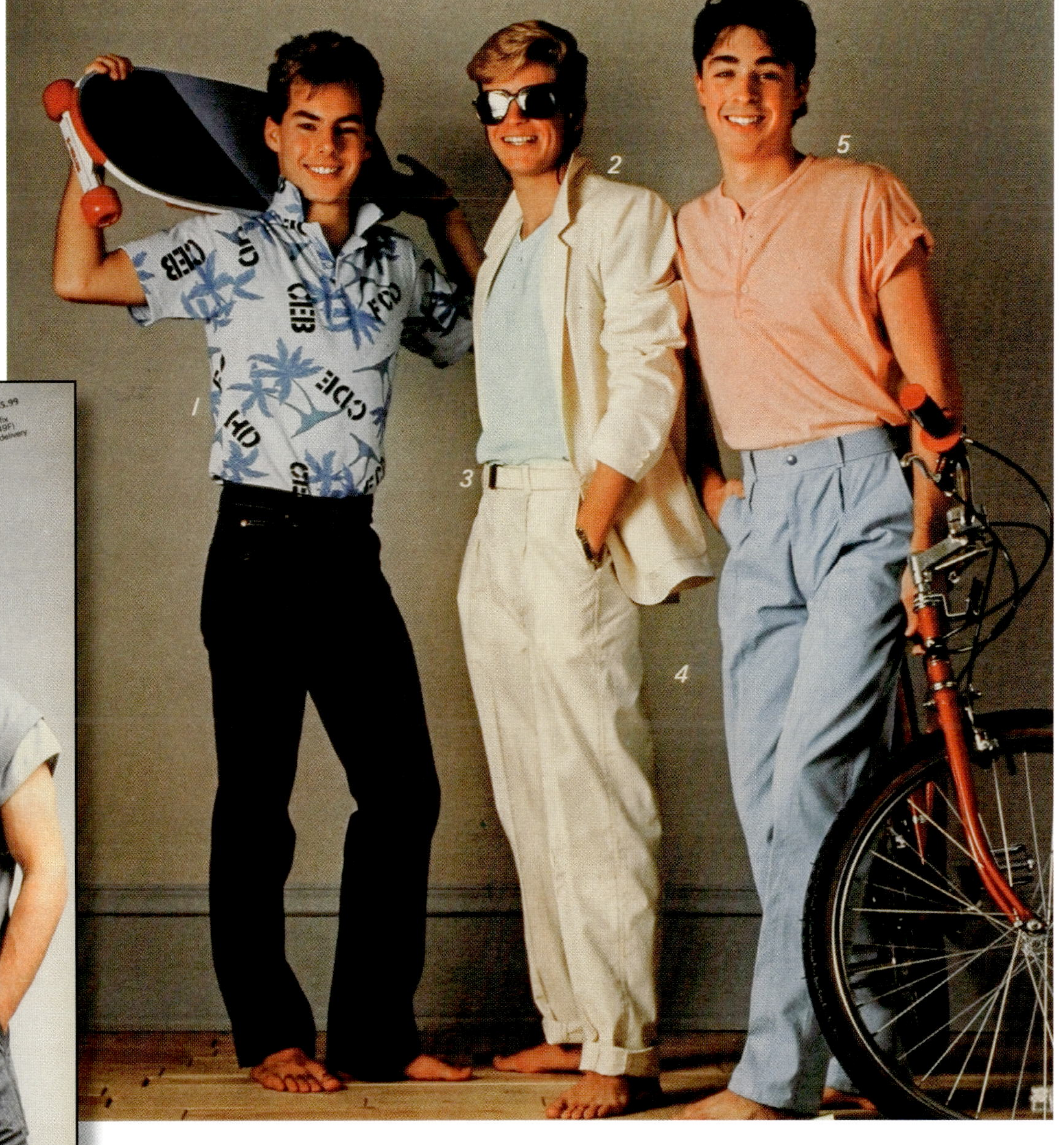

Shirt woven of lightweight polyester and cotton chambray, and layered knit shirts in polyester and cotton. *Fall/Winter 1985*

Sporty

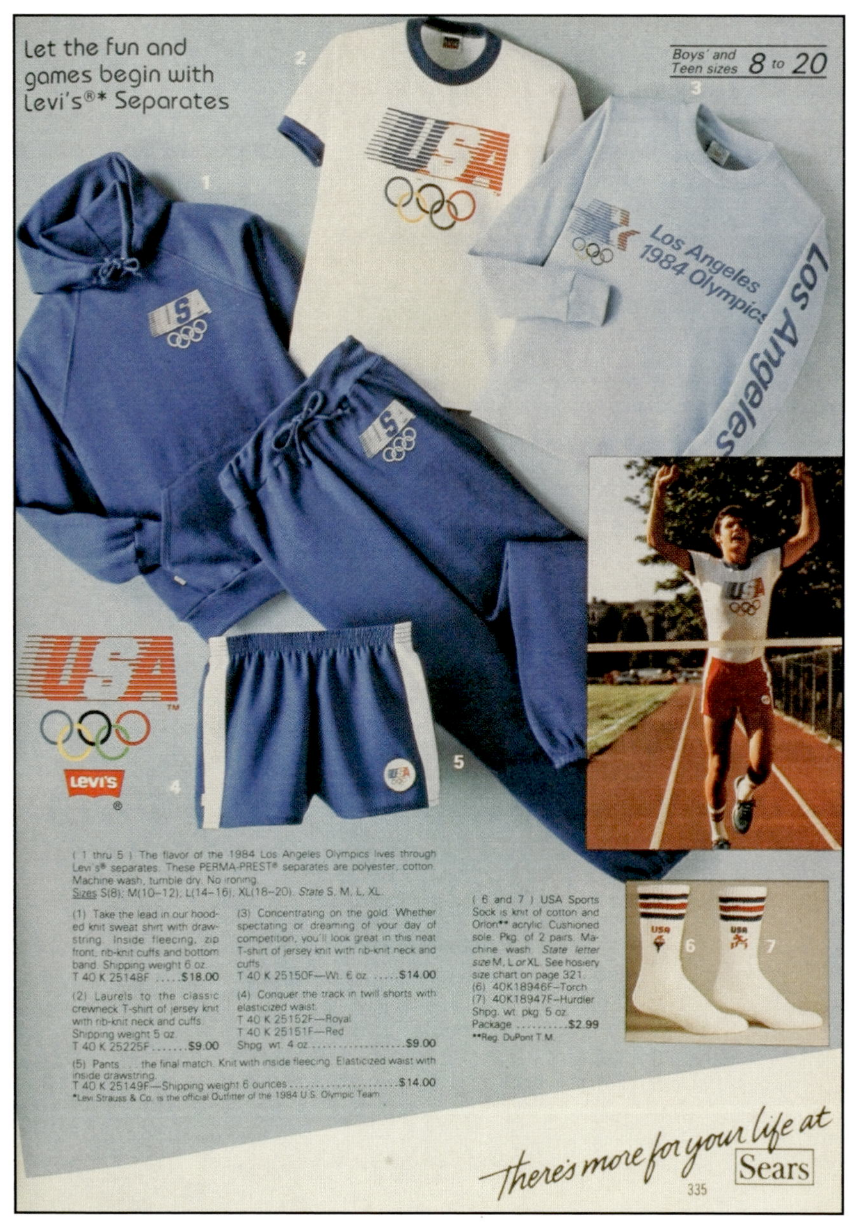

Levi's separates have the flavor of the 1984 Los Angeles Olympics. *Spring/Summer 1984.*

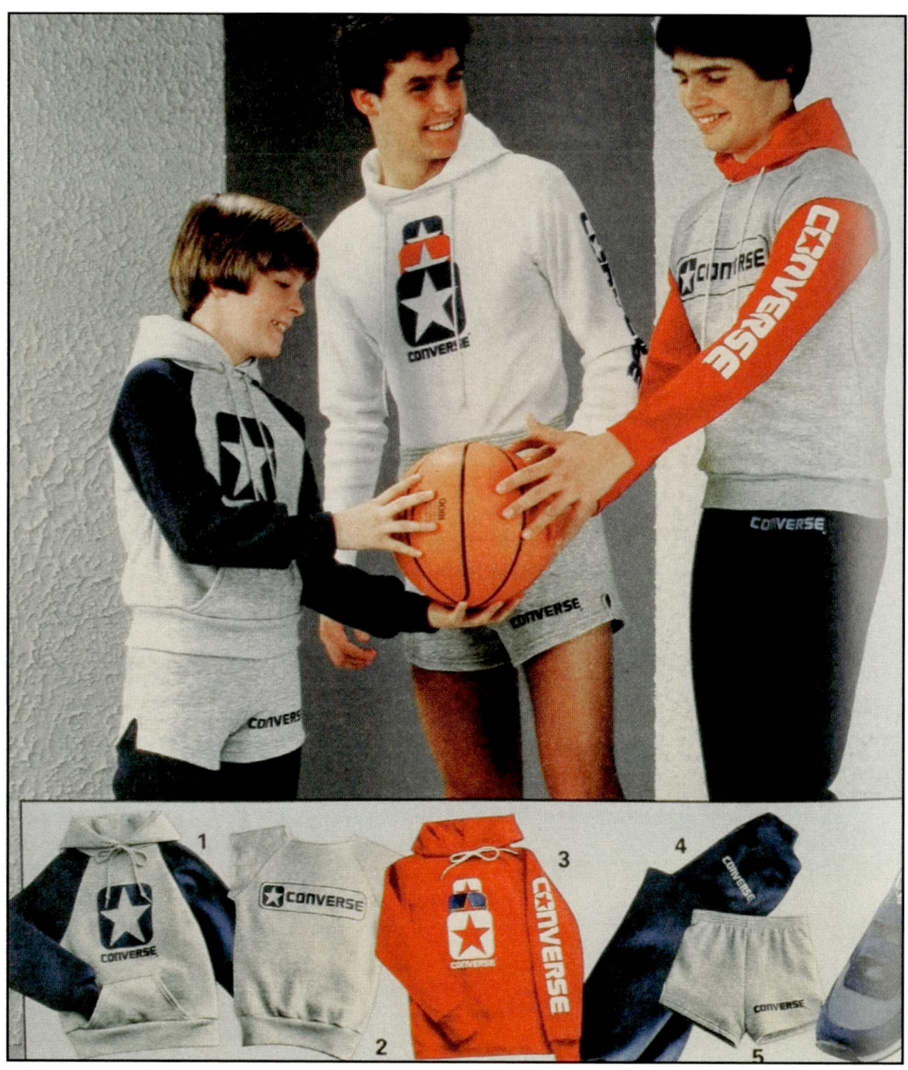

Athletic coordinates by Converse in cotton and polyester fabric. *Fall/Winter 1984.*

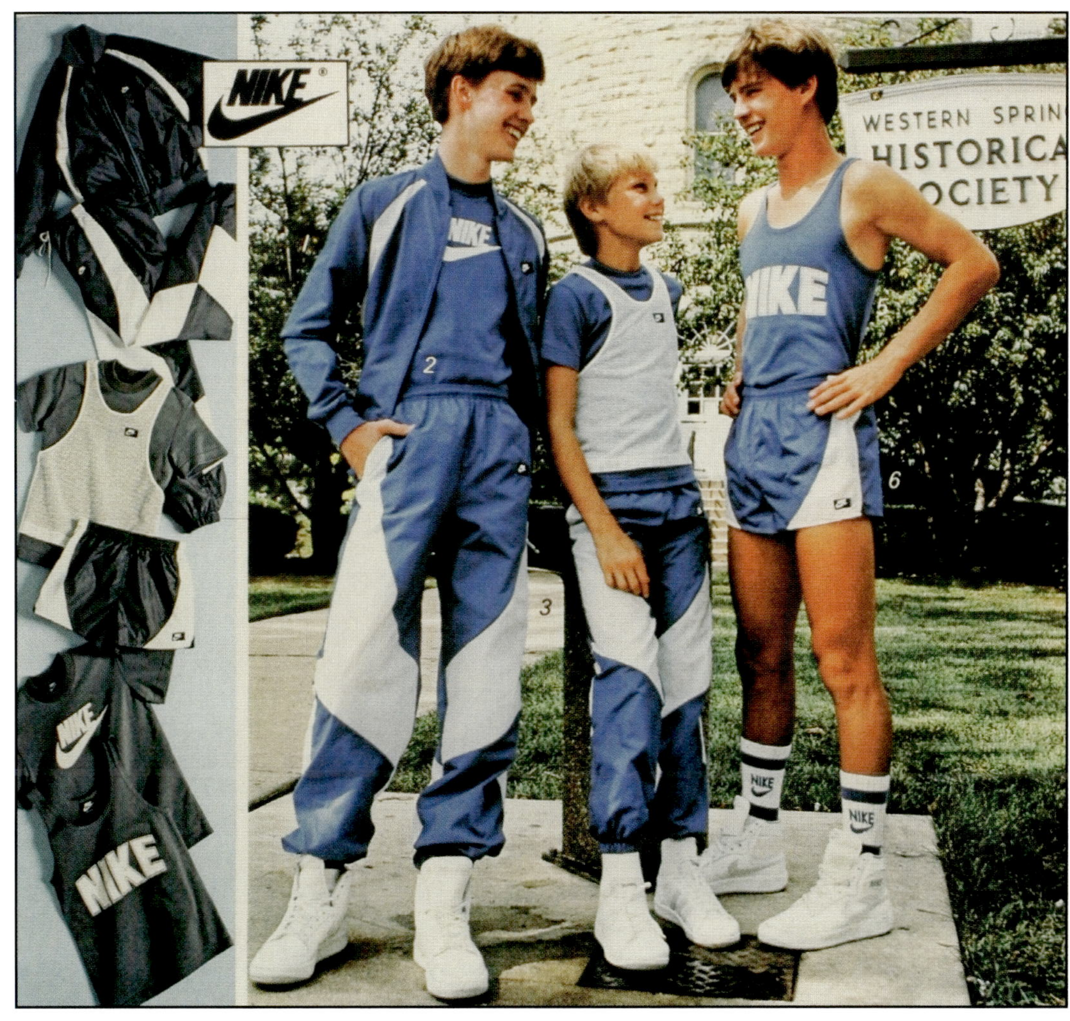

Nike athletic coordinates. *Spring/Summer 1986*

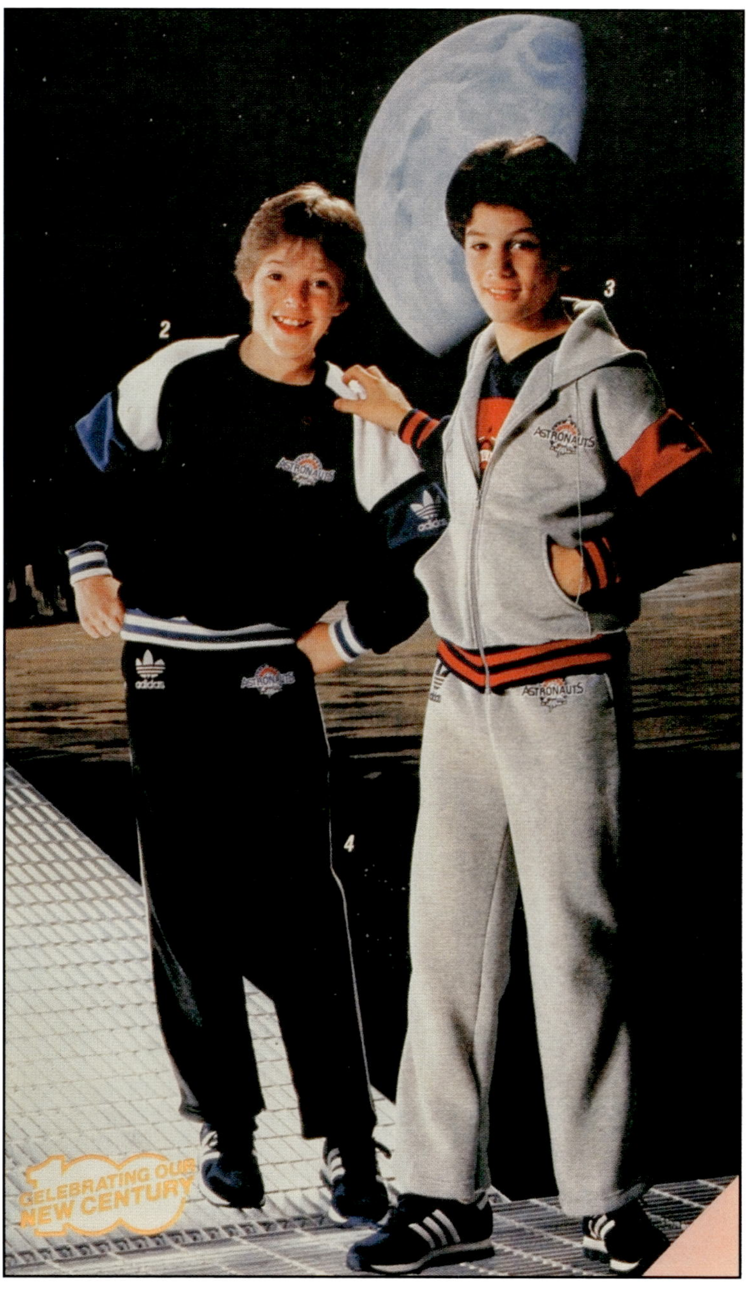

Fleece separates in polyester and cotton with the Astronauts and Adidas® logos. *Fall/Winter 1986*

Footwear

Brand name athletic shoes for men and teens. *Fall/Winter 1984.*

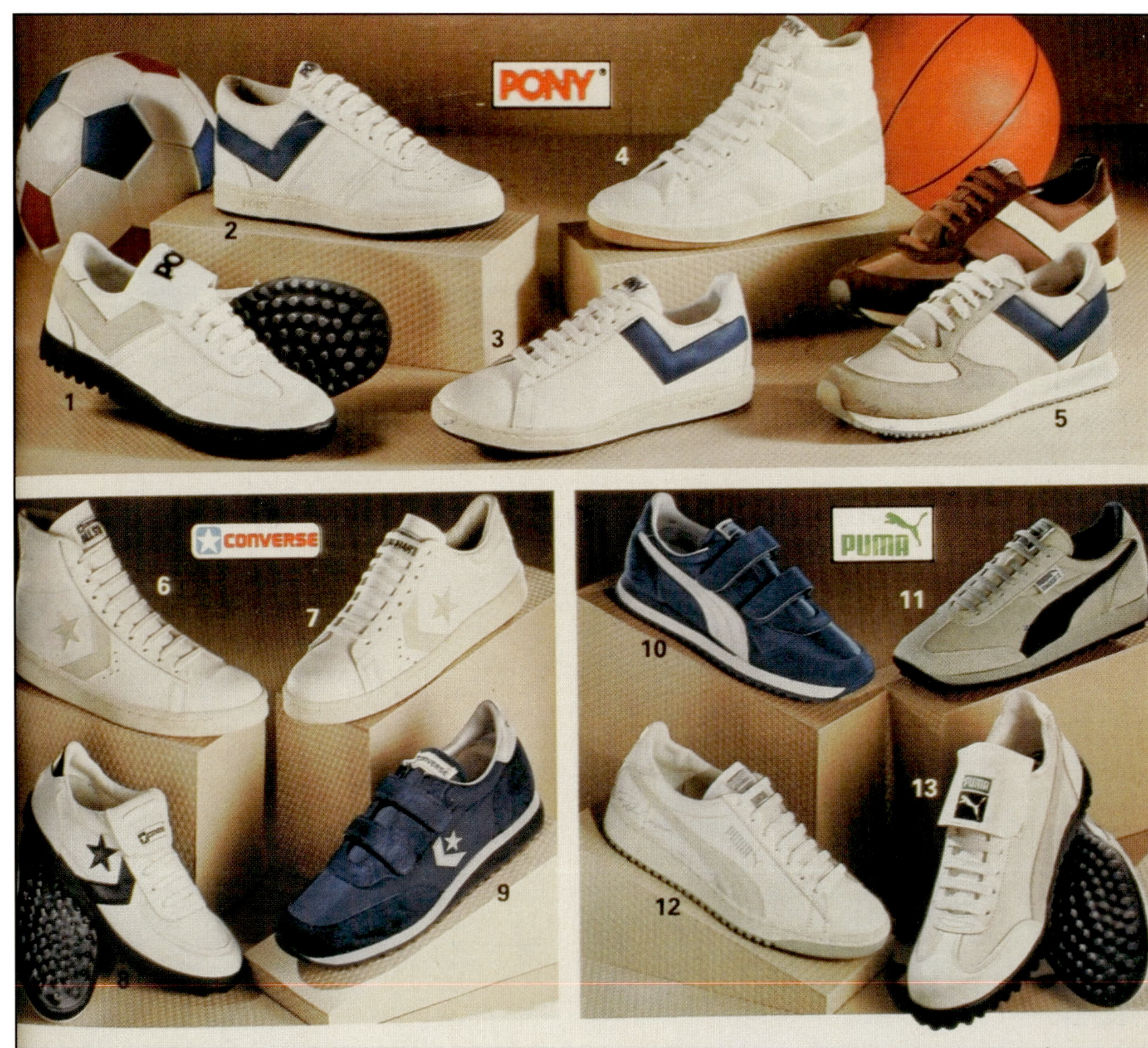

Coats

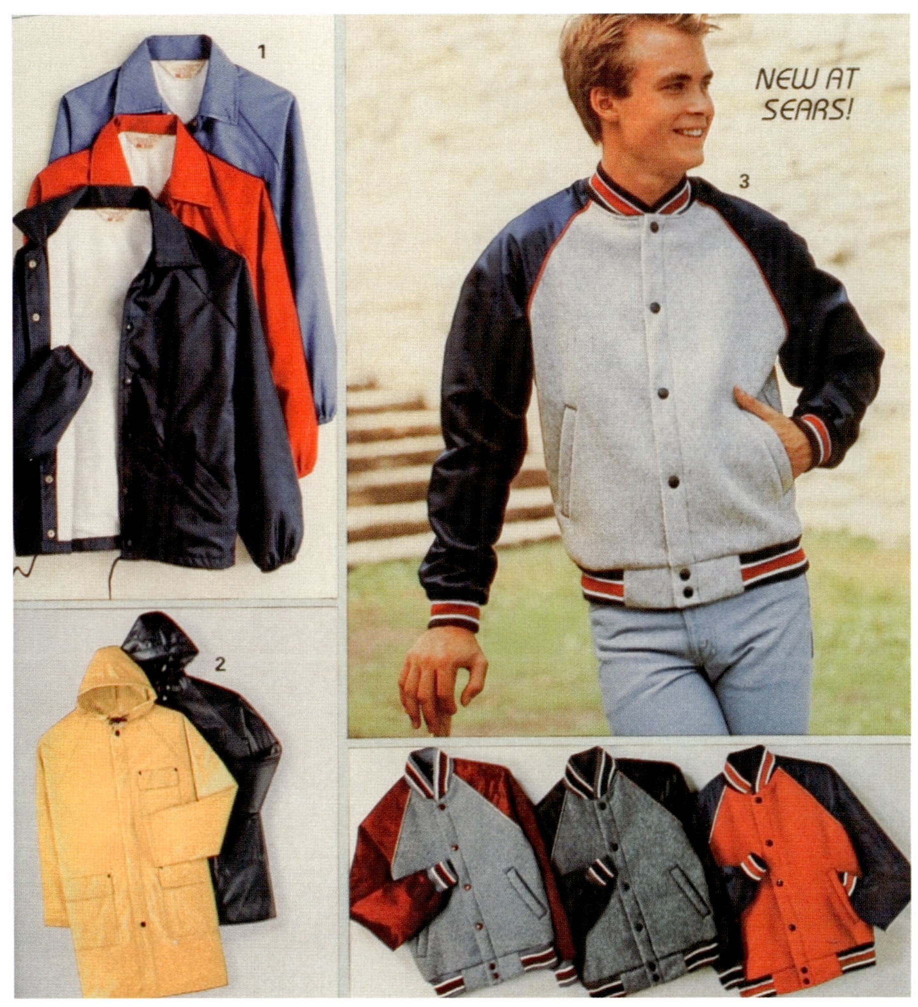

Warm-up jackets have drawstring waist, snap front, and slash pockets. Vinyl slickers with storm flaps are full length. Polar fleece of Celanese Fortrel® jackets create air pockets that hold in heat. *Spring/Summer 1984.*

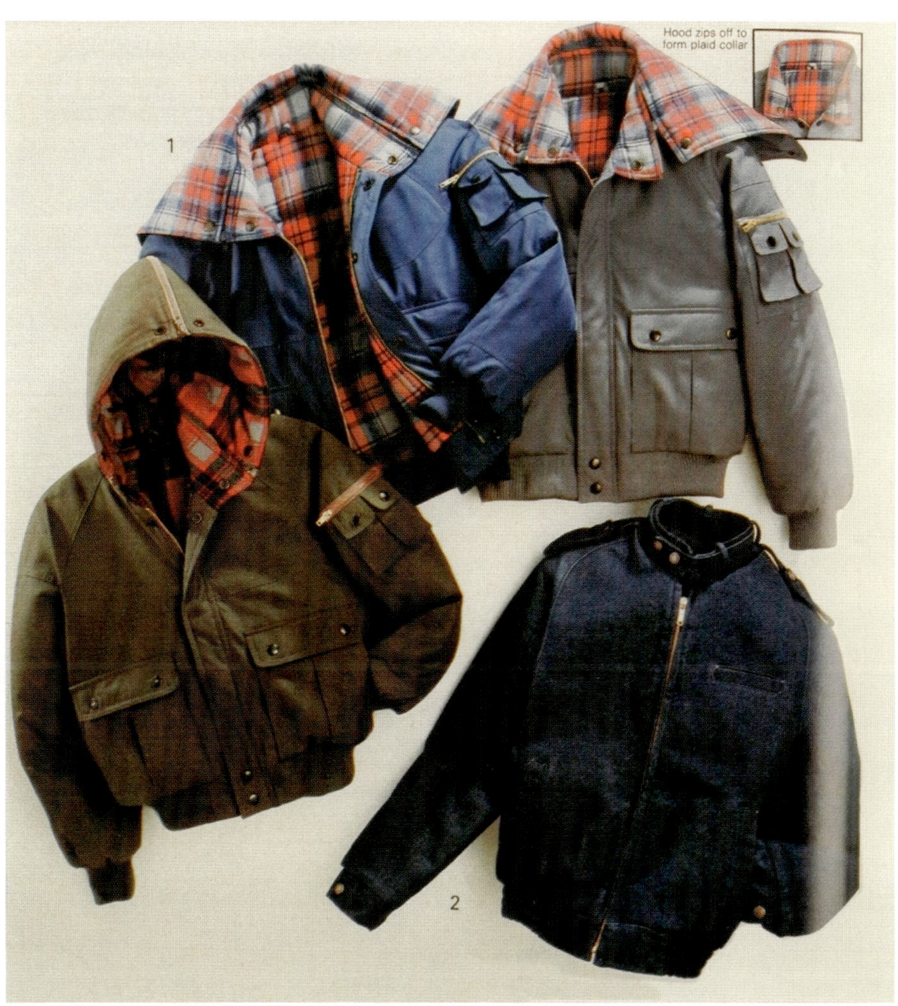

Poplin shell jacket of polyester and cotton with acrylic plaid lining and polyester fiberfill. Pre-washed 100% cotton denim jacket. *Fall/Winter 1984.*

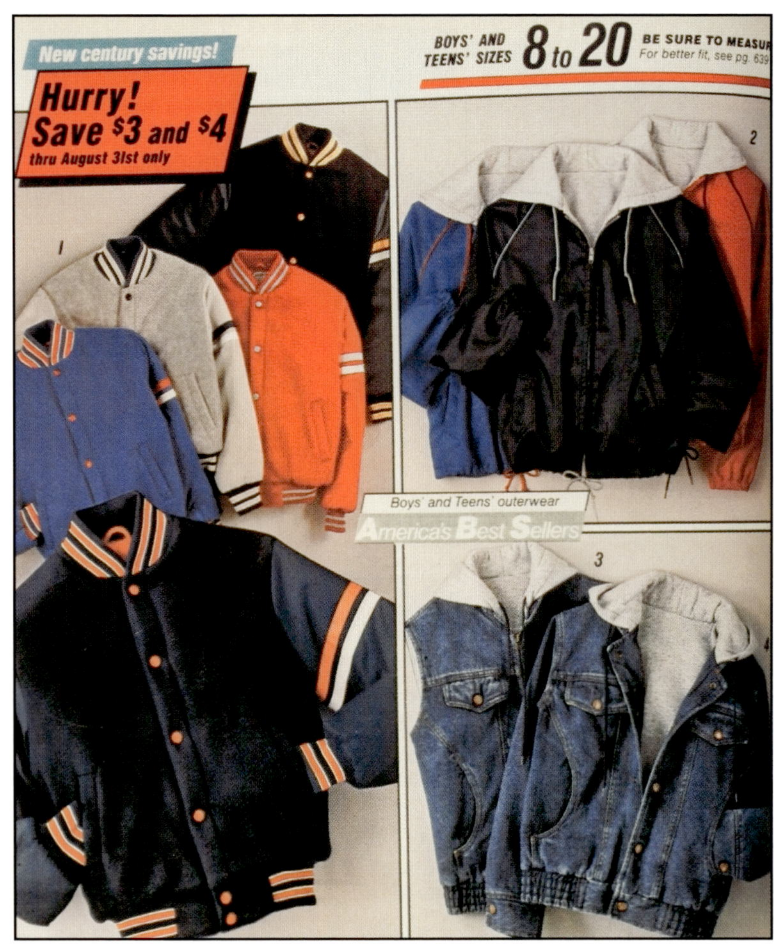

Team jackets, hooded jackets with contrast piping, jean jacket and vest, are all popular styles. *Fall/Winter 1986*

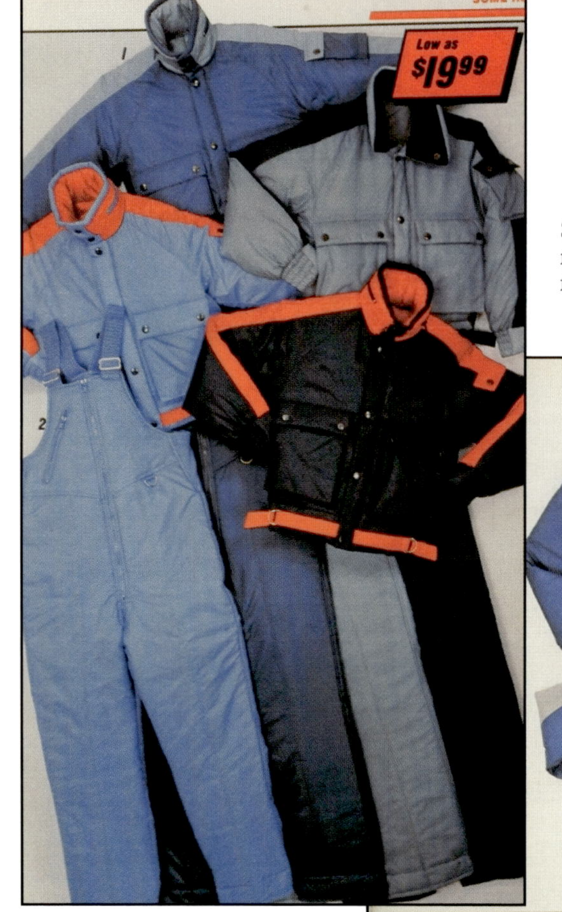

Ski jackets, vests, and bib pants have nylon shells quilted to polyester fiberfill. *Fall/Winter 1986*

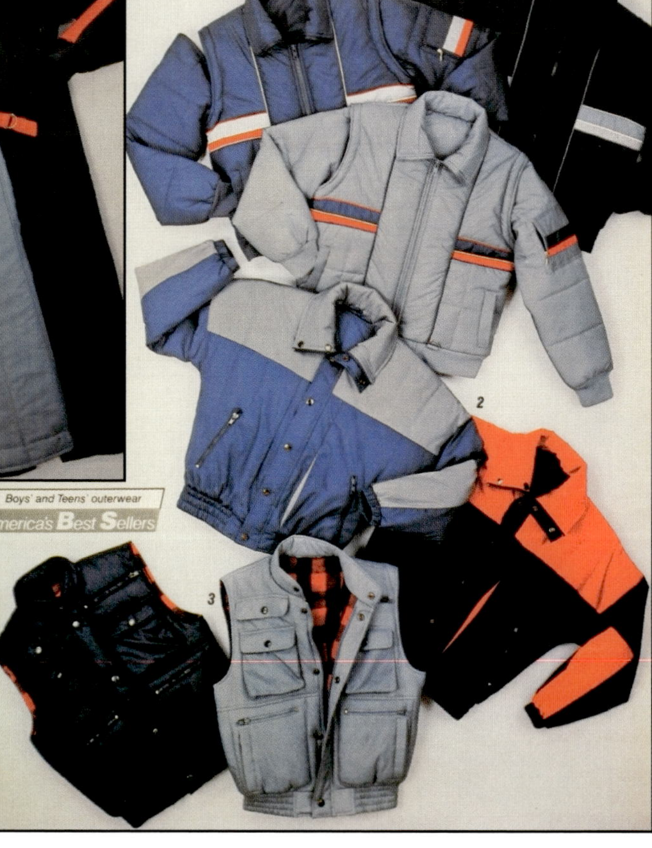

Little Girls' Fashions

Dressy

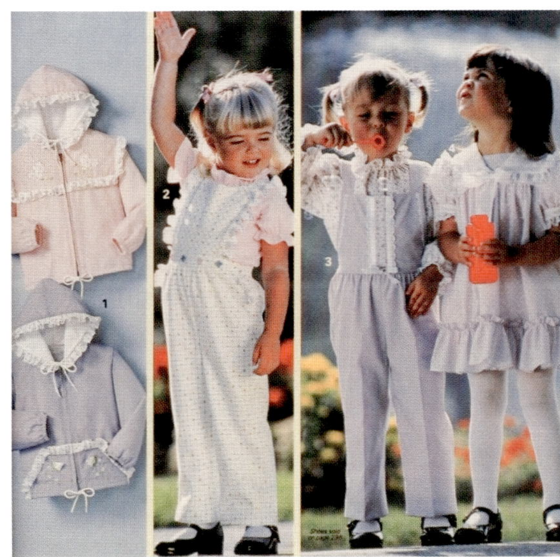

Woven nylon jackets with flannel lining and embroidered flower trim. Overall set is made of polyester and cotton. Lilac overalls with floral print blouse. High-waisted lavender dress with smock styling. Gingham apron dress in polyester and cotton. Tiered blue high waist dress with ribbon sash in polyester and cotton. *Spring/Summer 1984.*

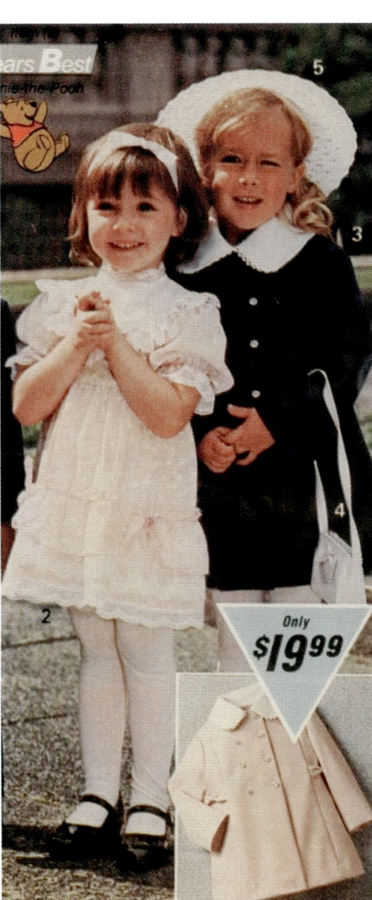

Winnie-the-Pooh pink ruffled party dress, and double-breasted dress with white poplin collar. *Spring/Summer 1985*

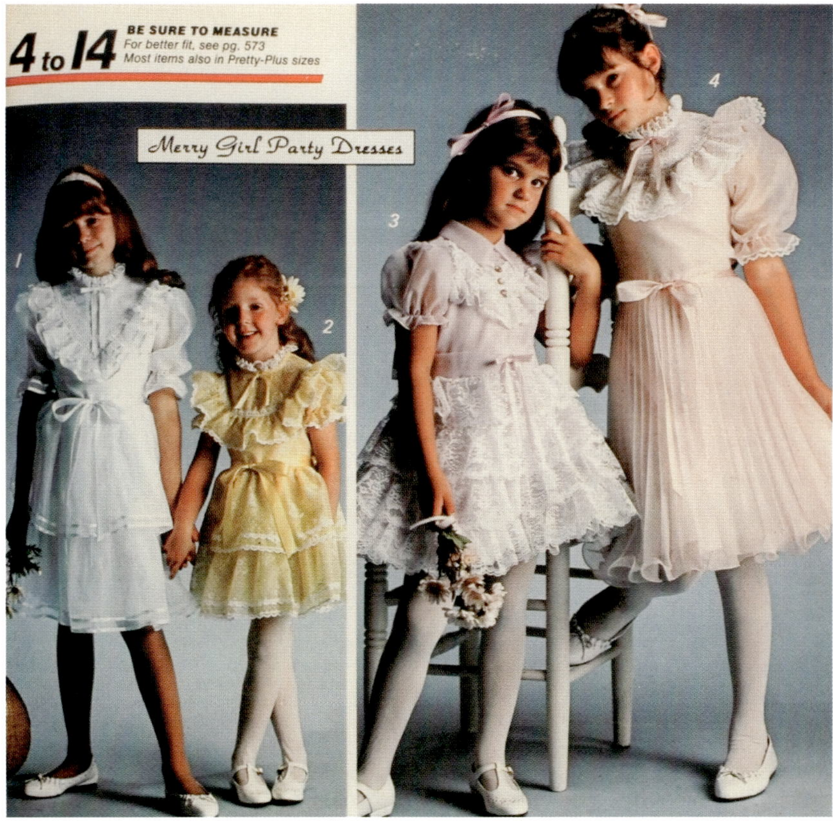

Polyester organza Merry Girl Party Dresses. *Spring/Summer 1986*

Casual

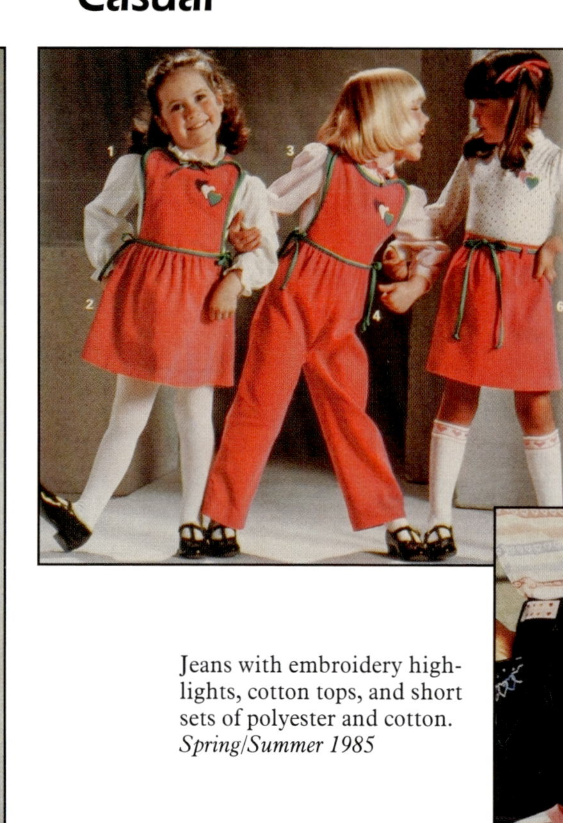

Cotton and polyester dress, jumper, and skirt with turquoise accents. *Fall/Winter 1984.*

Separates for infants are all made of polyester and cotton. *Fall/Winter 1984.*

Jeans with embroidery highlights, cotton tops, and short sets of polyester and cotton. *Spring/Summer 1985*

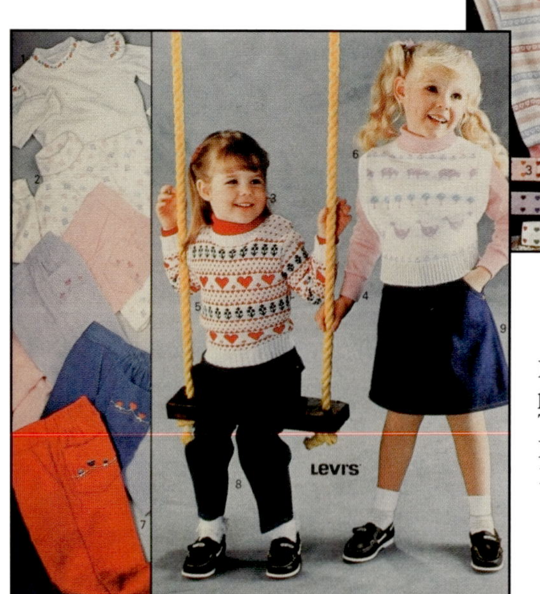

Polyester and cotton knit shirts, pull-over sweaters of acrylic, Toughskins® corduroy pants, and Levi's® baggy jeans and skirt in 100% rinsed cotton. *Fall/Winter 1985*

Sporty

Separates from the Struts line feature bright and fresh colors and styles. *Spring/Summer 1986*

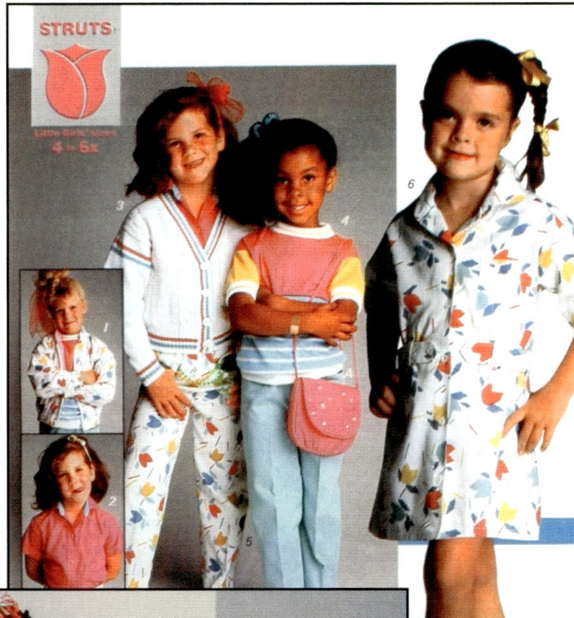

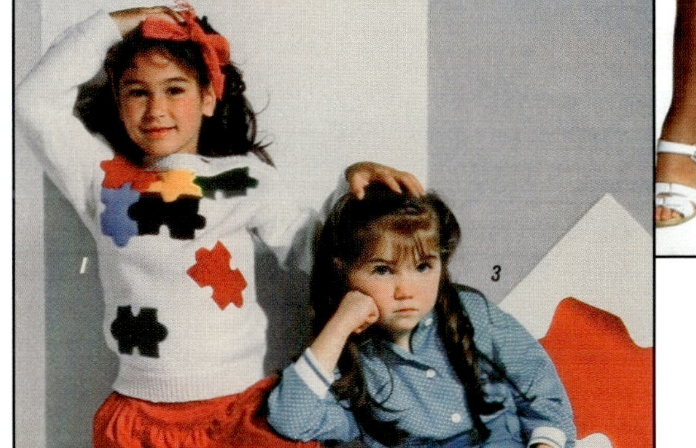

Struts mix and match coordinates. *Fall/Winter 1986*

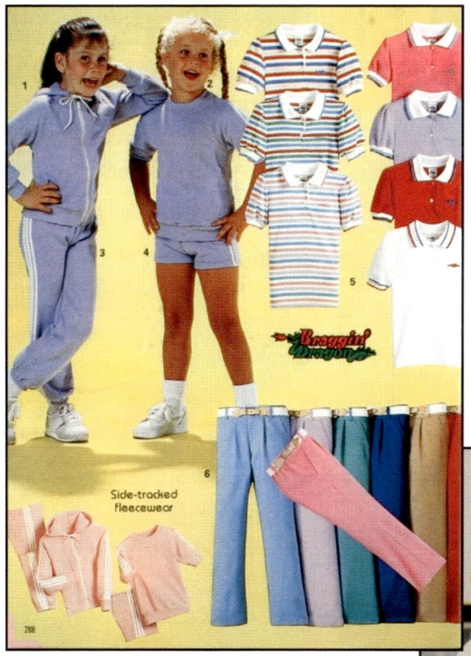

Acrilan® acrylic fleece active wear tops and bottoms. Braggin' Dragon PERMA-PREST® shirts and slacks. *Spring/Summer 1984.*

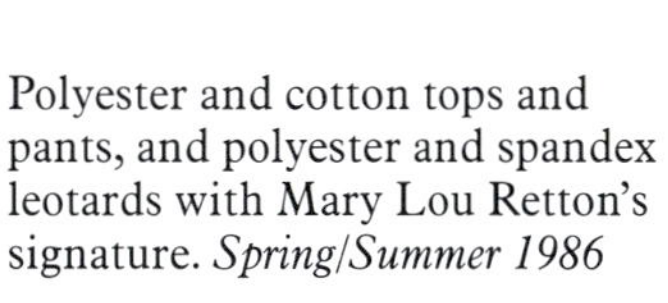

Polyester and cotton tops and pants, and polyester and spandex leotards with Mary Lou Retton's signature. *Spring/Summer 1986*

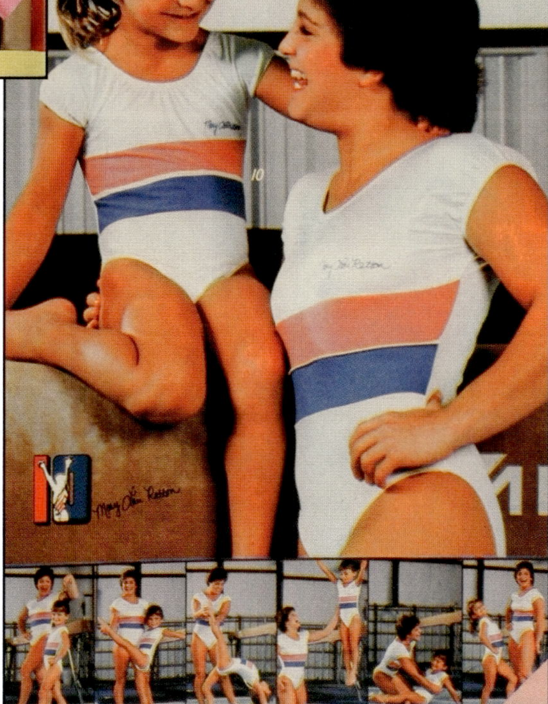

Pajamas

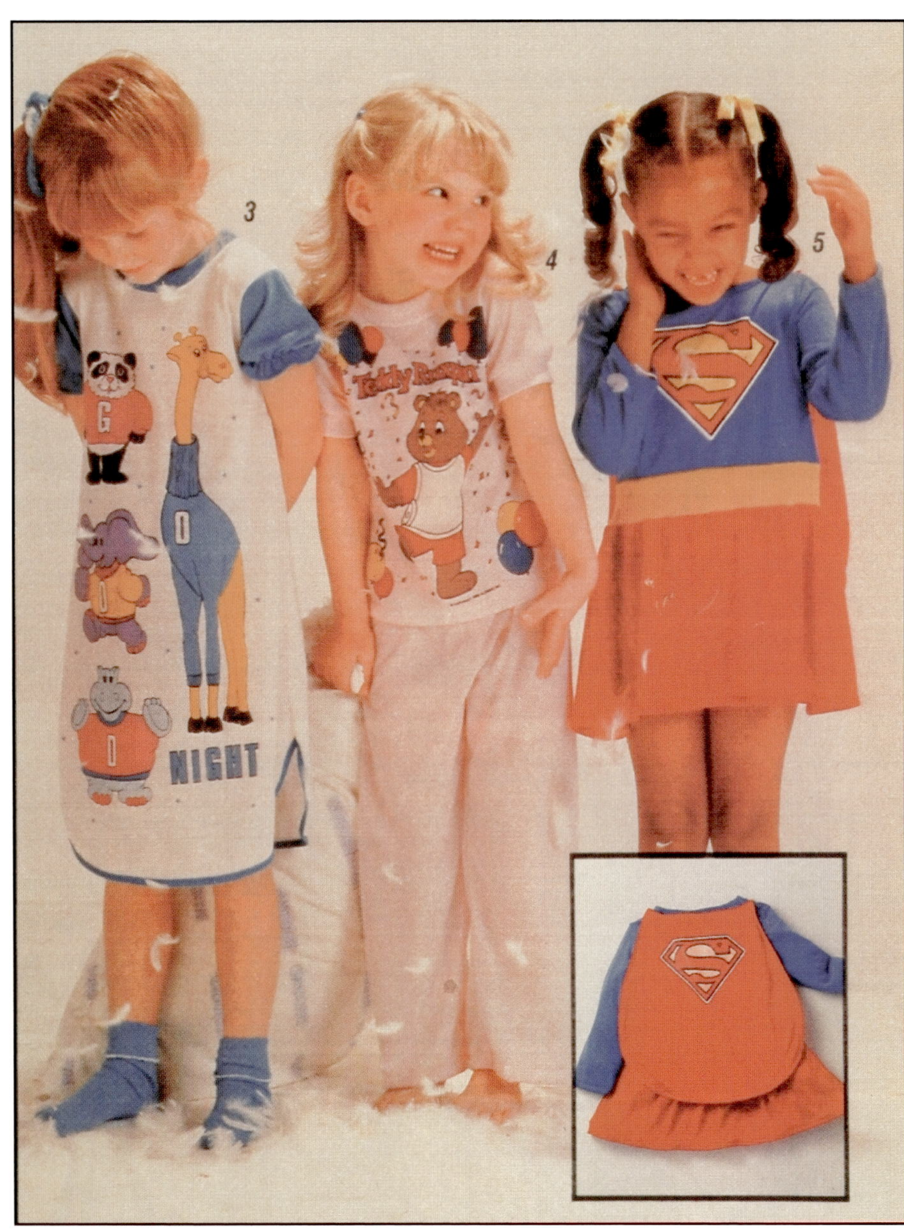

Bedtime wear comes with animals, Teddy Ruxpin, and SuperGirl in polyester knit. *Fall/Winter 1986*

Coats

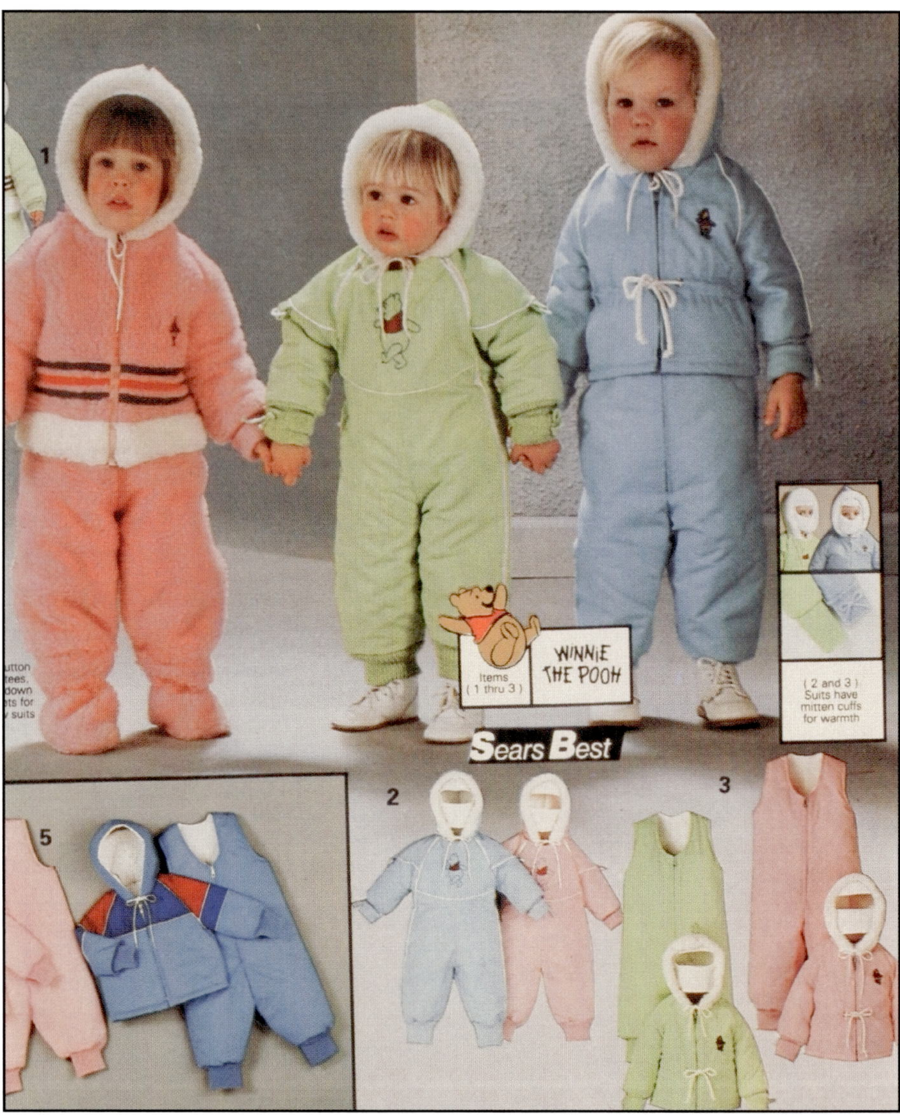

Wintertime one- and two-piece suits. *Fall/Winter 1984.*

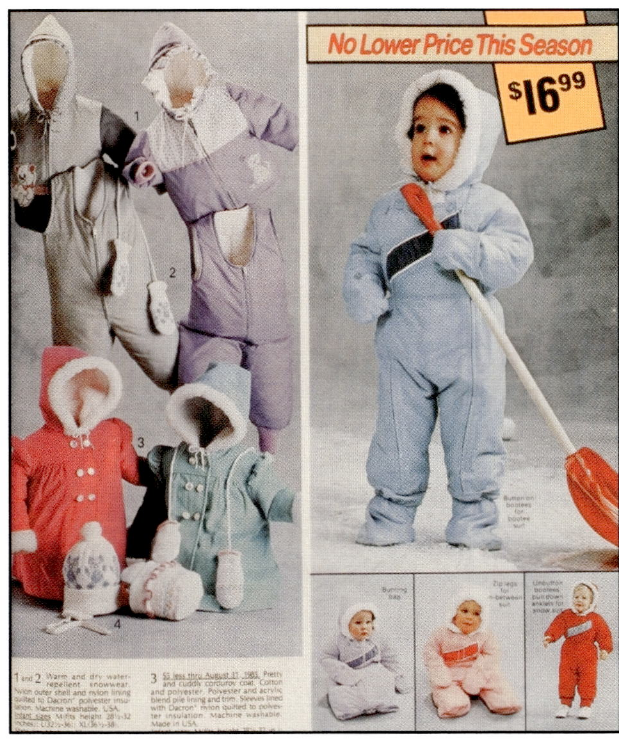

Snow wear in nylon and corduroy fabrics and a variety of styles. *Fall/Winter 1985*

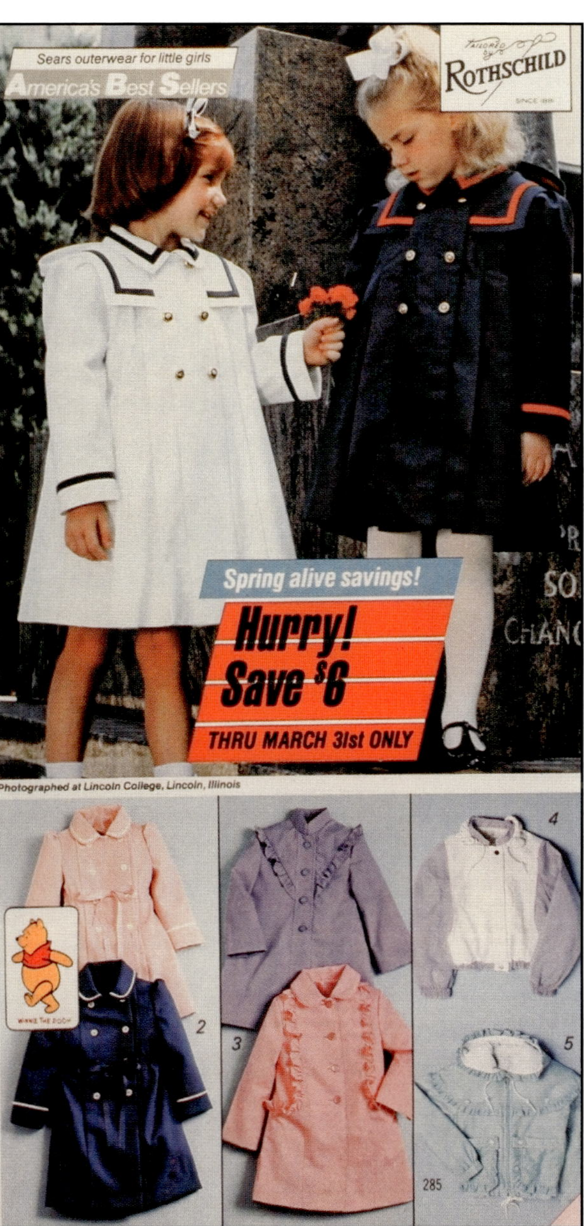

Coats with a regal sweep are tailored by Rothschild. Winnie-the-Pooh coats have elasticized empire waists and grosgrain ribbon tie. Coats with feminine ruffles in polyester and cotton twill. Vest-look jacket in crinkled nylon. Hooded jacket has a drawstring waist. *Spring/Summer 1986*

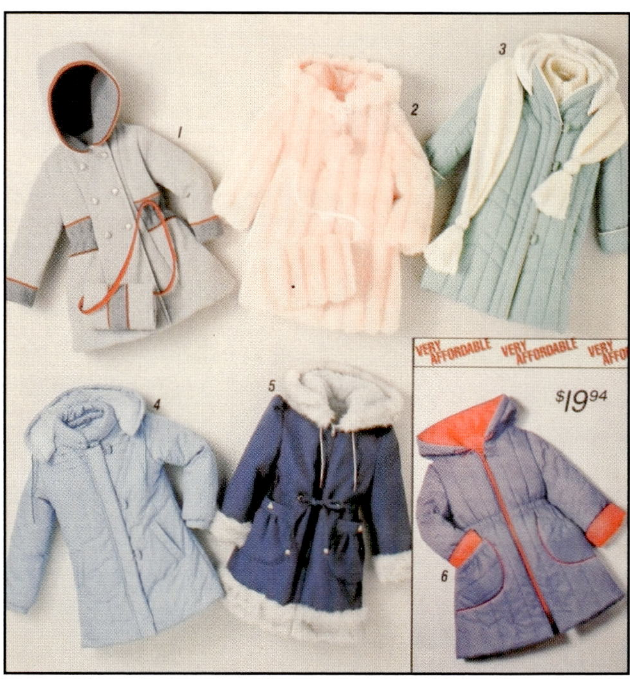

Coat and coordinating muff in polyester. Acrylic coat has pom tie hood and matching muff. Vestee coat in polyester and cotton has knit scarf and toggle closure. Pleated v-yoke coat in polyester and cotton with toggle closure. Polyester and acrylic coat is pile lined and has an attached hook and waist with drawstring. Quilted coat with contrasting color treatment. *Fall/Winter 1986*

Little Boys' Fashions

Dressy

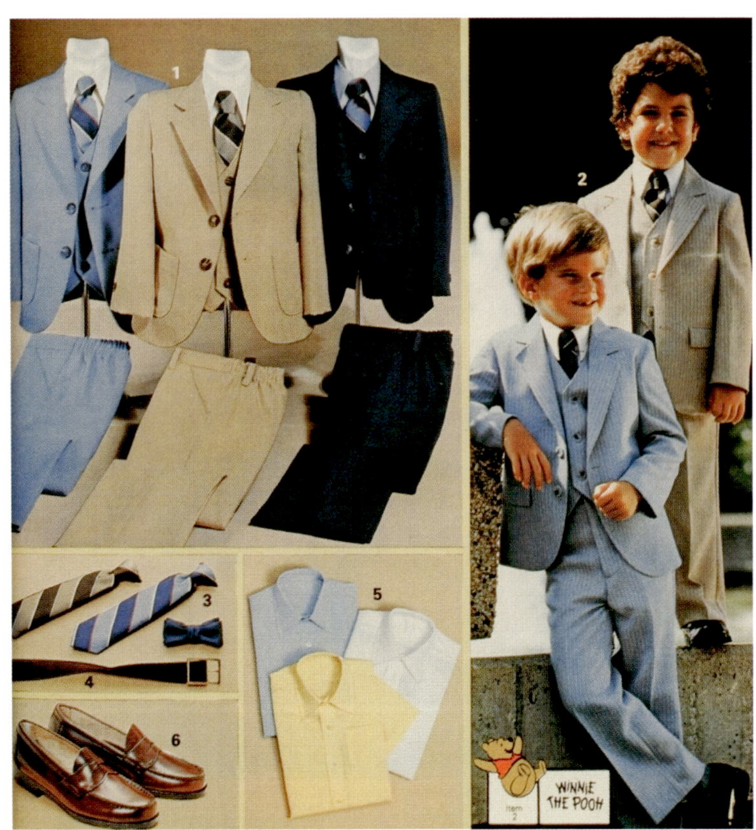

Winnie-the-Pooh 3-piece suits in solids or pinstripes are made of woven polyester and nylon. *Spring/Summer 1984.*

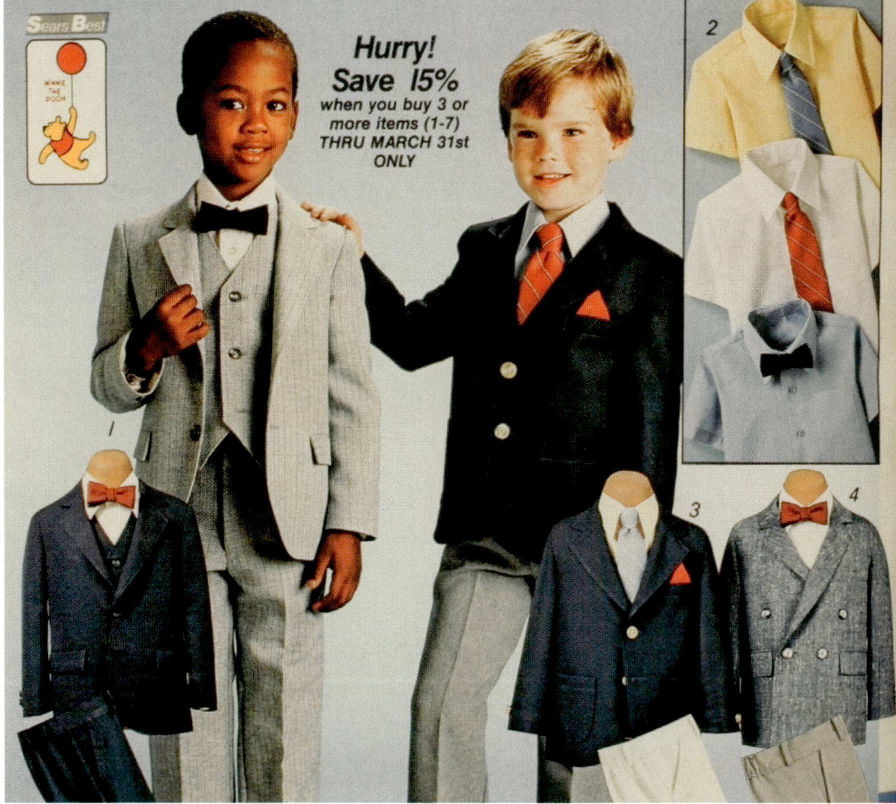

Winnie-the-Pooh 3-piece suits in solids or stripes. *Spring/Summer 1986*

Casual

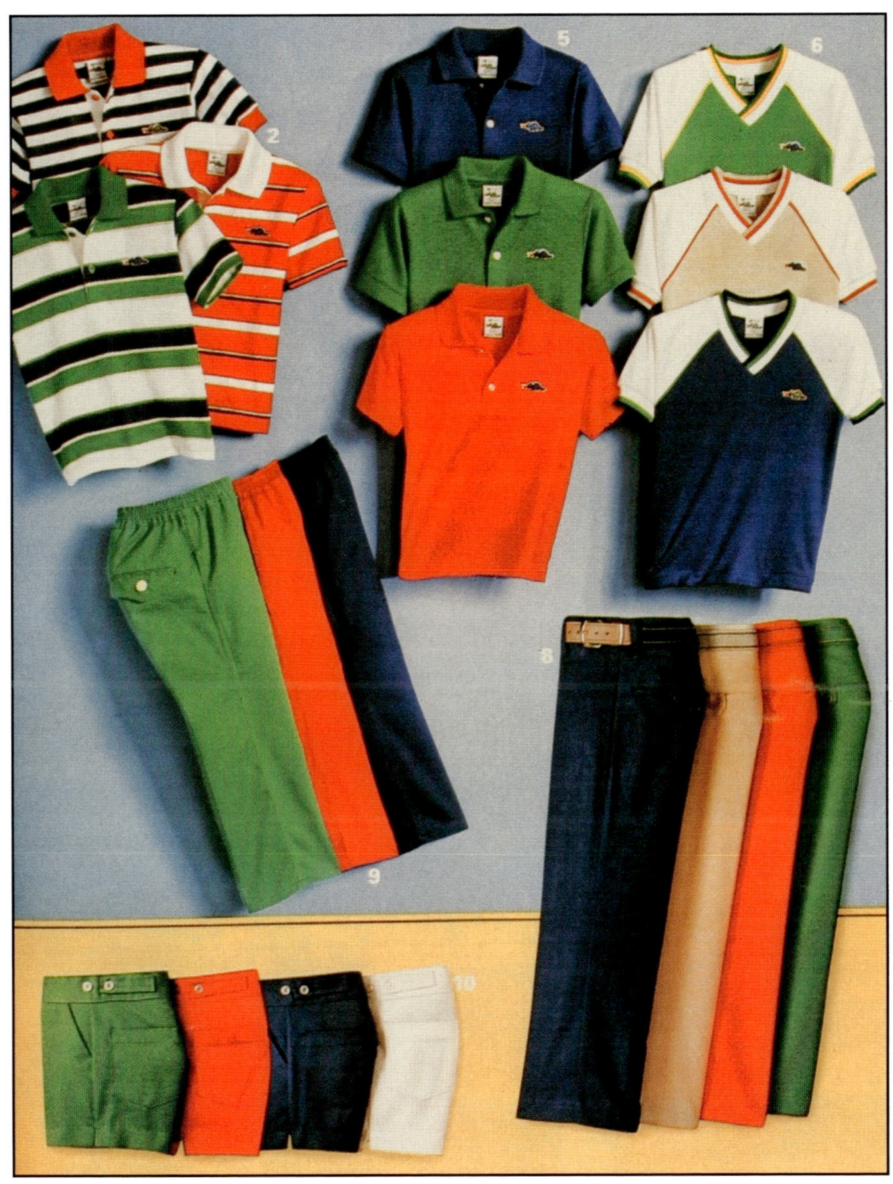

Knit shirts in solids, stripes, and V-necks in cotton and polyester. Cotton twill pants or shorts. Together they make a bright and sporty outfit. *Spring/Summer 1984.*

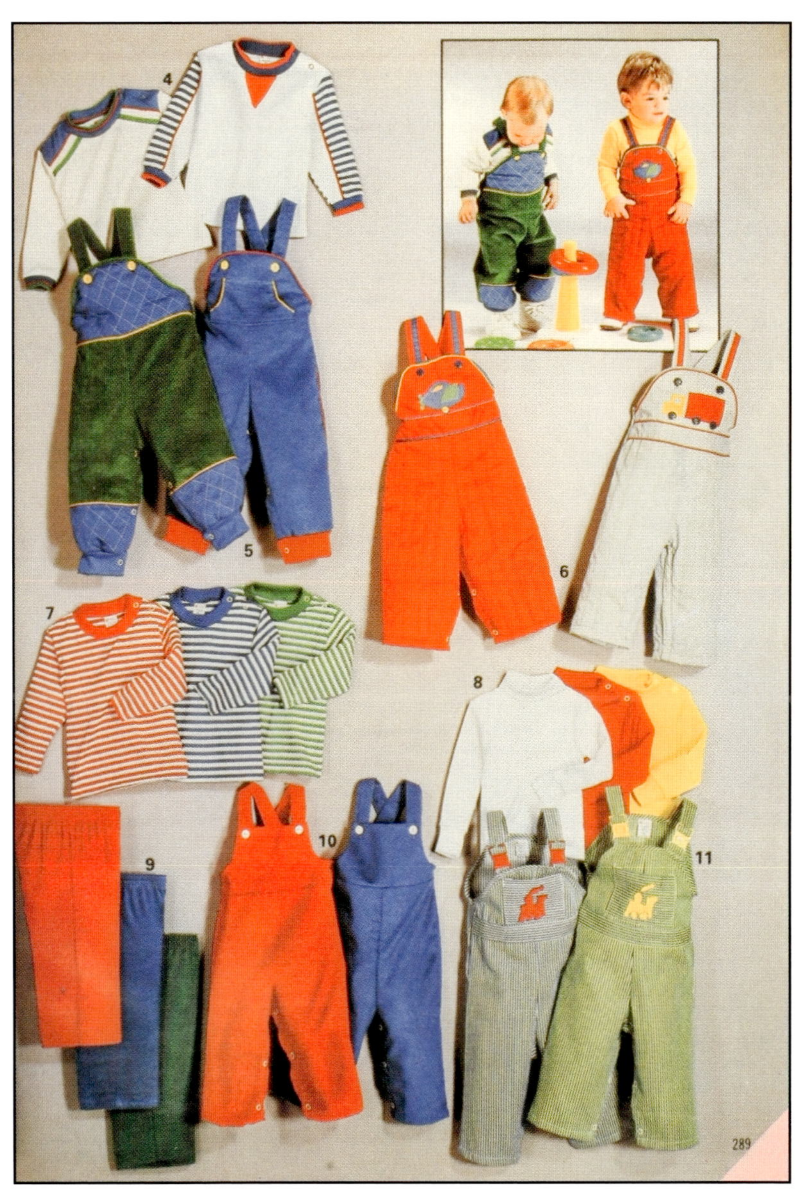

Shirts, pants, and overalls in polyester and cotton blends for toddlers. *Fall/Winter 1984.*

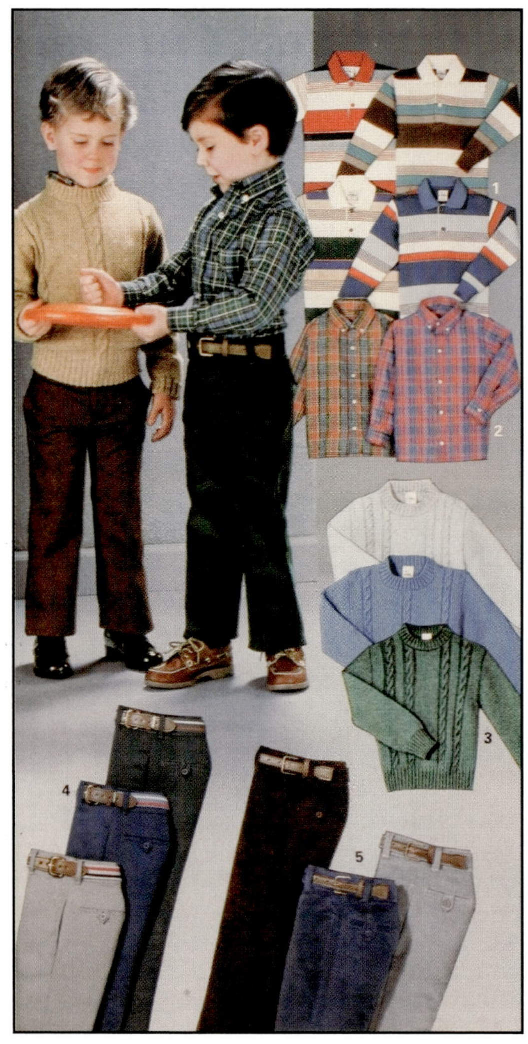

Sweaters, shirts, and pants from the Braggin Dragon collection for boys. *Fall/Winter 1984.*

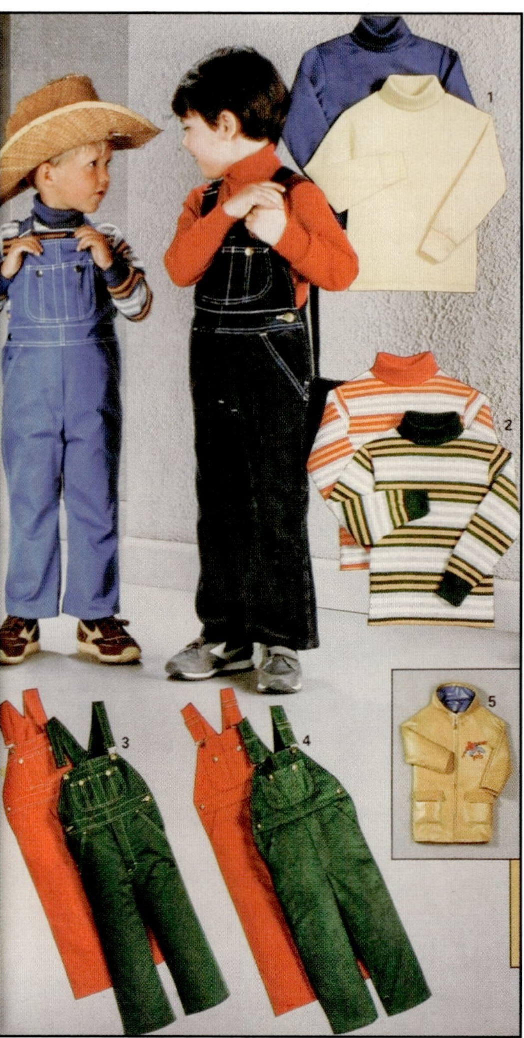

Polyester and cotton turtleneck tops and carpenter-style overalls in twill or corduroy. Waterproof slicker with Spiderman print on the front and back. *Fall/Winter 1984.*

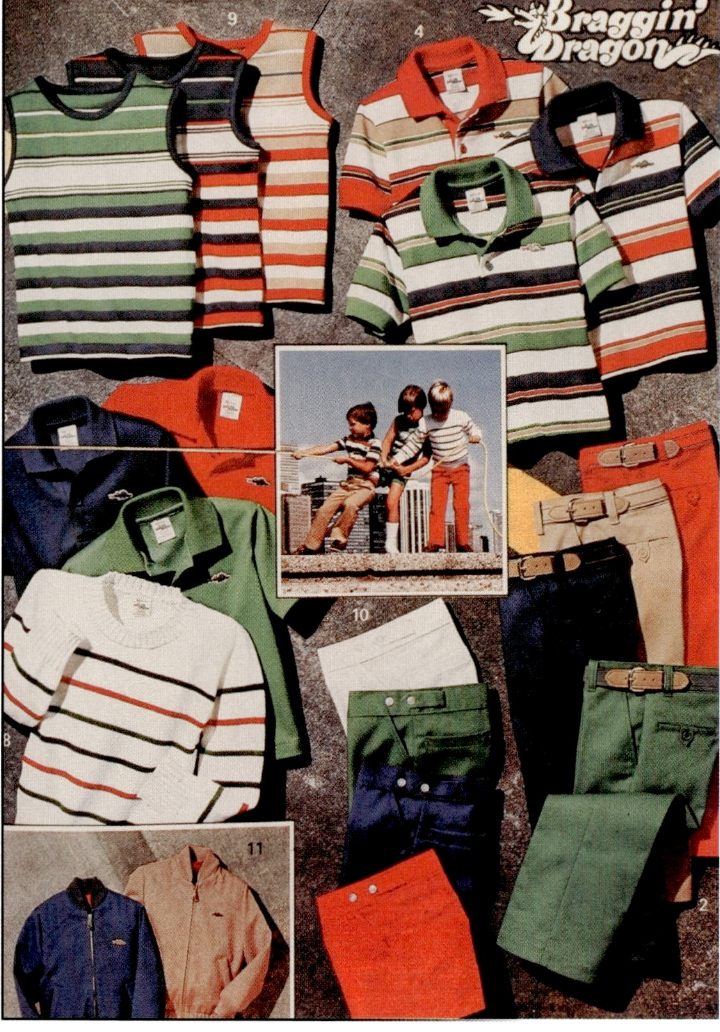

Braggin Dragon polyester and cotton tops, pants, and shorts. *Spring/Summer 1985*

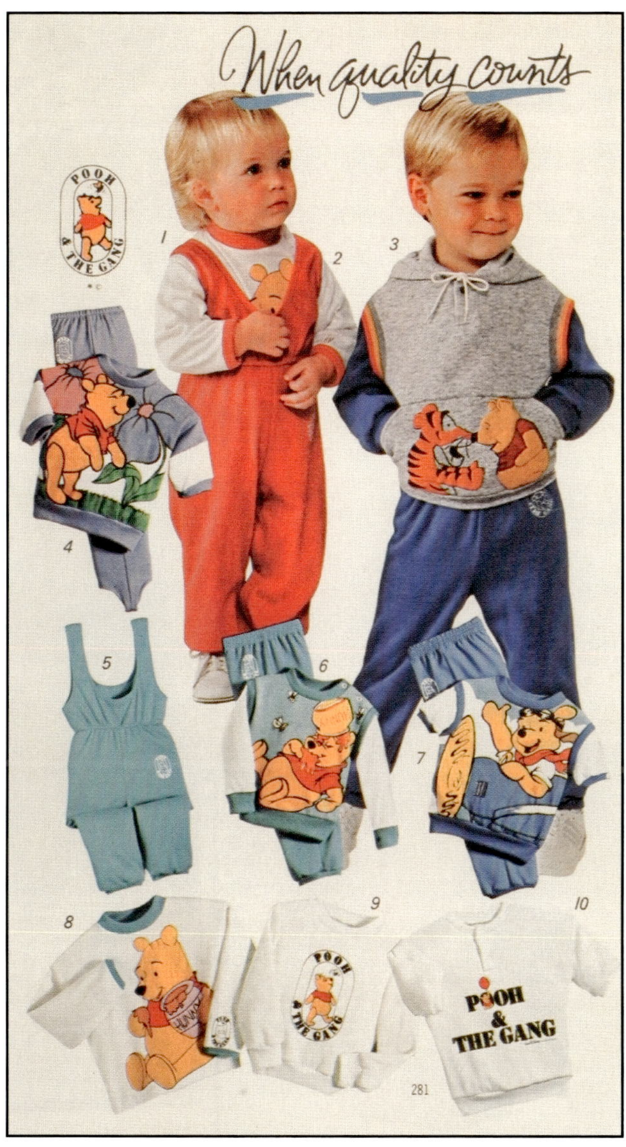

Winnie-the-Pooh separates feature soft combed cotton fabric blends. *Spring/Summer 1986*

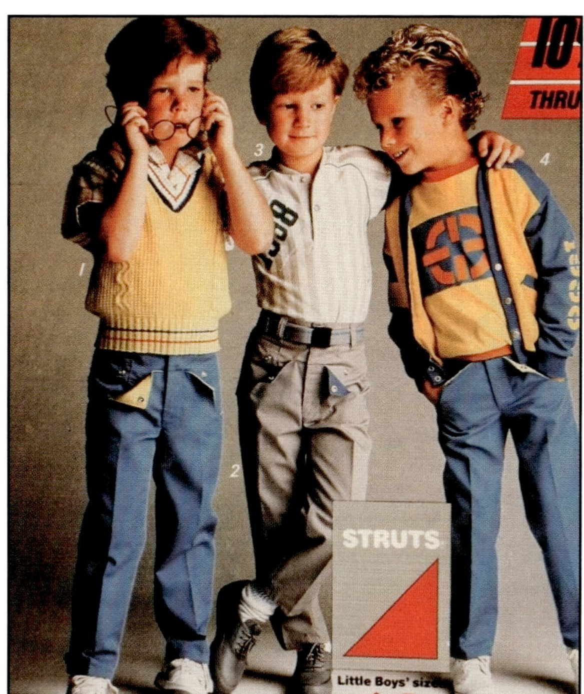

Separates in little boy sizes from the Struts collection. *Spring/Summer 1986*

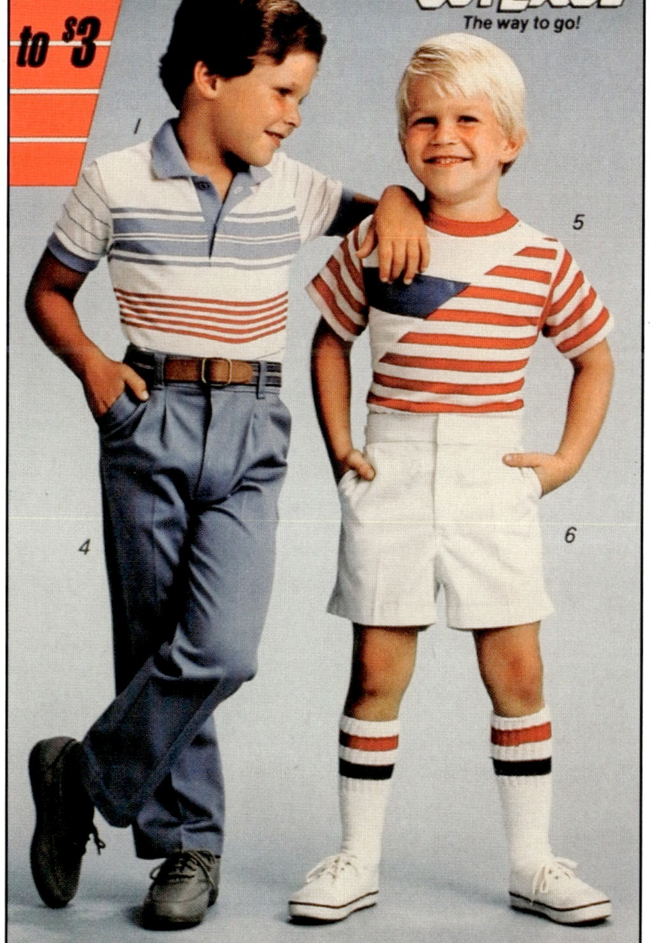

Cotton and polyester tops, shorts, and pants separates. *Spring/Summer 1986*

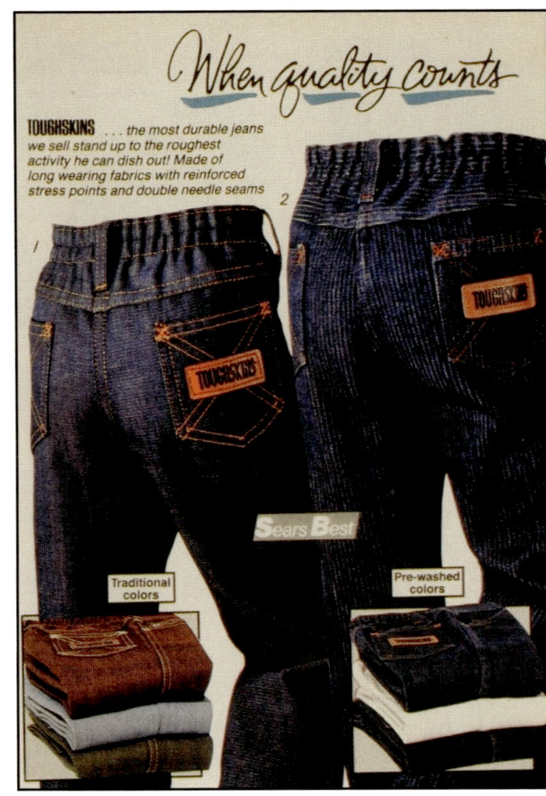

Toughskins® denim jeans have straight legs and elastic back waists. *Spring/Summer 1986*

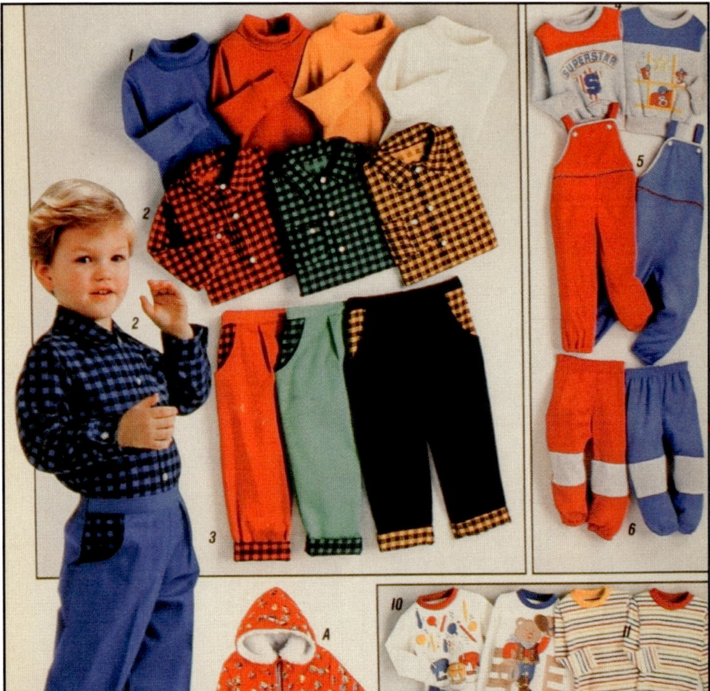

Turtlenecks, plaid shirts, and matching pants for a layered look. Fleece coordinates includes shirts, pants, and overalls. Knit tops and twill bottom coordinates. Polyester and cotton corduroy jacket. *Fall/Winter 1986*

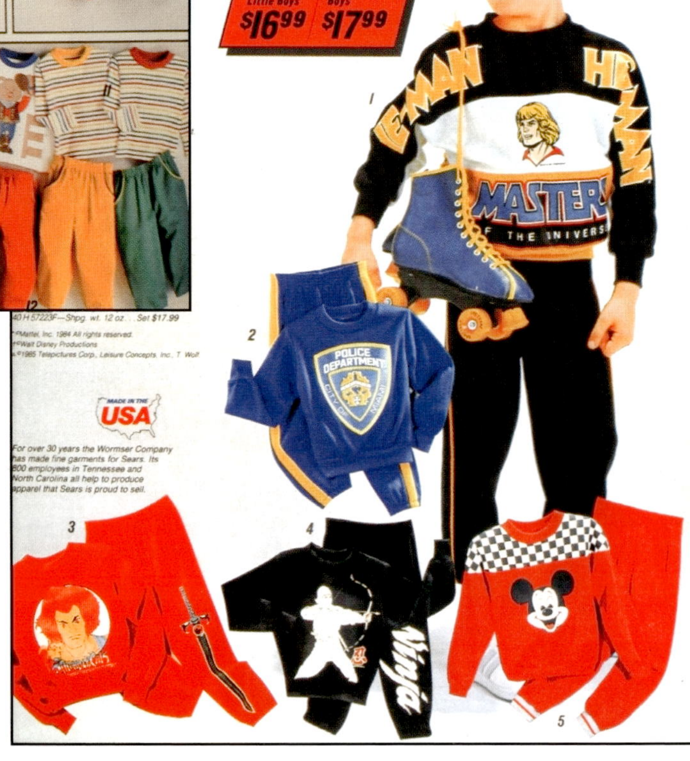

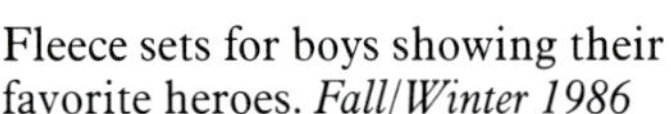

Fleece sets for boys showing their favorite heroes. *Fall/Winter 1986*

Sporty

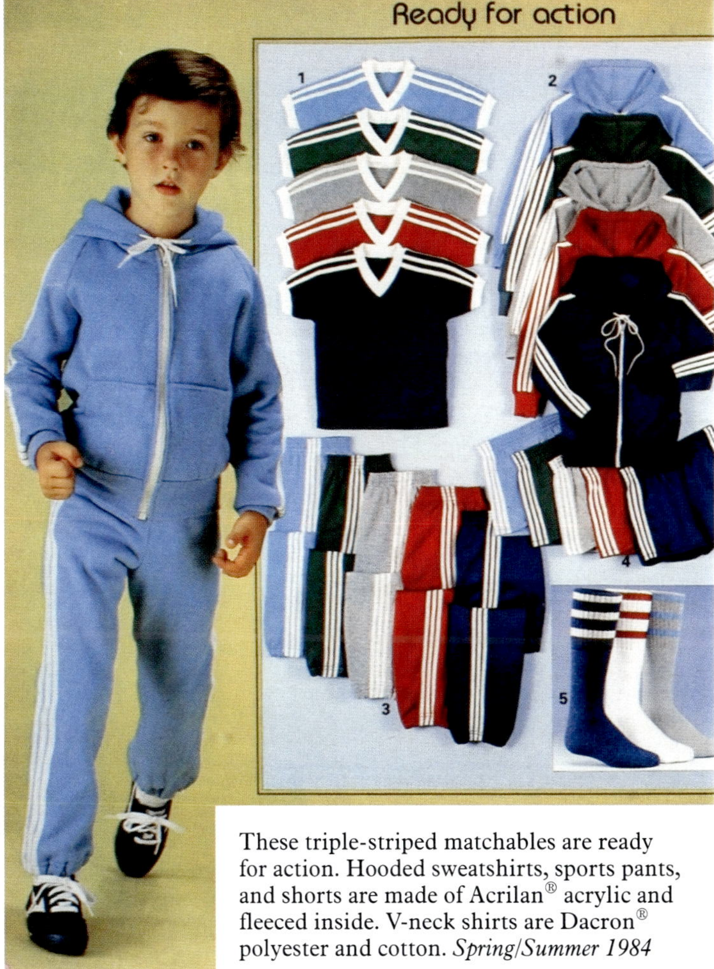

These triple-striped matchables are ready for action. Hooded sweatshirts, sports pants, and shorts are made of Acrilan® acrylic and fleeced inside. V-neck shirts are Dacron® polyester and cotton. *Spring/Summer 1984*

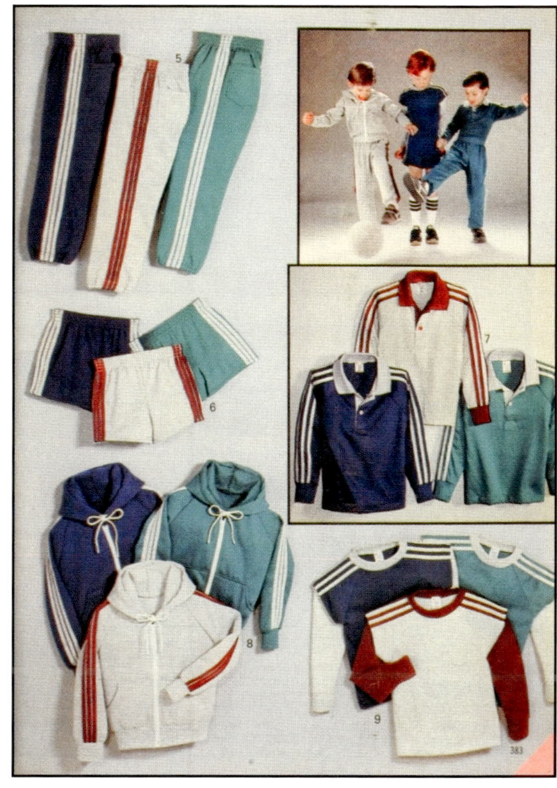

Triple striped matchables pants, shorts, shirts, and hoodies are ready for action. *Fall/Winter 1984*

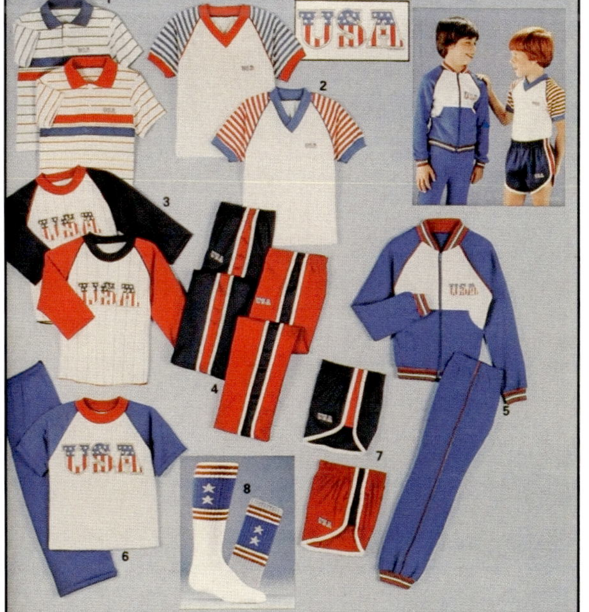

A variety of USA sportswear. *Spring/Summer 1984*

Pajamas

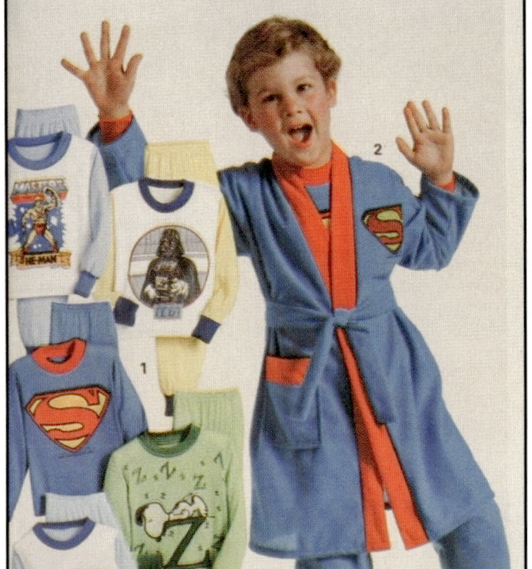

Ski style pajamas with heroic characters and knit flannel Superman robe. *Fall/Winter 1984*

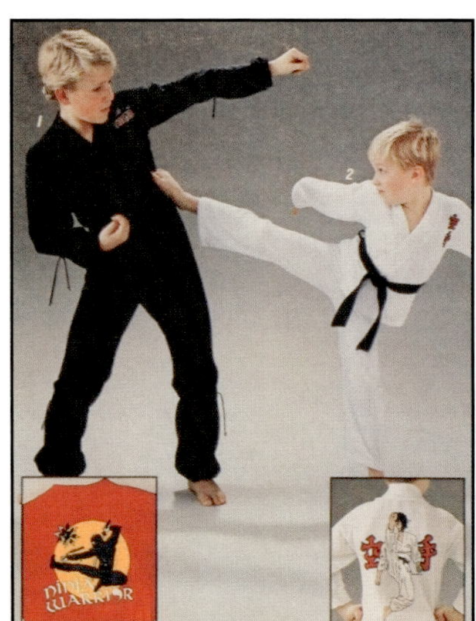

Ninja and karate polyester fleece pajamas. *Fall/Winter 1986*

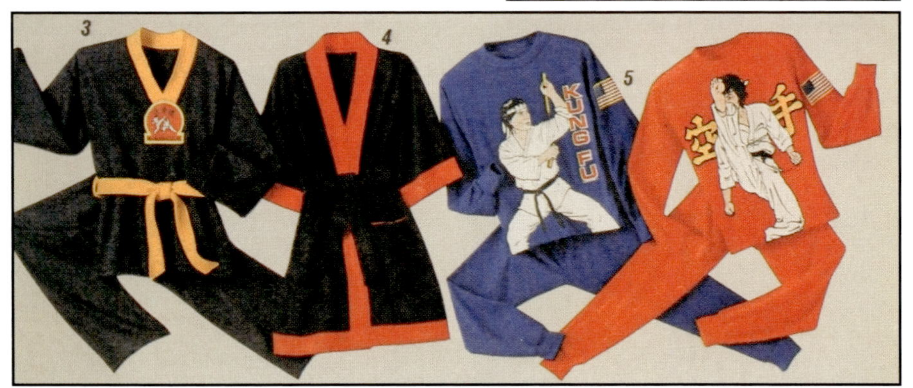

Coats

Jacket and snowpant outfits, bomber jacket, and quilted jackets for boys. *Fall/Winter 1984*

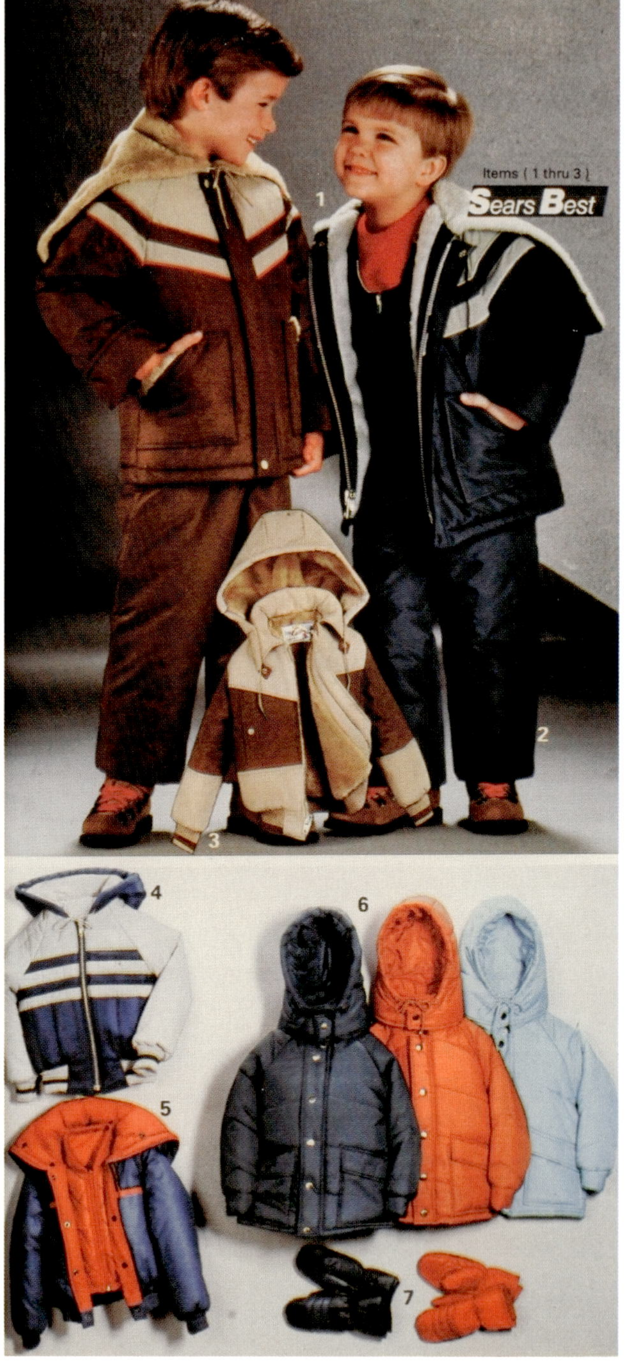

Girl Scouts/Boy Scouts/ Brownie Uniforms

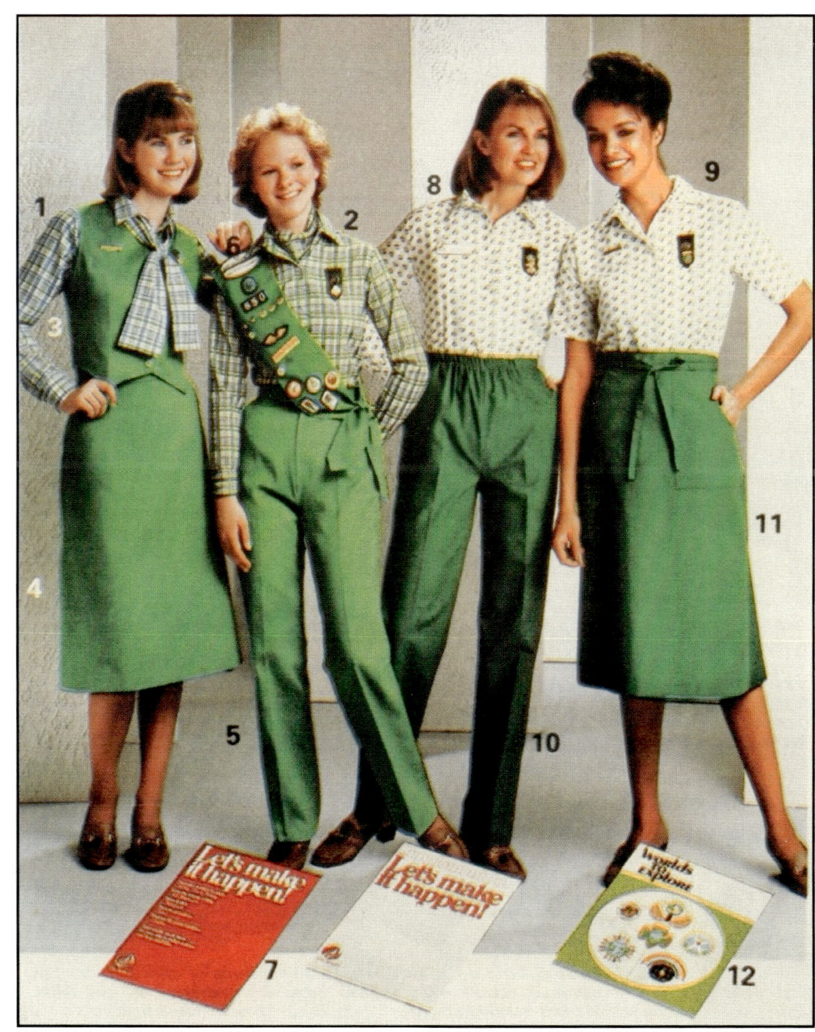

Official Girl Scouts uniforms. *Fall/Winter 1984*

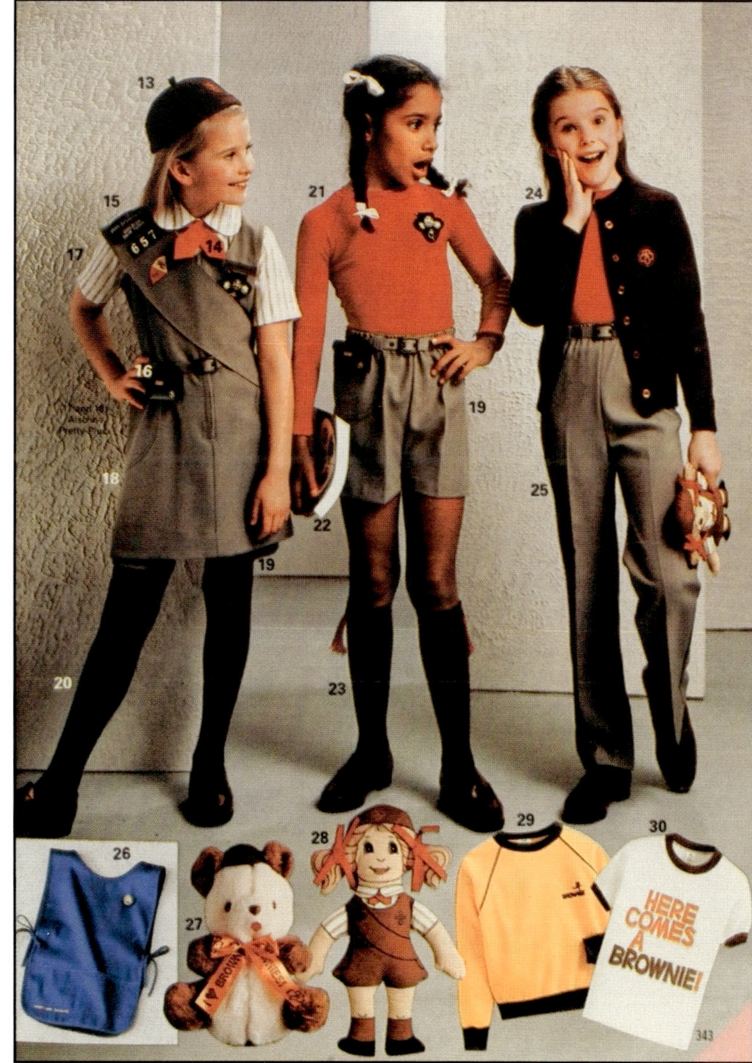

Official Brownie Girl Scout uniforms and accessories. *Fall/Winter 1984*

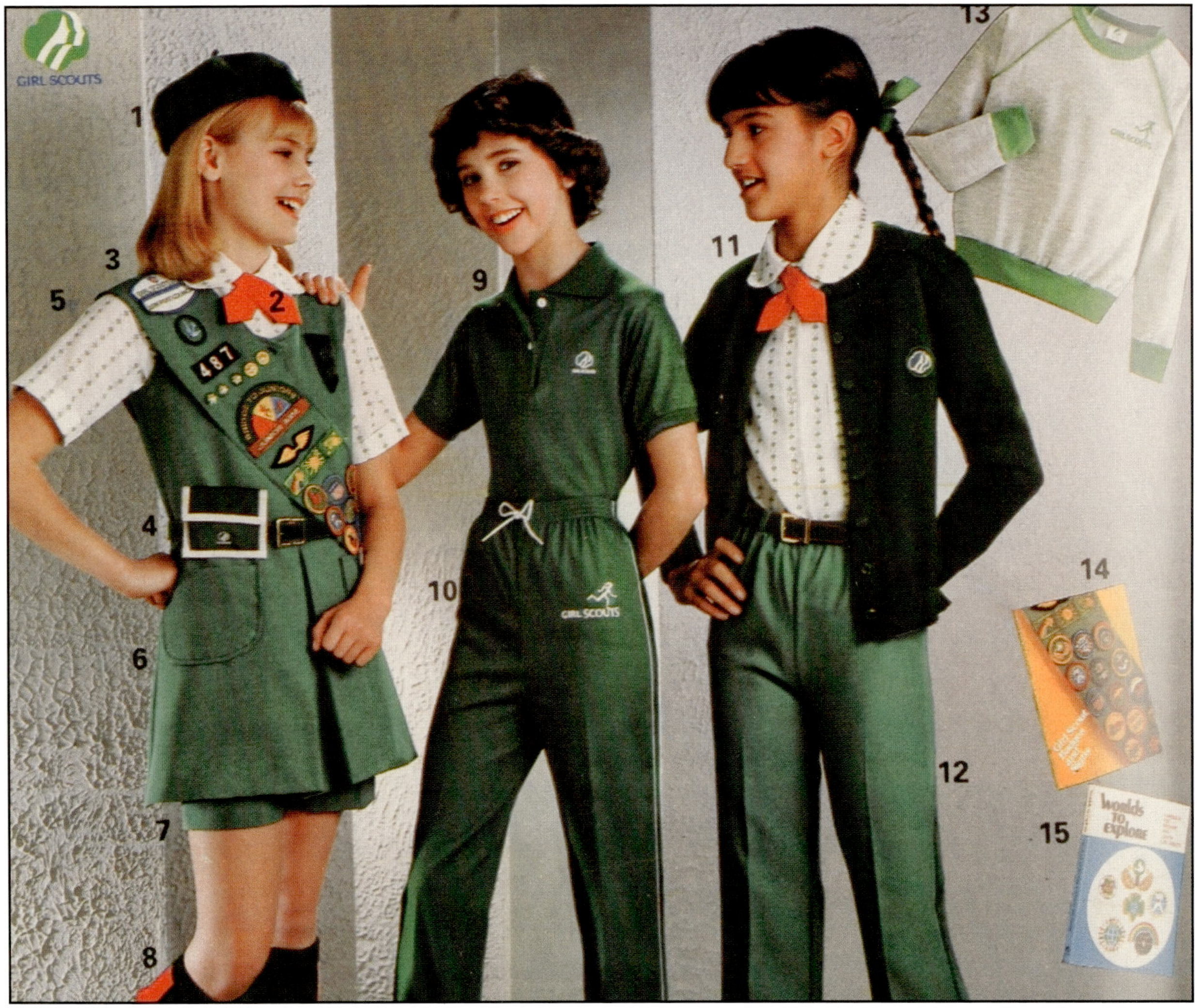

Official Junior Girl Scout uniforms and accessories. *Fall/Winter 1984*

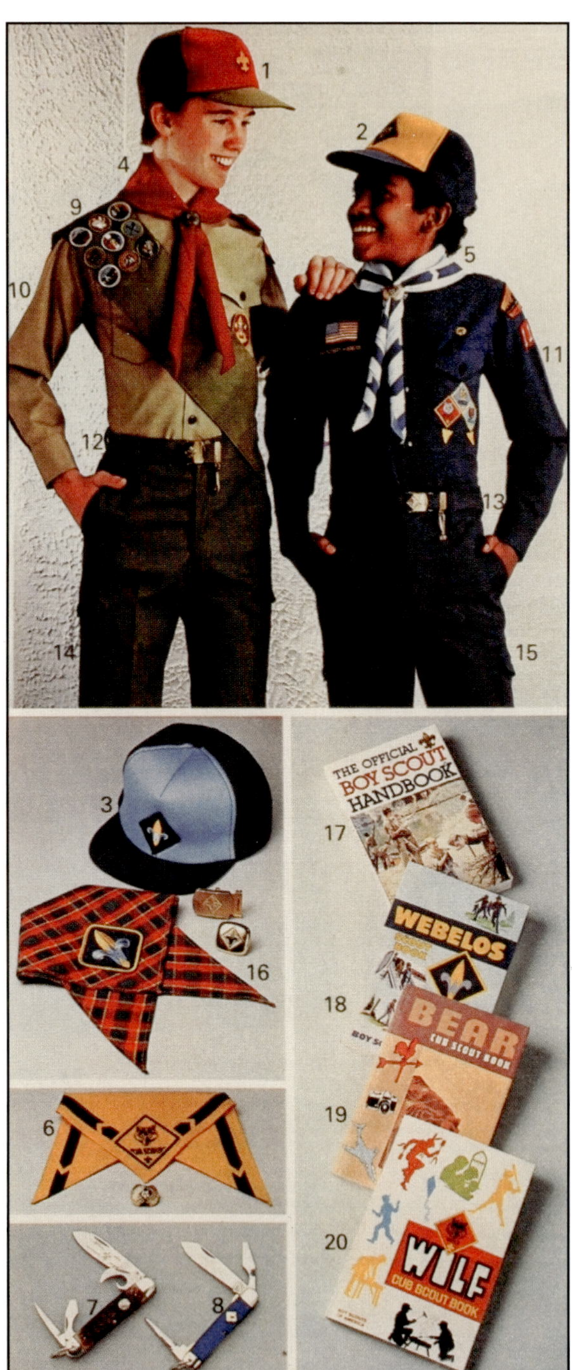

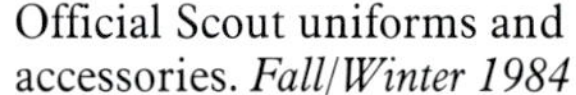
Official Scout uniforms and accessories. *Fall/Winter 1984*